Communication Studies in Canada

Études Canadiennes en Communication

Liora Salter

Butterworths
Toronto

Communication Studies in Canada/
Études Canadiennes en Communication

Canadian Cataloguing in Publication Data

Main entry under title:

Communication studies in Canada/Études
Canadiennes en Communication

Papers presented at the founding conference of the
Canadian Communication Association, held at the
Learned Societies meeting, Montreal, 1980.
Text in English and French.
Bibliography: p.
ISBN 0-409-86524-9

1. Communication - Congresses. 2. Communication -
Canada - Congresses. I. Salter, Liora. II. Canadian
Communication Association. III. Title: Études
Canadiennes en Communication.

P90.C65   001.51'0971   C81-094549-5E

Données de catalogage avant publication (Canada)

Vedette principale au titre:

Communication studies in Canada/Études
Canadiennes en Communication

Exposé présentées au congrès de fondation de la
Canadian Communication Association, tenu aux
congrès des sociétés savantes, Montréal, 1980.
Textes en anglais et en français.
Bibliographie: p.
ISBN 0-409-86524-9

1. Communication - Congrès. 2. Communication -
Canada - Congrès. I. Salter, Liora. II. Canadian
Communication Association. III. Titre: Études
Canadiennes en Communication.

P90.C65   001.51'0971   C81-094549-5F

The Butterworth Group of Companies

Canada:
Butterworth & Co. (Canada) Ltd., Toronto and Vancouver

United Kingdom:
Butterworth & Co. (Publishers) Ltd., London

Australia:
Butterworths Pty. Ltd., Sydney

New Zealand:
Butterworths of New Zealand Ltd., Wellington

South Africa:
Butterworth & Co. (South Africa) Ltd., Durban

United States:
Butterworth (Publishers) Inc., Boston
Butterworth (Legal Publishers) Inc., Seattle
Mason Publishing Company, St. Paul

Printed and bound in Canada by Hunter Rose

5 4 3 2 1 1 2 3 4 5 6 7 8 9/8

Acknowledgements

Editing a book that would help the Canadian Communication Association in the task of delimiting and defining the field was indeed a challenging task. It was manageable only because of the support of members of the association as a whole. Fifty articles were submitted, and 30 readers assisted in selecting the articles included herein. It took the willingness of everyone to work in two languages and the support of many universities. Simon Fraser University, the University of Quebec at Montreal, McGill University and Concordia University deserve special mention. The success of the work has depended upon the surprising strength of the field in Canada, despite its various guises at different universities. The book has drawn upon the skill of two editors, Kristin Jackson and Mireille Landry, and the skill and patience of two typists, Lucie Housden and Hugette Cote. As editor, I am grateful for their efforts.

Contents

Préface

L'événement à l'origine de ce livre — la création de l'Association Canadienne de Communications à Montréal au printemps 1980 — marque-t-il une nouvelle étape dans la reconnaissance officielle, au Canada, de l'émergence et du développement d'une discipline scientifique spécifique, celle des communications? Les communications: discipline ou champ d'études? Vieux débat . . . déjà! Mais académique, formel. Il en est de la promotion d'un champ d'étude au rang d'une discipline comme de la promotion d'une dialecte au statut de langue nationale: c'est davantage une question politique que scientifique.

Qu'on concoive les communications comme une science générale transdisciplinaire à la facon de Lévi-Strauss (1958), comme une science sociale spécifique, ou comme un objet éclaté appartenant à plusieurs disciplines différentes, force est de reconnaître que de plus en plus de chercheurs et d'étudiants de divers horizons se consacrent à l'étude des phénomènes de communication. Et il y a là plus qu'un engouement, plus qu'une mode. Il est évident pour tout le monde que les communications sont devenues un enjeu social, politique et économique important dans les sociétés contemporaines. Le congrès de Montréal a été l'occasion pour ses deux cents participants d'échanger sur quelques-uns des principaux enjeux et des nombreuses questions qui se posent actuellement dans le monde des communications au Canada: domination culturelle américaine, concentration croissante de la propriété des moyens de communication, consommation massive des mass-média, homogénéisation du savoir, développement de la télématique, etc. On en trouvera écho dans ce livre.

Les communications: discipline scientifique ou instrument de discipline politique? L'histoire et l'épistémologie de la science des communications restent à faire. Je ne peux donc m'en inspirer, encore moins prétendre les résumer dans le cadre de cette courte préface. Malgré cette lacune, on peut avancer que la machine a joué un rôle prépondérant dans le développement de la science des communications. Les premières théories de l'information, de la communication et du contrôle ont vu le jour dans les années quarante, suite aux travaux d'ingénieurs préoccupés par le réglage de machines énergétiques complexes (Wiener, 1961), par la transmission efficace et économique de l'information (Shannon et Weaver, 1949). Après avoir trouvé des techniques pour produire de grandes quantités d'énergie, il fallait découvrir moyen de les contrôler. Aux machines énergétiques, on a associé des machines à information. Ces machines productrices de travail sont devenues capables de poursuivre un objectif déterminé, et de s'autoréguler par rapport à celui-ci. Le mouvement s'est poursuivi vers une plus grande automation jusqu'à l'utilisation actuelle des micro-circuits intégrés.

On doit à ces premières théories plusieurs des concepts de base de la science des communications: émetteur, transmetteur, récepteur, quantité d'information, redondance, bruit, signal, code, feedback. On leur doit également une certaine perspective qui centre l'analyse sur la circulation de l'information, mettant entre parenthèses la constitution physique et les caractéristiques des différentes parties du système. On considère ces dernières comme des boîtes noires qui reçoivent des inputs et produisent des outputs. Elles sont définies uniquement par leur fonction dans le système de circulation de l'information.

La transposition de cette approche à l'analyse de la réalité psychologique et sociale, à partir des années 1950, ne peut s'expliquer totalement ni par la rigueur scientifique des concepts (entendre leur caractère mesurable), ni par une conception naïve et réductionniste de la réalité humaine. Par delà les espoirs et chimères des scientifiques, il faut reconnaître une certaine analogie entre le fonctionnement des systèmes sociaux contemporains et celui des systèmes mécaniques. Lewis Mumford (1962) a émis l'hypothèse que la mécanisation des hommes a précédé historiquement celle du monde physique, dans la constitution de la royauté en Egypte 4,000 ans av. J.-C. Si on définit la machine essentiellement comme un assemblage d'éléments résistants spécialisés dans une tâche fonctionnelle et capables de produire du travail sous direction humaine, il n'y a selon lui aucun abus de langage à qualifier la société industrielle moderne aussi bien que l'Egypte pharaonique de mégamachines. Dans cette perspective, la société n'est pas un produit de la machine. Elle se produit elle-même comme machine par l'instauration de rapports de domination et la consécration de valeurs sociales qui font de la majorité des hommes de simples engrenages dans le processus de production.

Cette analogie, société-machine, est sans doute boîteuse, comme toute analogie. Sans opération mystificatrice ou réductionniste, on peut tout de même voir une certaine parenté entre le concept de boîte noire et celui de "masse" (communication de masse). On peut reconnaître aussi que le concept de feedback occulte souvent, sous couvert de participation sociale, un mécanisme de contrôle de l'énergie humaine comme le feedback dans les machines sert à contrôler l'énergie physique.

Il faudrait se rappeler que plusieurs problèmes sociaux de communication résultent des nécessités de co-ordination et de contrôle à l'intérieur d'organisations de plus en plus complexes pour produire du travail ou de la destruction. Il faudrait voir que les campagnes politiques se modèlent maintenant sur les campagnes publicitaires et que l'exercice du pouvoir se fait de plus en plus par sondages d'opinion, pas toujours rendus publics. Il ne faudrait pas non plus oublier que l'idéologie de la libre circulation de l'information a servi à faciliter l'expansion internationale du capital américain et à établir la domination culturelle des Etats-Unis (Schiller, 1976). Il faudrait lire le rapport de la commission McBride et écouter la voix de ceux, individus ou peuples, qui tout en réclamant la liberté d'expression veulent aussi exercer un certain contrôle sur la définition de leur identité et de leur devenir.

Les premières études, mais aussi le courant encore dominant de la recherche sur les mass-media, ont été profondément influencés par cette approche behavioriste et fonctionnaliste de la communication humaine. Les problèmes de transmission et de contrôle de l'information dans les machines énergétiques complexes ont été à l'origine de la constitution d'une science des communications. Mais le développement de cette dernière a également été stimulé par les problèmes politiques liés à la complexification croissante des rapports de production et de la structure sociale dans les états contemporains. On a malheureusement trop souvent essayé de résoudre ces derniers en empruntant la grille d'explication et de solution des premiers. Une intention politique et des intérêts économiques y ont présidé.

La réduction principale du modèle mécaniciste à considérer les individus et les groupes sociaux comme des "boîtes noires", à les dépouiller de tout ce qui déborde leur fonction dans un système de production. Comment lire, en contexte de la dominance de ce modèle, le foisonnement des expériences et des théories de communication interpersonnelle et les diverses expériences de communication communautaires et collectives? Faut-il les interpréter comme prise en charge fonctionnelle des facteurs résiduels ou comme expérimentation et recherche d'un modèle plus organique? La réponse, encore à venir, est sans doute trop complexe pour être résumée dans une formule lapidaire.

On ne saurait expliquer entièrement les orientations actuelles de la science des communications en damasquant cette association et cette réduction de la société à la machine. Malgré l'hégémonie de l'empirisme et du behavorisme, la science des communications est traversée par des courants diversifiés, entre autres par des théories sémantiques et sémiotiques. Ces dernières empruntent beaucoup aux acquis de la linguistique structurale, pour la rigueur de la démarche méthodologique certes, mais aussi pour la définition de l'objet d'étude et, par voie de conséquence, pour l'établissement d'un ordre de pertinence des préoccupations. L'accent y est mis sur le jeu plus que sur les enjeux, sur la langue plus que sur la parole, sur la signification plus que sur le sens. L'objectif principal est d'établir la structure et les règles de fonctionnement des codes à divers niveaux de profondeur, et les règles de transformation de l'un à l'autre. De tels choix n'épuisent pas tout leur sens par simple référence aux "nécessités" méthodologiques. Ces "règles de la méthode", selon l'expression de Sartre, s'enracinent dans des postulats philosophiques, dans une vision de l'homme et de la société. Leurs manifestations de surface ne sont pas sans rapport avec certaines tendances abstraites et formelles des arts d'expression. Les jeux de code fascinent davantage que le rapport du sujet à sa parole. L'éclairage se porte plus sur la cohérence synchronique du système que sur la genèse du comportement des acteurs. On ne peut bien comprendre ces tendances et l'évolution d'ensemble de la science des communications sans faire référence au contexte global de la culture occidentale.

Les études historiques sont encore très rares en communications. Pour parler le langage d'Innis, la science des communications véhicule des préoccupations plus spatiales que temporelles. Sa nostalgie de la tradition orale grecque ne pourrait-elle être interprétée comme un appel à recréer des situations de communications où on peut difficilement faire abstraction de l'investissement du sujet dans sa propre parole? En serait-il de ces situations comme de ces matières premières si rares qu'on soit obligé de les reproduire en laboratoire de façon artificielle?

La science des communications gagnerait à s'inspirer davantage de l'anthropologie. L'étude de ces sociétés qu'on dit a-historiques—mais qui ont davantage le sens du temps et de la durée que nos sociétés dites historiques pour qui le temps est souvent synonyme de vitesse—ne vise pas à fournir des modèles passéistes, mais à faire ressortir par comparaison les caractéristiques de notre civilisation. L'interrogation de Lévi-Strauss (1958) sur le caractère "authentique ou in-authentique" des sociétés mérite approfondissement. L'essai sur le don de Marcel Mauss (1966) provoque la réflexion: existe-t-il encore dans nos sociétés des rapports de communication qui obéissent à ce modèle circulaire du donner-recevoir-rendre? Les échanges symboliques sont-ils tous à ce point contaminés par la marchandisation pour qu'on ne trouve en communications que des théories de l'échange inspirées de l'économie capitaliste?

L'anthropologie manifeste une égale préoccupation de l'universel et du particulier, un sens de la totalité culturelle et sociale que toute théorie générale de la communication devrait reprendre à son compte. Comme condition de la culture, la communication obéit à des règles générales, transculturelles. Mais comme partie et produit de la culture, elle prend forme dans une société spécifique dont elle est la création originale, résultant d'une dialectique des intérêts, des aspirations des groupes qui la composent et des rapports de pouvoir qui la traversent.

La science des communications existe. Il lui manque encore une histoire et une épistémologie. Ce n'est qu'au prix d'une explication critique de ses postulats, de sa démarche, de ses enracinements socio-culturels qu'elle saura devenir discipline scientifique et non instrument de discipline politique. C'est l'une des tâches importantes de la nouvelle Association Canadienne de Communication que de favoriser un tel cheminement.

REFERENCES

Lévi-Strauss, C. *Anthropologie structurale*. Paris: Plon, 1958.

Mauss, M. *Sociologie et anthropologie*. Paris: Presses Universitaires de France, 1966.

Mumford, L. *The Myth of the Machine*. New York: Harcourt Brace Jovanovich, 1962.

Schiller, H. I. *Communication and Cultural Domination*. New York: M. E. Sharpe, 1976.

Shannon, C. E., et Weaver, W. *The Mathematical Theory of Communication*. Urbana-Champaign: University of Illinois Press, 1949.

Wiener, N. *Cybernetics or Control and Communication in the Man and the Machine*. Cambridge: Massachusetts Institute of Technology Press, 1961.

Editor's Introduction

Part I

The proposal for a book on communication studies in Canada was first made at a planning meeting, held in March 1980, for the founding conference of the Canadian Communication Association as a Learned Society. Judging from the response to the call for papers for the conference, it was apparent that many people from a wide range of disciplines considered themselves part of this newly emerging field of study. The original notice for the conference was sent to the dozen communication departments in Quebec and elsewhere in Canada, but also to psychology, English, philosophy and cultural studies departments. The conference attracted participants from these fields and others.

What became evident at the planning meeting, however, was not simply the diversity of interests and work but also a growing convergence in approach taken by academics doing communication studies in various disciplines. In addition, some aspects of a coherent theoretical orientation became apparent. Those who submitted proposals may only have been partially aware of any emerging coherence in the field, but many commented later that they were acutely aware of a growing gulf between themselves and their colleagues in the established disciplines. In some senses, what brought people together was the experience of working at the margin of traditional disciplines, and the experience of being rebels in their fields. The conference, held in June 1980 in Montreal, provided the first Canadian opportunity for a discussion among those whose work had often overlapped.

A journal has existed in the field of communication studies in English-speaking Canada for some time, first as *Media Probe* and later as the *Canadian Journal of Communication*. A new association was formed in Quebec in April 1980 and a journal, *Communication et Information*, is published at Laval University. All of these efforts reflected, to a greater or lesser extent, the growing pains of the early years of a not-yet-formed discipline. However important their work, few thought that either journal could yet fully support the new level of growth in both French and English work in the field. For an association that sought to do just that, this was something of a crisis. Much substantive work in communication studies was appearing in the journals of other disciplines in Canada or was being published in communication studies journals in the United States or Europe. For obvious reasons, neither the other Canadian journals nor the communication publications outside Canada could be expected to be a catalyst for a new discipline in Canada. Without some additional push, it appeared likely that the field would remain underdeveloped and students would continue to ask, "what are communication studies?"

The association faced an additional problem. In other disciplines, French and English-language research usually was published separately. Proposals submitted for the conference showed the association that very similar research was being conducted in French and English. More important, the nature of the subject matter called for a bilingual approach. What might have been a social and political goal for any other academic association in Canada was seen as a necessity from the perspective of the Communication Association. Whatever the long-term arrangement between publications and conferences in Quebec and elsewhere, close collaboration in the initial efforts was deemed essential. The conference was successfully bilingual as is this publication.

Conference-based books have inherent weaknesses. Papers given at conferences seldom reflect fully the more substantive and broadly-cast work being done. The attempt to maintain a link between the conference and the publication tempts both author and editor to attempt to hasten publication. More important, as those working in communication studies are particularly aware, the structure of a conference and a book are very different. The reader does not take part in the drama of the event; the logic of oral presentation is lost when transferred into print on a page.

In recognizing these problems, the association defined specific goals for a book emerging from the founding conference. Any developing coherence of the field would have to be demonstrated in published form. A first volume could indicate something of the boundaries of the problems being addressed, the varieties of method and the span of research. The first volume could generate a perception of a field. The perception, if grounded in reality, would, in turn, encourage the publication of substantive work in the existing Canadian communication journals and the development of new publications in the field.

Part II

In preparing the manuscript, it became apparent that certain themes reoccurred in seemingly disparate articles. A discussion of the response of citizens living in remote communities to new satellite experiments, for example, raised many of the same questions as an analysis of the role of song in Maritime culture and even as a description of media strategies used by political parties in campaigning in federal elections. John Jackson's analysis of the thematic content of a CBC radio-drama incorporates some of the same concerns as Donald Theall's discussion of a telephone company advertisement, yet, as Theall argues, two more diverse cultural products could not be found. In almost every article, the tension between the social dimensions of experience and technology, between the centre and the periphery in the

Canadian experience, between expression and advertisement, and between regionalism and centralization, figured heavily.

From the perspective of an editor working in an as yet undefined field of study, the identification of these themes was a tenuous activity at best. It was much easier to locate the coherence of the emerging field of communication studies in Canada by indicating some of the distinctions being made by authors in the field.

It was, for example, becoming clear that boundaries were being drawn between communication studies and semiotics on the one hand, and communication studies and sociology on the other. Some aspects of communication-related problems had attracted significant attention in Canada while others had been relatively neglected. In organizing the founding conference, for example, it was agreed that a session on organizational communication was in order, but finding enough papers to fill the session was difficult. Although the identification of emerging distinctions or boundaries also must be highly tentative, it is worth the effort if it helps focus the debate. Without doubt, however, wide brush strokes will be used.

The distinctions between communication studies in Canada and in Europe or the United States are perhaps the easiest to define. Unlike their European counterparts, Canadians working in the field of communication studies combine some aspects of the strong theoretical orientation of their European colleagues with a surprisingly pragmatic and often specific policy interest. Rarely would one find an article in a European journal concluding with a list of recommendations. Among the papers submitted for consideration for this volume, such lists were common. They spell out or imply directions that government policy or political organizations should take. Even articles on discourse theory, working from an epistemological perspective, conclude with a relatively specific discussion of what might be done. Messages are analyzed not only in terms of the structuring principles that shape their content, or in terms of their epistemological roots, but also in terms of how those messages become, or might become, part of the social and political activities of their audiences.

In the Canadian work, the interplay between the public and private spheres of activity is seen as critical. Whereas much European communication theory provides discussions of questions arising from the interrelationship of the psychoanalytic and semiotic content of the message, here the analysis is extended to the concrete political situation where the message is first produced, then interpreted and used.

Two examples from this volume will illustrate the point. In one article, Serge Proulx calls for the development of a new analytical framework for a communication analysis of television. In that framework, he argues, must be a political economy, a study of the interpretive process being used by producers and audiences and a study of the technological forms of dissemination. In another article, Debra Clarke describes the operation of a Canadian television newsroom, leaving little question that the economic constraints of the news process, the organization of the newsroom, the interpretive framework of the reporters and even the organization of furniture in the newsroom are all reflected in what is broadcast on the evening news programme. Implied in both cases, then, is a methodology for a new, more comprehensive communication analysis, one that takes semiotics but also political and economic realities into account. Implied also, are recommendations for policies that might reshape the imperatives of the Canadian media system.

Canadian work may be more grounded than its European equivalent; it is, in general, much more broadly theoretical than the American variant of communication studies. The differences between American and Canadian communication studies go beyond the commitment or orientation to theory, however. Unlike their American colleagues, Canadian researchers have seldom attempted to isolate the effects of a communication process for study. One might easily cite as typical a study in an American journal that explored the effects of television violence or of stereotyping, or one that examined the impact of various organizational structures or group processes on what would be communicated to whom. The Canadian literature is striking for its neglect of similar problems, its neglect of mass media studies and, as noted above with reference to the founding conference, for the paucity of work in organizational communication. To be sure, some work has been done in these areas, but that work seems to remain peripheral. However significant the studies in themselves, they have yet to exert a formative influence on the field of communication studies in Canada.

More commonly, Canadian studies look at the media system rather than its specific content, at regulatory problems rather than media effects. Where content is discussed, it is often to take into account how Canadian consciousness is shaped by current political debates, by proximity to the United States, by Canadian commitment to state intervention in broadcasting or the economy. If, as Douglas Baer argues in this book, American communication studies make the assumption, usually implicitly, that a communication process can be studied in any context, Canadian work appears more historically and culturally specific. If the emphasis in the American discipline has been on *how* the communication process may get played out from culture to culture, here the orientation is often to the events and culture themselves. Media coverage, or any other communication process is seen as simply one more aspect of a larger problem to be considered. Again, examples will help. In two very different articles in this volume, Michel de Repentigny and Manar Hammad discuss how messages were used in shaping recent events in Quebec. The analysis is of the messages in each case, but the implicit discussion is about Quebec.

To take the Clarke article again, group process is seen in terms of its effect on practices of work and, in turn, on the news. The assumption of a culturally independent communication process, to be studied as it is shaped in its application or implementation in various cultural contexts, finds few takers in this book and indeed in the discipline as it appears to be emerging in Canada. Even the most highly empirical studies, work being done on the messages in election coverage by scholars at York and the University of Windsor for example, often combine an analysis of the data with a discussion of the context and of the constraints of the media system in Canada.

It is not surprising that these distinctions should have developed. Assuming that the problematic—the orientation of the field and the definition of problems to be addressed—of any discipline emerges as a consequence of the conditions of its development within society and within its parent discipline, communication studies in Canada should be different from its sister disciplines elsewhere. Understanding the genesis of the sister disciplines, in a most general way here, will shed some light on the emerging coherence of the field in Canada.

In the American case, psychology and engineering gave birth to communication studies. On one hand, systems theory, the study of the flow of information through large complex organizations, exerted a strong pull on scholarly interests. On the other hand, the humanistic bias of social psychology had an impact. The pervasive influence of television, particularly in light of its somewhat unique dependence on advertiser sponsorship, demanded explanation and analysis. The core question in every case was the nature and the impact of various forms of transmission of information. Whether in the structure of the group, or in the hierarchical organization of a major corporation, or even in the way in which programmes were designed, the emphasis was on the process of dissemination.

Perhaps the most commonly applied early model for the study of communication processes clearly was drawn from the combination of psychology and engineeering. It saw a sender, a receiver, a message and a means of transmission. Recent attempts have been made to elaborate the model—for example to include a process of encoding and decoding messages, public and private cues, and feedback loops—but the basic format remains the same.

A number of very concrete questions directed the research, however. If, for example, televison portrayed mainly violence, how had that violence been integrated in the perceptions and behaviours of individual viewers? If advertiser sponsorship was critical in shaping the media and their content, what effects did it have upon the viewer and within the capitalist process as a whole? The disparate nature of the audience, that is, the existence of many audiences simultaneously for any one message, was less important for analysis than the role and movement of the messages themselves. In its more conservative application, the consequence of the approach was an individualistic and behaviourist orientation to the analysis, reflecting both the origins of the discipline and also the way media were being used to generate very specific and limited behaviours. In its more radical formulation, the audience could be treated as a mass because, analytically at least, it was a critical mass from the perspective of those who sought to engineer information systems and human response for whatever purpose.

American television is, of course, world television, in a way that no other television can equal. The significance of being at the centre of a process of diffusion was not lost upon those who conducted research in the field. The study of radio and television was the core of communication studies in the United States for many years, but it was soon joined and, indeed, paralleled by research into the diffusion of technologies, of innovations, of development philosophies, etc. How messages would (and could) be spread, through what kinds of organizational or community forms, as subject to which group processes, as interpreted within which cultural context — these processes demanded and got attention.

Even among communication studies' more radical practitioners, the emphasis was on the dissemination of information. New critical work on the news production process — such as that by Gitlin, Tuchman and Epstein — appeared to argue, at least in part, that a less constrained and inner directed news production process might produce news more capable of reflecting reality to the people to whom it was disseminated. The argument was that the news production process had, for various reasons, been short-circuited; the constraints of production were being fed back into the content of messages before they could be sent out. Media were also analyzed in terms of their role in the reproduction of capitalist relations, but seen, even here, as systems of distribution capable of generating legitimation or demand for consumer services. For this latter group of researchers, the diffusion of *which* information and for what purpose formed the questions for study.

In Europe, on the other hand, communications often seemed synonymous with theory in general. The emphasis, among the most diverse writers, was on consciousness, the ways in which messages are structured by the epistemological systems of which they are a part. The structuring process had at least two main aspects — the production of messages themselves and the ways in which the messages were articulated and interpreted within the psycho-political consciousness of members of different groups or classes. The problematic was Marxist, at least in orientation, although communication analysis could often be read as a critique of more traditional Marxist theory. At the core of the study was the problem of revolutionary activity; consciousness was seen as a key element. The impact of failed revolutions, of fascism, of state socialism, of technological predispositions, of bureaucratization, of Euro-communism and of the growth of populist movements in the Third World or in Europe itself had a direct effect on what would be analyzed. If each posed a problem for Marxist theory, then the theory had to be reformulated to take account of changes in the historical process, the realities of psycho-social existence, the significance of epistemological perspective (of audience, producers and of researcher) and an increasingly sophisticated understanding of all aspects of the relations of capitalism itself.

In Europe, then, the root disciplines were literary, social and political theory. The policy implications of political activity were left to those who translated theory into practice, to national, social or workers' movements. The emphasis on consciousness was an outgrowth of the Marxist heritage, a product of the difficulties of translating theory into revolutionary practice. Psychoanalytic theory, semiotics, structuralism and linguistics were all tools necessary for the reformulation. The problem in many of the variants of European theory has been how the relations of discourse were structured.

In this volume, the influence of the European theorists is evident. Gaetan Tremblay draws upon Habermas, Bernard Schiele implicitly on the French structuralists, and Manar Hammad on semiotic theory. But the problematic is different and the underlying theoretical orientations have occasionally been stretched beyond easy recognition. The parent disciplines in English-speaking Canada and Quebec are sociology, literature, history and political science. The Marxist debate emerges from time to time, but is seldom at the centre of the discussion. Obviously Canadians are not at the forefront of social and political movements, except, in some senses, in Quebec. Nor are they often at the centre of a process of diffusion of information (although they are sometimes participants in it) or technologies. It might be argued that Canadians are often simply at the receiving end of all these processes—perhaps that is the problem.

It is not so simple, however. Communication studies in Canada are more than merely reactive and certainly more, already, than a shadow replica of work being done elsewhere. Whether intended or not, Canadian work in communication studies often parallels the approach of Harold Innis. Innis is the Canadian economic historian who studied, first, the fur trade in Canada and, later, the role of communication media in the consolidation and expansion of empires. He argued that economic history had to be combined with the analysis of the interpretive framework of the actors in that history. Communication studies, he said, demanded an analysis of the relations between the technological form (media of communication) and political systems (empires), between social experience and its economic context.

Certainly an Innisian perspective seems to have influenced the authors in this volume, at least implicitly, although few would consider the Innisian formulation sufficient. David Crowley in "The Bias of Communication and the Communication of Bias," explores the question of bias in communication systems, a problem that Innis discussed at length. Both Christopher Plant in "PEACESAT—A Classic Wolf in Sheep's Clothing," and Gaetan Tremblay in "Technologie de Communication: Démocratisation et Régionalisation," discuss communication satellite experiments by emphasizing the interplay between technological form, political constraints and what is communicated. George Warskett in "The Information Economy in Late Capitalism," locates the new information technologies in a system of economic forces. Several articles in this volume, and more that could not be included because of space constraints, discuss national sovereignty—in Quebec and in Canada. Although their authors might take issue with Innis, they appear to set the problem firmly within his terms: centre-periphery relations, regionalization and centralization. And, of course, Innis continually sought to combine his analysis of political economy with specific policy recommendations.

If, then, as Proulx argues here and Innis certainly claimed, an analysis of media must take into account their political economy, their epistemological dimensions and a discussion of the limits of the technological form, it is because for both Proulx and Innis, and for almost all the authors in this volume, those elements could not be seen as distinct. Unlike its sister disciplines in the United States and Europe, communication studies in Canada seldom focuses on communication process in the abstract. In Canada, even network analysis—tracing patterns of communication exchanges—often takes as the object of its study inter-corporate connections.

Once the elements of political economy, epistemology, experience and technological form are seen as intrinsically related, the subject matter of communication studies has been altered. It can no longer be encompassed by the study of processes in (and problems with) the dissemination of information or with the development of consciousness. To put the point in its simplest terms: communication studies in Canada takes culture itself as the problematic.

Obviously, in the sense it is being used here, culture is more than its literary or media products. James Sacouman, in an article in this book, defines culture as lived experience, but even that is too narrow a definition. Rather, culture is that experience as shaped by the messages and message systems of its participants. Culture is conceived as history and its social context, art and commercially produced artifacts, political debates and the activities they generate, experience and its interpretation by individuals as members of groups, regions, nations or classes. Culture, when seen in this light, draws heavily from the Innisian formulation.

Many disciplines study culture, of course, even from what might be seen as an Innisian perspective. What makes culture the focal point of communication studies in Canada requires further explanation. Certainly one factor is the unique status of culture in the Canadian context. Ask any television viewer what constitutes Canadian culture or even culture in general. The answer is likely to be troubled, more of a non-answer than a definition. Part of what narrows the subject for analysis and gives it focus is that culture in the Canadian case cannot be assumed. It cannot be used, by the television viewer or the research scholar, as a basis for comparison or as a starting point for an analysis of the significance of the transmission or dissemination of information.

More significantly, in the general Canadian context, culture does not seem to be clearly identifiable. To be sure, certain cultural forces can be identified, certainly in Quebec and, as James Sacouman argues, in the Maritimes. Such identification notwithstanding, what constitutes the content of culture eludes definition and articulation. Those who seek to delimit its shape and boundaries are confounded by problems. Policy-makers in Quebec or in the federal regulatory agencies who support cultural develoment understand the problem only too well.

That the public and governmental agencies have trouble identifying the parameters of Canadian culture (and occasionally deny its existence) should not lead one to suggest that culture is itself illusory. Neither at a theoretical nor at a practical level does a cultureless society exist. Despite problems in identification, whether or not the parameters are known, the reality of place, position, experience and practice shape not only what people do but how and what they think. Culture, whether understood or not, indicates not only certain problems but also the ways those problems seem amenable to solution. The problems faced by the Canadian television viewer in discussing culture or those faced by broadcast agencies in attempting to regulate for its development are real. Nonetheless, the full dimensions of location and situation are played out in experience and awareness, in activities and in ideas.

What gives culture its specificity as the problematic of communication studies is not simply that culture in the Canadian context cannot be assumed. After all, a significant number of people seek to reject culturally-given definitions of reality, although they usually do so on the basis of a prior identification of what is culturally given. It is not even that the identification of culture in the Canadian context is difficult. Again, people in cultures throughout the world do not seek to identify the shape and boundaries of their culture but simply assume them. Culture becomes linked to communication studies when it can neither be identified nor assumed, and when the cultural process is tied to a socially-valued process of determining and defining its boundaries.

Under these conditions what is culturally given is conceived mainly in terms of the *process* of its own production. Two examples will illustrate the point. The television viewer who answers the question by arguing that Canadian culture is bound up in the process of its own identification, articulates culture as a communication problem and argues, albeit implicitly, for a communicational analysis of its dimensions. Canadian cultural policies that identify cultural products in terms of the ingredients in their production process (the stars and director of a film, for example, make the film Canadian) again tie culture to a communication process. In each case, the way messages are being structured and produced becomes the key to understanding their cultural content.

When what constitutes culture is its definition and articulation, and when what constitutes the study of culture is the study of the process of the production of definitions and interpretations, then culture has specificity as the problematic of communication studies.

The communication process, as it is being conceived here, cannot be understood in terms of the old model of sender, receiver, message and mode of transmission, even if the model is made more sophisticated. Cultural experience is at the centre of what is being studied, not a variable in a process of encoding or decoding messages.

As such, the cultural experience has to be understood along three dimensions. First, it must be understood as a process of signification. Messages become meaningful within specific contexts and as shaped by particular forces. Both how messages assume meaning, and how the dimensions of meaning emerge from any message as it is articulated and used must be analyzed. Second, cultural experience must be understood as a process of expansion, shaped in part by epistemological perspective, but also by social, political and economic constraints and by the interpretive framework called into use. Finally, cultural experience must be understood in terms of its effects. How a message is used, for what intended and actual purposes, and to what effect, all become part of the message itself. From this perspective, messages are simultaneously cultural products and cultural forces; their study involves an analysis of the interplay between the two. Messages are themselves also message systems.

The study of advertisements used in the Quebec referendum campaign by Manar Hammad is again a good case in point. Hammad's analysis indicates clearly that the power relations between the federal Liberal party and the Parti Quebecois found their way quite directly into the structure and content of the advertisements themselves. Those who prepared the advertisements may or may not have been aware of how they were structuring the message, but they were without doubt aware of the intentions and positions of the actors involved.

Culture, as a communication study, must also be understood as an active process of construction and reconstruction. As an active process — as an activity — it takes place in the realms of the cultural product, of practices, of media and of consciousness.

Again, some examples will be helpful. In this volume, Donald Theall compares advertisements and films. He does so by taking account of both structural and interpretive elements in their production. The advertisement embodies a specific use of ideas, but is more than the embodiment of ideas because it actively seeks to construct (and succeeds in constructing) and limit activity in the social world and in thought. The advertisement is, as noted above, both a cultural artifact and a cultural force.

William Gilsdorf discusses the practices of political campaigners in the last federal election, for example the scheduling of the leadership tours. He shows how those practices, in themselves, became imperatives to the media about how the campaign should be covered in the news. Bernard Schiele analyzes the narrative structure of a television programme. He indicates how that structure transforms the scientific content of the programme. The structure of the programme is itself a realm of activity. Marilyn Taylor explores the process of adult education and argues that it involves a necessary change of consciousness. She suggests that this consciousness change can only be accomplished, and that adult education can only succeed, through social interaction. What brings all of these articles into the same volume is not their subject matter (which is clearly different) but their treatment of the communication process as active and of cultural experience as a process of reconstruction.

The emerging coherence of the new discipline of communication studies, I would argue, is located here, in the way advertisements, political practices, narrative structures, adult education programmes all constitute both messages and message systems, cultural artifacts and cultural forces. From this perspective, so too are satellite experiments and the new information technologies. Specific words, songs, television, technological form, organizations of activity, media of communication, radio-dramas and even an election are all conceived of, first, as messages and message systems in a cultural context.

It was made clear above but should be repeated that a message system never is simply a message and its means of transmission. Nor can an analysis of a message/message system, however important, be done in abstract. The message/message system is seen as a product of its process of production and a result of the conditions under which it is produced. It contains what is being said, but also what is *not* being said, and what might have been said instead. The intent of the producers, the intentions of the audiences and of those who frame what messages will be made available to whom are all fed back into the content of the message itself. Context becomes a crucial element in understanding the communication process; it cannot be treated as an independent variable.

Similarly, the transmission process and its technological form shape communication but cannot be understood as independent variables. They too are elements of the message/message system. Finally, a message must be understood not only as a description (not even primarily as a description) of cultural reality but must also be taken as a prescription for activity. John Lee makes this point clearly. The word "gay" (meaning homosexual) becomes both the focus and instrument of political conflict once a newspaper refuses to use the term. Culture as a communication study, is both reality and a command for its transformation. Inherently, its description contains elements of the prescriptive.

Part III

At the founding conference of the Canadian Communication Association, Dorothy Smith made a critical observation. The tools of communication analysis, she noted, had been lifted largely from interpersonal communication, but were now necessarily being applied to the activities of institutions. She might well have included many of the European theorists in her critique. A discussion of consciousness in terms of its linguistic, psychoanalytic and epistemological components still focuses on the individual as the subject and object of discourse. At the conference, Smith called for new models for communication analysis, certainly drawing on theoretical work going on outside Canada, but capable of taking into account the institutional context within which message systems shape and connote meaning.

It is certainly true that none of the authors in this volume had developed an analytic framework equal to the task Smith set. Nor perhaps would it be realistic to suggest they should, at this stage of the discipline's development. It is clear, however, that the particular problems posed in the Canadian context—in Quebec, the Maritimes, the North and elsewhere—may be advantageous in the long run. At the very least, the kinds of questions being asked by the authors in this book, and others at the founding conference, indicate that the development of such an analytic framework is possible and, indeed, is on the agenda. This volume, then, represents a first approach to this task.

The book is divided into three parts. In Part One, the emphasis is on the media of communication, the message systems themselves. John Lee provides a delightful but also thought-provoking discussion of the word "gay." Debra Clarke summarizes her research on news production in a Canadian television station. William Gilsdorf reports on his experience in trailing candidates in the last two federal political campaigns, particularly as those candidates planned and executed their media strategies. Bernard Schiele and Gabriel Larocque discuss how the scientific content of a television programme was altered by its presentation in the narrative form. Donald Theall uses several films and advertisements to indicate the nature of the advertisement as a cultural product.

In Part Two, the emphasis is on the role of communication. James Sacouman, Rob Brunton and Jim Overton analyze the popular culture of the Maritimes in the context of working conditions and workers' struggles in that region. Marilyn Taylor reports on a study of the adult education process. Christopher Plant and Gaétan Tremblay both discuss new experiments using satellite technology in remote areas, Plant in the South Pacific and Tremblay in Quebec. And finally, George Warskett provides a critical analysis of "the new information society."

In the last part of the book, the emphasis is on the analytical tools used in communication studies. Here, the authors engage in implicit debate. David Crowley starts off by suggesting that the problem of bias has been inadequately dealt with since Innis's pioneering efforts to locate its character. Doug Baer takes up the case for mass media studies in Canada, suggesting that, with some caution, Canadian researchers might link up with their American counterparts in the analysis of television messages. John Jackson lays out the case for both content analysis and structural analysis and provides a clear example of how each technique can be used to dissect a CBC radio-drama. Michel de Repentigny details a methodology for the analysis of messages in media coverage of an election campaign. Manar Hammad applies semiotic theory to the analysis of advertisements in the Quebec referendum campaign and Serge Proulx indicates where an epistemological analysis of television might be extended and used.

In all, the articles indicate the lively state of the art in the new field of communication studies in Canada.

Part One

The Medium of Communication

Chapter 1

Don't Use That Word! Gay, Meaning Homosexual

John Alan Lee*

L'auteur fait ici l'examen historique, linguistique et sociopolitique—en com- parant l'usage du mot "gay" avec celui d'homosexuel, homophile, etc.—de la thèse selon laquelle le mouvement de libération des homosexuels ("gay") s'est approprié le mot "gay" et l'a galvaudé. Une analyse de contenu de trois quoti- diens torontois de 1960 à 1980, une série d'entrevues avec des rédacteurs en chef, de même que des communiqués des media exposant leurs politiques, ont servi à examiner l'opposition de ces derniers à l'adoption du mot "gay." Une analyse théorique des positions favorables et opposées à l'emploi du mot "gay" pour homosexuel, s'est appuyée sur le "vocabulary of motives" de C.W. Mills, et sur le "political language" tel que défini par M. Edelman.

> Although we think we govern our words, yet certain it is that words . . . mightily entangle and pervert the judgement.
>
> Francis Bacon, 1605

> "When I use a word," Humpty Dumpty said in a rather scornful tone, "it means just what I choose it to mean—neither more nor less."
> "The question is," said Alice, "whether you can make words mean different things."
> "The question is," said Humpty Dumpty, "which is to be the master—that's all."
>
> Lewis Carroll

The motivation to write this paper arose out of a discussion with colleagues, all of whom know that I am gay. We were talking about the work of the Gay Academic Union, an officially recognized organization at many American and Canadian universities. "If you're really *academics,* why not use the cor- rect word to describe your condition?" a colleague asked. The correct word, to his mind, was "homosexual." He went on to deplore the "destruction of one of the nicest little words in the English language by militant homosexuals."

---

* I am especially grateful to Dr. Kathryn Kopinak, Dr. Susan Whalen, and Dr. Stephen Murray for their comments on an earlier version of this paper, and to the Canadian Gay Archives for access to their collection.

This paper is concerned with the resistance to adoption of "gay" as a term referring to same-sex orientation. The research methods include interviews, a content analysis of newspapers, and personal observations.

Resistance to the word gay (meaning homosexual) is widespread. Opposition is found among the most widely published and politically "liberal" authors. For example, one of Canada's best-known writers and commentators, Pierre Berton, told me when I appeared on his television programme, "The Great Debate," that "homosexuals have ruined the fine old English word gay." Canada's "national newspaper of record," the *Globe and Mail*, long maintained an official policy of banning the use of "gay" to refer to homosexuals. This ban was finally lifted by the newspaper's style editor, Alan Dawson, in a memo of July 1, 1978, in which he complained:

> The style guide [entry] dealing with the words gay and homosexual must yield to reality. A once precise word has been bastardized beyond recall and stolen. We yield to progress if that's what it is, and relax the ban on gay, particularly in features and entertainment stories.

Others have resisted "reality," or "progress, if that's what it is." The *Vancouver Sun,* for example, fought gay advertising all the way to the Supreme Court and won. It asked: "What should homosexuals be called? How about homosexuals? That seems to say it." (*Vancouver Sun,* March 28, 1977). Opposition to the use of the word gay, meaning homosexual, is still the policy of such large Canadian newspapers as the *Toronto Star* (confirmed with senior editor Borden Spears).

The hypothesis of this paper is that resistance to adoption of the word gay, meaning homosexual, involves more than determination to protect the purity of the English language. It involves a refusal to recognize the reality of a politically organized minority and its communities in many North American cities. The term "recognize" is used here not in the sense of perception, but of political acknowledgement, as in "the recognition of China"—that is, the Communist government of China.[1]

A Useful Ambiguity Lost

Ironically, those who resist the adoption of the word gay, meaning homosexual, do not necessarily deny that for many years the word "gay" had a covert, or insinuating, reference to homosexuals. Many argue that this was one of the advantages of the word. As a code meaning homosexual, it allowed those in the know to refer to the homosexual reality without the naive catching on. This ambiguity was useful both to homosexuals and heterosexuals.

A secret homosexual ("in the closet") could signal someone else he thought might be homosexual, by innocently but pointedly introducing the word "gay" into conversation. "What a good time I had . . . it was a really gay party." If the target of such usage was not homosexual, he was unlikely to pick up the double meaning. If he was, and was willing to disclose this information, he could respond in code: "Yes, a gay party is always great fun."

Heterosexuals aware of this ambiguity could have some fun too, at the expense of homosexuals. For example, a decade ago a Canadian newspaper reported a New Year's Eve party at which the star guest was an internationally celebrated ballet dancer who was known to be homosexual but who carefully cultivated a heterosexual image by publicly courting ballerinas. The reporter wrote that this star was having an "especially gay time at the party." A decade ago, he could have innocently replied to any threat of a libel suit that all he meant was that the ballet star enjoyed himself. Today such a defense is unlikely. As Borden Spears, *Toronto Star* senior editor, noted, "the word can't be used that way anymore . . . just about every reader is 'wise' to it."

The ambiguous tradition of the word gay had its risks. Author Donald Cory points out that a police detective could trick a secret homosexual with it:

> This man you were out with tonight — you know he's gay? A denial brings a torrent of new questions: What did you understand by the question? Did you understand it to refer to his being queer? How did you know that's what the word means?[2]

The very fact that those who resist the adoption of "gay" admit this ambiguous reference has long existed, is an admission that the use of gay for homosexual is not an entirely new invention of "militant homosexuals." Yet this myth persists, as in this transcript of a radio discussion between Canadian broadcasters Bill McVean and Gary Lautens:

> McVean: An individual's sexual performance is no concern of mine, just as long as he or she isn't sexually aggressive or exhibitionist. I rather tend to think that gays so-called tend to be both. . . .
> Lautens: I don't like that word . . . because I think they've taken a perfectly good word and misrepresented it. The old words "queer," "fairy," were ugly words but "gay" . . . they've assumed this word and I don't like it.
> McVean: . . . I refuse to surrender this word to a deviate world.
> Lautens: I'm glad you said that because it is an unnatural thing. Gays are unnatural. . . . For instance, Matlovich, who made the cover of *Time* magazine, and of course the Air Force asked to resign. . . . I personally wouldn't want to be in barracks and have a comrade in arms who was gay. . . . It's an unknown, unseen threat to me. . . .
> McVean: If they're to be called "gays" what are we? *Glums?*
> *CFRB broadcast, November 14, 1975*

Getting History Straight (or glum?)

History has been written almost exclusively by heterosexuals. For centuries, they have silently conspired to eliminate homosexual life from historical records.[3] The most recent example is Doris Faber's biography of Eleanor Roosevelt.[4] Referring to the lesbian Hickok-Roosevelt letters, Faber asked the Roosevelt Library's curator, "Why couldn't this collection be locked up again, at least for another several decades?" We are all familiar with the heterosexualized versions of high school history in which various kings (James, William, Edward II) are said to have "changed court favourites," and the teaching of literature, in both high school and college, in which homosexual authors and their works are expunged or bowdlerized. (For details, see *College English,* 1974.)

Thus, it is not surprising that the most educated people believe that "homosexual" is the correct (i.e., scientifically or medically correct) term, and that it precedes any recent expropriation of the word "gay." But this is not the case. The word "homosexual" was coined in 1869 by Karoly Maria Benkert, an Austro-Hungarian physician, himself gay, in an effort to provide a less derogatory label than the one current in his time—sodomite.[5] His neologism is hardly linguistically pure. It breaks the rules by combining a Greek root (*homo*—same or like) with a Latin root (*sexus*). It is a confusing neologism because *homo* in Latin means man. Thus, "homosexual" has tended to become a term of reference only for males.

American historian Vern Bullough[6] believes that the word homosexual caught on because it was adopted by two of the most influential and widely read sexologists of the late 19th century, Magnus Hirschfeld and Havelock Ellis.

The new word was not without its competitors. Another sexologist of the time, Karl Heinrichs Ulrichs (also gay), proposed the term *urning,* which enjoyed wide usage for a few years before disappearing. Another invention of the times, of yet unknown origin, was the term *homophile,* which at least had the claim of linguistic purity in combining two Greek roots. Still another term was introduced by the gay English author, Edward Carpenter, in his essay *Homogenic Love* (1873).

And what of "gay," alleged to have been stolen by 20th-century gay militants? Its use in reference to homosexuals long predates the word homosexual. It appears to have originated in the salons of 18th-century France, which tended to be dominated by women. These women especially enjoyed the company of certain witty and entertaining young men who were styled *précieuse* and *gaie.* The feminine form of *gai* was deliberately applied.

The historically contemporary English equivalent for such men was dandy or fop (cf., Oxford English Dictionary entries), used to refer to a man who cultivated precious and delicate (i.e., effeminate) manners. The best-known example is the fictional character, the Scarlet Pimpernel, who used an effeminate courtly role to disguise his secret adventures in France.

American historian David Pascoe claims to have found the earliest English use of "gay" to refer to homosexuals who congregated at a London inn called "Mother Clapp's."[7] However, the usage may have referred primarily to prostitution rather than homosexuality. In 1889 there was a notorious scandal involving young male prostitutes (also legitimately employed as telegraph boys) at a house on Cleveland Street in London. Since the scandal threatened to reach into the royal family via the retinue of the Prince of Wales, the London police hushed the matter, and court documents were sealed until 1975. When English linguist Philip Howard examined the released documents in 1977, he found that the young men in the scandal referred to themselves not in the historically current terminology, sodomite and bugger, nor in Benkert's newly coined word, homosexual, but as gay.

The Oxford English Dictionary has long recognized the use of gay to denote prostitution, but even its 1971 edition (appearing at least two decades after gay had become a common equivalent for homosexual) omits any indication of its usage for male homosexuals. The reference to prostitution is limited to women. Only in 1972 did the Oxford English Dictionary Supplement acknowledge gay as a reference to homosexuals. However, the OED maintains that the earliest use of the word in this context occurred in 1935.

Although the exact historical origin of the word gay, meaning homosexual, may never be clear (the OED is not even clear on the origin of general uses of the word gay in English) one thing is certain, for many decades the word has not enjoyed the "precise" meaning which Alan Dawson of the *Globe and Mail* attributes to it, nor has it always been one of the "nicest" words in the language. The Oxford English Dictionary includes, among its many definitions, "awkward," "immoral," "showy," and "impertinent."

In a path-breaking work which described gay life in America in positive terms for the first time, Donald Cory advocated general acceptance of the word "gay."

> Gay is simple and easy to say and free from the usual stigmas. . . . One of the most desirable purposes it serves is that it facilitates discarding the mask by offering a language free of odium. . . . One would seldom hear it said "At the age of thirteen I realized I was a *fairy*. . . ." One version might be "that I was a homosexual" but most frequently the word "gay" would be used.[8]

Cory was arguing as much with his homosexual as with his heterosexual readers in this early advocacy of using the term gay, because many homosexuals tended to regard gay as too superficial a term for an often oppressed minority and the resultant psychological depression.[9] When a militant gay movement emerged out of the general social activism and social change of the 1960s, it first rejected gay and resorted to the long-discarded 19th-century neologism, *homophile*. Militant homosexuals felt gay was too closely identified in the public mind, when used to refer to homosexuals, with effeminate men or "drag queens." The new militants wanted to shatter the stereotype that all male homosexuals were effeminate and, at the same time, to emphasize that homosexuals love each other, as well as have sex with each other. Homo*phile* seemed preferable to either homo*sexual* or gay, as *phile* is derived from the Greek *philia*—friendly love.

A New Vocabulary of Motives

Leaders of the various North American and European movements for social change in the status of homosexuals strongly felt the need for a new language to describe themselves. The old terminology limited discussion to two modes: the medical model of homosexuality as an illness, and the popular conception of homosexuals as deviates with abnormal sexual appetites, both in terms of sexual object chosen and the strength of the appetite. (See the McVean and Lautens conversation quoted above: "I rather tend to think that gays so-called tend to be both . . . sexually aggressive and exhibitionist.") In the popular stereotype, the trouble with homosexuals (a term generally referring to men) was not merely that they had sex with other men, but that they did so indiscriminately and with relentless importunity.

Although the language of the medical model pretended to be neutral (sometimes substituting invert for homosexual), the tenor of medical discussion of this "illness" was far from neutral. As for popular language, homosexual alternated with homo, faggot, queer, pansy, gearbox, cocksucker, fairy, cornholer, and numerous other derogatory terms. As one gay militant replied to a heterosexual objection about the expropriation of the word gay, "You can have gay back, if you'll also take back all the other words you've called us."

The motives for social change toward gay liberation required a new language. C. Wright Mills was one of the first sociologists to clearly recognize and describe the importance of linguistic change in social change.[10] In Mills' terms, homosexuals seeking liberation and public acceptance were choosing among "alternative programs . . . for situated action." Their motivation for change was a quest for words in which to conceive, perceive, and promote such change. "Motives are words . . . motives are programs of language related to situated actions in response to questions."[11]

Vocabularies of motives are social resources available in different degrees to different individuals, and in different degrees from one social system to another. Mills notes, for example, the lesser availability of religious vocabularies in the 20th century. Gay leaders were no more likely to choose a religious vocabulary to attempt a new conception and description of themselves, than to choose, say, the vocabulary of witchcraft and witchhunting. The vocabulary of law offered no liberation—most North American criminal law speaks only of "indecent assault," "sodomy," "buggery," and so forth.

The most articulate leader in the gay liberation movement of the 1960s was Frank Kameny, an American scientist. It is not surprising that he looked to scientific terminology for a new vocabulary to express (Mills would say "constitute") his motives. Kameny had been fired from his job in 1957 when his homosexuality was discovered. He spent several years attempting to secure reinstatement through legal channels. When all other recourse was exhausted, Kameny turned militant. In 1962, he founded a homosexual organization to promote his new vocabulary of homosexuality.

At the time there were already homosexual organizations promoting social change and greater tolerance, such as the New York Mattachine Society. But these organizations were disguised as civil liberties groups seeking "justice for the unfortunates suffering from the mental aberration . . . of homosexuality." Such groups accepted, at least in their public vocabulary, the medical model of homosexuality as sickness. Kameny rejected this model.

> In this society, rightly or wrongly, those called mentally ill simply do not get all their rights. . . . The entire homophile [sic] movement is going to stand or fall on the question of whether homosexuality is a sickness.[12]

Kameny was among the first to resurrect the word homophile. By 1962 there were several new homophile organizations, linked by ECHO, the East Coast Homophile Organization. By 1966 there was NACHO, the North American Conference of Homophile Organizations. In Canada, the first public gay liberation group, the University of Toronto Homophile Association, was formed in 1969. Various city-wide organizations soon followed, such as CHAT, the Community Homophile Association of Toronto, and HALO, the Homophile Association of London, Ontario.

To replace both the medical and popular vocabularies and models of homosexuality, Kameny invented a new term — sexual orientation.

> In the continuing absence of valid scientific evidence to the contrary, homosexuality *per se* cannot properly be considered a sickness, illness, disturbance, disorder or pathology of any kind, nor a symptom of any of these, but must be considered as a preference, orientation, or propensity, not different in kind from heterosexuality and fully on a par with it.[13]

Kameny's new vocabulary has since entered the language and the law. "Sexual orientation" now appears, for example, in the anti-discrimination provisions of various trade union contracts, university faculty agreements, and city regulations (e.g., Toronto, Ottawa) as well as the provincial law of Quebec (Human Rights Code).

When Frank Kameny first visited Canada in 1969, he still seemed reluctant to use the word gay and preferred homophile. He seems to have linked the word gay with effeminate homosexuals.[14] Kameny's preference accorded with language use in the subculture of homosexuals. For example, an underground newspaper was published at the time by Canadian homosexuals. Its name was *GAY*. It specialized in gossip, innuendo, and news of "drag" contests.

The famous Stonewall Riot of the summer of 1969 in New York City was eventually to change the attitude of the new homophile leaders to the traditional "drag queens," and thus to the use of the word gay. This riot is now celebrated annually as the "Bastille Day" of the gay liberation movement. It was the first recorded incident in history in which homosexuals, congregated at a bar (the Stonewall Inn in Greenwich Village), did not flee from police harassment, but struck back with force.

The riot galvanized the homophile movement with a new "masculine pride." Ironically, it was the "drag queens" (homosexual men who enjoy wearing feminine garb) who led the battle. Homosexual militants who had previously felt defensive and apologetic for comrades who showed effeminate manners and taste, now recognized that for many decades the "drag queens" had been almost the only courageously public, if also outrageously blatant, homosexuals. They had formed the only overt gay community.

C. Wright Mills asks what social conditions are likely to lead to the adoption of a new vocabulary of motives by individuals.[15] He hypothesizes that shifts in language use occur when people find their actions "in some way frustrating . . . in situations, the new vocabulary becomes a program of action which constitutes awareness of anticipated consequences."

Despite more rapid change in the status of homosexuals in one decade than in a previous century, leaders of the new homophile organizations became increasingly impatient and frustrated with both popular and medical stereotypes. The movement split, as the more impatient leaders advocated a full-scale confrontation with heterosexuality. Homophile became a dirty word to the new radicals; it seemed to express a willingness to compromise with the old vocabularies. Kameny, still in the forefront of change, borrowed from the black civil rights movement to invent the slogan "Gay is Good," patterned on "Black is Beautiful." Both slogans conceded nothing to the opposite category of heterosexual and white. Homosexuality was no longer merely on a par with heterosexuality. Homosexuality was good in its own right.

In Canada, the movement divided into relatively conservative "homophile" organizations, and politically confrontationist "gay" organizations such as GATE, the Gay Alliance Toward Equality in Vancouver and Toronto. The transition is documented in gay publications of the time and occasionally in the non-gay press. For example, the "hippie" underground newspaper, *Guerrilla,* reported in its December 1970 issue: "The University of Toronto Homophile Association is trying to remain apolitical, it holds dances, it is not a gay liberation group."

The same conflict was taking place elsewhere. Thus, a group of American, Dutch, French and German authors combined in 1970 to publish a series of essays, *Les Minorités Homosexuelles.*[16] These authors argued for the use of the word homophile rather than gay. They expressed distaste for the "homosexuals in the streets, wearing placards proclaiming: 'We are gay and we are proud.' "

The Public Media Respond

If a "vocabulary of motives" is to bring about the desired social change, it eventually must be adopted by the decision-makers and opinion-molders of society. As one means of examining this process, a content analysis was made of the use of the terms "homosexual," "homophile," and "gay" in the news columns of the three daily newspapers of Toronto from 1960 to 1980. The clipping collections of the Metropolitan Toronto Reference Library and the Canadian Gay Archives were used for this purpose.

"Homophile" has only rarely been employed by the editors and reporters of the three newspapers, except when it is part of the name of an organization. In fact, the only two instances I could discover occurred in the *Globe and Mail* in July 1964.

"Gay" appeared in news stories prior to 1970 only when the author was discussing the special argot of the homosexual subculture, or occasionally, when a clever and "wise" reporter insinuated that a person was homosexual (as in the ballet party mentioned earlier). The Toronto daily press, until 1970, almost universally preferred the term homosexual when reporting regular news.

As the use of the word gay became more broadly acceptable in the homo-sexual-homophile-gay liberation movement, the term began to creep into the daily press. At first the editors appear to have had no clear policy on its use, apparently not anticipating the extent to which homosexuals would adopt this term. There was already the precedent of black for Negro. The reporters and editors even appear to have considered the early use of the word gay by homosexuals as amusing and offering new opportunities for ambiguity and puns.

Thus, on August 31, 1970, the *Toronto Star* reported a "gay march" in New York City. On November 1, 1971, the same paper reported the events of the previous night, Halloween, in the city. Halloween had long been the one night in the year when Toronto police took no action against men in drag on the streets. Indeed, a substantial number of police were employed to hold back the now-bemused, now-jeering, now egg-throwing crowds of heterosex-ual spectators while homosexuals in drag entered two downtown bars which held annual drag queen contests. The *Star* described these events rather tolerantly and used the word gay without quotation marks. The following year, on November 1, 1972, the *Star* even went so far as to headline its Hallo-ween story, "Now We Don Our Gay Apparel," a cute pun on the Christmas carol. A few months earlier a critic reviewed one of the first new books on militant homosexuals with the headline, "Study of the Gay Liberation Move-ment."

In an interview, the senior editor of the *Toronto Star*, Borden Spears, could not recall the exact date when an editorial directive was issued to ban the ordinary use of gay as an equivalent of homosexual. The ban appears to have come after 1972, but certainly before 1974, by which time the *Star* shows no use of the word gay. The precipitating incident may have been an attempt by a new and militant gay newspaper, *The Body Politic*, to place a classified advertisement in the *Star*. The ad read:

> Body Politic, Gay liberation journal. $2.00 for six issues. 4 Kensington St., Toronto.

The *Star* refused this apparently innocuous advertisement on the grounds that it would contribute to the "recruitment" of homosexuals. *The Body Politic* appealed to the Ontario Press Council, an ethical association which the *Star* had been instrumental in organizing. The *Star*'s marketing director argued that it had the moral right to reject the ad because it was a "family newspaper." A gay bookstore then submitted an equally brief and non-provocative ad and, when it was rejected, also appealed to the Press Council. The Council eventually found the *Star* guilty of discrimination, but its findings were not binding.

On October 19, 1974, the *Star* published an editorial headed, "Where the *Star* Draws the Line." It argued that the paper was tolerant of homosexuals but "we stop short of encouraging the spread of homosexuality. We have no wish to aid the aggressive recruitment propaganda in which certain homosexual groups are engaged." However, the *Star* initiated a review of its advertising policy and in April 1975, issued a set of guidelines. Under the heading "Homosexual," the *Star* staff was instructed that, "[T]he word 'gay' is not acceptable except in the name of an organization."

The Political Use of Apparently Non-Political Language

"The fundamental influences upon political beliefs flow from language that is not perceived as political at all," argued Murray Edelman.[17] He notes that such language is especially potent when words denote "a personified threat."[18]

The *Star's* use of a "family newspaper" argument is nicely couched in non-political language. "Family" is expected to conjure up traditional images of the nuclear family, despite the changing reality of families in Canadian society (which has led even relatively conservative institutions such as the Vanier Institute of the Family to recognize a variety of alternative living arrangements as equivalents to "the family").

The *Star's* argument allows it to appear as a tolerant but non-political corporation, serving and protecting its "family readership" by opposing a political intrusion into its otherwise non-controversial advertising columns; an intrusion by homosexuals "aggressively recruiting" sexual partners. There is, in addition, the implication that the *Star* purveys only "news," objectively reported, but the militant homosexuals purvey "propaganda."

The realities of newspaper editing also bear on the issue and the subsequent use of "gay" in the *Star*. News copy is often hurriedly composed, without careful reference to official style guidelines. Headlines are tacked on to reporters' stories by editors, who may have time to read only a few lines. Headlines must also be visually attractive, by employing short, catchy words. They must fit the space available, in column widths, without leaving too much white space.

These considerations are clearly at work on occasions when the word gay continues to slip into the *Star* and other newspapers which officially oppose its use as an equivalent for homosexual. It is beneath the dignity of the *Star* and similar "family newspapers" to force a headline to fit by reducing "homosexual" to "homo." (It is not, of course, beneath the dignity of the "yellow press" to do this.) Thus, a harried editor simply writes in "gay," as in the headline, "Gay Lib seeks Place in Military" (*Toronto Star*, September 17, 1975).

By contrast, when the editor works at a leisurely pace, as in the case of the editor who selects letters from readers to publish on the "Letters to the Editor" page, there is an opportunity to accomplish a political goal with apparently non-political language. Edelman argues that this is often achieved through the use of "problematic categories" which enable people to dismiss and negatively characterize those who are threats to the established order. "Though symbolic cues are not omnipotent, they go far toward defining the geography and topography of everyone's political world."[19]

One of the means editors may employ is simply to discard letters from readers which express opinions contrary to those of the editor, especially if the views are articulately and persuasively written. The *Star* also employs a difficult, more surprising method. Whenever a reader writes and uses the word gay as meaning homosexual, the *Star* editor simply transforms this to "homosexual," a term clearly regarded as politically more acceptable.

This amazing practice was finally protested by a university English professor, Michael Lynch, in 1978. Failing to receive a satisfactory reply from the *Star*, he complained to the Press Council. His arguments included: (a) letter writers have a right to refer to themselves as they wish, providing there is no offence to taste or law; (b) various dictionaries now define gay to include a homosexual meaning; (c) the *New York Times*, America's "newspaper of record," uses the term gay to denote homosexual; (d) the *Star* itself acknowledged the homosexual meaning of the term gay in its April 1975 advertising guideline; and (e) the Modern Language Association has accepted homosexual as being among the correct meanings of "gay."

At the time of publication of this article, the *Star* continues to reject these arguments. Moreover, even in its news columns, when reporting a scholarly paper on homosexuality in which the scholar uses "gay," the *Star* transforms the word to homosexual. Thus sociologist Brian Miller's paper, "Gay Parents," became "Homosexual Parents."[20] The *Star* has accepted "black" as an equivalent for Negro, and does not transform one to the other.

The *Toronto Star* policy forms an interesting contrast with that of the other two Toronto dailies. The *Globe and Mail,* a national newspaper with satellite editions across Canada, banned the use of gay until the style guide change (cited earlier) of 1978. But the editors appear to have been much less dedicated to enforcement than those at the *Star.* Everyday usage in news columns had altered so much by 1978 that the style guide change simply accepted a *fait accompli.*

In the early 1960s, the *Globe and Mail* not only used the word homosexual, it also reported news relating to homosexuals in words such as deviates, sexual perverts, and aberrations.[21] A headline of July 25, 1964 refers to homosexuals as "Sex Deviants." But the *Globe* began using "gay" soon after it became politically popular in the gay liberation movement. Indeed, the Oxford English Dictionary Supplement (1972) cites the *Globe* as a source of an early use of gay in its *substantive* form (e.g., meaning homosexual person). The example is "a coffee shop where the gay congregate." By 1975 the *Globe* was using both the substantive plural form, and the possessive form. Thus, "Publicity over Homosexual Ring prompts Protest by Ottawa Gays," was a headline which appeared on March 2, 1975. In a story of March 12, 1979, under the headline, "Are there Gay Genes?" the phrase "the gay's post-birth environment" occurred. The *Globe* even introduced an antonym in the headline, "Rally gives Anti-gays a Chance to Vent Anger" (January 8, 1979).

The *Toronto Sun*, one of a number of *Sun* newspapers in Canada, has used "gay" and "homosexual" interchangeably since it began publication in the early 1970s. The *Sun* editors seem to be guided by two considerations, one simply pragmatic and the other openly political (in contrast to the *Star's* covert politics of the family). In headlines, "gay" is used when it fits conveniently, which is rather often, since the *Sun*, a tabloid newspaper, deliberately aims for a more sensational presentation of the news. Thus the headline, "Gays Ok Carter" appeared on March 27, 1977.

But when political considerations enter, the *Sun* is explicitly and passionately opposed to gay liberation and its goals. Whenever public funds are provided to a gay group (for example, in the arts or recreation), the *Sun* protests editorially. It strongly opposes any legislation to ban discrimination on the basis of sexual orientation. News stories and headlines dealing with gay liberation politics are therefore likely to evoke the "problematic categorization"[22] of homosexuals. For example, a headline reads, "Homosexual Mag Gets Art Grant" (*Sun*, August 11, 1977). The same information could have been communicated in the same column width with the headline, "Gay Magazine Gets Art Grant." "Homosexual" in this instance is more "vivid and memorable . . . in depict[ing] a personified threat . . ."[23] especially when combined with "mag" which detracts from the image of the publication brought to mind by "magazine." The *Sun* has not hesitated to use even more provocative language, referring to a gay political group as "the limp wrist lobby"[24] and gay spokespersons as "radical homosexuals laying seige to society."[25]

The Quantitative Effect of Language Use

Changes in the vocabulary of references to gay politics, culture, and lifestyle, are of increasing importance in their impact on society, simply because of the enormous increase in the number of media references. Only a decade or so ago, any reference whatever to the existence of homosexuals was unacceptable in certain media. For example, in 1969 some 39 Canadian daily newspapers subscribed to *Weekend Magazine,* a glossy insert added to their weekend editions.

On September 13, 1969, *Weekend Magazine* published a feature article on "The First Canadian Organization for Homosexuals." Fourteen of the 39 subscribing newspapers assigned staff the onerous task of ripping this article out of every copy of the magazine before it was inserted into their Saturday editions.

In Toronto in 1974, the three daily newspapers published a total of eight articles on homosexuals (90 column inches). By 1979 the coverage of homosexuals had greatly increased. The clipping count at the Toronto Reference Library and the Canadian Gay Archives is as follows:

Year	Articles	Column Inches
1974	8	90
1977	39	450
1979	113	2,000

The Politics of a Word

In an interview with Borden Spears of the *Toronto Star,* I commented that the word gay seemed to be perceived both by gays and non-gays as having political overtones not present in homosexual. Of course, as Edelman argues, homosexual only appears non-political. Spears agreed with my suggestion, but put it differently: "Gay is a political word, but homosexual has a precise meaning." The *Star*'s official position is explained in more detail in a letter from editorial page editor David Crane to the Ontario Press Council[26] which reads in part:

> We agree entirely with the rejection of such terms as queer, faggot, and pervert. They are pejorative words and we do not employ them. For precisely the same reason, but in the reverse sense, we do not admit gay as a description of homosexuals. To do so is to use the wrong word where the right word exists. . . .
>
> If the homosexual community had coined a new word and it won general acceptance, the *Star* would have no difficulty in accepting it. This is not the case here. The arbitrary misappropriation of any honest word debases the language. It may be that in time, gay will have lost its historic meaning and acquired another. If that happens, the language will be poorer. We do not intend to assist in its impoverishment.

Using an approach similar to Murray Edelman's *Political Language,* this argument is analyzed in detail below. First, it must be remembered that the same *Star* editors have no objection to the fact that Negroes have not "coined a new word" but simply given new use to an old one—black. (The same editors, however, *do* object to the feminist movement coining a new word, Ms., and there has been considerable media resistance to its use. But that is another story, worth a research paper of its own.)

There is apparently no feeling among *Star* editors, and those who make the same argument against gay as a "misappropriation of an honest word," that black, meaning Negro, is a misappropriation. The implication is that the editors find Negroes fully on a par with whites and are prepared to align themselves with the liberal conscience and the civil rights movement by adopting the word black liberation leaders have adopted for themselves. The editors apparently do not consider the supplementary meaning for the word black as a loss to the English language, because the older meanings of black remain.

In the case of the term gay, there is different sentiment, forthrightly expressed by the colleague who argued that I should use the academically correct word for myself. When I replied that he had adopted black for Negroes, he retorted that, "Using black that way doesn't ruin its other uses. But now that 'gay' means homosexual, I can't use it any other way. Homosexuals have ruined the word."

The same argument lies buried in the *Star* letter. It states "for precisely the same reasons, but in reverse . . ." and contrasts pejorative terms (e.g., faggot) with gay. But the reverse of pejorative is approbative. Use of the word gay for homosexual is too approving, too positive, when applied to an allegedly sexually deviant group. It puts homosexuals on a par with heterosexuals (as Kameny explicitly argued).

Now the *Star* claims to be a family newspaper, and in this case, family is a symbolic cue for heterosexual. (Those who reject homosexuality as "fully on a par with heterosexuality" never concede that homosexuals living together constitute a family.) In short, "black" meaning Negro does not ruin the word, because blacks are no longer considered as inferior to whites. "Gay" meaning homosexual ruins the word gay because it still refers to what is considered a deviant and inferior lifestyle. Any other use of the word thereby carries the odium of association with social inferiority.

There is a more fundamental level of meaning which leads to resistance to the use of gay. Edelman observed:

> People can communicate in a public language when they sufficiently share norms that they need not be explicit about premises and meanings. Simple and sometimes unfinished sentences . . . demonstrate implicit understanding. . . .[27]

There is an implicit meaning in "homosexual" which is important for those who dislike and disapprove of homosexuals. Homosexuals are considered sexually aggressive. They "recruit" heterosexuals "to their perverted way of life." Homosexuals are morally subversive. The word gay is not considered to carry the same implicit meaning. The choice between the two terms is politically motivated, just as editors and writers must choose whether to call a certain act of violence (such as a bombing) an act of liberation, resistance or terrorism.

At best, insistence on "homosexual" constitutes an argument for a medical model rather than a lifestyle model. Those with a same-sex orientation must be categorized as a medical constituency rather than a political community. They may be pitied (like the handicapped or slow learners) but no one would deliberately want to be one.

The advocates of the word gay, on the other hand, argue that a person might well want to be attracted to the same sex, that one might find it enjoyable and morally rewarding. The slogans insist "Gay is Good," "Gay is Proud," and the marching songs repeat:

> Two, four, six, eight,
> Gay is just as good as straight.
> Three, five, seven, nine,
> Lesbians are mighty fine.

The use of "gay" or "homosexual" has ceased to be a matter of preservation of the English language, if it ever fundamentally was such a matter. The struggle is now a political contest between one word, which is regarded as scientifically correct by its advocates and as a humbling reminder of a medical model by the opposition, and another word, which one side regards as aggressive propaganda, and the other side considers morally correct. As Foucault observes:

> As if in order to gain mastery over it in reality, it has first been necessary to subjugate it at the level of language . . . (1978:17).[28]

There is wide agreement among social scientists today concerning the political power of language. Out of the pioneering work of Sapir and Whorf has developed the awareness that "words have enormous power over us, including the power to prevent recognition of alternative conceptions of the real."[29]

It is not merely a question of conflict over definitions of the real; language shapes and limits our ability to grasp a particular reality. Hertzler argues, "Language . . . powerfully conditions all our thinking about our social problems and processes."[30] Mueller agrees, ". . . language and political consciousness go hand in hand. . . ."[31]

Many years passed between the accession to power of the Communist party in China and the recognition of that reality in our political language. During the interval, many diplomats and civil servants had to screen out some words and "police their statements."[32] The most politically acceptable reference in many circles was "Red China." Those politically tolerant of the new regime but not prepared to be seen as "fellow travellers" would refer to "Mainland China." Sympathizers with the new rulers used the new rulers' own label, "The People's Republic of China." Yet in time, this latter title has prevailed even among the political opponents, with the small exception of an extreme-right fringe who continue to call the island of Taiwan "China."

Much the same political process is involved in the contest between "homosexual" and "gay." The battleground is not limited to the media and everyday speech. It includes a wide variety of walls where Humpty Dumpties strive for mastery, such as dictionaries and encyclopedias. Webster's editors have recognized a different political reality than Funk and Wagnalls by including gay as meaning homosexual. The latter dictionary includes a homosexual reference under such words as fag, faggot, queer and pansy, but not under gay.

Alice in Wonderland must realize that words do mean different things, and the editorial decision to admit different meanings is not merely one of mastery over language. The editors of Funk and Wagnalls and the *Toronto Star* may prefer to argue their choices of words as evidence of their protection of the purity of language. But as Hertzler notes, "a change of language is a change of world stance."[33] If it is true, as Mills argues, that social change requires a new vocabulary, once the new vocabulary is invented, it may in turn require social change. "Motives are words," Mills summed up his analysis. But an analysis of the arguments for and against the use of the words homosexual and gay suggests that the reverse is also true—words are motives.

NOTES

1. For a discussion of political recognition and homosexuals see Edmund White, "The Political Vocabulary of Homosexuality," in *The State of the Language*, edited by L. Michaels and C. Ricks (San Francisco: University of California Press, 1980), pp. 235-246.
2. Donald Cory, *The Homosexual in America* (New York: Paperback, 1951), p. 106.
3. Cf. Vern Bullough, *Sexual Variance in Society and History* (New York: Wiley, 1976); and Jonathan Katz, *Gay American History* (New York: Crowell, 1976).
4. Doris Faber, *The Life of Lorena Hickok: Eleanor Roosevelt's Friend* (Toronto: Gage, 1980).
5. Bullough, *Sexual Variance*, p. 637.
6. Ibid., p. 670.
7. *Globe and Mail*, June 22, 1978, p. 8.
8. Cory, *Homosexual in America*, p. 107.
9. Cf. Marion Foster, and Kent Murray, *A Not so Gay World* (Toronto: McClelland & Stewart, 1972).
10. C. Wright Mills, *Power, Politics and People* (New York: Ballantine, 1963), p. 440ff.
11. Ibid., p. 440.
12. K. Tobin and R. Wicker, *The Gay Crusaders* (New York: Paperback, 1975), p. 98.
13. Ibid.
14. Cf. report of Kameny speech in Toronto, *The Ryerson*, January 27, 1970.
15. Mills, *Power, Politics, and People*, p. 441.
16. S. de Batselier, and H. L. Ross, *Les minorités homosexuelles* (Brussels: Ducat, 1973).
17. Murray Edelman, *Political Language* (New York: Academic Press, 1977), p. 21.
18. Ibid., p. 14.
19. Ibid., p. 41.
20. *Toronto Star*, May 25, 1979.
21. *Globe and Mail*, November 14, 1963.
22. Edelman, *Political Language*, p. 41.
23. Ibid., p. 15.
24. *Toronto Sun*, August 10, 1978.
25. Ibid., January 9, 1980.
26. September 21, 1976.
27. Edelman, *Political Language*, p. 110.
28. Michel Foucault, *The History of Sexuality* (New York: Vintage, 1978), p. 17.
29. Austin Turk, "Law as a Weapon in Social Conflict," in *The Sociology of Law*, edited by C. E. Reasons and R. M. Rich (Toronto: Butterworths, 1978), p. 213.

30. J. O. Hertzler, *A Sociology of Language* (New York: Random House, 1965), p. 440.

31. Claus Meuller, *The Politics of Communication* (New York: Oxford, 1973), p. 19.

32. Foucault, *History of Sexuality*, p. 18.

33. Hertzler, *Sociology of Language*, p. 126.

Chapter 2

Second-hand News: Production and Reproduction at a Major Ontario Television Station

*Debra Clarke**

Le présent article vise à exposer les résultats d'un projet d'observation (sans participation de la part du chercheur) mené en Ontario, dans une des plus importantes stations de télévision privées. L'examen détaillé de la production des nouvelles à l'intérieur de cette station suggère la possibilité que des différences visibles existent entre le phénomène canadien et la production de nouvelles en Grande-Bretagne et aux Etats-Unis. La première consiste dans le fait que le flot unidirectionnel des nouvelles tend à se centraliser hors de la métropole (Ottawa, Toronto, etc.) où il paraît concentré, selon le modèle de transmission de l'information observable au niveau international. L'article suggère qu'une bonne part de ce qui constitue les informations au Canada, traite d'événements survenus hors du pays et de nouvelles produites au-delà des frontières canadiennes. C'est ainsi que le processus de production des nouvelles en devient un de distribution. Il apparaît que trois contraintes immédiates pèsent sur la production (le temps, l'argent et la technologie), et déterminent ici son caractère distributif. Spécifiquement, le temps manque, les moyens financiers sont rares et la technologie est inadéquate ou limitée.

Toutes ces conditions se retrouvent à la station "A", l'objet de cette étude. La structure physique de la salle des nouvelles, la division des tâches, la coordination de la production des actualités et les bulletins d'informations eux-mêmes, portent tous les effets de ces contraintes. Cependant, la production est marquée par un grand nombre de contraintes plus subtiles parmi lesquelles on retrouve: les priorités budgétaires et de programmation pré-

---

* A lengthier version of this article was prepared for presentation at the founding conference of the Canadian Communication Association, Montreal, June 1980 (see Clarke, 1980). Acknowledgements are extended to Philip Elliott, Graham Knight, and Liora Salter for their comments on various formulations of the material.

établies, l'influence des autres medias, le contrôle social des producteurs de nouvelles, le caractère visuel de la télévision et le contexte de divertissement dans lequel les informations sont produites, l'action des valeurs des nouvelles, le concept de fabrication des actualités en fonction d'un auditoire, la nature des sources d'information, la compartimentation des nouvelles, la pratique journalistique et son code professionnel (c.-à-d. les lois de l'objectivité et la nécessité de preuves à l'appui), et l'intervention directe de la direction ou des propriétaires dans la production de nouvelles. Un bulletin d'informations pris comme échantillonnage a été examiné et discuté, bien que la nécessité de procéder à une analyse textuelle étendue s'impose, afin de déterminer pleinement les causes de ces contraintes.

Les rédacteurs aux informations de la station "A" ont été soumis aux huit "mesures de contrôle du travail" de Marchak, à l'aide d'entrevues traitant de leur emploi. Quoique la plupart d'entre eux soient expérimentés et hautement qualifiés, la division des tâches rudimentaire et le travail rendu routinier, en partie à cause du caractère distributif de la production, réduit le rôle des rédacteurs à celui de simples reproducteurs d'actualités ne disposant que de peu ou pas d'autonomie vis-à-vis de leur travail, et d'un contrôle restreint sur l'information produite dans sa totalité. Par conséquent, l'aliénation et le découragement règnent chez les rédacteurs qui ont tendance à trouver dans leurs loisirs des compensations à leurs frustrations.

Une discussion des moyens que prend chaque type de contrainte pour affecter la production de la station "A", et des comparaisons avec d'autres études sur la production aux Etats-Unis et en Grande-Bretagne, présentent d'autres preuves de l'importance des contraintes de production. Les conclusions de l'étude suggèrent que de nouvelles recherches s'imposent afin de définir la place du Canada à l'intérieur du flot international d'informations et d'examiner plus complètement les ramifications idéologiques importantes qu'impliquent les deux opérations de production et de reproduction en présence.

What emerges most clearly and most emphatically out of the recent wave of British and American publications regarding television news is the crucial point that news production must above all be understood as a social process. News production, or rather news construction, is first and foremost a *social* construction. While news producers[1] seemingly have little sense of either process or structure, their work ties them into a process that is both structured and itself a structure, that is, the larger institution which is the mass media.

The institution of the mass media is in turn tied within the structure of the still larger social order through its dual economic/ideological operations, its productive/reproductive activities, and its simultaneous base/superstructure location. News production and media production at large must at all times be understood in terms of this social location, and this double articulation that links production and reproduction constitutes, in Murdock's words, "one of the key conditions for the continued existence of prevailing productive relations."[2] However, this link between production and reproduction still needs to be wholly elaborated and documented, and the present analysis is restricted to the immediate social world of news production.

News production is a process that differs little in its essential character from the production of other commodities. It is fundamentally integrated into the economic base and it features a division of labour, a technological scheme (a relatively skilled and disciplined work force, a highly bureaucratized organizational scheme), and a raw material that is transformed through the course of production into the news commodity. The raw material of news production is, at least in theory, the world. (Consider the number of news programmes pretentiously titled "The World at Six," "The World this Week," etc.) To understand the most basic constraint operative in the news production process, one needs to consider how "the world" is delimited at the hands of news producers, since it is impossible to display all that there is to the world at any one point in time across the television screen. The world, as it is, must be taken as pre-given. It is not, in itself, news. (This alone speaks volumes about the structured-in ideological operations of the media.)

Moreover, since each new day starts anew, what already exists, what existed the previous day, cannot be said to be new and therefore is not "news." "News," then, is not "the way the world is today." Instead, since the world is pre-given, "news" is "what is new about it," or "what has taken place today" in this pre-given world; that is, the "event." Hence the *prima facie* delimitation of the world for news producers is its reduction to events.

However, "all that has taken place in the world today" may be "news," but it is not necessarily *newsworthy*. The world is thus again reduced to "what has taken place today that will interest and/or be important to the audience"; that is, newsworthy events. It must also be added that the event *itself* is not the news. It is still just the raw material, which remains to be processed into the *report* of the event. It is the news report of the event which is the finished product of the whole production process. During this process, the event will be further reduced, in line with journalistic practice, to the "angle" of the coverage, and still further reduced to the five basic "Ws" of news reporting: "Who" comes to mean the representatives of legitimate, official institutions; "What" is the extraordinary, dramatic, tragic, or humorous event; "Where" is at the legitimate, official institutions (Parliament Hill and so forth) where journalists are positioned; and "When" is in time to be processed for the newscast. "Why," if not somehow pre-given, is derived from the angle that the journalist has pre-determined.

Each of these acts can be seen to further delimit or reduce the world as the original raw material of news production. Events, for example, will also be compartmentalized according to their locales and their apparent implications; that is, into international, national, and regional or local news categories. All of these things and more—the nature of news sources, the rules of "objectivity," the conception of the audience, and so forth—carry consequences for what is produced, and for the way that the world is revealed, and therefore all these things act in some fashion to *constrain* the presentation of the world in the news programme. In this broad sense the term "production constraints" is used here.

These constraints can themselves be categorized according to the magnitude of their consequences for news production and for the news programme. Time, money, and technology[3] are probably the most immediate and the most pressing production constraints that news producers face, and those to which producers will most readily admit.[4] Yet there are others that, while not so immediate, have more extensive consequences. These include: the operation of news values; conception of the audience; visual imperative (which transforms news into "show business"); compartmentalizing of news stories; social control of news producers; nature of news sources; role of news managers; the influence of other media; rules of objectivity; and the historical legacy of the television enterprise. All of these broad and not so broad constraints are operative in the case of Station "A."[5]

Most production constraints are rooted in news practices and the organization of news production, and should be understood through a consideration of the emergence of journalistic procedures through time, within the parameters of capitalist production relations. Such an exercise becomes important to understanding the means through which ideological themes appear and reappear through the cultural form of news products. Obviously there can be no attempt here to either theorize or demonstrate the operation of the process; without doubt, it is much less plainly observable than the concrete process of news programme manufacture. Nevertheless, the analysis that follows strongly suggests its operation at the level of concrete practices of news production. A concomitant textual analysis of the news *product* would more fully highlight its operation. These are all crucial tasks that need serious attention, especially in respect to the case of Canada, where so little work has yet been undertaken in this area.

Therefore, while limited in its range, the present study is one of the first to detail the specifics of Canadian news production. Although existing studies of news operations apply equally to Canadian production, additional considerations are at work here. Some originate from the organization of the Canadian broadcasting system and more generally to Canada's position as a nation that is at once imperialist victor and victim. In terms of news production, it means that much of what constitutes news in Canada takes place elsewhere and is originally produced outside the national borders (by international news agencies, British and American television networks, contractual correspondents, etc.).

It can be tentatively suggested (since this still needs to be demonstrated) that Canadian news production is highly centralized, to the extent that, outside the metropolis (such as Toronto) where news is concentrated, news production is largely reduced to the *distribution* of news, or, at the very least, to the *reproduction* of news commodities produced elsewhere.

The Station "A" case bears witness to these dual processes of production and reproduction. Moreover, it suggests that the three most immediate production constraints may underline Canada's distribution-oriented production, particularly when time is short, money is sparse, and the technology is poor or otherwise restrictive.

THE STATION "A" CASE

Station "A" is a private non-affiliated television station operated by Niagara Television Limited which in turn is controlled by Selkirk Holdings Limited, the major broadcasting arm of the Southam communications empire. The station operates within and is accessible to the Toronto/Hamilton/Niagara region of Ontario. Indeed, due to its location and its access to most of the lucrative southern and central Ontario broadcasting market, its (real and potential) audience is the largest of all television stations in Canada (3.7 million according to a 1978 BBM survey). Its independent status vis-à-vis the three principal television networks that operate in Ontario and its competitive position within the most densely populated region of the country make the station a fruitful and interesting case.

This study documents the actual process of news production, the means by which the raw material at the disposal of news producers is shaped into the evening news programme, the activities of the various news workers who contribute to the process, and how other factors—economic, technological, organizational—figure within the process and/or affect the end product.

Observation at the station was non-participant and loosely structured. The activities of the production staff were observed and recorded. Informal and formal taped interviews were conducted with news management, news editors, and other assorted staff members. All material related to the production of the evening news programme (used and unused Broadcast News wire copy, Visnews and NBC network feed copy, staff-assigned story copy, programme scripts, etc.) was collected for the two weeks (11–15 December 1978 and 8–12 January 1979) and retained for later analysis.[6] Some preliminary foci that first directed the observation included: the division of labour within the newsroom and how it is determined; how specialities or "beats" are categorized and how flexible these are; how work is routinized; the degree of autonomy exercised by news workers; career aspirations of news workers and their attitudes towards their work; and, indications of constraints operative in the production process that altered or otherwise affected the news programme itself.

The Newsroom

The Station "A" news department occupies the ground floor of a three-storey renovated brick house situated in a downtown area close to the city hall. The second floor accommodates sales and administrative offices. Studio facilities are housed within a large building across the street. The news department includes two rooms plus a separate small office for the news director. The newsroom itself occupies what was the living room of the house, while the original kitchen or pantry is now the film-processing room. The newsroom is small (approximately 12 x 20 feet) and its space is further reduced by the assistant news director's office which is partitioned off at one end of the room. At the opposite end a corkboard wall holds wire-copy clippings and memos and leads to the film processing room. Against this wall are the three wire service machines, the police radio monitor, and a large colour television set which rests above a tall file cabinet. Along the sides are more file cabinets, a bulletin board for administrative notices, a coffee machine, and a bookcase that holds newspapers, style manuals, dictionaries, and other assorted reference books. One large and long table serves as "the news desk" and fills most of the remaining space, making movement around the room frequently awkward and cumbersome. On the desk are three large manual typewriters, a six-button telephone, a file box, and scattered papers. There is no fixed seating arrangement for the staff, and this often causes confusion and irritation when all chairs placed before typewriters are occupied, particularly close to air time.

The noise level within the newsroom is constant and medium to high in volume (depending primarily on the number of people in the room). The television, at medium volume, is tuned to the Station "A" channel at all times, with two exceptions. Hockey games and other sports events broadcast on other channels are watched for late scores which are then telephoned to the studio and passed to the sportscaster just prior to air time. Often during the evenings newsroom staff will watch their favourite American game shows either on American stations or on the Station "A" channel. At one side of the newsroom a radio constantly monitors local and regional radio stations for news stories. Both the radio and a wall-mounted telephone are wired to a tape recorder (the telephone is used to produce audio reports for Parliament Hill stories). The noise of the radio, together with the television, the typewriters, and personal conversations, makes the police radio monitor barely audible.[7] After 9:00 p.m., however, the radio is kept at a low volume or shut off, typewriter noise is (at best) intermittent since little typing is done, and there are no more than three to four staff members on duty, so that the noise level is considerably lower at this time of day.

The physical structure of the newsroom is important to the extent that it reflects, in some interesting ways, the newsroom's organizational and, as it were, social structure. Most blatantly, the cramped quarters of the room and the otherwise poor and meagre facilities available to the department reflect its economic organization; that is, the budgetary limitations that apply to news at Station "A." Relative to other departments, especially the programming department, budgetary allocations to the news department are slim. (The Station "A" case is somewhat unusual in the sense that the news department commonly breaks even or manages a small profit, whereas at most television stations, news is the single greatest expense and the news department "either operates in the red or barely breaks even.")[8] This in turn reflects the station's programming priorities, its historical legacy, and its management-styled image: Station "A" management regard the station as first and foremost an "entertainment station" and only secondarily or peripherally a "news station."

This management position was so frequently stressed (and lamented) throughout the interviews that it soon became a predictable, inevitable, and unavoidable subject of conversation, *both* with news workers and with some news management staff. Indeed, one reporter suggested that Station "A" was a poor choice for a case study of television news production since "this station doesn't care about news, and if it weren't for the CRTC, I bet it wouldn't even bother to do a news show."

Interestingly enough, the limited newsroom facilities set off a chain reaction in respect to other features of the news operation. The cramped space of the newsroom, the awkwardness of movement, the absence of a formal seating arrangement around the news desk, and the related noise level, all contribute to the appearance of frenzy and excitement (especially during shift overlaps, 2:30–5:30 p.m.), despite what is a highly routinized production procedure and (to most of the news producers), outright boring news work. At the same time, it places the news workers in a somewhat ambiguous position vis-à-vis their attitudes to their work and to the news operation at large. On the one hand, the news staff seem tense and excited during these periods and persist in their perception of the newsroom as chaotic, frenzied, and replete with excitement. On the other hand, this same physical organization, or rather disorganization, aggravates their already alienated and dispirited position as non-autonomous, de-skilled television journalists, who, in the words of one news editor, "have been reduced to clerical workers."

Finally, the location of the news studio across the street also symbolically reflects the sharp division between the news staff and the technical staff who operate and supervise the technical aspects of news production. Technical staff, it should be noted, are not responsible exclusively to the news department, but are shared with programming and other departments. Tenuously situated outside the structure of the news department, and holding sharply distinct job classifications according to the union contract, the technical staff operate within a clearly separate work world. Hence the phrases "across the street" and "the guys across the street," frequently invoked during the course of the interviews with news workers, had a significance that referred much more to relations between workers and between departments than the location of the news studio. This will become clearer through the following discussion of the division of labour within the newsroom.

The Division of Labour

The station employs more than 100 organized workers (excluding management, clerical, and maintenance staff), but the news department consists of only 17 permanent staff members. This reflects the station's self-styled image which dictates that it is an "entertainment station" by desire and a "news station" only through necessity. Budgetary allocations correspond to this self-image and to this set of priorities.

The news director and the assistant news director are the two management representatives, while all other news staff are non-management and, with the exception of the news department secretary, all are unionized and belong to the Canadian Association of Broadcast Employees (CABE).[9]

The news director, who has held his position for more than 15 years, is directly responsible to the station manager, and is the ultimate overseer of the newsroom and its news programmes. His most immediate responsibility is the 6:00 p.m. newscast, which is considered the most important news programme that the station broadcasts. Outside news source material is channelled to the news director and he supervises the Monday to Friday day staff who produce the 6:00 p.m. newscast. Most importantly, he supplies the sources and assigns all local and other staff-covered stories, despite the presence of a staff member whose official title is "assignment editor."

The assistant news director has held his salaried management position for 12 years, and for the same period has simultaneously acted, through a contractual agreement with the station, as the provincial parliamentary (Queen's Park) reporter. His most immediate responsibility, other than the Queen's Park reports which he covers during weekday afternoons, is the 11:00 p.m. newscast. He decides which stories from the 6:00 p.m. newscast will be re-broadcast at 11:00 p.m., selects the wire service stories that will be broadcast at that time, assigns the few local stories to be covered during the evening, and determines the day stories as well as the order of all stories included in the 11:00 p.m. programme. The assistant news director also acts as the unofficial public relations director for the news department, and occasionally conducts tours of the department for interested outside groups.[10] Like the news director, he is responsible for handling all viewer complaints with respect to "his" 11:00 p.m. programme.

The actual news staff consists of eight reporters officially titled "news editors," four "film photographers," and two "film editor-processors." The day staff typically includes five news editors (one of whom is designated "assignment editor"), two film photographers, and one film editor-processor. The evening staff includes two news editors, a film photographer, and a film editor-processor.

The so-called assignment editor will allocate stories to the day staff in the absence of the news director. Otherwise, like the other seven reporters who are officially titled news editors, his work mainly consists of re-writing wire copy. The news editors are all quick to criticize the lack of a beat system at Station "A" (the journalist's equivalent to a "specialized division of labour"). Under this system reporters are encouraged to develop specialized knowledge of a particular category of news—such as labour, education, crime, municipal politics—and are regularly assigned to cover such issues. It would appear that staff size *alone* prohibits the implementation of this common scheme to organize the labour process.

All reporters, in theory and in practice, are assigned to report all categories of stories, with the exception of one (woman) reporter who is always assigned to sports stories. Another reporter who is also a volunteer firefighter likes to report fire stories, although these are usually initiated by him through his own sources within the local fire department. (Significantly, this was the only instance in which a reporter identified any outside contacts as his own personal sources.) Another reporter tends to report City Hall activities, yet his assignments are not restricted to municipal politics. Finally, the station has a contractual agreement with a journalist in Ottawa who supplies daily reports from Parliament Hill.

When asked why the station had no official beat system, the assistant news director responded that it *did* have a beat system, pointing to the "tendencies" listed above. Yet discussions with each of the reporters revealed that, in reality, there is no such system and that all reporters are general reporters, or more precisely, general news editors. Their official title is a telling admission. It will be argued later that their work consists more of editing copy prepared elsewhere than of reporting either self-initiated or assigned stories. Indeed, it will be argued that the division of labour is primitive and simplistic, and that the real news producers—the reporters, photographers, and film editors—although in most cases experienced and highly qualified, have been de-skilled through the imposition of this rudimentary division of labour and through the routinization of production. As a result they are reduced to news *re*producers or news distributors with little or no autonomy, freedom, or control with respect to their work.

Like the journalists who have been reduced to mere news editors, the film photographers are mere photographers with even less autonomy and little involvement in the journalistic aspects of production. Photographers, for example, must always be accompanied by a news editor at each story,[11] and rarely make decisions about news events or even about the angle of shots.[12] Similarly, the film editor-processors are not film *editors* but mere processors, since all film editing decisions rest with news management. Appropriately therefore, reporters will hereafter be referred to as news editors, film photographers simply as photographers, and film editor-processors as film processors.

This completes the list of permanent full-time news department staff, which totals 17: the news director, the assistant news director/Queen's Park reporter, the eight news editors, the four photographers, the two film processors, and the department secretary. The listing also reflects the status system or prestige order within the newsroom. The remainder of those associated with the production process are linked less closely to the news department through (generally) special contracts. These include: the 6:00 p.m. newscaster; the 11:00 p.m. newscaster (whose regular position is with a local radio station); the evening sportscaster (a newspaper journalist who, unlike the newscasters, both prepares and reads his own copy); and, a substitute sportscaster who holds a renewable six-month contract with the station.

It is indicative of the station's "entertainment" image that, while reluctant to commit monies to the production of news, station management prefers on-camera staff who are, in the words of one news worker, "name people." Both newscasters, for example, are well known in the region and both (particularly the newscaster who appears on the more important 6:00 p.m. programme) exude a stern, authoritative, and conservative presence. The 11:00 p.m. newscaster, while still stern, authoritative, and conservative, attempts a witty and sarcastic style, and at the conclusion of each programme engages in a short "ad lib" dialogue with the sportscaster. The dialogue typically consists of light humour or sarcasm that is clearly intended to entertain the news audience. Moreover, the sportscaster, although not highly regarded by his peers in the field of sports journalism, is considered "a colourful character" and is best known for his strange and often outlandish attire.

Finally, the news department utilizes the technical staff based "across the street." This includes the show director (who, for the purposes of the news programme, is no more than a technical supervisor), two videotape recorder (VTR) operators, an audio operator, and the booth announcer who opens the news programme. The technical staff work at all times at the studio across the street, and supervise the technical aspects of all programme production at the station.

The Organization of News Work

Station "A" produces two 30-minute newscasts Monday through Friday at 6:00 p.m. and 11:00 p.m., in addition to hourly news bulletins throughout the day until 6:00 p.m. Weekend production is limited to a 15-minute newscast Saturday and again Sunday at noon, with a staff that includes the weekend supervisor and two news editors.[13] The weekday 6:00 p.m. newscast is considered the major news programme, and is produced with a staff that includes the news director, four to five news editors, two photographers, and a film processor. The news editors and photographers work either 9:00 to 5:00

or 9:30 to 5:30 shifts. Staff associated with the 11:00 p.m. programme include the assistant news director, who arrives after his afternoon at Queen's Park at 4:30 or 5:00 p.m.; two news editors (one works 2:30 to 10:30 and the other 3:30 to 11:30); a photographer (if required); and a film processor. The evening newscaster and the sportscaster arrive at the newsroom at 9:30 or 10:00 p.m. Day and evening news staff rotate weekly.

Originally, it was planned that the project would be restricted to the production of the 11:00 p.m. programme, since this seemed more manageable at the time. However, it was not significantly more demanding to document the total production process, for three reasons. First, it was clearly important to observe the production of the earlier newscast as well, since the later programme is largely its offspring and a sizeable proportion of the 11:00 p.m. stories are produced during the day and by the day staff. Secondly, the work is so highly routinized that a thorough and detailed understanding of both productions can be quickly acquired. Thirdly, in any case, there is little to distinguish what are in reality two stages of the same production procedure. Therefore, the complete day and evening routines will be outlined, although it will first be necessary to identify the "raw material" of these productions.

News Sources

At Station "A," categorizations of news stories (international, national, etc.) directly correspond to the categories or types of news sources. International news is exclusively supplied by the Visnews satellite/wire service and the American NBC television network. The former service, based in London, England, and associated with the BBC, is used mainly for overseas news. With bureaus in various world capitals, it supplies a satellite transmission from London to New York, which is then re-fed to Toronto and from there to the Station "A" newsroom. For the 4:45 to 5:00 p.m. line, NBC, CBC, and Station "A" share the transmission costs, which are charged at a flat monthly rate of approximately $15,000.

Most other international and specifically North American stories are obtained through contractual agreement with the NBC television network, which provides a daily feed of approximately 15 news items listed according to their pre-determined priority order. The feed is actually a slightly lengthier version of the national NBC network news programme in the United States, from which Station "A" news workers select an average of three to five news stories (including the corresponding visual tapes) that will later be re-broadcast on their own news programme. Feature stories are often retained for the weekend newscasts. Audio portions of the NBC stories are usually re-written, and the visual tapes are edited to shorten their length and to delete the NBC journalist's sign-off, so that the item will appear to be originated by Station "A."

Other than the daily Parliament Hill reports submitted by the Ottawa journalist, national news is exclusively obtained from the Broadcast News

(BN) wire service. Broadcast News, with major offices in Ottawa and Toronto, is the broadcasting division of Canadian Press (CP), and was originally established to circulate news stories to its radio station subscribers. Since its subscribers are still primarily radio stations, BN wire stories are short, radio-oriented, capsule reports. This is the single most important news source for the Station "A" news programme, and most BN wire stories are re-written for broadcast. Major exceptions are the hourly newscasts, where the news director or the assignment editor takes stories directly from the wire and pastes them onto a large sheet for the newscasters to read. This is the extent of the production process for these regular news bulletins.

Provincial news consists mainly of the Queen's Park reports supplied by the assistant news director, although provincial news is also available through the BN wire service. Regional and local news is supplied through five sources: (a) newspapers like the *Toronto Star* and the Toronto *Globe and Mail* are perused daily, and various weeklies are scanned for feature stories that often appear at the end of the news programme or on weekend broadcasts; (b) as discussed earlier, the newsroom radio monitors a number of radio stations for local stories, such as traffic accident and fire reports;[14] (c) the police radio monitor is "officially" a news source (that is, according to the assistant news director), although throughout the observation no stories were derived from it and no one paid attention to its regular messages;[15] (d) the four stringers situated in surrounding localities will from time to time submit reports of events in their vicinities; and (e) the Station "A" news editors will prepare reports about events that take place in the immediate municipal region. The latter stories are determined by and originate almost exclusively with the news director, who receives all press releases, letters, and telephone calls from those who seek news coverage.

To summarize, three wire services supply the majority of the news stories broadcast on Station "A" news programmes: Visnews, the NBC News Programme Service (NPS), and Broadcast News (BN). One additional wire service, the Canada News Wire, is supplied without charge to Station "A" (and to numerous other broadcasting stations across Canada). Terminals are installed in the offices of the federal and provincial governments, major Canadian corporations, charitable associations and some trade unions. The stories most often are prepared by public relations officials within these organizations, and transmitted regularly across the wire to those media outlets that are equipped with the free service. Additionally, the federal and provincial governments each record their respective parliamentary sessions and send these, without charge, to all Canadian broadcasting stations (Station "A" receives the cassettes for the federal and Ontario sessions only).

News Programme Production

The Station "A" news day starts at 9:00 a.m. when the news director, the news editors, photographers, and film processor arrive at the newsroom. One of the news editors will immediately go to the BN wire and rip off copy printed out during the night. The first important event of the day, however, is the assignment of local stories to the news editors and photographers. The news director sits at the news desk with the others gathered around it, and reviews the "leads" for the day. His leads are obtained from three sources: (a) his own ideas for stories, which in turn are derived from the press releases, letters, and telephone calls he has received and the newspaper he has read the night before; (b) the futures file; and (c) the daily log of staff-covered stories. The futures file contains mostly press releases regarding forthcoming events, meetings, conferences, festivals, that are dated upon receipt (with the date of the event) and filed. The news director reviews this file and decides which events will be covered and who will cover them. The log partially duplicates the contents of the futures file. It lists the "pre-scheduled" events that have been pre-planned for coverage that day, such as sports award banquets, parades, conventions, scheduled news conferences, and speeches due to be delivered to local organizations. Events are listed and identified by a catchline that will continue to signify the story with respect to all references to it throughout the day until its final broadcast. Beside each catchline the time of the event and the name of the news editor (and photographer, if necessary) are listed, so that the log also serves to indicate the whereabouts of news editors and photographers at any point during the day. All of the stories actually assigned by the news director are listed here, as well as the expected topics of the reports from Ottawa and Queen's Park.[16] Occasionally, a news editor will suggest a story of his own to the news director and ask permission to cover it. If approved, the news editor will then enter it into the log, sign his name, and leave with a photographer.

Shortly after noon, the preliminary Visnews listing is available, which identifies the tentatively scheduled international news items that will appear in finalized form on the actual Visnews feed at 4:45 p.m. The preliminary listing is scanned by one of the news editors and some items are tentatively selected. Later, the news editor's selections will be reviewed by the news director, the assistant news director, or both. In general, the news editor who first takes the preliminary Visnews listing thereafter assumes responsibility for all international and national (NBC) news stories, while the others will handle BN wire stories and write up local news items.[17]

At 1:30 p.m. a flight from Ottawa arrives with the Parliament Hill report for the 6:00 p.m. newscast. The report is delivered to the newsroom, and if film is associated with the report, it will be edited according to the enclosed directions of the Ottawa reporter. Both the audio and visual portions of the report will then be checked for total time.[18] Between 2:00 and 3:00 p.m. the preliminary NBC line-up is available and items are tentatively selected (typically three, or a maximum of five). The complete feed is available at 5:00 p.m.

At mid-afternoon most if not all of the news editors and photographers have returned to the newsroom and have started to write up their stories. Film is passed to the film processing room where the news editor, and/or photographer, and the news director will supervise (and often argue about, with the news director's decisions being final) the editing, advising the processor where to cut or slice the film, whether to delete the sound for a voice-over, etc., and making note of the "in cue" and the "out cue" which will be indicated on the script for the benefit of the newscaster. At 2:30 and 3.30 p.m. the two evening shift news editors arrive and help to write up the stories selected from the four wire services and any others that need to be re-written. All of the typewriters are in use at this time, and the number of people typing, moving back and forth from the news desk to the wire service machines, and from the news desk to the film processing room, sets the illusory picture of chaotic frenzy and excitement. In reality, however, by 3:30 or 4:00 p.m. the 6:00 p.m. news programme is all but ready for broadcast. Any stories taken from the BN wire after this time will be saved for the 11:00 p.m. programme, and all the remains to be done is the odd last-minute re-writing of either BN or staff-covered stories.

By 5:30 p.m. the day staff has left the newsroom. The assistant news director arrives at 4:30 or 5:00 p.m. and starts to check the BN wire for stories that will be broadcast at 11:00 p.m. He then scans the script for the 6:00 p.m. newscast, and decides which of these stories will be re-broadcast on the later evening programme. He also checks the log to see what stories have been covered during the day and to see if there are any stories to be covered during the evening (such as city council meetings). These assignments have already been cleared through the news director, and if a photographer will be required during the evening, this will be pre-arranged by the news director. However, few evening stories are covered since there are only two news editors on duty after 5:30 p.m. The assistant news director will also prepare his Queen's Park report and oversee the editing of any accompanying film. Along with the two news editors, he will re-write the wire and other stories that he has selected for the 11:00 p.m. programme. As each tentative or potential news item is prepared, it is timed and placed with its associated key slide in the file box at the centre of the news desk. (Key slides, the still visuals that will appear on the screen behind the newscaster, display either a headline/catch-line title, the name and position of any person interviewed, or the scene of the event.)

At 6:00 p.m. the first evening news programme is broadcast. Although the newsroom television set is usually tuned to the Station "A" channel, those in the newsroom pay little attention to the programme. (However, on two occasions when the assistant news director was not in the newsroom at the time of the broadcast, the news editors on duty watched the "opinion piece" at the end of the newscast and jokingly remarked about the newscaster's conservative views.) At 6:30 p.m. the NBC network news programme is watched, taped, and the visual portions of the newscast are edited. Selected stories are re-written for broadcast on the 11:00 p.m. Station "A" newscast. When there is a second Parliament Hill report regarding stories that "broke" during the afternoon, it will arrive with the 6:30 p.m. flight from Ottawa.

Between 7:00 and 9:00 p.m. the actual production of the 11:00 p.m. newscast takes place. It consists entirely of re-writing prepared news items: the selected items from the 6:00 p.m. programme, NBC stories, BN wire stories, and the Ottawa and Queen's Park reports. At the same time, the film processor screens and reviews all films and videotapes likely to appear on the 11:00 p.m. newscast and completes any editing work that remains to be done. The assistant news director periodically glances through the potential news stories, and by 9:00 p.m. is ready to establish the line-up. All of the stories have been typed in large print on yellow pages that will together make up the script which the newscaster reads. The assistant news director gathers the stories from the file box and spreads them out on a small table at one side of the room. Of the average 25 to 30 stories that have been re-written by the evening news editors, the assistant news director will select approximately 20 stories and arrange them in what he decides should be the broadcast order. Items will be shuffled to avoid extended periods in which the newscaster steadily reads copy without visual accompaniment.

After numerous observations of this procedure and later analysis of the used and unused items which were retained during the project at my request, it is still difficult to determine what criteria the assistant news director uses to make decisions. It is clear that the visual stories are of prime importance. The disdain for "talking heads" that television producers harbour has been well-documented. Visual stories will more likely be broadcast than non-visual stories, and are more likely to be placed at or near the top of the line-up. Other than simply stating that the stories he selected were "the most important" (without being able to explain why—this was always "obvious"), the assistant news director repeatedly stated that television was a visual medium, that news was essentially show business, and that people (the audience) did not want to watch "talking heads." In regard to the order of the items, there is no necessary correlation between their type (international, national, etc.) and their position within the line-up (as Table 2-1 will illustrate).

Once the items have been placed in their broadcast sequence, the accumulated time of all the news items is calculated and verified to ensure that it meets the total time allotment for the news portion of the programme: 1,020 seconds or 17 minutes. (The remainder of the 30-minute newscast is dedicated to seven minutes of sports and six minutes of advertisements, the maximum commercial time allowable according to CRTC regulations.) Any necessary adjustments to the line-up are done. This usually means rejection of one or two additional stories. Often (yet not always) the rejected items are features or human interest stories originally placed at the bottom of the line-up and are sometimes saved for the weekend news programmes. In some cases, stories that had made it into the line-up are again re-written by the assistant news director to shorten them. Only rarely is film re-edited to conform with the news time allotment.

By approximately 9:30 p.m., when the script is finalized, a film list is prepared as well as a video list that will be used by the VTR operator at the studio across the street. The stories, which have been typed on four carbon copies, are assembled and separated into four script copies.[19] Any additional key slides are pulled from the files, either by the assistant news director or one of the news editors. The script pages are numbered and checked against the visual list, and films and videotapes are checked to ensure their correct order. Occasional delays at this point are usually due to the sportscaster who arrives at 9:30 or 10:00 p.m. to start preparing his copy. Neither the assistant news director nor any other news staff take part in the production of the sports portion of the programme, apart from saving BN sports stories for the sportscaster to review. Once prepared, the sportscaster submits his copy to the assistant news director, who adds it to the news script in its proper sequence and re-numbers the script pages. Sports films and videotapes are checked, added to the visual list, and sports key slides are pulled. The news visuals are frequently re-checked at this time to avoid technical errors, which will be attributed to the VTR operator.[20]

At 10:00 p.m. or shortly after, the show director and the newscaster (who takes no part in the production of the programme) arrive at the newsroom. The show director takes two of the script copies and indicates the camera angles throughout.[21] One of these copies is then passed to the newscaster, who reads through the script, changes words and phrases to better suit his broadcast style, and underlines the words that he intends to stress.[22] The newscaster, sportscaster and show director proceed to the studio across the street. On their way into the building, a thermometer is checked and the present temperature is inserted into the blank space that has been left for it in the weather portion of the script.

Once in the studio, if time permits, there will be a short rehearsal. In practice, this rarely occurs as both the newscaster and the sportscaster balk at the need for rehearsal.

Meanwhile, there is still one news editor on duty at the newsroom until 11:30 p.m. He checks the final scores on hockey games and other sports events which are passed to the sportscaster. In theory (that is, according to the assistant news director), the news editor also checks the wires for late-breaking stories up to 11:30 p.m. However, throughout the observation, news editors on duty at this time remained at the news desk (sometimes watching televison) and did not check the wires. In reality, it would be impossible to prepare such stories in time for broadcast (as detailed above). The newscast is "fixed" at least two hours prior to air time.

At the studio, the show director checks all films and videotapes for time and sequence and runs through them with the VTR operator. The Telecine operator (projectionist) then inserts them into the slide drums, so that all films and videotapes can be automatically aired at the appropriate time according to the script cues. The newscaster and the sportscaster take their seats in the small studio, facing the three cameras that are operated remotely from the control booth. At precisely 11:00 p.m., the newscast begins.

The News Programme

Table 2-1 outlines the show order of a sample 11:00 p.m. news programme that was broadcast 15 December 1978. A few observations regarding its composition and its structure can be made at this point.

First of all, 13 of the 19 stories were broadcast earlier on the 6:00 p.m. programme. Of the six new stories, five were printed out on the BN wire after 5:00 p.m. The sixth story, the headline or lead news item, referred to a televised speech by (then) American President Jimmy Carter that was broadcast on the American NBC channel in the early evening. In this case, the assistant news director watched the pre-scheduled speech on the newsroom television set, prepared the copy, and edited the tape of the speech down to the 28 seconds that he had decided to use. The inclusion of this late-breaking story at the top of the 11:00 p.m. line-up is the only sense in which the sample is not representative of a typical Station "A" programme.

Second, the order of the items for the 11:00 p.m. newscast does not correspond with their line-up at 6:00 p.m. The fifth story at 6:00 p.m. becomes the next to last story at 11:00 p.m. The 6:00 p.m. headline story becomes the third item at 11:00 p.m. The third story at 6:00 p.m. regarding the Simpsons/Bay take-over becomes the second-last story at 11:00 p.m. The nineteenth story at 6:00 p.m. is promoted to position nine at 11:00 p.m. and the sixteenth story at 6:00 p.m. is promoted to become story seven at 11:00 p.m. All of the news programmes analyzed reflect this fundamental inconsistency between the order of the news items at 6:00 p.m. and 11:00 p.m. It would be difficult to attribute the discrepancies to differences in the news values of the assistant news director and the news director (who establishes the 6:00 p.m. line-up). If this were the case, one would assume that the assistant news director might reject more of the 6.00 p.m. stories and use a greater number of new BN wire stories. Nor can the discrepancies be explained in terms of international, national, or regional news categories. The only discernible pattern is a tendency for headline items to be either international or national in their implications.[23]

Third, and this is one of the most striking features observed, the individual news items are remarkably short. In this sample, the length of each item ranges from 11 seconds on the story regarding the appointment of the new Ontario Hydro chairman to a maximum of one minute and 55 seconds for the Queen's Park report about the proposed airport expansion plans. Rarely do news items exceed two minutes in length. Stories without an accompanying visual tend to be much shorter than visual news items, due probably to the "talking heads" phobia. Indeed, it has been seen that where the total

Table 2-1: Sample Station "A" News Programme (Friday, 15 December 1978, 11:00 PM)

Item	Source	Position in 6:00 p.m. Line-up	Visual Time (Min:Sec)	Total Audio & Visual Time (Min:Sec)
1. *Audio Opening:* "And now, (Station "A") News with ___ and ___"	—	—	—	:05*
2. *Headline Tease:* "Tiny Taiwan is abandoned by the United States . . . ___?"	—	—	—	:05*
3. *Sports Tease (ad lib)*	—	—	—	:10*
4. Headline Story 1: Carter speech	NBC	—	:28	:53
5. Story 2: Mid-East peace talks failure	NBC	Story 5	1:30	1:40
6. Story 3: Kerr affair	Queen's Park	Story 1	—	:41
7. Story 4: local airport expansion	Queen's Park	Story 2	1:31	1:55
8. Story 5: mayor re airport	staff (weekly news conference)	—	—	:56
9. Story 6: Air Canada appointment	Parl. Hill	Story 4	:36	1:25
10. Story 7: provincial welfare benefits increased	BN wire	Story 11	:54	:21
11. Story 8: Cottman Transmission scandal	BN wire	Story 16	—	:36
12. Story 9: cops shot — Italy†	Visnews	Story 19	:55	1:10
13. Story 10: OPEC oil hike†	BN wire	Story 6	—	:27
14. Story 11: Ontario drug arrest	BN wire	—	—	:20
15. Story 12: new Ont. Hydro chairman	BN wire	Story 14	—	:11
16. Story 13: new Ont. Ombudsman	BN wire	Story 15	—	:13
17. Story 14: Brantford fire†	local radio	Story 17	:55	:57
18. Story 15: Canada sells nuclear reactors to Rumania	BN wire	—	—	:20
19. Story 16: Anik B satellite†	BN wire	—	—	:30
20. Story 17: Ont. special ed legislation	BN wire	—	—	:23
21. Story 18: Simpsons/Bay take-over	BN wire	Story 3	—	:28
22. Story 19: Lord Snowdon remarries	Visnews	Story 12	1:20	1:35
23. Weather	BN wire	—	—	:23
24. *Sports Tease:* "___ will be back with the sports"	—	—	—	:03*

Table 2:1: (cont'd) Sample Station "A" News Programme (Friday, 15 December 1978, 11:00 PM)

Item	Source	Position in 6:00 p.m. Line-up	Visual Time (Min:Sec)	Total Audio & Visual Time (Min:Sec)
25. Commercials	—	—	—	3:00
26. Sports Intro (newscaster introduces sportscaster)	—	—	—	:05*
27. Sports	BN/NBC	—	4:10	7:37
28. Tease: "Don't get too high on this balmy banana weather. _____ updates a light dusting dandruff snow . . . when we return"	—	—	—	:03*
29. Commercials	—	—	—	3:00
30. Weather Update: "The weekend weather may bring us light snow tonight and Sunday. _____?"	—	—	—	:03*
31. Close: ad lib discussion between newscaster and sportscaster	—	—	—	:25
TOTALS			12:19	30:00

* my estimate
† original catchline

line-up must be shortened in order to meet the 1,020-second time limit, visual
stories are least likely to be revised and non-visual stories are often re-written
to shorten their reading time. In the case of the sample, stories 15, 16, 17 and
18 were grouped at the end of the programme with a total time of one minute
and 41 seconds for all four stories. This also reflects the preference for visual
rather than non-visual stories. The stories contained no films, videotapes, or
other visual elements except key slides. Story 15 was accompanied by a still
file photo of a nuclear reactor and story 17 included a file photo of the Ontario education minister. The two other stories included neither film nor
videotapes nor key slides.

The headline story is not necessarily the longest. Indeed, it was shorter
than at least two other items in all of the 10 programmes studied. In the case
of the sample, the longest news item, and the story with the longest visual accompaniment (one minute and 31 seconds) was story four, a Queen's Park
report, which consumed a total of one minute and 55 seconds. The assistant
news director is Queen's Park reporter, supervisor of visual editing, *and* the
person who determines the 11:00 p.m. line-up. It is probably not coincidental
that Queen's Park stories usually appear within the top five news items at
11:00 p.m. Other staff stories, however, usually are shorter. In this case, the
two stories were 56 and 57 seconds. Moreover, at no time during this two-week
period did a staff report attain a position higher than fifth, with the exception of the Queen's Park reports. It might be assumed that this is due to
their local nature, yet it was seen that there is little correlation between the
site of the event and the position of its associated news report within the
broadcast sequence.

Despite the tremendous emphasis on visual stories and the visual
elements of the news programme, the visual time for news stories (in this case
eight minutes and nine seconds) consumes roughly half the total 17-minute
news time allotment. Of the total 30-minute newscast, less than half (in this
case, 12 minutes and 19 seconds) is consumed by the news and sports visuals
combined.

Finally, the sample programme outlined in Table 2-1 is representative of
a typical pattern with respect to the number of news items selected from each
available news source. In this case, two Visnews stories made it to broadcast,
as well as two NBC stories, two Queen's Park reports, one Parliament Hill
report, two staff stories, and ten BN wire stories. It also should be noted that
the two staff stories were not self-initiated: one derived from the regular
weekly City Hall press conference. The other story on a fire was obtained
through the regular monitoring of a local radio station, which originally
reported the fire.

While it is clear that news management (i.e., the news director and the
assistant news director) fulfill a substantial role in the production process, and
make most of the major decisions about the composition of the news programme, the news workers, particularly the news editors, also carry out im-

portant tasks, and would otherwise be considered "the real producers" of Station "A" newscasts. Regardless of how one decides to categorize them, it is important to investigate further their fundamental position as news workers and their position within the Station "A" news operation, since this also influences the ultimate news product.

The eight news editors are all relatively young (the oldest is in his mid-forties), but most have considerable experience in the field of television journalism, and at least three are graduates of college journalism programmes. Their length of employment with the station ranges from 4 to 12 years and averages 6.3 years. Like the photographers and film processors, all belong to the station's union. Significantly, all but one are of middle or upper middle-class origin,[24] and all but three are men. The three female news editors have each worked at the station five years or less. Before 1976, the news department was virtually an all-male operation.

Despite their position as news editors, it is possible to argue they have less impact on the composition of the news programme than news management. This leads to a questioning of their autonomy and the general significance of their role in the news production process. Marchak[25] has usefully identified eight "job control measures" that she applied to a sample of workers in British Columbia. They can be utilized here with respect to the news workers at Station "A." The measures include the degree to which a worker exercises control over task content, the pacing of tasks, the sequencing of tasks, quantity and quality of the daily product, subjection to direct supervision, and discretion with respect to one's time and spatial arrangements at work. One need not recapitulate all that has been discussed of the news production routine in order to demonstrate that Station "A" news workers score poorly on all these counts. Task content, pacing and sequencing are each pre-determined according to the established routine and, while the news editors and photographers are sincerely concerned about the quantity and quality of the daily news product, their control over its ultimate character is limited, their suggestions are consistently unheeded, and their capacity to affect either its quantity or quality is minimal. Indeed, the news workers are frustrated in their attempts to improve the quality of the news programme. They tend to blame station management for what is perceived as a distorted set of programming priorities.[26]

The news workers' level of concern about the quality of the news programme is nowhere more evident than in the fact that, throughout the interviews, responses to questions regarding unrelated matters would inevitably drift towards this topic. It occurred with all eight of the news editors and the two photographers interviewed. When asked about his perception of the differences between newspaper and television news writing, one news editor responded this way:

> Basically, newspapers tend to be *developing* material, where we don't develop anything. We react. All we're doing all the time is reacting: to what the news-

papers are doing, to what the radio stations are doing, and to whatever hard news stories are out there happening all by themselves. We're reacting all the time, we're not originating anything at all. That's one of my biggest complaints, is that we, collectively, in this room . . . [names all the news editors] . . . have some kind of grey matter available that's never collectively employed. Nobody ever sits down and says, "Hey, this week let's look at this problem, let's try to put together a well-rounded, in-depth look at a situation" — not necessarily even a *problem*. But that's never done. There is no collective approach, there is no teamwork approach, no brainstorming approach. [original emphasis]

The absence of a collective or teamwork approach to newsmaking generally, or even to the coverage of a single news event, was confirmed throughout the observation. Moreover, the decision-making structure within the newsroom tends more towards autocracy than democracy, with the decisions of the news director (and, in his absence, the assistant news director) being final in all cases. Supervision is direct yet carried out in a subtle, casual, and seemingly friendly fashion, although, in light of the statements of news workers made in the absence of news management, it seems accurate to state that the degree and scope of supervision is resented.

Lastly, the news workers exercise little discretion with respect to their time and spatial arrangements at work. Shift periods or working hours are pre-established and invariable. When outside the newsroom, news workers must at all times sign out and indicate their whereabouts. In terms of spatial arrangements, only the film processors can be said to have their own personal work space (that is, the film processing room). Since there is no formalized seating plan around the news desk, the news editors often must scramble for a seat and a typewriter in order to proceed with their work. This compounds their frustrations with their working conditions.

Like the workers in Marchak's study, the news workers make relatively few decisions, work primarily with machines most of the day, and have little significant involvement in the total production process. Their work time is consumed by the task of re-writing news stories that have been initiated, covered, and originally prepared by journalists elsewhere (at Visnews, at NBC, etc.). Since most of the news staff defined the basic journalistic skills as a "news sense" or "nose for news," the ability to "follow through leads," investigative skills, interviewing skills, and writing skills, it is apparent that few of these fundamental skills are required during the course of their work at Station "A." The raw material for these news workers is the completed news report — reports of events that have been investigated, covered, and prepared prior to their arrival at the Station "A" newsroom. In the newsroom, these news reports are simply re-written, processed, and (if selected by management) broadcast on the Station "A" news programme.

In summary, the Station "A" news workers exercise little or no control over the content of their work, the pacing of their work, the sequencing of their work, the quantity of the product, the quality of the product, their work time, or their work space. Moreover, the organization of production denies them the capacity to utilize and exercise their journalistic skills. This is a fundamental source of their alienation. The extent to which these conditions prevail at other Canadian stations cannot be determined here, and, for the purposes of this analysis, the question is largely immaterial. It remains that these conditions are part and parcel of the social control of Station "A" news producers and hold serious consequences for Station "A" news programmes—a consideration to which the news audience, the largest television audience in Canada, remains oblivious.

Other studies have found that news workers attribute equipment inadequacies to management indifference about news quality[27] and that news workers are caught in a tension between the craft of news writing and the demands of television production.[28] However, there are additional factors to which Station "A" workers attribute their discontent. Three principal and interrelated conditions were most regularly cited. First, the quality of the news programme was criticized, including the lack of in-depth reporting, the incompetence of the news director, and the "wishy-washy" or "garden party" nature of staff-assigned stories. Second, the low quality was attributed to the station's programming and budgetary priorities. Third, the lack of a beat system renders the news staff generalists and not specialists. The last condition most clearly indicates their sense of having no control over their work, and the feeling that no work can be considered their own. This is illustrated in the following interview with one news editor who compared his work at Station "A" with his previous experience at a Regina station where there was a beat system.

> It [the beat system] gives you scope as to what you can do, what you can put on the air is much more left up to you. In Regina there was a very dynamic system. That machine, that system, gave you a lot of freedom. Here, there's no system, and virtually no freedom, because there's no initiative. . . . There, anything I could find out there was *mine*. That was my baby out there. Here, well, here I'm a general reporter.

The news workers attempt to reconcile their alienation in various ways. The response of the above news editor is akin to a sort of deferred gratification. Although employed with the news department since 1969, he describes his position at Station "A" as "only for the time being." The same news editor also owns a local restaurant where he sometimes works during weekends, and plans to establish a travel agency (with a partner) that will enable him to use his journalistic skills by writing and producing travelogues.

Another news editor stated that he tried to regard his occupation as a "hobby" and concentrated his thoughts on his numerous leisure activities. Significantly, both news editors offered this information without prompting. A third, when asked how he unleashed his frustrations with his work, replied that his "answer" was to create outside interests. Two of the photographers seek compensatory satisfaction in their free-lance work, and a fourth news editor discussed the plight of one of the film processors who has held his "dead-end job" for 16 years, identifying this as the cause of the man's alcoholism.

Production Constraints

Most of the production constraints operative in the case of Station "A" are self-evident in the discussion to this point, and will only be briefly reviewed here. In addition to the three most immediate constraints—time, money, technology—10 less specific production constraints can be identified: (a) the historical legacy of the station or its established record of budgetary and programming priorities; (b) the influence of other media; (c) the social control of news producers; (d) the visual character of the television medium and the entertainment context within which news is produced; (e) the operation of news values; (f) the concept of the audience that news producers hold; (g) the nature of news sources; (h) the compartmentalization of news stories; (i) professional journalistic practice and its codes (objectivity rules, the "evidence" requirement, etc.); and (j) direct owner-management intervention. Needless to say, these constraints do not operate independently or in isolation; instead, all of the constraints tend to congeal, in various combinations, in order to produce their restrictive consequences for the processed news commodity.

Of all the constraints that operate upon television news production, time is the most pressing and the most directly visible. The time element pervades all aspects of production. It affects both the news programme (renders reports incomprehensible rather than comprehensive) and the routine of news production (requires that "news" must be pre-planned). Along with the economic and technological limitations, it is a major, overriding concern for news producers. Tracey notes the old cliché that "the number of words in a broadcast news programme wouldn't even fill the front page of most newspapers."[29] In the case of Station "A," the expression is remarkably accurate. The 17-minute news time allotment, and the 10 to 100-second length of individual news items, make inconceivable any notion of in-depth news coverage. Furthermore, the completed news reports that make up the raw material of Station "A" production, like the Visnews stories or NBC stories, originally average 100 to 150 seconds and are substantially reduced to fit within the scant time concession. It is often pointed out that the time constraint leads to a dehistoricized and generally decontextualized picture of the world. At a different level, however, the time factor also works to make the news rather old. It also demands that news consists largely of pre-scheduled events. In Altheide's words, "while news will ideally be new, organizational considerations preclude too much newness."[30] Thus, the time constraint interacts with other less direct constraints and culminates both in the pre-determination of news events and the pre-determination of their significance.

This problem was well illustrated throughout the observation at Station "A." On one occasion a news editor and photographer were observed during their coverage of a local news story. Christmas was nearing and the news

editor, a volunteer firefighter, had learned from associates at the fire department that some local Christmas tree dealers were spraying their dried-out
trees with green paint and selling them as fresh trees, thus creating a fire
hazard. When first requesting the news director's approval to do the story, the
news editor explained that he planned to investigate two or three of the
suspected dealers and then interview the public safety inspector at the fire
department.

The case is well worth detailed discussion, since it illustrates several of
the production constraints at work. It shows not only the interaction of time
constraints with other organizational factors, but also the pre-definition of
the event and its significance, the routinized nature of event coverage, the importance of the "evidence" requirement, the operation of news values, and, to
some extent, the concept of the audience that news producers hold.

As we left the station and drove to the first Christmas tree dealer, the
news editor explained the story (also for the benefit of the photographer, who
was driving):

> There's a tree dealer that has some trees, and what we gotta do is try and spot
> some of these painted ones and get some shots. We will go in there telling this
> tree dealer we are doing a story on Christmas trees and we will find painted
> trees. And then I will whip out the microphone and say, "Sir, why are you paint-
> ing your dying trees green?" [laughter] And then I'll go to the fire department
> and we've got the fire department safety inspector who's going to tell us that, uh,
> this is quite a common practice that they're trying to crack down on and uh . . .
> nail these bastards to the wall. *So we've got the problem and we've got what
> they're trying to do about it.* Uh, I don't know if it's a widely known thing—the
> fire department seems to think that people get sucked in . . . okay, so *it's your
> basic consumer story*, where people are being ripped off, with a hazard involved.
> [added emphasis]

The news angle that the journalist pre-determined could not have been more
succinctly expressed. His tone during the explanation was one of stating the
obvious, the straightforward, the routine, to such an extent that it evoked
laughter at the point indicated. This was probably due more to the routinized
nature of event coverage than to any feeling that the story was not newsworthy
(after all, it was he who suggested the story). The news editor indicated this
shortly thereafter:

> Now I know there are going to be *some* people out there who know what's going
> on. But by the same token there are *also* going to be people out there saying,
> "No kidding? I didn't know that." It's not hard, hard news, but it's something
> that uh . . . you know, it's conversational, people will pick up and talk about
> over coffee.

Later, still en route:

> Question: What sort of film coverage are you going to do?
>
> News Editor: As little as possible.
>
> Photographer: (simultaneously) Not much. (laughter) This camera is . . . not
> exactly inconspicuous.

News Editor: Well, that's no problem. We'll go in there and we'll say, "Look, we want to do some Christmas tree shots, do you mind if we take some shots?" and he'll say, "Oh, fine, take all you want" and what I'll be doing while B's [the photographer] filming is looking for green spray paint cans and trying to find trees. And then when we get them, B [the photographer] will show the paint, and maybe even we can talk the guy into painting some. So we've got *the actual evidence* of this asshole doing the job. And then we go down to the fire department and do an interview with the man we're going to talk to, and have him rip a strip off him for doing it, and then we've got film of him doing it. And then we wrap the whole thing up, I'll come on camera at the end and say, well, you know, buyer beware type thing, whatever. [added emphasis]

Question: Do you know at this stage that what you're essentially going to do is shoot silent footage with a voice-over?

News Editor: No, *I know exactly how I'm going to do it.* I'm going to do silent film with cart, interview with the guy, why he paints the trees green, and then I have a choice of either putting his interview tight to the fire department man saying "this is awful, this is a rip-off, this is dangerous" or, doing more silent film of the fire department guy and have his interview on, and then I might just do a three, four, five second extra. . . . [added emphasis]

Later, still en route to the first Christmas tree dealer, the news editor repeated the value of evidence.

The fire department guy is aware that it's going on, but I'd like to have something on film to back it up. That's the key. I mean, it's fine to make allegations and accusations, but if you haven't got the print on film, forget it.

After stopping at five different Christmas tree dealers, no "evidence" of painted trees could be found, and the team concluded that it was probably still too early in the holiday season to detect any dried-out and subsequently painted trees on the lots. When asked if he would try again at a later date, the news editor responded that the news director probably would not allow it, since this would be akin to a follow-up and a new story would take precedence.

At this point the news editor called in to the newsroom, was told that there were no new stories to cover, and decided to proceed to the fire department to at least film the planned interview. However, since neither the fire department nor the news team had evidence that trees had been painted, the public safety inspector preferred not to discuss it. Instead, the interview was restricted to a discussion of "special Christmas safety measures." (The film was ultimately shelved and broadcast two weeks later during the annual public service announcement about Christmas safety.)

Apart from the visible operation of news values, the incident also illustrates the operation of economic and related technological constraints. Laughter erupted when the team was asked about planned film coverage points. This relates to the high costs of film coverage, and the fact that, for Station "A" producers at least, film is at a premium. The department's film costs amount to roughly $100,000 annually, and more than 60 per cent of all film footage is deleted through editing and discarded.[31] The film is packaged in 10-minute rolls, and the photographers typically shoot no more than five to six minutes for each story. At municipal council meetings, where the event may span two to three hours, the news editor will cue the photographer to start shooting only when particular individuals (the mayor or others who can be expected to say something newsworthy) rise to speak. The important point is that a tight film budget "precludes shooting enough film for an optimum presentation."[32]

A more subtle constraint concerns the visual nature of the television medium itself, although the real constraint lies in the way in which production is organized to overcome the problem. Table 2-1 demonstrates some of its consequences for the selection, length, and ordering of news items. It is unquestionably difficult for news producers to reconcile the visual obsession with events (especially events that signify complex social processes) that are neither intrinsically nor potentially entertaining. To illustrate the absurd consequences of the visual imperative, note the following solutions recommended in a CBS News style manual:

> For the sake of time and interest, on-camera sections need to be kept short and concise. Yet many major stories, such as political controversies, debates, and conferences, belong to the difficult and complex world of ideas. Good writing may help to cut through to the essentials of the story. Art work or library film may sometimes provide illustration and video relief to hold interest. Sometimes, it may be useful merely to register the fact that there *is* a controversy without going into complete details. This much, at least, television owes its viewers.[33]

The constraints of the visual imperative are closely related to the operation of news values and the perception of the audience that news producers hold. Elliott (1974: 88-89) makes the important point that television production is not a process of "communication" between producer and consumer, but a relationship between production and mere *reaction*. Three major sources of audience reaction are available to news producers in general and Station "A" news producers in particular: (a) audience research reports (concerned with demographic characteristics and purchasing habits); (b) letters or telephone calls; and (c) personal contacts. At Station "A," audience research reports are mostly used by the sales department and occasionally by the programming department. The news department makes no use of the material. Letters, telephone calls, and personal contacts, however, do evoke a response by news (and station) management. This kind of feedback necessarily contributes little to a genuine or meaningful understanding of audience composition. Nor is it necessarily important. To cite Tracey's cogent phrase, "there is no organizational emphasis on *knowing* the audience, only on *having* one."[34] The absence of a precise or even imprecise knowledge of the audience leads producers to depend on themselves as a point of reference. The audience is conceptualized as a large, anonymous but homogeneous middle-class unit. This is remarkable given that Station "A" purports to serve what is widely regarded as a predominantly working-class or union town.

The importance of audience reaction varies for news management and news workers. While management spoke of the need to retain audience interest and was most concerned about audience reaction, news workers were less concerned about the audience. In fact, they tended to regard the audience as illiterate fools who would not know good news if they saw it — quality news was something only journalists could know about. Some suggested that journalists produce for other journalists, who constitute their real and most critical audience[35] and who together make up a type of legitimacy network. What is legitimate news to one journalist will doubtless be legitimate to others. There is a curious kind of reproduction of journalistic practices at work here, made possible in an occupation where the work of one's peers is always open to view.

The legitimacy of a news story in the eyes of journalists will depend in part on another production constraint — the nature of the news source. The point is often made that journalists position themselves (or are positioned) close to institutions guaranteed to regularly produce a stream of newsworthy events, including courts, sports grounds, government offices, and which, not coincidentally, tend to be established or official institutions. The compartmentalization of news according to specific beats or categories, with their associated institutional news suppliers, is also related to professional journalistic rules about reliable sources and objectivity. Hall et al. argue that these very rules (which require that news reports be grounded in objective and authoritative statements from acquired sources) command that journalists seek out and thus *reproduce* the definitions of these powerful institutional authorities.[36]

Such rules are reflected in the organization of news-gathering at Station "A." Parliament Hill, Queen's Park, and City Hall are prime sources and prime sites for events reported by Station "A" news staff. Hall et al. explain that time constraints and the constraints imposed by objectivity "combine to produce a systematically structured *over-accessing* to the media of those in powerful and privileged institutional positions."[37] At Station "A," economic constraints compound these two to produce a reliance not only on accredited, legitimate sources but also on readily available (and with no staff cost) sources, like wire service reports, where the requirements of objectivity, evidence, and so forth, have already been met and where the legitimacy of news stories has been pre-established. Moreover, the "structured over-accessing" to the media of those who hold legitimate institutional positions is reflected in the regulated time periods for news-gathering. Station "A" news happens between 9:00 a.m. and 5:00 p.m., Monday to Friday, and is dramatically absent during those periods (evenings, weekends, summer months) when official news suppliers are not fully in operation. Recall that weekend news production is limited to two 15-minute newscasts, filled mainly with shelved feature items. One news editor explained that Christmas is also a slow news period since "all the newsmakers go away on holidays."

The last production constraint is perhaps (although arguably) the least significant of all the constraints discussed. One of the news editors described the usual manner in which direct management intervention takes place.

> Occasionally, we've had situations where (the station president) will call and say "I'm not trying to tell you what to do, but I've heard that there's such and such a thing happening . . ." the message is there. Or you'll get little letters from the president of the local garden party who in the letter will say, "I was talking to (the station vice-president) who indicated that it would be quite appropriate for me to call you and suggest doing a story about. . . ."

The assistant news director also related a number of instances where station management telephoned to "informally request" that particular stories be added or deleted. This occurred most often when these stories favoured or conflicted with management's interests, especially if it was concerned with organizations to which they were affiliated. A more critical and all-pervasive type of control (and a tactic often attributed to the Thomson and Irving media organizations in particular) is simply to hire what are seen to be less well-qualified persons. This ensures, at a concrete level, that quality investigative reporting of the sort that might threaten the interests of owners and managers at large, will not be undertaken.

CONCLUSIONS

If there is an incompetence in Station "A" news production, it cannot be reducible to individuals. Rather, it is structured into the organization of the production process and aggravated by each and all of the production constraints that have been identified. Few of these constraints, however, are immutable or irreconcilable. It is still possible to imagine alternative ways in which production might be organized. If news workers, for example, were to exercise some control over the fate of the news product and the means of news production, a very different kind of news programme could emerge.

What sets this case apart from other news operations (at least, those that have been studied to date) is the news producers' redistribution of news commodities produced elsewhere, and their reproduction of the work of other news producers, complete with its own prepackaged limitations. Throughout the project, it was clear that Station "A" is not alone in this redistribution and reproduction. As a news distribution centre, it is merely one point of juncture in a larger network of production and distribution that extends well beyond the borders of a single station.

Canadian news production needs to be examined empirically within the international flow of news products. Once this task is done, it should be possible to explain how stations like Station "A" come to operate fundamentally as reproductive mechanisms, and why its news progammes simply distribute the work of others, just as its entertainment programmes distribute the work of American and other producers. These are the programming realities of private broadcasting in Canada, only partially explained by the need to obtain and retain audiences while simultaneously pursuing private pecuniary interests.

Station "A" news programmes are produced with a minimum of skill and economic and technological resources but with a maximum of routine. Cheaply produced, routinized stories form programmes that connote and promote continuity and stability. This may well be their most potent ideological feature. While the present analysis illustrates to some extent the operation of ideology through and within concrete practices, a full-blown textual analysis of the completed news product would specify its operation more precisely. With these tasks ahead, it is obvious that much work remains to be done.

NOTES

1.   "News producer(s)" is used throughout in its generic sense, without reference to a specific position or occupation.
2.   Graham Murdock, "Blindspots about Western Marxism: A Reply to Dallas Smythe," *Canadian Journal of Political and Social Theory,* Vol. 2, No. 2, Spring/Summer 1978, p. 116.
3.   Michael Tracey, *The Production of Political Television* (London: Routledge & Kegan Paul, 1978), p. 95ff.
4.   However, the Glasgow University Media Group (GUMG), in their study of *Bad News* (Vol. 1. London: Routledge & Kegan Paul, 1976) encountered some reluctance: "The technology of television news production itself helps to determine the shape and content of bulletins to an extent which the newsroom personnel seem reluctant to admit" (p. 59).
5.   In the interests of anonymity, the television station in question is referred to simply as Station "A." Wherever possible, all other identifying references have been eliminated.
6.   Due to problems of access and videotape recorder (VTR) breakdowns, it was not possible to obtain a complete set of programme videotapes for the same two week period.
7.   This may be just as well. As Altheide explains: "Police radio monitors . . . provide crime news involving street crimes which frequently involve lower class and minority group youth. But the story of crime is incomplete if it is only learned about from these sources. The image is presented, albeit unintentionally, that certain kinds of crime are not only committed by certain groups of people, but that this is what the crime problem is all about. White collar crime and corporate rip-offs are not presented via police monitors, even though more money is involved than in dozens of $25 to $100 robberies." David L. Altheide, *Creating Reality: How TV News Distorts Events* (Beverly Hills: Sage Publications, 1976), p. 191.
8.   Altheide, *Creating Reality,* p. 15.
9.   Station "A" workers were formerly associated with the National Association of Broadcast Employees and Technicians (NABET). However, in 1973 the station's local entered into a dispute with NABET through its refusal to support a CBC strike, was subsequently disaffiliated, and established its own union for Station "A" workers only.
10.   It was the assistant news director who conducted the initial guided tour that led to this undertaking. Shortly after the more extensive observation began, it was evident that his presentation did not reflect the realities of the newsroom operation.
11.   This is actually a requirement specified in the union contract.

12.   One photographer, who will be discussed later, represents the exception to this general rule.

13.   Weekend programmes entail little preparation, consisting largely of BN wire stories and "features" that have been saved throughout the week.

14.   Altheide speculates that other media are monitored for three reasons: (a) other media may broadcast/publish different or more current news reports and possibly conflict with or challenge the station's own news reports; (b) other media provide a basis of comparison in terms of news competence; and (c) other media often compete within the same market as the station. (Altheide, p. 55.)

15.   In fact, few news editors were familiar with the police codes or aware that the bookcase contained a police code book.

16.   The topics of these reports are usually known well in advance, and entered by the Queen's Park reporter/assistant news director.

17.   During the evening, when two news editors are on duty, the one who is loosely responsible for international and national stories will handle the 6:30 p.m. NBC feed and most of the BN wire stories, while the other will check the radio and/or cover local evening events.

18.   The Ottawa reporter forwards both his own film and the cassette recording of the House of Commons debates. He also decides what portion(s) of each will be broadcast.

19.   Script copies are distributed as follows: copy 1 to the newsroom, copy 2 to the audio operator for sound cues, copy 3 to the show director, and copy 4 to the newscaster, to be later filed and retained for a period of one year.

20.   All errors (usually technical ones) that take place during the broadcast are logged on "fault sheets" (e.g., splice breaks, which are blamed on the film processor). The news director receives a copy and periodically reviews these sheets.

21.   This is a straightforward procedure that takes no more than a few minutes, since the cameras are fixed and camera angles are inflexible: Camera 1 presents the newscaster with a key slide; Camera 2 is used where there is no visual or key slide, simply the newscaster against a plain background; and Camera 3 is used for the sportscaster only. Thus, camera shots are invariable and determined by the script itself.

22.   It is symptomatic of the newscaster's broadcast style that on one occasion a headline tease which originally read "The final tribute to a former Prime Minister . . ." (regarding Golda Meir's funeral) was changed and broadcast as "Shalom, Golda!"

23.   This is illustrated through the following list of headline teases for the ten programmes:

Monday	11 December 1978:	"A big heist at Kennedy Airport . . ."
Tuesday	12 December 1978:	"Shalom, Golda!"
Wednesday	13 December 1978:	"The Cross kidnappers are back in Canada. . ."
Thursday	14 December 1978:	"The PM says he is not stepping down . . ."
Friday	15 December 1978:	"Tiny Taiwan is abandoned by the United States . . ."
Monday	8 January 1979:	"A Vietnamese takeover in Cambodia is all but complete . . ."
Tuesday	9 January 1979:	"The Vietnamese are now bombing Thailand . . ."
Wednesday	10 January 1979:	"Ottawa's Liberals rejoice over the latest opinion poll . . ."
Thursday	11 January 1979:	"The U.S. withdraws support from the Shah of Iran . . ."
Friday	12 January 1979:	"Good evening, a hijacking is underway over North African skies . . ."

24.   See Debra Clarke, *The Significance of Mass Media Ownership for the Process of Ideological Reproduction: The Canadian Case,* M.A. Thesis, McMaster University, 1978, pp. 214-221 (especially Table 23, p. 220, re class origin) for a discussion of similar findings with respect to a sample of news directors and news editors at broadcasting stations across Canada.

25.   M. Patricia Marchak, "The Canadian Labour Farce: Jobs for Women," in *Women in Canada* (rev. ed.), edited by Marylee Stephenson (Don Mills: General Publishing, 1977), p. 149.

26.   Space limitations demand that much of the interview material be excluded here. See the longer analysis (Clarke, 1980) for statements by the news producers that illustrate this and subsequent points.

27.   Altheide, *Creating Reality,* p. 52.

28.   GUMG, *Bad News,* p. 61.

29.   Tracey, *Political Television,* p. 93.

30.   Altheide, *Creating Reality,* p. 67.

31.   This is similar to Altheide's case where the photographers shot a 3:1 ratio.

32.   Altheide, *Creating Reality,* p. 84.

33.   Columbia Broadcasting System (CBS), *Television News Reporting* (New York: McGraw-Hill, 1958), p. 93.

34.   Tracey, *Political Television,* p. 129.

35.   GUMG, *Bad News,* p. 68.

36.   Stuart Hall et al., *Policing the Crisis* (London: MacMillan, 1978), p. 59.

37.   Ibid., p. 58.

Chapter 3

Getting the Message Across: Media Strategies and Political Campaigns

William O. Gilsdorf

Cet article fait partie d'une étude plus considérable portant sur les élections canadiennes de 1979 et 1980. Réalisée grâce à une subvention de l'Université Concordia et du Conseil de recherches en sciences humaines du Canada, cette étude explora les thèmes suivants: (1) l'organisation mise sur pied et la stratégie élaborée par le Parti libéral pour imposer aux medias des thèmes électoraux spécifiques: et (2) l'organisation mise sur pied par les medias pour couvrir ces deux élections ainsi que la perception que les medias eurent de ces deux campagnes.

Cet article, basé sur une soixantaine d'entrevues avec des travailleurs de l'information après chaque élection, ainsi que sur une monitorisation systématique des medias et une tournée avec les chefs de parti, est une analyse descriptive des stratégies utilisées par les partis pour imposer des thèmes électoraux précis, de même qu'une analyse de ces thèmes qu'on a cherché à imposer. L'emphase est tout particulièrement mise dans cette étude sur les stratégies du Parti libéral, même si à l'occasion, et lorsque cela s'avère nécessaire, des références sont faites au Parti conservateur et au NPD.

Selon les membres des media, les stratégies du Parti libéral ont réussi, au cours de ces deux campagnes, à imposer leurs thèmes et ce, tout particulière-ment lors de la campagne de 1980. Le thème privilégié par les Libéraux fut celui du leadership. Alors qu'en 1979 ce thème présentait la forme d'un mélange de pro-Trudeau et d'anti-Clark, en 1980 il était essentiellement anti-Clark. Les autres thèmes que les Libéraux voulurent exploiter furent, en 1979, celui de l'unité nationale et, en 1980, le thème du "18 cents de taxe par gallon d'essence" avec tout ce que ce thème symbolisait. L'inter-action entre l'effort de communication du Parti libéral et la couverture des medias semble avoir eu des effets variés sur le thème du leadership, avoir considérablement réduit la crédibilité du thème de l'unité nationale et augmenté celle du thème de la taxe sur l'essence.

En plus des efforts qui sont normalement déployés pour s'assurer une presse favorable, les partis utilisèrent à l'égard des media des stratégies qui épousèrent plusieurs formes: tous les partis (sauf, peut-être, le Parti conservateur en 1980) mirent surtout l'emphase sur le reportage national et tout particulièrement sur le reportage des activités de leur chef. De tous les partis, c'est le Parti libéral qui fit le plus de discrimination entre les stratégies qu'il adopta pour le Canada anglais et le Canada français. Partis et medias s'accordent à affirmer que les medias visuels—télévision et photographie de presse—furent ceux qui eurent le plus d'importance dans les campagnes. Tous les "événements critiques" des campagnes, tels que perçus par les partis et les media, furent orchestrés en fonction des medias ou conçus pour eux. La campagne libérale de 1980 apparaît comme une véritable distillation du rituel et du contrôle électoral. Elle est devenue, en quelque sorte, le modèle parfait de la stratégie destinée à projeter l'image d'une campagne nationale active. Une étude approfondie démontre que cette campagne, qui a réussi à imposer ses thèmes aux medias et à "communiquer son message", était beaucoup moins active, substantielle et nationale qu'elle voulait bien le paraître (toute axée qu'elle était sur l'électorat du Toronto métropolitain).

Cette étude des stratégies des partis a donné naissance à un certain nombre de préoccupations. Cette forme d'activité de communication des partis et des medias qui influence le choix des thèmes électoraux et l'orientation de la campagne elle-même n'encourage-t-elle pas l'aliénation régionale, ou encore ne donne-t-elle pas naissance dans la population à des attentes irréalistes à l'égard des chefs de parti? L'emphase mise sur le thème dominant du leadership, qui peut encourager la formation de coalitions à court terme et provoquer des succès électoraux immédiats, ne peut-elle pas aussi avoir des conséquences à long terme sur différents aspects du processus électoral, comme favoriser l'apathie ou l'instabilité des électeurs?

La télévision, qui s'impose comme le médium électoral par excellence, devra résoudre certains dilemmes auxquels elle se confronte en acceptant, tout particulièrement, de contribuer si activement à la formation du rituel électoral. Enfin, la conception de l'électeur comme "consommateur d'images" qui influence la stratégie de communication en politique laisse présager que de moins en moins de Canadiens pourront participer à la formation du message politique. Ceci est important si on considère que le système politique se veut une consécration du processus démocratique.

Introduction

Even the most casual observer of the 1979 or 1980 Canadian federal election campaign event could see that accommodating the media was the top priority of party leaders. At meetings or fund-raising events, it frequently was difficult to see the party leader because of the photographers and cameras clustered in front. Television lights flicking on and off made concentration impossible, particularly when directed at audiences to get the "cut-away" crowd reaction.

To make matters worse, the television announcers sometimes cut into the middle of the candidate's speech in order to meet a press deadline "back East" or because he or she already had known what the candidate was going to say. Most campaign appearances have become media spectacles. At least five camerapersons with lights, five soundrecorders and three photographers were usually involved.

The media (both print and electronic) were accorded the front position in most halls—that valuable space between leader and live audience. Television camerapersons sometimes were put to one side (often in the 1980 Liberal campaign camerapersons were moved to the rear) but the raised, highly visible and highly distracting camera platform still prevailed.

Television crews were in constant motion during a campaign speech. A regular pattern of English network camerapersons was to go for cutaways if the party leader lapsed into French. Perhaps they assumed the leader would say nothing important in French or, if he did, that it would be repeated in English.

Surprisingly, there were few complaints from the live audiences about the sometimes noisy and insensitive actions of camerapersons, photographers or stand-up television announcers. It is as if most spectators enjoy being part of the spectacle, accepting the priority of the "out-there" audience and their own diminished role. The politician even may have a diminished role in the mind of the audience. The audience invariably spent as much time watching the media (especially at the beginning of events) as watching and attending to the speaker. The spectacle was often the overriding characteristic of the campaign events.

The importance of media to current federal campaigners is evident in many ways. A large staff is assigned to accommodate media personnel and to set up and orchestrate events. Candidate's reactions to media reports are often paranoiac and they eagerly court reporters, editors and publishers. The media are monitored closely during and between campaigns—press summaries are prepared daily by the Liberals, Progressive Conservatives and the New Democratic Party—with a priority on the television reports. The media's criticisms or praise heavily influence scheduling strategy—deciding whether the "game plan" for the campaign should be maintained or changed.

Canada has entered an era in which the priorities, processes and structure of the media, especially television, dictate party strategy. Ironically, it also works vice versa.

This paper is part of a larger study exploring the symbiotic relationship between press and political party during the 1979 and 1980 federal election campaigns, which was funded by grants from the Social Sciences and Humanities Research Council and Concordia University. This paper focuses on part of that larger study, and analyzes the Liberal Party as a primary source of communication strategy. Party intent, preference and activity around key issues and strategies are examined. Reference to the communication activities of the NDP and PC are made for purposes of comparison with Liberal party strategy.

The major approach of this paper is descriptive analysis, based on 60 interviews with media and party personnel after each election, observations during travel with each of the party leaders, and content analysis of media coverage during each campaign. Certain phenomena are isolated and an attempt is made to draw some conclusions about the implications of certain strategies and the consequences for the political and communication processes.

This paper begins with a discussion of the efforts of the Liberal party to set an agenda for discussion of issues in both elections and general press liaison. The national versus regional focus of both campaigns, French and English strategies and television as a priority medium which emphasizes the appearance of campaigning then are discussed. Finally, suggestions for further research are made.

The Struggle to Set the Agenda for the Discussion of Issues

Much of the competition in both campaigns was between the parties and the media and it exceeded even the expected competition among the parties. This was particularly true for the Liberal party as it was rooted in the historical relationship between Pierre Trudeau and the National Press Gallery.

Despite the loss of the 1979 election, there was much convergence, in both elections, between what the Liberals wanted as an election agenda and what the media perceived as important issues. In both the 1979 and 1980 elections, the Liberals most wanted attention to leadership. In 1979, relying on the slogan, "A leader must be a leader," the emphasis was on the strong, statesmanlike qualities of Pierre Trudeau and compared his qualities with the inexperience of Tory leader Joe Clark. In 1980, the Liberals preferred to focus even more sharply on the ineptness and indecisiveness of Joe Clark, contrasted to the experienced professionalism of Pierre Trudeau. The media followed suit.

In 1979, the Liberals' secondary preferred campaign issues were national unity and energy. Despite the advice of most of his aides and the anglophone members of his cabinet, Pierre Trudeau felt strongly that national unity must be a key issue. The energy issue usually took the form of discussions about Petro-Can.

In the 1980 campaign, in the words of one of his aides, Trudeau "readily accepted" the diminished priority of national unity as an issue. Instead, the recurrent theme was the 18-cent excise tax on gasoline proposed by the party in power, the Conservatives. This simply and forcefully subsumed both the problems of energy and the Tory budget. Lastly, the Liberals paid some attention in the final weeks of the campaign to an industrial strategy for the Canadian economy.

It is important to emphasize that the Liberals desired close identification between leadership and national unity in the 1979 campaign and between leadership and the 18-cent tax in the 1980 campaign. In 1979, the campaign emphasized that Pierre Trudeau, a forceful French-Canadian federalist, was the best leader to deal with problems of unity and a strong central government. In 1980, the emphasis was on Joe Clark who, with the help of a bungling cabinet, was deemed a disaster for the Canadian taxpayer and energy consumer.

Campaign structure is linked with effort to set the agenda for the discussion of issues — both the structure of media coverage and party campaigns. The 1979 Liberal campaign was a campaign in which all the major policy issues and the party position on these issues were established and made public before the election was called. Many issues had already been extensively debated in Parliament and the media (especially through the televising of Parliament, the effect of which needs to be studied and better understood). In the 1980 campaign, most party positions already were established, having been debated and originated in the earlier campaign. In addition, most reporters assigned to cover the election had covered Parliament for several years.

There were at least two false starts to the 1979 campaign and many members of the media had been preparing and re-preparing for 18 months. Weariness and cynicism emerged from the interviews with reporters and editors. Most felt the decision already was made — that voters were going to opt for a change. In any event, it seemed apparent that Pierre Trudeau was going to suffer a loss, and that would represent a change. Though most reporters respect the intellectual abilities of Trudeau, few expressed any feelings of warmth toward him. Not surprisingly, the Conservatives won.

In 1980, many reporters were angry and frustrated by an election call. This was compounded by the fact that media organizations were not geared up for an election and that most had just finished eulogizing the retiring elder statesman, Pierre Elliott Trudeau. The prospect of his return was not greeted enthusiastically, although the Liberals, with Trudeau as their Prime Minister, won easily.

Though the Liberal campaign was decentralized for organizational purposes and made use of provincial chairpersons, most communication and strategy decisions (especially those involving the media) were centralized and focused on the campaign of the leader. This was true for both the 1979 and 1980 campaigns, with the exception of the campaign in Quebec. Strategists in Quebec were given a great deal of autonomy, although their work was coordinated with the rest of the campaign.

All the major media organizations devoted at least half their energy and resources to covering the activities and utterances of the leaders. Some devoted almost all resources to this purpose.

Many members of the media covering the 1979 campaign feared they would be manipulated, as they believed they had been in the 1974 Liberal campaign. In that election, policy statements frequently were released just before filing deadlines, forcing the media merely to report the Liberal position without analysis.

Thus, the CBC organized for 1979 in an interesting manner. On a daily basis part of the coverage would be a "conduit" for the leaders. Thus reporters were assigned to cover each of the leaders and file daily reports. In addition to this "leader team," the CBC established an "issues team," responsible for analysis of party positions, key ridings and/or geographic areas, voter profiles and special features. Few media organizations were so elaborate or deliberate in their planning. Most chose to concentrate on the activities of the leaders. The centralized, leader-focused campaign seems to have had different effects on the success of the Liberal party's preferred issues of national unity, leadership and energy.

On national unity, the very structure of the Liberal Party campaign, specifically a separate and almost autonomous Quebec campaign, seems to have undermined the viability of national unity as an issue. Campaign structure revealed acceptance of a separate Quebec provincial fact. It is difficult to communicate strong central government from a bifurcated structural base.

The leader-focused structure of media coverage, combined with Trudeau speaking out on national unity more frequently in Quebec, may have undermined the effectiveness of unity as a Liberal party issue. A higher percentage of English media coverage of the unity issue originated from Quebec. More and more this may have underscored that unity was really a Quebec problem, a problem for and of French Canadians, especially in the context of an issue that was not "catching on" in the minds of the voters.

In addition, the decision to emphasize strong central government during the opening of the campaign and the greater freedom allowed Pierre Trudeau may have led to a further undermining of both the unity and leadership issues. It was during the "free rein" of the early 1979 campaign that Trudeau strongly attacked the provincial premiers, those drawing unemployment insurance, and farmers. The context for the reporting of the campaign of this stage was: (a) a structure that spotlighted the leaders; and (b) weary reporters who already knew the policy positions, anticipated a change, and had personal reservations about Trudeau. Trudeau's attacks were the most colourful element in the opening stages of the campaign and were reported widely. Disunity rather than unity was understood. Arrogance and combativeness rather than co-operativeness and statesmanship were emphasized. An electorate composed of many former Trudeau voters who were uncertain about supporting him again was reinforced. Thus an unfavourable "set" for receiving campaign communication during the last six weeks was established.

On the other hand, the decision by so many media organizations to concentrate on covering the leaders' tours strengthened those Liberal strategies designed to make leadership a preferred issue. Moreover, an organizing assumption of the television networks and many of the newspapers is that they must give equal time or space to every party, particularly the party leaders. The Liberals knew this and exploited it in both campaigns—especially in 1980.

At first examination, energy seems to have been one issue least affected by the structure of campaign or media coverage. The clarity with which the Liberal position on the 18-cent gasoline tax was transmitted during the 1980 campaign is attributable to the Liberal strategy of exploiting media organizing guidelines of equal space and time. This is discussed further in the section on media strategies.

Media Strategies, General Press Liaison and Accommodation

The services provided for the media by the Liberals, Conservatives, and NDP during the campaigns can be listed:[1]

(1) All parties provided personnel to schedule hotel rooms, handle luggage, place wake-up calls, etc., while on the road.

(2) All parties provided filing facilities such as phones and typewriters. Phone access varied widely depending on the town or city visited. In the 1980 campaign, the Liberal party provision of filing and writing space was particularly impressive although the number of events each day was fewer than either of the other two parties.

(3) Only the Liberal party utilized press passes. The other parties were more informal except at certain crucial events such as the television debate or a large rally.

(4) Free food and drink, at least at lunchtime, was generally available. Reporters had varied feelings about accepting gratuities from the parties. On the airplanes, where basic expenses were covered by the media organizations, food and liquor were abundant.

(5) News releases were occasionally provided by the Tories and Liberals. The NDP had a regular system of news releases, more cynically called "gainesburgers" by the press, ready for distribution most days in the 1979 campaign and on the average of two to three days a week in 1980. These news releases were part of an integrated, thematic day, where attempts would be made to emphasize an issue through several events on the same day.

(6) All three parties made a master tape of most speaking and interview appearances by their respective leaders. In 1979 and particularly in 1980, the Liberal Party provided transcripts within two days of the event. Only occasionally were advance texts provided. The Liberals regularly provided riding and candidate profiles to the media in advance of a scheduled event.

(7) The frequency of press conferences varied considerably, depending on the standing of the party in the advance opinion polls. In 1979, Joe Clark avoided press conferences until the last weeks of the campaign. In 1980, there were frequent scrums and a weekly, Friday morning press conference in Ottawa. In 1979, Pierre Trudeau had weekly press conferences and frequent

scrums. In 1980, there were only three or four scrums, cut off abruptly after Trudeau was forced to state a position on the Olympic boycott in mid-January. There was only one Trudeau press conference, in Sherbrooke, in response to a petition signed by 29 reporters. Most regretted the conference since Trudeau proceeded to filibuster reporters with long answers of up to 12 minutes to only eight questions. The NDP on average granted weekly press conferences with a number of organized scrums under strict topic limitations.

(8) Interviews were granted sparingly and under controlled conditions by Clark in 1979, but were profusely given to local and national media in 1980. Trudeau was generally available for interviews in 1979 but granted only eight to select "national media" in 1980. Neither the Liberals nor the NDP engaged in spontaneous interviews in either campaign. The NDP easily granted interviews if requests were made in advance. The NDP clearly tried to avoid making exclusive statements to any member of the media. Other members of the media often had the chance to listen in on interviews as they were conducted.

(9) Informal access to the leaders was limited but varied according to candidate. Trudeau was almost never approached on the airplane except through an aide. He only came to the back of the airplane to talk with reporters on one or two occasions and there was no banter or exchange between him and reporters. Joe Clark was a frequent visitor to the back of the plane in an attempt to be one of the boys. However, this was a characteristic which a number of reporters held against him, seeming to prefer the distance of Pierre Trudeau. The banter between NDP leader Ed Broadbent and reporters was frequent. His visits to the back of the plane seemed carefully designed but occurred regularly on long flights. For all parties, informal access and exchange was expected to be off the record.

(10) Access to aides was generally very free and open, though different aides were trusted to different degrees—witness a suit between Jim Coutts of the Liberals and Alan Fotheringham, a columnist for the Canadian news magazine, *Maclean's*. This easy access sometimes had negative consequences. Occasionally an aide would become irate at a reporter's treatment of a news item or policy statement. Conversely, a reporter sometimes would discover he/she had been manipulated by an aide. At any rate, most events had an abundance of aides present. My personally observed record was 15 aides at a Clark event in Scarborough in January 1980.

(11) Most parties provided an audio multifeed for radio and television. Many print reporters also relied on tapings for accurate quotations. The only significant exception was the decision by the NDP in the 1980 election to provide a multi-microphone stand. Reporters had to supply their own mikes and cables. The effect was interesting. In contrast to the other leaders, Broadbent appeared to be surrounded by eager media mikes, while Clark and Trudeau would be behind a single or, at most, double microphone.

(12) The frequent practice of the press aide tipping the television reporters in advance, persisted throughout both campaigns. An aide would

indicate the key elements of a speech, making certain the media did not miss the important clips. CTV was more dependent on this service since they could not afford to shoot an entire speech.

(13) Perhaps the fullest accommodation of the press was the NDP's "dead-heading" of a DC9 from Timmins, Ontario to Toronto, loaded only with a television crew, two television producers, several videotapes, several film cans and two rolls of film, in order to make evening deadlines. The NDP then flew the plane back to Earlton later that evening to pick up the candidate, his aides and the press.

Media Strategies: National vs. Regional

In both elections most of the resources of the federal parties went into reaching voters through the national media. The term "national media" is one that is resented by many reporters. It suggests a certain elitism and escapes precise definition, for it seems to refer to both the media or certain reporters and columnists. Generally, party personnel consider the wire services, news services like Southam, television and radio networks, the Toronto *Globe and Mail*, syndicated columnists, *Maclean's* and certain large city newspapers as part of the so-called national media. The papers from cities of central Canada, Toronto, Ottawa and Montreal, are those considered national. And the national media also are taken to include most of the reporters working out of the press gallery in Ottawa.

However, when Michael Valpy, political writer for the *Vancouver Sun*, wrote from Ottawa requesting an interview with Trudeau in the 1980 campaign, his request was dismissed by an aide on the grounds that interviews were only being granted to the national media. This reply created a ripple of resentment, along with a few wry smiles.

The parties' decision to focus on the national media also seemed to suggest that most resources would be devoted to the leaders' tours. The intent in releasing statements, scheduling events and otherwise "making news" was to reach a national audience. As often as not that meant reaching the critical voters of south-central Ontario. In any event, the leader's tours became the focal point of campaign activity and media strategy in both campaigns.

Although maintaining an emphasis on the leader's tour in the 1980 campaign, the Progressive Conservative Party attempted to switch in focus, leap-frogging the so-called national media to contact directly representatives of local newspapers, radio and television.

For a variety of reasons, the two major television networks—CTV and CBC—were not covering the leaders with daily reports during the first three weeks of January 1980. In the case of CTV it appears to have been due to a combination of limited resources and a conscious attempt by news executives to avoid becoming prisoners of the leader tours and the parties. The same fear of being manipulated by the parties and concern about overcoverage of the campaign appeared to have motivated CBC news executives to use 20-second "windows" (short visual footage with a studio voice-over by the anchorperson) from the tours and/or thematic pieces replacing the daily "itinerary" pieces of the previous campaign.

The NDP and Conservatives were particularly upset by the lack of coverage and let management of both news organizations know. The Liberals seemed less concerned, perhaps content as frontrunners and knowing that both networks would eventually go to daily coverage, which they did. The Tories decided to employ a new strategy — to schedule as many hot-line radio and television shows as possible and grant exclusive interviews to local media outlets. This strategy consumed a great deal of Clark's energy and took a long time to have much impact. To some degree, other parties utilized this tactic in key ridings. In the case of the Liberals, prominent ministers and second-level candidates utilized the local and regional media for interviews and radio-television appearances, especially in Quebec. Yet, the NDP basically rejected this strategy as being too risky.

The 1974 Liberal campaign had left many media personnel feeling manipulated. Advisors to Trudeau in the 1979 campaign felt they could not "get away" with controlling media access and response as they did in 1974. Thus, Trudeau was given freer rein. There were few close-to-deadline releases. Reporters had easier access to aides and Trudeau. In the 1980 campaign, everything tightened up again except that policy (what there was) was released largely through early afternoon luncheon speeches, well ahead of late afternoon deadlines. Party strategy concentrated on daily media coverage. The structure of the leader's tour did not encourage feature stories, nor analytical, reflective or background pieces. A number of media organizations were aware of this but had little success in producing analytical studies.

Media Strategies: French and English

All three parties gave nominal attention to both languages. Releases, texts and schedules were prepared in French and English. Liberal press aides were bilingual while the NDP doubled up with a press aide for each language. Both Clark and Broadbent spoke in French to the French media or at events where French-speaking Canadians were present. Broadbent and especially Clark used French more frequently and easily in 1980 than in 1979. Paid media campaigns and party organizational structures were divided, to varying degrees, along linguistic lines. All three parties relied on French as well as English advertising.

The Tories and NDP generally reflected the English themes, with the notable exception of stridently anti-Trudeau "coupable" television ads launched by the Tories in Quebec in 1979. These were the first of the negative or "anti" ads to be employed — a strategy soon dropped by the Tories in Quebec as it seemed to backfire. However, both Liberals and Tories relied heavily on the negative approach in the first major advertising series launched in English in the 1980 campaigns.

As indicated earlier, because of their strong support among the voters of Quebec, the Liberal party's separate campaign in Quebec differed from the rest of Canada. In both the 1979 and 1980 campaigns the creative package was distinct, as was the organizational structure. Whereas the English media ads in 1979 were leery of stressing the economy as an issue, Quebec media ads proclaimed the "Economic Olympics." Whereas English strategists in 1980 were concerned about "low-bridging" Trudeau, the Quebec ads prominently displayed him as the chief engineer of the Liberal train. If Trudeau was counselled to speak less and less of national unity in English Canada in 1979, he was encouraged to step forward and "parle fort" on federalism and unity on behalf of Quebecers.

Media Strategies: Television and the Appearance of Campaigning

To the communication student, it is a cliché to say that North American campaigns are television-oriented. Given the changes in the Canadian Elections Expenditure Act, the growing sophistication of party aides and strategists, the increased use of marketing techniques, the increased viewing of television and a complex of other reasons, television entered the 1979 Canadian federal election in full force. It entered with such a force that there was frequent, and often resentful, comment in the written press about the strategy of events for television and the cynical use of the press itself as "print props" for television clips.

It is obvious that most aspects of the national campaign were geared for television. Key aides of all the parties unabashedly admitted the television orientation. Scheduling, policy statements, speeches, rallies, sleigh rides, paper mill visits, farm visits and Chinatown visits were all designed with the visual media in mind. There seemed to be a general ranking order: television (CBC first), wire service photographs, radio, wire service reporters, selected columnists, the *Globe and Mail,* the *Toronto Star* and, finally, the rest of the print media. After the 1980 election, there were some aides in the Liberal party who relegated the columnists to the lowest rank. In the words of one aide, "The 1980 election was the worst kick in the teeth for the pundits of this country in the last 25 years."

The Liberals and the NDP acknowledged that the print medium had a limited effectiveness. Adapting the frequent dictum of David Halberstram in his book *The Powers That Be*[2]—a book that was recommended to me several times by Liberal aides after the 1979 election and may have influenced 1980 strategy—print was acknowledged as an influence on television and the television reporter. Columnists were believed to influence other reporters. The influence was perceived as defining issues, legitimizing tone and selecting leads. My own observations confirmed an almost incestuous desire on the part of all reporters to consume each others' reports. Print also seemed to serve as an interpreter and legitimizer of voter interpretation of the significance of events.

For example, the reaction to the televised debate in 1979 seemed to change as interpretation and analysis by the print medium became widespread.

Both campaigns were essentially eventless, at least in terms of those happenings that had a critical effect on changing votes. In the 1980 campaign, reporters and aides interviewed generally agreed that there were no critical or key events. The few that were cited were non-events; that is, the lack of a television debate, the absence of effect on voters of the closing of the Canadian embassy in Tehran, and revelation of the smuggling out of six Americans.

In the 1979 campaign, a few incidents were singled out as "events" with regularity; Trudeau's admission that he might try to stay in power if he had fewer seats than Clark, Trudeau's responses to hecklers early in the campaign, the Maple Leaf Gardens rally of the Liberals and the televised debate. What is interesting about all four of these events is that television played a very large role in each. The debate, for example, was staged by the media and was of significance because of the immense spectacle it created—the many columns of copy and feet of film used for pre-comment and post-comment. The rally was staged for the media as a Liberal demonstration of "drawing power."

The 1980 Liberal party campaign was a distillation of this campaign ritual and control. It merits further discussion, as it represents the quintessence of media strategy. Private and public polls showed the Liberals ahead of the Progressive Conservatives by at least 20 points by late November 1979. The Liberal plan, as developed after the fall of the Tory government, was to "low-bridge" Trudeau by limiting the events per day, severely controlling the media's access to him, carefully scripting speeches and minimizing the number of new policies and positions presented. Strategists admitted that the media strategy was to limit exposure of Trudeau to avoid vote-costing mistakes and to prevent his personality and style from overwhelming other important aspects of the campaign, such as the negative image of Clark. Essentially, "the print media did not matter" (in the words of a Liberal aide), as long as the daily file occurred. What did matter was that the CBC, CTV, Radio Canada and Global had the requisite one minute, 30-second clip on the nightly news. There was always an event from a different location in the country to ensure material for that news clip. The simpler the message, the better chance the message would get across.

Most days there was one event, usually a noon-time luncheon speech to a mostly partisan crowd. The parallels to the 1972 Nixon campaign (as Dalton Camp tried to suggest in the now-famous censored column by the *Toronto Star*) are striking. Both Nixon and Trudeau tire easily, requiring a full night's sleep to be at their best. When tired in a campaign, both seemed more prone to mistakes. The Nixon and the Trudeau campaign strategies were to limit campaigning to single media events, located in various parts of the country. The appearance of movement, the appearance of an active, legitimate and ritualistic campaign were reinforced by each successive television report, ending with a different deadline. Preliminary examination of the 1980 schedule showed that on only three occasions did the Trudeau tour remain more than one day in a targeted area, as opposed to the other parties that worked key areas, like southern Ontario, for several days.

Another scheduling addition to the 1980 Liberal campaign was the inclusion of a Saturday event. Most Canadian papers have no Sunday edition, but television still has weekend reports. The added day would not overly tax Trudeau, already on a one to two event per day schedule. The extra day added to the appearance of heavy campaigning.

The standard scripted speech read by Trudeau was usually preceded by short speeches by two candidates or sitting members of Parliament. Though paid scant heed by reporters, the introductory speeches underscored the team concept and reduced the prominence of Trudeau. Within the standard 18-cent gas tax speech would be light attacks on Clark (the paid media ads on television and radio carried the heavy attacks), attacks on the budget, and a localization of the effects of the budget/energy cost to the area where Trudeau spoke.

The result was a bored, frustrated and angry press corps who frequently commented in their daily reports about how controlled and lifeless the campaign was. This did not bother Liberal aides because they knew that reporters and editors would still feel that they had to give equal time and space and that they had to include some comment from the set speech and its local application. Several editors told me in interviews that even though they felt the Liberals were saying little, they still felt bound to give them equal time and space. The rules of fair play overrode the concerns about a cynical campaign.

As part of the game plan, Trudeau began to depart from the standard 18-cent gas tax speech in the last two weeks, revealing several new Liberal economic schemes. A few departures from the formated appearance occurred, interviews were granted to several selected reporters (especially television) and an additional event or two was added. Suddenly, bored reporters came to life. They had new things to write and report about. The struggle for a new angle in a lifeless campaign was reduced. The campaign appeared to be gaining momentum.

One of the results of the general Liberal strategy and the limited, ritualistic campaign was a series of nightly television reports with clear focus—a simple, often repeated, message. This contrasted favourably with the Tory and NDP reports. Clark, with many events in a day, seemed to feel compelled to comment on a variety of topics. Broadbent, also with several events per day, controlled the topic variance within a single day more successfully than Clark, but each day brought a new issue. NDP aides complained of being pushed to comment on many different areas, especially by representatives of the political left. Tory aides expressed concern about a lack of focus in the Clark campaign. This was confirmed by interviews with reporters who were more confused by or unaware of the preferred issues of the

Tories and NDP. However, the reporters agreed on the preferred issues of the Liberals.

Conclusions

Looking back on the two campaigns at the issue and media strategies employed, several conclusions, or rather concerns, can be formulated. They are filtered through my skills as an observer and my experiences as a communication analyst and political practitioner and sometimes do not yet have an obvious factual basis. Further exploration is needed, as is better understanding of the interdependence of media, political parties, and the political communication system.

Earlier in this paper, the ways in which the campaign structure of the federal parties either reinforced or undermined the viability of their own strategies were discussed. In those campaigns where most resources were put into a leader tour and most press strategies concentrated on a national media focus, efforts to make leadership a central campaign issue were reinforced. Current organizing assumptions of most media organizations dictate a commitment of major resources to the leader's tour for daily coverage. This also enhances the primacy of the leadership issue. Despite the outcries of many editors, producers and reporters, the media enter into willing collusion in their own entrapment.

Campaigns structured around leaders with a national media focus often are reflections of the more day-to-day decisions on covering Parliament. The prime target audience in these days of short-term coalition building appears to be south-central Ontario. This means structure and strategy enter into an uncomfortable relationship that may lead to greater centrism in values, lifestyle and beliefs. If pressures toward a strong, central federal system really communicate Ontario values, then Eastern, Western and Quebec alienation will be further strengthened.

A structure of accentuating the leader and national media focus may have another unwelcome side effect similar to the negative aspects of the American political system. Continued prominence of the national leaders, in addition to eroding the base of the parliamentary system, may increase voter expectations of the performance of national leaders. As attention turns to the executive so do increased powers and increased demands for accountability. In this context it is not surprising that Americans have presidents who last for one or one and a half terms and Canadians a prime minister voted out after a mere eight months in office. Again, the media co-operate with party strategy that sells leadership as the dominant issue and structures campaigns to further this concept.

Leadership has always been one of the components of the Canadian voter decision. Examination of *Political Choice in Canada* by Harold Clarke,[3] reveals interesting aspects of voter response to leadership and the resulting effects of leadership. The Canadian electorate is highly flexible, he argues, displaying a minimum of long-term party loyalty. In the past several elections prior to that of 1979, the Liberal party maintained power through short-term coalitions of transient voters, new voters and party regulars. A high degree of voter switching among the parties from election to election has occurred. Those who desert a party tend to do so more for negative reasons than positive ones.

Clarke suggests that personality and style are the most salient factors in assessing leadership image. These characteristics far outweigh a leader's position on issues and policies in the final image implanted in the mind of the voter. The emphasis on personality and style produces instability. The desire by the Liberals and other parties to make leadership the key issue in both campaigns resulted in a strategy of building a short-term coalition on an issue of style rather than substance. In 1980, the Liberal goal was immediate return to power. The most successful way to achieve that goal was to reinforce negative reasons for deserting Joe Clark, pushing heavily the medium with the greatest potential for showing the negative and positive aspects of personality and style—television.

Political campaign strategy—in this case strategies for promoting the issue of leadership—and the medium of television are inextricably linked. The Liberal party in 1980 was particularly fortunate (as they have been historically) to have a leader with a clearly defined personality and style. Pierre Trudeau has served party strategies well in this sense for many elections. Party strategists also know the medium of television very well. The exploitation of television guidelines in successfully communicating the 18-cent a gallon tax is a vivid example. But Trudeau is going to retire. In the long-term, the continued use of a process issue (leadership) in a process medium (television) can only increase the instability of short-term coalitions. Long-term loyalties and commitment are not established through continued exploitation of the personality and style of a party leader.

A contradiction of television is its ability on the one hand to plunge the viewer into the actuality of an event and on the other hand to make things appear as they are not. Though most of the comments in this section are based on the 1980 Liberal campaign, they reflect many aspects of the other party campaigns in both elections. However, the Liberal Party campaign, with its tight format, limited number of events, emphasis on television and daily coverage and careful control of Trudeau, was the essence of the campaign ritual followed by all mainstream parties. Because of the low-key nature of the campaign, it is easier to see its basic structure and strategy. And it became easier to see that, at the level of basic structure, what was communicated was the *appearance* of many things.

Television and the other media, especially the wire services, are easy accessories to promoting the appearances of a campaign. With a commitment to daily coverage, the media help to legitimize strategies like those used in the 1980 Liberal campaign. With commitments to equal coverage, the media make it difficult for the viewer or reader to tell the difference between the real thing and the appearance of the real thing. With all three parties following much the same ritualistic structure, it becomes difficult even for an attentive analyst to discern what the real thing is. The media also gain their own legitimacy by regularly giving exposure to the leaders of the nation. With a mandate to serve the country's interest, as in the case of the CBC, there is added importance to daily coverage. There is also excitement, glamour and action. It may be correct that the only truly Canadian stars are political leaders.

In communication terms, consumerism means presenting the concept, the issue or the candidate in a form already fashioned, and already finished. This puts the participative function in the hands of the initial creators — that is, the political strategists. The receivers of political communication (voters) have little opportunity to function as co-producers. They have even less chance if the creators have relied on the latest of political marketing techniques, such as polls, targeting, lifestyle appeals and so forth. For example, polling techniques have moved away from demographic and issue-orientation questions to aspects of lifestyle orientation. After reviewing the Tory television ads in the 1979 election a number of students interviewed felt as if they had just seen a beer ad.

As political parties become more centralized in their decision structures and with the rise of the political technocrat in Canada, fewer and fewer people are functioning as co-producers of federal political ideas. Already there is evidence, for example, of a decline in successful door-to-door canvassing and other grass-roots techniques. People with an inclination to participation have been turning to the special one-issue interest groups instead of the political parties. Within the interest groups there are issues of substance and there is still an opportunity to co-create the communication message.

In political parties, especially the Liberal party, the consumer issue has become leadership because it is easier to pre-fashion. It "cuts" with the electorate. The short-term coalition can be established for a return to power. It succeeds. In the meantime the electorate becomes more volatile. The political process has been sacrificed to the more immediate goal of getting the message across.

NOTES

1.   For a more complete account of this, readers might refer to Dalton Camp, *Point of Departure* (Deneau and Greenberg, 1979). He includes a sample day's activity of Brad Chapman, the "Wagonmaster" for the Tories. A less satisfactory account of some reporters' experiences is contained in Clive Cocking, *Following the Leaders* (Toronto: Doubleday, 1980).
2.   David Halberstram, *The Powers That Be* (New York: Alfred Knopf, 1979).
3.   Harold Clarke, Jane Jenson, Lawrence Leduc and Jon H. Pammett, *Political Choice in Canada* (Toronto: McGraw-Hill Ryerson, 1979), Chapters 7, 8, 9, 11 and 12.

Chapter 4

Interpretive and Structural Analyses: The Advertisement and the Film

Donald F. Theall

Tandis que la structure, les signes, les éléments dramatiques et mythiques, les aspects fantaisie et rêve, et particulièrement la naissance du désir sont tous présents dans la séquence d'une publicité bien conçue de même que dans une oeuvre d'art "véritable", la création distance ou aliène l'action symbolique de son contexte normal, ébauchant déjà une critique. Utilisant comme points de départ une publicité de Pepsi-Cola et une séquence de publicité de la compagnie de téléphone Bell—telle que racontée par l'écrivain de science-fiction Arthur Clarke—cet article examine le message publicitaire en se référant aux films de Fellini et de Dusan Makavejev et aux écrits, entre autres, de Joyce, Bateson, Kenneth Burke, Nietzsche et Ricoeur.

Alors que la publicité échafaude un mini-récit qui, si possible, essaie d'enfermer le spectateur en lui-même, de l'emmurer, l'oeuvre de Joyce (ou n'importe quelle oeuvre d'art) invite le participant-lecteur à s'engager dans la recherche d'un sens qu'il réalise à travers une libre participation du corps, de l'esprit et des sens. L'une produit un effet de claustration (enclosing) tandis que l'autre libère (disclosing).

Cette théorie dramatique-poétique de la communication provient d'une conception écologique, avant tout, de l'activité artistique. La théorie conçoit les autres types d'activités de communication comme des reflets des procédés que privilégie la présentation artistique. Cependant, il est important de noter que même les langages utilisés par la communication dramatico-poétique sont indissociables des sphères sociale, politique, économique, et biologique de l'activité humaine. Par conséquent, toute analyse de l'élément dramatique devra nécessairement tenir compte des relations analogiques complexes qui le lient au domaine des arts et au rapport langage-vie en société. Un tel procédé de liaison tranversale des fragments entre eux permettra l'émergence d'une série de perspectives nouvelles dans l'examen d'une publicité, ainsi, l'impor-

*tance qui s'y trouve de vendre d'abord un mode de vie, avant même de pro-
mouvoir un produit.*

Recently the Pepsi-Cola Company presented an advertisement on television
which seemed to be a parody of the Oedipal triangle. The ad, which
dramatizes a family visit to the grandparents' ranch, is roughly structured in
three segments. The first segment shows the children arriving by car at the
ranch. The second shows the family riding on powerful horses, with close-ups
of the youngest son on a black stallion, accompanied by the music "Come on,
come on, come on . . . ." The third shows the family and friends at an old-
fashioned barbecue with the camera paying considerable attention to a variety of food-making machines which emphasize the eroticism of the foods. The
sequence concludes with the mother taking the youngest boy on a horse with
her and pulling a large black stovepipe-style hat over his head.

It is highly charged symbolism and a blatant sketch of the Oedipal situation. And it is hardly the kind of situation in which the interpreter "reads
into" the advertisement, for the ad is almost comic in its invitations to engage
in Freudianized analysis, including the phallic Pepsi-Cola bottle. It is the type
of material that has furnished film-maker Dusan Makavejev and others like
him with their targets for satire, and easily reminds us of the role of sugar in
Sweet Movie.[1]

Without analyzing the particular ad in greater detail, although this
easily could be done, a number of questions arise. Here is a narrative involving a psycho-social dimension and employing traditional historical and myth-
ological symbols. The narrative is dramatized, cinematically shaped and accompanied by sound and music. Superficially it is a film in miniature. In fact,
apart from being shorter and more condensed, it is not unlike many films on
television or the audio-visual sequences that are the regular fare television
series provide. As such it certainly can be analyzed either semiologically or in-
terpretatively or both, for it is dependent on a continuity shaped from various
series of signs and joined into a unity. The Pepsi ad has cultural, intellectual
and historical dimensions involving the familial, the psychiatric and
American mythology. It is engaged in a process of making sense both by inter-
preting part of the world and its relations with Pepsi-Cola and also by being
itself interpretable as part of a world in which Pepsi-Cola has a significant
place in the social and economic structure as well as the cultural and
ideological superstructure. What difference is there between this and the
analysis of the director as artist in Federico Fellini's film *8½?*

To answer the question, the concept of the "ecology of sense" that
developed from James Joyce's literary practice will be useful. Certainly common sense suggests that the activity of the Pepsi-Cola ad, which is contrived
and manipulated in the narrow interests of selling a specific product, is not a
contribution as art, a contribution to some ecological process by which
human relates himself to human in the desire to be interacting with his

natural world. Yet the structure, the signs, the dramatic and mythical elements, the ingredients of fantasy and dream and especially the arousal of desire are all present in the ad as they would be in other types of productions like Fellini's $8^{1}/_{2}$.

The first and most obvious aspect of an answer could take the films of Makavejev or the writings of Kurt Vonnegut or William Burroughs as examples. Such productions incorporate the type of symbolic action involved in the Pepsi-Cola ad and estrange or alienate it from its normal context. Such a process of decontextualization becomes the beginning of a critique, a destruction of the facile and superficial Oedipal triangulation implied in the ad. Consequently, Makavejev's play with milk and sugar in *Sweet Movie* makes sense of the Pepsi-Cola ad in a way in which the creator of the ad did not conceive and did not intend. Yet this is just the first stage, for the process in the ad differs in other ways from the process involved in the true ecology of sense. Here the signs and structures all have an uncomfortable familiarity, a feeling that they have been borrowed after being used many times before. Conventions become conventional. Whatever play may be present is the play of repetition rather than the playfulness of discovery.

But how can such allegations be grounded in the objects of the ad itself? The strategy of Joyce's *Finnegan's Wake* provides a guide to the very extent that it is a work of masterly destruction as well as masterly construction. The novel backs Joyce's claim of being the greatest engineer that ever lived. From the perspective of the *Wake*, the mode in which desire is developed in the Pepsi-Cola ad depends on a seductive continuity which does not invite us to consider any *polyvocity* or polymorphousness, much less any ambiguity or ambivalence which might create breaks in the continuity of effect. The ad constructs a superficial mini-narrative which would, if it were possible, try to enclose the spectator within his own limits, to wall him in. The desire for sense aroused by Joyce's work invites the participant-reader to engage in the making of sense, permitting him a free play of his body-mind-feeling in the process. The signs generated by the one are *enclosing*; the signs generated by the other are *disclosing*. The ad could not sustain the dark laughter of comedy which is precisely what the work of wit, as a work of the ecology of sense, invites.

The Pepsi-Cola ad is a relatively simple example, and it is necessary to consider another example with complex roots in the film and literary worlds and dependent on an extended sense of the ad, that is, the extended sequence of ads used on some individually sponsored specials. The particular example used here occurred during a made-for-television presentation of a new version of the classic Hollywood film, *The Man in the Iron Mask*. The programme is an expensive period costume extravaganza of 18th-century France, including location filming at Versailles, that stars Richard Chamberlain. It was a pseudo-cultural vehicle with considerable nostalgic interest for the older portion of the viewing audience who remembered the original 1939 version, or for those hooked on Hollywood film history.

The sponsor was the Bell "family" of companies, and their advertising consisted of an interrelated group of ads. One presented a single unified tale, which was narrated by Arthur Clarke, the science fiction writer who collaborated with Stanley Kubrick on the film *2001* and also provided commentary for the CBS presentation of the real-life moon landing—the Moon Odyssey. Science fiction therefore provided a way of uniting technology and culture, as well as uniting film, literature and the real event of the first landing on the moon. Through the ad sequence, Bell played on virtually every theme, motif, key and subject area possible. Clarke's presentations ranged from historical and nostalgic glances at the growth and development of Bell services through their operators, to comic presentations of computers as new members of the office's communications staff. There were impressive presentations of Bell's super-technology, culminating in a final futuristic-cultural *pièce de résistance* in which Arthur Clarke (who might also suggest in this role Sir Kenneth Clark lecturing on art history and culture) takes us back to the works of architecture and sculpture in ancient Ceylon while speculating on the possibility of extra-terrestrial, inter-galactic communications sometime in the future. And so Bell's ads show that technology can provide both images from the historical past for an immediate present through transmitted image and computerization, and its technology also points the way to inter-galactic communications and transportation. This grand finale comes complete with visions of the stargate from Kubrick's *2001* and all the accompanying innuendoes of Beyond Jupiter and its mysticism imported via Arthur Clarke himself.

At first consideration, this appears to be advertising on a different order than the Pepsi-Cola version of back to grandpa's ranch and the family hang-ups. Here the ad sequence offers a vision of a world where the scientific, technological, social and cultural unity is offered through the hegemony of a multinational corporation—the phone company. Yet the strategies used in the actual presentation still play fundamentally with human desire, with a technology that itself is subtly eroticized in a parody of the artistic productions of "high culture." The series of ads ends with Clarke in a sensuously erotic cultural setting, amid the art of ancient Ceylon. Narrating the wonders of the past in this ancient environment, Clarke subtly shifts from the distant past to the distant unpredictable future. He associates with the ancient culture new possibilities of inter-galactic communication—an encounter with the mystery of a totally unimaginable "other" whose possible existence evokes the fear and fascination aroused by our preoccupation with UFOs.

This Bell ad sequence leans heavily on the connections between art, reality and futurology which the image of Clarke as narrator focuses through the roles he has played in the media treatment of the moon shot and in the making of *2001*. Kubrick's film seeks to raise complex questions about technology and its future, which ironically the Bell ad sequence attempts to suppress. This attempt at suppression is achieved by the introduction of more stock virtues of the everyday world—the myth of the small home-town, family and children, pseudo-erotic camaraderie in office by-play, and the pseudo-liberating power of business. To the extent that the suppression is successful, the ad has reduced the polyvocity which characterizes Kubrick's film as well as the most intense and successful contemporary science fiction work.

Both the film and science fiction are co-opted in the interest of the large corporation by a strategy in which the full potential of possible sense is suppressed. More significantly, desire is re-directed in the interests of a technologically organized universe. The dominating aspect of the technological imperative and its socio-economic foundation is concealed by linking the technological imperative to a life in which eros is allowed a free rein. This is realized in images such as the sequence of cars flowing along a throughway at night, which becomes a mobile artistic metaphor of the flow of messages through the Bell system and thus of the beauty of the power of modern telecommunications technology.

The one difference between the Pepsi-Cola ad and the phone company ad is Bell's totalistic approach and tendency to exploit the language of the arts involved. Clarke (whatever his value or significance) becomes a sell-out — not because he accepts money to be a huckster, but in his willingness to destructure the language of the artistic and historical activities in which he has previously engaged. The genuine danger of the phone company ad is precisely a function of its "artistic" value, its apparent similarity to a work of art in miniature, its aping of art. This is true regardless of the standard audience reaction of irritation or amusement with the ad itself, for these very reactions are a response to a response, an awareness of the seductive nature of the presentation even while attempting to reject it as a repetitious and over-simplified approach to reality.

One extreme case leads to the essential difference between this advertising "art" and the liberating creative activity which produces the ecology of sense. In the province of Quebec, it was possible to view two very similar visual presentations of Coca-Cola advertisements, one in English and one in French.[2] They were obviously made from the same footage, but edited with subtle differences and accompanied by different sound tracks. Each of these ads shows nearly identical visual material, with a summertime sun beating down on the earth. But the messages are drastically different. The English advertisement appeals to Coca-Cola as a "saver of life." It is a practical way of beating the sun's unpleasant effects, a way of quenching thirst. The French ad, on the other hand, plays on the life-giving powers of the sun, associating the sun and Coke as two good life-giving sources in nature. The English ad finally appeals to a practical, instrumental sense of dealing with the summer sun; the French ad shows the sun as sustainer of life, creating a kind of transcendent symbolism.

These ads originally were isolated and analyzed in a comparative study of French and English advertising, but the point here is not the difference between French and English approaches. Rather, these examples show how the polyvocity of the symbolic material is necessarily suppressed when it is placed in the advertising context. The art becomes an art of selection, which mutes the undesired associations. It would not do to have the sun which endangers life become associated with the sun that sustains it, even though in nature itself it is the very same sun. Ads tend to minimize ambiguity and avoid ambivalent reactions. A full-scale analysis of these ads only can be achieved by placing them in the context of the historical development of advertising. That clearly would show how the ad sequence Bell used represents an entirely new approach to what advertising does in society. Such knowledge is assumed in part in our interpretive activity, but such a historic approach also requires a socio-aesthetic theory by which to undertake the rhetorical analysis of the advertising.

Throughout this paper, the important interrelations of drama, game, play, language and symbolic systems have been stressed, for within that nexus lie the insights essential to developing a socio-aesthetic basis for understanding communication as symbolic action. Gregory Bateson recognized the importance of these in developing a theory of schizophrenia as a theory of communication and distortions of communication.[3] Yet each of these metaphorical ways of building a theory of communication has different and important aspects to contribute to the understanding of communication. *Drama* involves action, plot, conflict, tension and peripety or surprise. It stresses the importance of the inevitable and the unexpected. *Game* involves a logic based on mutually agreed rules or regulations governing controlled conflict between two or more parties. Play, while sharing aspects of the game and the drama, differs in directly emphasizing the freely creative and mimetic aspects of these other activities, at the expense of the controlled rules of the game in its more rigid forms, and the formal structure of dramatic action. Language is among the most complex and it also can be the most misleading, as language is only part of a total human communication system. Language is most likely, as Sapir argued, communications *par excellence,* but it is always supported by the presence of the total system of symbolic communication.[4] Those aspects of a theory of communication that are borrowed from language are concerned with the principles of structuring formal properties so as to make them meaningful. Language has, as Wittgenstein recognized, important relationships with games, but it also has relationships with drama and with the mimetic qualities towards which much play is directed. As Roman Jakobson has shown, there are important interrelationships between psychiatric disorder and language, yet it is notable that Bateson does not isolate language in the way he does drama, game and play (as well as other "artistic" forms) when discussing his theory of schizophrenia. In fact, the comic and laughter, the joke and wit, are more specifically points of his focus.[5]

In developing these ideas into a theory of communicative action based on a theory of poetic action, it is important to stress the work of John Dewey,

George Herbert Mead and especially Kenneth Burke. But one of the strongest statements of the theme of art as an ecology of sense appears in Friedrich Nietzsche's *The Will to Power,* in which art is attributed a privileged role in respect to communication. Nietzsche observed that "all art works like a suggestion to the muscles and the senses which were originally active in the ingenuous artistic man."[6] Such art, he declared, works as a "tonic," negating ugliness and dismissing the bluntness of logic.

> The aesthetic state represents an overflow of *means of communication* as well as a condition of extreme sensibility to stimuli and signs. It is the zenith of communion and transmission between living creatures, it is the source of languages. In it, languages, whether of signs, or glances, have their birthplace. The richer phenomenon is always the beginning: our abilities are subtilized forms of richer abilities. But even today we still listen with our muscles, we even read with our muscles.[7]

Such a sense of the artistic or poetic state is ecological, for it suggests an interdependence within human society in shaping its means of communication, a sharing between those who can attain a condition of extreme sensibility and others who shape their abilities from the "subtilized forms of richer abilities." The relation noted earlier between art and advertising, especially modernist art and advertising, would then be explicable in the role that art played in the generation of languages. But reciprocally, artistic works would be a way of returning to those languages and seeing through or breaking through their constraints and limitations.

The dramatic-poetic theory of communication depends on this privileged ecological position of artistic activity. It sees other types of communicative activity as a reflection of the processes which are intensified in the artistic presentation. It is important to recognize, however, that even the languages used in dramatic-poetic communication cannot be divorced from the social, political, economic and biological spheres of human activity. Kenneth Burke in his writings insists upon an interrelationship between art, society and nature. His criticism, as exemplified in such essays as "The Rhetoric of Hitler's Battle," is directed towards the unmasking of power relationships concealed within symbolic actions.[8]

Analogy is central to the way poetry functions as well as to the way that any social phenomenon can be susceptible to dramatic analysis. The analogical perspective insists that the work of art is connected with something other than the symbolic or linguistic world through the polyvocity of its language or its signs. There must be an awareness of both the particular construction of the work and the web of relationships that the work invokes beyond it. A thorough poetic-dramatic analysis of social and communicative phenomena (or objects) necessarily will involve complex analogical relationships to the realm of art and to the relationship of language and social activity.

An analysis of the Pepsi-Cola ad requires not only careful attention to its relationship with the type of dramatic categories Burke proposed, and to the dramatic-narrative form of the ad (including naturally, the linguistic and figurative aspects of the ad), but it also must insist on an interrelationship of the matter of the ad with the patterns of social process with which that ad is enmeshed. An analysis must be concerned with invoking the disjunctions which arise when the ad is placed in a relationship with these social processes. For example, the way the Oedipus relationship and the interlocking structure of the family and grandparents is used in the interest of a specific manipulation of desire would be an important aspect of the interpretation of this ad. But this would be extended to the broader relationship between economic imperatives and the investments of desire on the part of individuals.

Such observations rise directly from dramatic-poetic explication of the ad in question. From this base the overt intent of the ad, in regard to the reinforcing of the Oedipal nature of society, arises from the use of images, the movements, the relationships of sounds, words, images and movements and the sequential unfolding of the action. It is only by not allowing the ad to create its own exclusive world, but by relating it to a world of which it is a part, that it is explicated and exposed. The type of explication required by a dramatic-poetic theory of communication insists on a conception of analogy which leads to relating fragments of the ad as object (or preferably machine, for it is a "machine" in the sense in which Gilles Deleuze speaks of desiring machines in *Anti Oedipus*,[9] to fragments of the social and natural world in which it occurs. Such an approach is termed an interpretation, but it is an interpretation in a new sense from that of Paul Ricoeur because it is concerned with how the machine is constructed and operates. It is understood through its function, which is why Burke rises from the pragmatic traditions of Dewey and Mead and preserves a delicate set of contradictions between his idealism and his materialism. Such an explication, relating fragments to one another transversally, allows a whole new series of perspectives to appear in relation to the ad: the importance, for example, to Pepsi and Coke to sell a way of life even before they promote a product, for the whole direction in which desire is invested only becomes clear through such fragmentation of the continuities established by the ad. Such strategies make clear the way the Oedipal content of the Pepsi ad is used in the interest of motivating the type of social production and consumption desired by Pepsi's manufacturers.

Besides, such poetic-dramatic explication shows that the advertisement cannot be separated from a body of advertising. Through interrelating parts of ads with one another the purpose or motivation of the advertising industry begins to emerge. Many of the statements above can only be made in the awareness of a body of advertising, including items such as the phone company ad sequence. The relationship between a life style, a technological imperative and a set of politico-economic aims rises more immediately from such an ad sequence. When the interrelationship behind which the pattern of power in the phone company ad is concealed, then the phone company ad can be analogically related to the pattern of life style and the Oedipal imagery of the Pepsi-Cola ad.

Analogy has become more central to discussions of method in the human sciences, since it has been clearly recognized that metaphor is central to theory building.[10] In fact, the socio-aesthetic domain is important to understanding human communications, because it provides various metaphors which are crucial in the analysis of communication events and objects produced as communications. Without fully accepting all of Ricoeur's views of interpretation, the way in which he develops his distinction between "explanation" and "interpretation" is helpful in understanding what is at stake in the analogical perspective of this poetic-dramatic theory of communication. In "Metaphor and the Main Problem of Hermeneutics," Ricoeur relates explanation to the way that a metaphor creates meaning, or makes sense through the emergence of meaning. He relates interpretation to the way that this emergent meaning of metaphor can only come about through the relationship of the metaphor to a work as a whole and to the relationship of that particular work to its world.[11] An explanation of an isolated object is not able to achieve the understanding required for communication, which must involve interpretation.

Kenneth Burke discussed the same problem in relation to analogy in his discussion of metaphor and perspective by incongruity. He naturally warned against the great danger of analogy in which similarity is taken as evidence of identity,[12] but simultaneously stressed its centrality.

> I do not see why the universe should accommodate itself to a man-made medium of communication, particularly when there is so strongly a *creative* or *poetic* quality about its goings-on. . . .[13]

Burke in the 1930s questioned the possibility of any kind of thinking that did not involve analogy or metaphor. Metaphor is as natural to scientific or philosophical work as it is natural to poetry. But that phenomenon was linked in Burke's mind to dissonance, nonsense and the grotesque.

He could rightly stress the importance of the world of nonsense to modern art for the "nearest approach to modern art which can appeal to the naive and sophisticated alike is perhaps this ambitious and creative nonsense."[14] This corresponded to the immense contradictions which permeated the social life of the contemporary period. Media analysis involves metaphor directly as well as depending on a theoretical base which involves metaphor. While it is possible such theories lead to analogical over-extension, just as did the mediaeval search for essences, Burke argues for their necessity and stresses the importance of "an incongruous assortment of incongruities" in the modern avant-garde. He used the image of the mediaeval gargoyles as "typical instances of planned incongruity."[15] The "incongruous assortment of incongruities" of the avant-garde multiplied gargoyle elements previously played an important role in Marx's formula of class-consciousness and was the basis of Joyce's later work *Finnegan's Wake* which provided "the most striking instance of modern linguistic gargoyles."[16] A concept of analogy related to such a sense of planned incongruity naturally stressed difference more than similarity, employing the difference to intensify the process of emerging meaning. Along with this insistence on planned incongruity, Burke recognized the most important fact of the double-edged nature of analogy, which related metaphor to sense as well as relating the social world to the work. Such an account of analogy had been propounded previously in the history of rhetoric: the discussion of Puttenham's theories in the 16th century shows the presence of this theory.

Admittedly, Burke always had a certain awkwardness in dealing with this "dramatistically," for the categories as enshrined in his pentad suggested some set of absolutes rather than clearly recognizing the importance of the dialectic between convention and innovation in all artistic activity. as Nietzsche observed, "Convention is a condition of great art, *not* an obstacle to it. . . ."[17] Consequently, Burke tried to develop his dramatic pentad loosely, so as to permit the greatest flexibility of explication and the greatest freedom from rigid categorization. This pentad, composed of act, agent, agency, scene and purpose, permits other broad concepts related to drama and narrative to be useful, such as action, plot, character, thought (as an intellectual-emotional nexus related to Joyce's "feelful thinkamalinks") and language (including rhetoric, poetry and stylistics). But Burke tries to avoid the overwhelming specificity of Frye or some of the more rigidly systematic structuralists. All of this, he argues, ideally ought to be developed within a fundamentally comic perspective, though he admits that he himself was attracted to the ritualistic rhythms of tragedy. One way of approaching the telephone company television ad sequence would be to "read" it in conjunction with a satiric artwork such as Flicker's film, *The President's Analyst.* A seriously underrated film, starring James Coburn, *The President's Analyst* uses the strategies of "incongruous assortments of incongruities" to satirize "the extremism of both the left and right, cold war logic, hippies, the corporate mind, the psychiatric mentality, and middle-class, suburban mores." What *The President's Analyst* does, and what the Bell ad does not do, is place the corporate and institutional realities in a broader context of the social realm with its rich range of contradictions. The realm of government, political movements and social drives form the context for the overwhelming power of the corporate persona.

The President's Analyst, which begins with a psychiatrist being drafted into the service of the White House, ends with a view of a Washington Christmas party being monitored by a room full of computer-like androids shaped in a replica of the president of TPC (The Phone Company). While the Flicker film pre-dates the Clarke-Bell ad by a number of years, it assists in the analysis of the ad sequence, just as the ad sequence provides an example of aspects of the film. James Coburn plays the role of a psychiatrist drafted by the CIA to serve as analyst to the President of the United States. The unfolding action is comic, avant-garde and surrealistic, leading from New York to the White House and then following the psychiatrist's flight from the White House to suburbia, the underlife of New York, hippiedom, the world of international espionage and the corporate power of the phone company. The treatment is low-key and traditionally comic. At least one major critic, Juan Rodriguez, described it as superior to *Dr. Strangelove*, a view which unfortunately has not been widely recognized.[18]

The film leads to a climax in which the multinational communications organization, TPC, becomes the epitome of the whole network of violence, hysteria, disorientation, espionage and distrust which vitiates the modern world. In *The President's Analyst*, the phone company comes to be treated as an institution creating its own kind of total culture, which immediately relates it to the conception of the Bell system ad sequence.

Written sketches of the film can hardly convey the complexity of the low-keyed way it penetrates the follies of the late 1960s without appearing either partisan or abrasive. Nor can a description of the film properly represent the superb quality of comic acting, the excellent sense of visual presentation and design, and the by-play between stereotyped convention and penetrating revelation which recur again and again. The way suburbia is depicted is typical of the general thrust of the film. The analyst escapes from the White House by tagging along with a group of tourists, three of whom are a family on a visit from New Jersey. He cons them into believing he is on a special mission and they take him back with them to their "typical" New Jersey suburban dwelling. The visual images combine modes of kitsch with plasticized examples of bad taste in their living environment. The father carries a gun, the mother has taken judo lessons and the son has his own playtoy kit for bugging rooms, tapping the phone and other such covert activities. On an evening out in New York, the mother floors a Chinese individual who accosts her while they are leaving a restaurant in Chinatown. Each member of this family becomes a satiric reflection of what Harlan Ellison described as middle America, a world closely associated through its own paranoias with the production of violence.[19]

Kubrick's satire of the nuclear British family in *A Clockwork Orange* is less successful than Flicker's even though Kubrick presents a magnificent image of the tastelessness of the petit-bourgeoisie in the plasticized world. Since *The President's Analyst* moves from suburbia to the dropouts of the 1960s, the hippies, then to the luxury of the international world where espionage agents co-opt luxurious yachts, it embraces a totality of lifestyles. Yet the climax of all these occurs in the manipulations of The Phone Company, which views itself overseeing the life of the nation, a situation satirically realized by showing that TPC can even bug the President and the CIA.

The climax of the film centres around the presentation of TPC's plot to implant communicators in the brains of everyone in the world, thus providing an instantaneous network of communication and monitoring. Such a technological advance provides an incongruous analogical comment on the super-serious presentation of the advantages of extended technology with which the Clarke ad sequence concludes. The film subtly plays with other Bell devices, such as instantaneously replaceable equipment. When the analyst is kidnapped while placing a phone call in a phone booth, men with a TPC truck merely pick up the booth (containing the analyst), place it on the truck, and then replace it with a new booth.

Because a use of dramatic-narrative structure underlies both the film and the ad sequence, they provide by juxtaposition, a complex critical comment. In the Clarke sequence, Clarke acts as a story-teller, thereby providing a narrative structure, while Flicker's film presents its story directly. Each individual ad within the sequence contributes to the claim being established in the narrative; that is, the phone company offers and participates in a total way of life and makes things better through technology, including the technocratic mode of organization. The film parallels this thrust towards the "total" by including a wide variety of scenes encompassing professional activity, politics, suburban, urban and rural living. And the film deals with the counter-culture, the corporate world and the jet set, but it also questions that total way of life which might be achieved by making things better through technology.

Clarke, as narrator of the ads is also the agent of action, which is made possible by the fact that he is able to unite popular media success, futurological knowledge, technological know-how and ability as a maker of fiction. The President's psychoanalyst, played by James Coburn, provides a counter-image of a co-opted interpreter of the hidden agenda of the society. His acts, not statements, unfold as the action of the film. Such an image is a foil for the complacency of the Clarke image. However, the film shows ways in which the ad sequence must of necessity function in terms of a series of imposed constraints which repress the ambiguities and ambivalences — in fact, the fundamental contradictions involved in the signs which the creator of the ad uses. The way the ad sequence uses *2001*, for example, must be rigidly controlled — the signs must be constrained in the lexicon of the ad — for otherwise *2001* will produce a fundamental questioning of elements of the ad sequence, such as the value of unlimited computerization of society or the use of the "stargate" imagery as a positivistic, optimistic type of image, rather than as ambiguous.

The President's Analyst serves as a poetic-satiric commentary on the type of activity that Bell presents in its ad sequence. Admittedly such a function is subjective and ethnocentric, but it is the only dialectical process by which man can generate the intellectual-emotional complexes required to place such experiences in a broader ecological perspective. This is why Lionel Tiger can associate the poetic and artistic with the "biology of hope," providing an optimistic future-oriented critique of what is.[20] Such a view does not endorse without qualification the position taken by Flicker in his film, but it does draw on that experience as a way of encompassing in the intellectual-emotional spectrum of everyday life such manipulative experiences as the Bell ad sequence. Sign production is not a sufficient cause of change, but it is a necessary cause. The process of bringing these two exhibits into a relationship with one another brings forth the significance of considering both symbolic actions as dramatic and narrative, and thus using concepts of drama and associated concepts from play, humour, game and poetics in the process of interpretation.

Frederic Jameson has recently argued that drama is less desirable as a stance for analysis in such situations than narrative, because drama is more immediately related to the prevailing ideology. Consequently, Jameson challenges Burke's dramatism with respect to its idealistic susceptibility to ideological contamination.[21] Yet this evades both the historical and structural association of drama and narrative. It creates theoretical divorces between the poetic, the dramatic and the narrative which have been too prevalent in the history of artistic criticism. Dramatic conflict can be used as a demystifying strategy, just as narrative form (as in the Bell sequence) can be used as a strategy of mystification. In either case, there is an ideological orientation, for ideology is always prevalent in the type of world in which we live. The point is rather the difference between an ideology that is self-reflective enough to invite questioning and one that, while it may permit questioning unintentionally as in the case of Riefenstahl's film *Triumph of the Will,* does not really welcome such questioning.

The argument of this paper is not that *The President's Analyst* provides the exclusive work that has to be brought into play in dealing with the Bell ad sequence. First of all, the ad sequence must be placed in a historical context in which it represents a certain kind of evolution in the advertising activity, shifting the emphasis from product sales to the selling of a total way of life. This is a process in which the propaganda effort of the Second World War played a role in accelerating, even though the primary motivations for the process were implicit in the evolution of advanced industrial capitalism and the multinational companies such as ITT. In addition to placing the ad in its appropriate historical context, the historical context of the growth of the sign systems employed in the act are also relevant. Those works that contribute to the production of a sign system that strives to liberate the mind from the constraints imposed by such ad sequences are especially relevant. Some examples of such works are to be found in Makavejev's films, Dada, surrealism, Pop Art, Fellini and Joyce. In fact, such phenomena obviously help produce a context that directs the analysis which must necessarily take account of what it knows from all such sources when discussing the media production that dominates everyday life. In the process, it ought to be remembered that just because such acts as the Bell ad sequence have power to influence everyday life, they represent an ambiguous and contradictory approach to everyday life and are by no means necessarily totally wrong or misleading. The fundamental problem is one of a distorted system of communication, not a thoroughly perverse or wrong-headed one.

NOTES

1.   Dusan Makavejev, "Nikola Tesla Radiated a Blue Light," paper prepared for the 1976 International Conference, *The United States in the World,* September 27 to Oc-

tober 1, in Washington, D.C., at the Smithsonian Institute. Track 3, Session D, *Film and Television*, Thursday, 9:30-11:30 a.m., September 30, Freer Auditorium, p. 8.

2. Donald F. Theall, "The Development of Models of Interpretive Analysis and Structural Analysis to Study the Social and Cultural Effects of Television Advertising on Viewers in the Montreal Area," report to Le Service de la Recherche, Le Ministere des Communications, Gouvernement du Québec, March 1978.

3. Gregory Bateson, *Steps to an Ecology of Mind* (New York: Ballantine, 1972).

4. Edward Sapir, *Language: An Introduction to the Study of Speech* (New York: Harcourt, Brace, 1921).

5. Roman Jacobson and Morris Halle, *Fundamentals of Language* (The Hague: Mouton, 1956).

6. Friedrich Nietzsche, *The Will to Power*, trans. Walter Kaufmann (New York: Random House, 1967), p. 252.

7. Ibid., p. 253.

8. Kenneth Burke, "The Rhetoric of Hitler's 'Battle,' " *Philosophy of Literary Form: Studies in Symbolic Action* (1941, rev. ed. New York: Vintage, 1957), pp. 164-189.

9. Gilles Deleuze and Felix Guattari, *Anti-Oedipus: Capitalism and Schizophrenia* (New York: Viking, 1977), passim. Trans. Robert Hurley, Mark Seem, and Helen R. Lane.

10. Richard Brown, "Metaphor," *A Poetic for Sociology: Toward a Logic of Discovery for the Human Sciences* (Cambridge: Cambridge University Press, 1977), pp. 71-171.

11. Paul Ricoeur, "Metaphor and the Main Problem of Hermeneutics," *New Literary History*, pp. 95-110.

12. Kenneth Burke, *Permanence and Change: An Anatomy of Purpose* (New York: Bobbs-Merrill, 1965), p. 97.

13. Ibid., p. 99.

14. Ibid., p. 111.

15. Ibid., p. 112.

16. Ibid., p. 113.

17. Nietzsche, *Will to Power*, p. 253.

18. Juan Rodriguez, Review of "The President's Analyst," *Take One*, Vol. I, No. 9, (1968): 22.

19. Harlan Ellison, "Middle America," in *The Glass Teat* (New York: An Ace Book, 1970).

20. Lionel Tiger, *The Biology of Hope* (New York: Simon & Shuster, 1979).

21. Frederic Jameson, *The Prison House of Language: A Critical Account of Structuralism and Russian Formalism* (Princeton: Princeton University Press, 1972), pp. 62-63.

Chapter 5

Narrativité et scientificité dans le message vulgarisateur scientifique

*Bernard Schiele et Gabriel Larocque**

C'est un sujet épouvantablement complexe, mais à cause de son importance, à cause de ses conséquences théoriques et pratiques, j'aimerais vous en parler ne serait-ce que pour vous montrer une partie bien superficielle du problème général. Encore une fois, je vais simplifier à l'extrême.
F. Seguin, Science-Réalité, 10 décembre 1976,
Société Radio-Canada.

It is generally acknowledged that television is a cultural means facilitating the learning of scientific knowledge otherwise not accessible to a large public. The postulate of the "mass-media" power of television as a vehicle of knowledge derives its strength from the sense of learning television generates among viewers. In fact, the power for transmitting scientific messages by means of television programmes is limited.

---

* a) Il n'est pas dans notre intention d'entamer ici l'examen critique de la démarche scientifique. Nous admettons d'emblée, indépendamment de toutes les questions légitimes que quiconque est en droit de poser à cette démarche, que les règles d'énonciation régissant la mise en circulation des produits scientifiques, sinon la démarche présidant à leur élaboration, constituent un discours cohérent susceptible d'être appréhendé. L'article examine les relations nouées entre les modes mass-médiatiques et scientifiques de mise en circulation des informations, chacun d'eux considéré comme un ensemble cohérent de procédés discursifs. L'article entend montrer, une fois posée l'articulation nécessaire des règles de formalisation et d'énonciation du discours scientifique aux objets qui en ressortissent, que le discours vulgarisateur, tout en se référant à ces mêmes objets, les distord, et ainsi leur assigne un sens différent, en les incorporant à un ensemble de règles d'énonciation propres au système mass-médiatique. Peut-être ne s'agit-il là que de l'un des aspects du processus de socialisation auquel la science, comme tout produit culturel, est astreinte. Néanmoins, s'il est permis de s'interroger sur l'objectivité de la science, il faut tout autant examiner la transparence du processus mass-médiatique de diffusion des informations scientifiques.
b) Une version légèrement différente du présent texte est incorporée à un numéro spécial de la revue *Communications* (Revue du CETAS, Ecole des Hautes Etudes en Sciences Sociales, Paris) consacré aux problèmes de l'apprentissage par les media.

First, the situation of the viewer facing the task of learning remains ambiguous. His desire for knowledge is intermingled with his search for pleasure. The audience wishes to be entertained while being informed.

Second, the medium of television imposes upon presentation the information-specific focus of processing, choice, organization and ways of presentation. Information is directed towards a vague audience; it does not aim towards specific goals in terms of learning; it is not evaluated nor spread in time. Information in a television programme is characterized by its range and its almost random distribution within time segments. The programming process therefore produces a first form of decontextualization.

This situation also prevails for scientific information. Scientific popularization as analyzed here, provides us with the opportunity to bring out the differences between the forms of the statement of the scientific message and those of the popularized message. We will dismiss the idea that the popularized message might be just a simpler or more "vulgar" scientific or didactic message. Our study does not deal with the objectivity of the messages nor with their validity. Rather we looked for the comparison between the process of the formal scientific message as well as the televised popularized scientific message.

The scientific statement seems to be regulated by a set of rules similar to those involved in the television production process with respect to scientific information. This is not the case, however, for the popularized statement, especially for the television messages analyzed here. The weaknesses in the television message appear first at the iconic level. The television programme, while calling forth objectivity, carries little visual information. The verbal aspect dominates. Moreover, the redundant visual information calls to mind the commonplace features of the scientific world: characters, special clothing, instruments, etc. A fictional referent acts as a substitute for the symbolic one. Speech falls into an empty materiality.

But the image on television gives an effect of "likelihood." The programme, through the interplay of dramatic linkages, transforms the scientific message in a subtle way, breaking the information chain into narrative sequences. Under these conditions, information acquires a new meaning and substance. The popularized message voids the actual object of scientific knowledge; there is only a ritual recognition of the constituent steps of the scientific process. The television message only reproduces the steps. The illustration of the procedures and strategies by which knowledge becomes scientific is not given. Hence, the scientific knowledge conveyed by a popularized television message undergoes a second decontextualization.

Finally this decontextualization takes place because of the narrative form used in television, or the organization of the information sequences forming the television message. The narrative structure of the television message involves resorting to alternating a heightening and a popularization process. Facts and information draw their scientific credibility implicitly from the organization of the framework of this television "quasi-account." The nar-

rative form changes scientific information by recontextualizing it. The popularized message stands in the narrative form; as such, it acquires in return a new form of intelligibility and an apparent truthfulness.

The television screen thus distorts the scientific discourse by giving it the attributes of narration. Through a rhetorical device, the meaning of the popularized message comes from the homology of its replication: the narrative reflects the discursive. True mirror effect? It matters little. The television message manages to deprive the viewer of actual scientific knowledge. It generates the illusion of knowing by manipulating the signs of knowledge.

Society thus remains paradoxically under-informed while having to deal with a constant flow of new information. How, then, can a new economy of diffusion of knowledge emerge based upon mass-media?

Il est généralement admis que la télévision est une instance culturelle facilitant l'apprentissage d'un ensemble de connaissances autrement inaccessibles à un vaste public. Le postulat de la puissance mass-médiatique de la télévision comme véhicule de connaissance tire sa force du sentiment d'apprendre qu'elle génère chez les téléspectateurs.[1] Nous abordons et analysons dans cet article un des aspects controversés de l'influence culturelle dévolue à la télévision. Il s'agit, en l'occurrence, d'interroger et d'examiner sa capacité de mettre en place un dispositif produisant un savoir réel chez les téléspectateurs. Pour circonscrire au mieux le lieu de cette analyse, convenons d'emblée avec V. Morin que "seule l'information (actualités, reportages, interviews . . .) pose en audiovisuel un problème spécifique d'énonciation",[2] et que les autres messages (téléromans, feuilletons, films . . .) s'insèrent dans le champ télévisuel sans transformations majeures de leur "statut structural."[3] Et ce, non pas pour sous-entendre que nulle représentation ne découle de la fréquentation des émissions de divertissement, ce qui serait évidemment faux (que l'on songe par exemple aux apprentissages vicariants), mais bien pour souligner que par-delà le sentiment d'apprendre éprouvé par le téléspectateur ou, plus précisément, grâce à la médiation opérée par ce sentiment, se profile celui de la prégnance d'une positivité dont serait empreinte l'émission dite d'information et, a fortiori, celle ayant pour objet la science en son achèvement.

LE CONTEXTE MASS-MÉDIATIQUE

Le point de vue de pertinence adopté pour aborder le problème traité ici découle de l'articulation de trois considérations, à savoir: le primat de la télévision, le couple distraction-apprentissage et les contraintes de production-diffusion.

Le primat de la télévision

La dynamique du milieu urbain (industriel et urbain) régit et uniformise la répartition du temps consacré aux diverses activités quotidiennes. Le temps libre, c'est-à-dire le temps non contraint par les obligations courantes tend progressivement à s'équivaloir d'un pays à l'autre.[4] La télévision, virtuellement présente dans tous les foyers, accapare l'essentiel du temps consacré au loisir et au repos.[5] Souvent qualifiée d'ouverture au monde, elle représente pour la très grande majorité de téléspectateurs le moyen privilégié, sinon le seul, d'accès à la culture, car prenant le pas sur les autres moyens de diffusion de masse, elle est devenue en moins de trois décennies un des lieux cardinaux où convergent et s'articulent les composantes du fait social, et à partir duquel il se donne à penser.[6]

Le couple distraction-apprentissage

Pour la plupart, la fin de la période de scolarisation marque la fin de la période d'apprentissage formel des connaissances dispensées selon un processus suivi, gradué et cohérent. Dès lors chacun oriente ses choix selon ses besoins ou au gré de ses intérêts. La télévision occupe tout naturellement une place prépondérante parmi les instances culturelles auxquelles peut se référer l'individu soucieux d'élargir ses connaissances. Cependant, mises à part quelques émissions didactiques, présentées sous la forme de cours télévisés et suivis d'exercices ou de lectures complémentaires, chaque série d'émissions dont est composée la grille de programmation s'assimile à une série de blocs jouxtés les uns aux autres dont la continuité est assurée plus par un enchaînement thématique que par une articulation ou une gradation des contenus entre eux. En outre, la télévision s'inscrit non seulement différentiellement parmi d'autres media en proposant un traitement spécifique des contenus qu'elle véhicule, mais surtout elle s'approprie et diffuse des contenus qui, il y a quelques années, appartenaient en propre à d'autres institutions. Par exemple: jouissant d'une grande autonomie envers l'école, elle n'est contrainte ni par le jeu des programmes ni par la gradation des contenus de ces programmes; véhiculant à sa façon un contenu "scolaire" comme pourrait le faire n'importe quel autre medium, elle imprime cependant à celui-ci une torsion spécifique en vertu des contraintes inhérentes au medium lui-même et aux conditions particulières de production dont il est l'object: dès lors, le modèle télévisuel coexiste avec le modèle institutionnel traditionnel.[7]

Or, au besoin de s'informer ou de s'instruire exprimé par le téléspectateur correspond le besoin corrélatif de se distraire. Le couple distraction-apprentissage caractérise le leitmotiv se dégageant de l'ensemble des recherches ayant pour objet l'étude des attentes et des motivations du téléspectateur.[9] Ces travaux soulignent à juste titre que la télévision distrait, divertit et détend: c'est ce qu'on attend d'elle. Par l'ouverture au monde qu'elle procure, elle informe et instruit, et l'on souhaite apprendre davantage. Toutefois, s'il lui est demandé de continuer à nous instruire, c'est à la condition expresse de la faire sans cesser pour autant de nous distraire. La télévision lie donc d'un seul tenant deux fonctions opposées: instruire et divertir. La mouvance des thèmes et leur traitement lors de la mise en forme des émissions caractérisent le double rapport du ludique au savoir. Eléments de connaissance et de divertissement se succèdent, s'amalgament, s'enchevêtrent sans laisser transparaître, dans le message télévisuel, la coercition de ce lien. L'école, au contraire, rend manifeste la lecture des contraintes imposées pour accéder au savoir.

Les conditions de production-diffusion

Le medium télévision

a) Les messages produits demeurent marqués à la fois par les lieux au sein desquels ils s'élaborent et par ceux où ils s'échangent. Le contexte de production-diffusion-réception propre aux mass-media influe sur l'élaboration de l'émission de vulgarisation au même titre que les contraintes du medium de diffusion retenu; il marque aussi les types et les lieux de cette diffusion comme il détermine, à un second niveau, les attitudes et les attentes du récepteur. Tout nous porte à croire que ces conditions prévalent sur toute autre considération lors de la mise en forme du message vulgarisateur. Il est évident, par exemple, que la stratification des auditoires visés et la ventilation des contenus des émissions, dans les grilles de programmation, ne se comparent pas dans leurs découpages aux procédés employés par l'école. Ses groupements sont mutuellement exclusifs (populations stratifiées, contenus dispensés selon un processus gradué et continu des apprentissages); ceux engendrés par la composition du public-cible de la télévision ou déterminés par les contenus offerts ne le sont nullement. La fonction mass-médiatique ne recouvre pas la fonction scolaire, du moins jusqu'à présent. Le message subit des torsions lui conférant un ensemble de caractères spécifiques, et ce, au-delà de l'identité virtuelle des contenus ou des populations visées.

Ces conditions posent sous un angle particulier l'analyse de l'organisation interne des contenus à caractère scientifique proposés par le message télévisuel, et l'analyse de ses effets: le sentiment d'apprendre attesté par le téléspectateur et un savoir réel présumé. L'on peut même licitement soutenir que toute évaluation des apprentissages fondée sur des critères accordés aux stratégies de l'école, en occultant le fait télévisuel, grève l'interprétation des résultats obtenus. La composante distraction-apprentissage et son corollaire, les lacunes pédagogiques, caractérisent en propre le fait et la pratique télévisuels courants.

Le message vulgarisateur

b) Le message vulgarisateur n'est pas un message lacunaire dont il suffirait de corriger les imperfections ou les erreurs pour le faire accéder au statut de message scientifique ou, à la rigueur, de message didactique. Il n'est ni un message scientifique dégradé, ni un message didactique tronqué. L'écart qui le sépare du message scientifique ne procède pas non plus de la complexité de l'information traitée et mise en circulation: les formes les plus élaborées relevant du message scientifique, les autres plus élémentaires, du message vulgarisateur. En un mot, l'écart entre le message scientifique et le message vulgarisé ne relève pas des lacunes d'une mise en forme qui n'actualiserait que certains éléments constitutifs d'un contenu, ni, non plus, d'une dissociation des sujets abordés en contenus complexes et en contenus élémentaires. Le message scientifique et le message vulgarisé n'occupent pas les pôles extrêmes d'un même continuum. L'un et l'autre procèdent d'univers discursifs distincts. Le discours vulgarisateur obéit dans son agencement à des règles et procédures de mise en forme autonomes ne reproduisant pas celles du discours scientifique. Conséquemment, il n'en véhicule pas les contenus.

Le discours vulgarisateur

c) Le discours vulgarisateur se réclame à la fois de la science et de l'école, mais se défend bien de succomber à leurs excès. S'il espère diffuser et expliquer la pensée scientifique et technique, il entend le faire hors de l'enseignement officiel sans former ni perfectionner des spécialistes. Il souhaite pourvoir à l'élargissement de la culture de tous et chacun en dehors du champ spécifique de leur compétence.[9] Il serait futile de ravaler ce discours au seul investissement idéologique, de n'y voir aucune autre efficience que celle d'alimenter un cortège d'images-à-disposition renforçant l'illusion d'une science omnipotente ramifiée jusque dans la moindre des pratiques quotidiennes. Le juger non conforme aux normes du bon usage de la conception et de la réalisation du message didactique, et pour cela le rejeter hors du champ de l'école et de ses stratégies, équivaut à occulter les transformations profondes que subit cette institution sous la poussée du développement des industries culturelles. Ce serait oublier que les modes de diffusion et les formes préconisées d'assimilation de connaissances ressortissent à une commande sociale spécifique.[10] Il devient loisible à une société qui incorpore plus de savoirs opératoires dans l'objet technique qu'il n'en faut à un utilisateur pour en maîtriser le fonctionnement, de dissocier l'agir du savoir qui le fonde, d'exorciser l'angoisse de l'ignorance par le spectacle du savoir.

CONTEXTES ET SAVOIRS

Le corpus

Pour satisfaire aux contraintes inhérentes à l'objet même de notre recherche, l'analyse de l'organisation des contenus mis en forme dans le message vulgarisateur, les émissions choisies se devaient d'être culturelles, c'est-à-dire qu'elles n'étaient pas conçues et réalisées à des fins didactiques ni ne s'incorporaient dans un ensemble cohérent et progressif, sinon elles auraient été qualifiées d'éducatives. Cependant le contenu de ces émissions devait être à caractère scientifique et allier à la nécessité de distraire une volonté pédagogique d'informer. Nous nous limitions à la fonction mass-médiatique.

La recherche a consisté en une analyse du système textuel de toutes les émissions composant le corpus.[11] Cette analyse a été complétée par une analyse de contenu et une analyse structurale. Une fois la grille d'analyse mise au point, elle fut appliquée à des émissions de vulgarisation de provenances diverses pour en dégager les caractères généraux. Les quelques structures signifiantes mises en évidence par l'analyse désignent un ensemble de régularités propres au message de vulgarisation. Sans pouvoir affirmer que ces régularités définissent les relations fondamentales structurant le message vulgarisateur, il est néanmoins licite de soutenir qu'elles en représentent les formes dominantes. Toutefois elles n'en épuisent pas la complexité.

Les quatre dispositifs

G. Jacquinot (1977)[12] a montré que le système textuel du message didactique composé de trois procédés distincts d'énonciation articule en un tout, l'instance didactique, trois contextes de référence (système textuel tri-référentiel): *le monde de tout le monde, le monde de la classe* et *le monde du spécialiste.* Le basculement d'un monde à l'autre, appelé "rupture diégétique", se produit lorsque l'introduction dans le champ perceptif et cognitif du téléspectateur d'un indice visuel ou sonore, déclenche un processus de mise en correspondance avec l'un des trois contextes référentiels. Par exemple: l'apparition à l'écran de cartons, de schémas, de graphiques, expliqués et commentés à l'aide d'une baguette, d'une flèche mobile ou de tout autre procédé dirigeant le regard, réfère au monde de la classe et à ses stratégies de traitement de l'information. D'une certaine façon le message didactique est limpide. Les ruptures qu'il instaure demeurent franches. Il en va de son intelligibilité et des apprentissages qu'il entend faciliter.

Quant au message vulgarisateur, il présente par l'organisation de son système textuel une certaine similitude avec le message didactique. Il se compose de quatre dispositifs. Outre l'effet de réalité (premier dispositif) qu'il partage avec le message didactique et le message narratif, filmés ou télévisés, le message vulgarisateur articule ensemble, au fur et à mesure du déroulement temporel de la chaîne filmique, le référent-objet (deuxième dispositif), le référent-médiateur (troisième dispositif) et le référent-sujet (quatrième dispositif).[13]

L'effet de réalité (premier dispositif)

L'image par son caractère analogique perpétue l'illusion d'une transparence entre l'objet et son référent. La télévision innocente la réalité qu'elle construit. Diffracté en images, le monde s'offre au téléspectateur en un cortège de représentations successives. La vue d'un laboratoire où travaillent des chercheurs invite le téléspectateur à y pénétrer. Puis celui-ci, l'ayant déjà vu, pourra ensuite le reconnaître et par là même s'imaginer connaître.

Le référent-objet (deuxième dispositif)

a) D'une manière générale, l'élaboration de la connaissance scientifique procède d'une interrogation systématique face au réel. Au terme de cette démarche, elle construit un objet désigné et spécifié par le noeud des relations opératoires qui le circonscrivent. Conséquemment, la démarche scientifique conceptualise un fait en l'inscrivant dans un tissu de relations. La matérialité du fait importe moins que les modifications auxquelles se voit contraint l'objet. C'est pourquoi ce fait n'est significatif qu'inséré dans un processus de vérification, infirmant ou confirmant l'ensemble des propositions relatives à un objet.

La démarche scientifique vise à réduire l'incertitude. Par ses énoncés et ses modèles, elle élabore un objet, savoir nouveau, à la fois aboutissement de la démarche génératrice et relance d'un procès inachevé du développement des connaissances. Les objets du savoir émanent de l'application des règles de structuration propres au mode de connaissance scientifique; l'énonciation de ces mêmes règles dans l'opération de mise en forme du message scientifique en assure la validité. Le renvoi au "connu"[14] en reste tributaire puisque les règles de structuration s'assimilent à celles de l'énonciation lors de la fabrication du message. La mise en forme du message scientifique demeure isomorphe à l'objet scientifique produit, parce que la structuration de l'énoncé révèle la structuration des relations constitutives de cet objet. Et ceci quel que soit le mode d'expression retenu. Cet isomorphisme est exigé par la spécificité du mode de connaissance scientifique lequel, assujettissant l'objet à ses relations opératoires constitutives, en exige l'énonciation dans le message.

b) L'intrusion momentanée d'un laboratoire où s'activent des chercheurs dans l'univers familier du téléspectateur évoque une matérialité immédiatement connaissable, celle de la réalité concrète de la science incarnée dans un lieu et des agents. Mais cette image renvoie aussi à une réalité seconde, celle des notions, des concepts, des règles et des stratégies dont l'ensemble constitue le discours à partir duquel s'élabore le savoir scientifique. Les apparitions discontinues à l'écran de chercheurs, d'instruments, de graphiques, etc. réfèrent à ce discours et au procès spécifique de mise en forme qu'il institue. Le discours de la science matérialisé en une infinité d'images et de propos est le référent-objet de l'émission de vulgarisation; il est le terme de l'émission en tant que telle. L'espace-temps, le lieu et le moment où s'effectue une recherche, et le processus-agent, la confrontation d'une logique et d'une expérience, tous les deux pris en charge par le message vulgarisateur, réfèrent à un univers distinct de celui qui préside au déroulement de l'émission.

Le référent-médiateur (troisième dispositif)

a) Le chercheur interviewé en studio, sa participation à une table ronde, les questions-interventions du commentateur, l'opinion des autres participants, assignent un lieu et fixent les modalités de la mise en circulation des informations scientifiques. Par les tables rondes, les émissions-débats, les interviews contradictoires, l'émission de vulgarisation instaure un dispositif de mise en forme des contenus, sélection et combinaison, qui réfère au contexte massmédiatique de traitement de l'événement. La présence à l'écran d'un chercheur (médecin, biologiste, chimiste) exprime un double rapport paradoxal au savoir: celui d'un savant qui sait mais doit oublier pour découvrir, s'adressant à un téléspectateur qui ne sait pas et doit apprendre pour découvrir. La fonction de médiation du message vulgarisateur consiste précisément à articuler ces deux savoirs et ces deux ignorances. Ainsi le message vulgarisateur met-il en correspondance deux mondes étrangers: le monde de la science, attesté par la vue des universités et des laboratoires où s'exerce l'activité de production de connaissances, et le monde familier du téléspectateur.

Mais le message vulgarisateur enferme le téléspectateur dans la reconnaissance d'un principe interne de finalité inhérent à l'objet même du procès de production de connaissances: l'usage. Car c'est par l'usage télescopant ainsi le savoir, que la science pénètre dans la sphère quotidienne du téléspectateur. La manie de l'utilitarisme qui assure au message vulgarisateur la prégnance d'un sens riche et plein, donné d'emblée, subsume toute explication, toute information sous l'anecdote. Le message vulgarisateur ne relate pas les étapes d'une démarche signifiante; il illustre et commente une démarche signifiée. Prenons un exemple:

Quelle est l'étrange créature qui pourrait naître du croisement d'un chou-fleur et d'un homme, ou d'un poireau et d'un chien? Eh bien la chose peut sembler bien farfelue et irréelle, eh bien, c'est (sic), peut-être pas tant que ça, parce qu'incroyable ou non, il y a des savants qui cherchent aussi dans ce domaine. C'est le propos de Fernand Seguin, ce soir . . .
L'animal-plante, ça n'est pas une chose que vous allez voir dans les semaines ou même dans les années qui viennent, mais ça correspond à un vieux rêve de l'humanité, un rêve qui se retrouve même dans la mythologie classique, la, la sirène par exemple. . . .
Alors on cherche, depuis très longtemps, à essayer de contourner le processus habituel de la reproduction, aussi bien chez les plantes que chez les animaux. . . .
Mais dans le cas qui nous occupe et la découverte qui vient d'être annoncée, et ça c'est amusant parce que ç'a été annoncé indépendamment par trois laboratoires, un de Cambridge, un des Etats-Unis et un de Hongrie. On a réussi à faire la fusion de cellules non sexuelles, encore une fois, de cellules ordinaires en quelque sorte, de plantes et d'animaux. . . .
. . . si on veut parler d'applications pratiques, mais encore une fois, ça n'est pas pour demain, on se trouve en présence d'un système, animal-végétal, qui, si on réussit à le faire vivre assez longtemps et à le faire se multiplier, aurait cette propriété extraordinaire, de combiner à la fois les pouvoirs de synthèse des végétaux et les pouvoirs de synthèse des animaux, c'est-à-dire que, les plantes, elles, utilisent l'énergie du soleil pour fabriquer des protéines, des protéines, qui, dans la plupart des cas, ne sont pas complètement nutritives, ces animaux mangent ces plantes, et eux fabriquent des protéines animales. Cette fois-ci, on aurait une cellule, qui pourrait directement grâce à ses propriétés végétales, fixer l'énergie solaire, et qui pourrait en même temps fabriquer des protéines animales. Ça supprimerait, en sorte (sic), toute l'agriculture. Et ce qui veut dire que, de temps en temps, la science-réalité dépasse la science-fiction.[15]

Ces diverses bribes d'informations enclenchent-elles un processus d'intégration des connaissances? Comment et dans quelle mesure les connaissances préalables du téléspectateur sont-elles réorganisées? Le sont-elles?

b) On peut affirmer, toutes choses étant égales par ailleurs, que la démarche didactique s'arrête là où débute la démarche scientifique. L'objectif de la didactique n'est pas la production de connaissances nouvelles, mais la transmission des habiletés cognitives nécessaires et suffisantes aux manipulations symboliques exigées par le degré d'avancement d'un champ. Accéder à la maîtrise d'un champ du savoir scientifique, c'est en quelque sorte assimiler les relations fondamentales le structurant. C'est reconnaître "les objets auxquels il a affaire, les types d'énonciation qu'il met en jeu, les concepts qu'il manipule, et les stratégies qu'il utilise (. . .). (C')est ce dont on peut parler dans une pratique discursive qui se trouve par là spécifiée (. . .)."[16] C'est, somme toute, accéder à la pratique théorique d'un discours scientifique. Dans la mesure où il n'y a pas à proprement parler de degré zéro de la connaissance, toute connaissance nouvelle se constitue à partir d'une connaissance résiduelle préalable qui lui offre une résistance. La transmission de connaissances et subséquemment l'apprentissage qui en résulte consistent en la réorganisation des connaissances antérieures ou en la mise en place d'une nouvelle capacité d'organiser. Toutefois si l'acquis présente après coup l'aspect d'un ensemble structuré et ordonné (eu égard à un champ spécifique), il est nécessaire de distinguer le système cohérent des relations qui le caractérise, des multiples relations partielles auxquelles est confronté le sujet tout au long de son apprentissage et dont l'assimilation graduelle et progressive concourt à l'édification de ce même acquis. Dans le cas de la connaissance scientifique, pour que la réorganisation d'une *représentation*[17] procède d'un état moindre à un état supérieur de connaissance, il est nécessaire de dépasser la simple modification combinatoire de notions anciennes ou l'ajout combinatoire de notions nouvelles. Toute réorganisation qui ne porte que sur des éléments, bribes ou notions éparses, c'est-à-dire toute réorganisation qui substitue, ajoute ou retranche des éléments à une *représentation* sans modifier son processus d'intégration cognitive ne peut être considérée comme un progrès. Nous constatons alors une simple variation ponctuelle du niveau des connaissances dont on peut mesurer l'amplitude. Une telle variation, spécifiée par les objets qu'elle désigne et par les opérations qu'elle permet de conduire, agit au niveau de la performance mais laisse intact le niveau de la compétence. Nous restons en face d'un sujet plus possédé que possesseur d'un "savoir", car il ignore en quoi la réalité qu'il pense objective provient de l'actualisation des catégories d'un champ théorique cohérent de connaissances ou en quoi elle provient de notions étrangères à ce champ.

A la différence du sens commun, la connaissance scientifique, structure signifiante, énonce ses principes d'organisation et de structuration. Elle exige pour son apprentissage l'assimilation des relations constitutives de ses objets. Ce savoir ne correspond pas à une simple connaissance des objets, c'est une structure générant l'objet comme événement. Si le fait, phénomène porteur de sens, représente la dimension sémantique de cette connaissance, c'est qu'il actualise en tout ou en partie, en les nommant rapports objectifs, les règles qui président à l'élaboration de la définition opératoire d'un objet. Ainsi se trouve constitué un savoir sur lequel le sujet a prise et par rapport auquel il peut se distancer.

Toutefois, l'acquisition des connaissances propres à un champ se heurte à plusieurs obstacles: connaissance de la terminologie des conventions, des principes, des lois, des théories, etc. Même chez des sujets formés à l'exercice d'une discipline se côtoient, d'une part, des éléments parfaitement assimilés permettant de saisir et d'expliquer un phénomène par la mise en place du système de relations dont il découle, et d'autre part, des éléments imparfaitement assimilés interdisant la compréhension de relations multiples. En ce cas, une série d'informations fragmentaires pallie l'inculcation d'une structure d'accueil objectivée. Les notions mal comprises ou mal assimilées, c'est-à-dire les notions (éléments, concepts, lois, etc.) imparfaitement rattachées au contexte relationnel dont elles découlent, se trouvent du même coup décontextualisées et font l'objet d'une rétention qui ne peut être que sélective. Aux relations circonscrivant les objets du cadre théorique initial se substituent alors des entités concrètes décontextualisées perçues comme des manifestations tangibles du réel.[18] Il s'agit alors en quelque sorte de signifiés libres, d'ensembles de relations particulières isolées de leur théorie d'origine, disponibles pour toute restructuration éventuelle à l'aide d'une chaîne signifiante leur conférant un sens indépendamment des liens logiques qui les articulent les uns aux autres.

Le référent-sujet (quatrième dispositif)

Par les retombées concrètes qu'il engendre, le travail de la science transforme l'environnement familier du téléspectateur. Cette transformation s'impose même comme le terme nécessaire du processus d'élaboration des connaissances. Par la connaissance de l'usage, le sens s'investit tout entier dans la reconnaissance d'un objet enfermé dans son mode d'emploi. C'est donc empreint d'une positivité que cet objet pénètre dans la vie courante. La mise au point d'un matelas d'air pour le traitement des grands brûlés, d'une technique chirurgicale, la vagotomie proximale, pour le traitement des maladies ulcéreuses, ou encore l'installation d'un attrape-piétons sur le capot des voitures pour réduire les risques d'accidents mortels, etc., sont autant de modes d'emploi de la préservation de l'existence. Toutefois, le message vulgarisateur réfère au monde du téléspectateur selon un mode allusif. L'utilisation des codes implicatifs favorise la mise en correspondance de l'univers du locuteur avec celui de récepteur sans qu'il soit nécessaire de l'évoquer. Bien qu'absent de l'écran, le monde du téléspectateur pris comme référent participe à la mise en forme du message vulgarisateur. Il est l'univers visé: celui dont on affirme la transformation.

QUELQUES PROCÉDÉS DE MISE EN FORME

L'émission[19] de vulgarisation est bavarde: considérants, explications, commentaires, interviews, témoignages, etc., se succèdent sans répit. Aucune pause, aucun silence ne ménagent l'attention du téléspectateur. La parole accapare complètement le message. Même la musique s'estompe en sa présence. Elle se confine à souligner les génériques, les clôtures et quelques rares silences. Quant au bruitage, il est virtuellement absent: de rares cliquetis ou ronronnements émanent des machines que la caméra fixe. Le message vulgarisateur refuse de se laisser distraire par l'irruption d'un univers étranger à l'image et à la parole. Quelques mentions écrites apparaissent à l'écran: *titre* du thème abordé (Le Parkinson), *liste* des participants interviewers et interviewés, *localisation* d'un lieu (Allan Memorial Institute, entrance), *identification* d'un chercheur ou d'un commentateur (Dr. Claude Bertrand, neurochirurgien, Hôpital Notre-Dame). L'émission se pare des signes de l'intemporalité. Aucun artifice de montage (flash-back, surimpression, ellipse) ou de ponctuation (fondu au noir, fondu enchaîné) ne la déroute de sa démarche. Elle se déroule de façon continue, sans errance, à la manière d'une démonstration. L'utilisation systématique d'un nombre restreint de mouvements de caméra durant le tournage, principalement le *plan fixe,* le *zoom* et la *panoramique,* et la *coupure franche* lors du montage, crée l'impression d'une articulation logique des informations successivement énoncées ou débattues devant le téléspectateur. L'exploitation parcimonieuse des matières de l'expression télévisuelle reste sobre, évoque l'objectivité.

L'image et le texte

a) L'image, dit-on, assure à l'information télédiffusée une force et une qualité inégalées auparavant. En d'autres termes l'image subsumerait l'information verbale. Celle-ci ne représenterait plus qu'une forme résiduelle d'un mode antérieur de communication. Or l'analyse de la composition des séquences démontre, à l'encontre de cette prétention, que tel n'est pas le cas. Dans le message vulgarisé, le support verbal s'accapare l'édification de la trame informative principale. La visualisation, pour sa part, joue un rôle secondaire au niveau de la progression du contenu informatif. En décomposant le contenu des émissions en unités verbales[20] et en unités visuelles[21] l'analyse transversale a pu démontrer qu'à deux unités d'information verbales correspondait en moyenne une seule unité visuelle (le plan). Ceci s'explique par la nature du plan fixe. L'unité visuelle peut demeurer inchangée ou constante dans son contenu pendant que la durée de projection augmente. Les commentaires et paroles se multiplient: la télévision supporte mal les silences. . . . Le nombre d'unités verbales semble donc croître en raison directe de la durée de présentation à l'écran des unités visuelles. Il y a donc une relation entre la durée de projection de l'unité visuelle et l'augmentation du nombre d'informations verbales. D'autre part si l'on accepte le principe de l'accroissement de la valeur informative de l'image en raison directe du nombre d'éléments contigus, il s'ensuivrait qu'un même plan livrerait par le jeu des articulations entre les éléments, une multiplication des significations intraiconiques.[22] Mais l'analyse intraiconique,[23] dans le cas des émissions de vulgarisation de notre corpus, n'aboutit pas à ce résultat. Au contraire, la valeur informative des éléments iconiques semblait se distribuer aléatoirement relativement au nombre d'occurrences verbales concomitantes dans le même plan. Ceci démontrerait, semble-t-il, l'absence de tout projet de mise en relation formelle des éléments composant une séquence. Un accroissement systématique des valeurs iconiques et proportionnel à l'augmentation de la durée d'un plan ou encore d'une séquence eut amoindri la prépondérance verbale. Tel n'est pas le cas. Les séquences les plus longues (et comptant le plus grand nombre de gros plans de personnages) confinaient plutôt le téléspectateur au seul contenu verbal du message. Il est curieux aussi de constater que les images les plus riches apparaissaient brièvement en début ou en fin d'émission ou encore se glissaient sous forme d'inserts dans une séquence de gros plans. L'analyse de la répartition des plans, classés selon une échelle ordonnée en fonction de l'augmentation de leur durée respective, révèle que la moitié d'entre eux demeurent à l'écran 7 secondes ou moins, mais totalisent seulement 11% de la durée cumulée de toutes les émissions. A cette répartition, il faut opposer celle des gros plans de longue durée qui confirme la primauté de l'information verbale (un plan très long dure 5 min. 6 sec.). Les gros plans sont un phénomène modal: 60% des plans sont de ce type, tous les autres se ventilent dans des types à très faible fréquence: beaucoup de paroles, peu de variation dans les images. L'émission de vulgarisation évoque irrésistiblement l'idée d'une radio illustrée.

b) L'on est en droit de s'attendre que dans une émission de vulgarisation l'image et le texte en relation de complémentarité vont converger en un syntagme unitaire intégrant leurs apports respectifs. Or, pour une moitié des cas (52%), l'image et le verbal en disjonction véhiculent des contenus différents. La partie visuelle du message revêt alors l'aspect d'une théorie d'informations simplement jouxtées les unes aux autres. L'intelligibilité de ces images n'émane pas de leur contiguïté mais de la succession et de l'enchaînement des éléments verbaux. Ces derniers subordonnent les éléments visuels et assurent leur concaténation. Le reste des cas (48%) des images et du verbal en conjonction se ventile en relations d'ancrage (20% par l'image, 8% par le texte) et de relais (4% par l'image, 16% par le texte). La forte proportion des relations d'ancrage par l'image éclaire la fonction de condensation que lui attribue le message vulgarisateur: l'image confinée dans un rôle d'adjuvant métaphorique sélectionne et actualise un des possibles du texte. Elle assure le téléspectateur de la fixation constante d'un sens. Les relations de relais par le texte articulent les composantes iconiques et discursives du message: l'intelligiblité de son contenu nécessite cette complémentarité. C'est pourquoi il est à noter que dans tous les cas il s'agissait de schémas ou de graphiques nécessitant explications ou commentaires. Mais dans quelle mesure le schéma est-il encore une image? Outil de la scientificité, le schéma situe le discours vulgarisateur dans la vraisemblance de la démonstration.

c) L'analyse de contenu des éléments iconiques révèle la redondance de l'information visuelle. Une image sur trois présente un élément humain (et 60% des plans sont des gros plans); une sur quatre propose un extérieur ou un intérieur; une sur cinq, un instrument ou un appareil; une sur six, un intérieur spécialisé; une sur dix, un extérieur rural ou urbain. Cependant cette redondance relève plus de la forme que de la nature du contenu. Elle ne s'appuie pas sur la répétition constante des mêmes valeurs iconiques (redondance pure), mais bien sur la rémanence d'un aspect formel de l'image: lieu "spécialisé"; "spécialiste" associé aux "objets" de son art: les noms du laboratoire, cytologie, bactériologie, du spécialiste ou de l'objet, sphygmomanomètre, importent peu, peuvent glisser dans l'oubli. Le visuel développe une paradigmatique informative restreinte: intérieurs spécialisés, antres du savoir; instruments scientifiques, symboles de la scientificité; appareils sophistiqués, signes de la complexité de la recherche. Information verbale et information visuelle se dissocient en deux discours parallèles. L'image-du-laboratoire (ou de la-blouse-blanche) déclenche un code de reconnaissance. Elle semble contextualiser un discours par la représentation des lieux institutionnels où s'exerce la scientificité. Par son cortège de signifiés-à-disposition, le dire visuel recueille, condense et oriente le sens chaque fois que celui du contenu verbal échappe au téléspectateur, et cela indépendamment des rapports de relais ou d'ancrage noués entre le texte et l'image.

Nous pouvons comprendre, en partie, pourquoi le téléspectateur a le sentiment d'avoir appris quelque chose: le message télévisuel élude. L'économie profonde du message vulgarisé réside dans la présence constante de ces images-à-disposition, au départ banales et sans articulation véritable avec le contenu scientifique mais dont l'aspect formel leur confère une force d'abstraction: images quasi magiques capables de ressaisir et de canaliser tout glissement, toute incompréhension. On comprend alors pourquoi l'émission de vulgarisation opte pour deux grandes formules (fréquemment concomitantes): le commentaire ou l'interview. Dans les deux cas, le discours scientifique éclaté en opinions ou en commentaires fonctionne comme un référent imaginaire que l'image exorcise en lui assignant un lieu symbolique. L'émission de vulgarisation enferme le discours scientifique dans une matérialité vide qu'elle revêt d'un prêt-à-penser.

Le trajet du sens

Outre l'effet de réalité que partagent la télévision et le cinéma, le message vulgarisateur se compose de deux énoncés concomitants qui cheminent au fur et à mesure que progresse le déroulement temporel de la chaîne filmique. L'un, le *vraisemblable scientifique*, découpe, isole et condense en autant d'unités singulières les phases par lesquelles s'achemine le procès scientifique. L'autre, le *vraisemblable narratif*, substitue une logique des attributs à une logique des relations.[24]

Le vraisemblable scientifique

Le message vulgarisateur opère un *effet de focalisation*: il n'entend pas être dérouté par des propos hors sujet. Il demeure obstinément centré sur le thème traité. Il s'enclenche brutalement. L'énoncé d'un fait, la relation d'un événement ou le rappel d'une situation qui perdure arrache le téléspectateur à sa quiétude. La réalité crue, sans fard, s'impose d'elle-même. Le simple *constat* pose un problème qu'il faut résoudre:

a. "Chaque année, des milliers d'enfants se font tuer . . .";
b. "L'hypertension: 2 millions de Canadiens en souffrent . . .";
c. "Vous vous souvenez que tout a commencé en avril, lorsque, dans un camp militaire à Fort Dyks, au New-Jersey, s'est déclarée une épidémie de grippe et même qu'un soldat en est mort . . . ."

A ce constat succède l'énoncé d'une *démarche* qui articule ce problème à une série de mesures ou de procédés visant à le résoudre:

a. A propos du traitement des fractures complexes ou infectées—"Nous avons formulé une hypothèse; je supposai (W. Kraus, ingénieur-physicien) que des champs électriques étaient en mesure de mettre en oscillation l'os, de la même façon que le produisent des pressions ou des charges mécaniques sous les forces de la gravité";
b. "Les ingénieurs anglais ont pensé que si on pouvait empêcher la victime de tomber de la sorte, on pourrait atténuer ses blessures . . . ."

Puis la description et l'illustration des *moyens* et des *techniques* mis en oeuvre actualisent la démarche entreprise. Le processus d'élaboration de la connaissance se signifie par l'identification des objets techniques dont il s'entoure (curseurs, imprimantes rapides, électrodes sur la tête d'un chat) et la reconnaissance des lieux où il s'exerce. Il devient visible.

a. "Ils ont fixé dans les sabots du cheval des microphones spéciaux qui renvoyaient à un magnétophone le bruit de la respiration de l'animal, dont les chercheurs pouvaient ainsi étudier le rythme . . .";
b. A propos de la maladie de Parkinson. Vue d'un singe, cou et torse solidement fixés à une potence—il est agité de tremblements—
"Alors nous avons constaté, à l'aide d'approches multidisciplinaires, que nous pouvions reproduire ces troubles moteurs, par exemple, le tremblement, la rigidité et l'akynésie. On peut reproduire ces troubles moteurs en, en inactivant ou en interrompant certains circuits nerveux dans le système nerveux central. . . ."

Les conclusions ne suffisent pas: un fait concret implique des *résultats* tangibles, sans équivoque.

a. ". . . on a découvert que le plus souvent ce n'est pas le choc de la voiture qui est fatal, mais le fait que la victime soit projetée sous les roues. . . ."
b. "Et alors, les conclusions ont été lesquelles? Les conclusions ont été que les populations du Var, c'est-à-dire, cuisinant à l'huile, (. . .) ces populations-là ont moins de maladies des coronaires, et que cette maladie des coronaires, vraisemblablement, passe par l'intermédiaire des plaquettes sanguines;"

Enfin l'on est en droit d'espérer de ces travaux et de leurs résultats des *retombées* pratiques, immédiatement incorporées aux activités quotidiennes.

a. "Après des expériences minutieuses, les savants ont conçu un siège de tracteur réglable qui filtre toutes les vibrations nuisibles. . . ."

b. ". . . même si on ne peut encore guérir cette anomalie (la cécité nocturne), les médecins utilisent le miniscope pour permettre aux handicapés de jouir d'une vision utile en attendant qu'on ait trouvé le moyen de les guérir. . . ."

Un *constat* pose un problème; l'énoncé d'une *démarche* articule ce problème à une série de mesures ou de procédés visant à le résoudre, et ce, par l'intermédiaire de *moyens* ou de *techniques* dont on espère, après expérimentation ou mise au point, généraliser les *résultats* par des *retombées* concrètes. Analogue et symétrique au message scientifique, le message vulgarisateur en épouse la forme. Simulacre, il reconduit et actualise, en autant d'effets consécutifs, les principaux moments charnières du procès scientifique. Mais comment articule-t-il ces divers moments entre eux?

Evidemment, on ne s'attend ni à la structuration, ni à la rigueur d'une communication scientifique formelle; de toute façon, tel n'est pas le but poursuivi par l'émission. Il s'agit de savoir si le message vulgarisateur, par son organisation intrinsèque, satisfait minimalement aux conditions du procès scientifique: l'implication réciproque des éléments du contenu.

L'articulation des contenus dont est composé le message ne correspond en rien à la dépendance logique qui unit l'objet à sa définition opératoire dans le procès de production des connaissances scientifiques. Au fur et à mesure de son déroulement le message télévisuel offre un flux continu d'informations décontextualisées, discontinues, contiguës les unes aux autres. Les opinions, les déclarations, les témoignages, les vérités de fait, les chiffres, les résultats, etc. se télescopent: la mise en forme n'implique pas les contenus, elle les jouxte. Chaque élément de contenu présenté selon un mode assertorique garantit aux faits rapportés un statut d'évidence, mais en masque la contingence. Le tout confère au message un caractère linéaire, sans épaisseur. Donnons deux exemples:

a. "Oui, nous avons étudié le chlofibrate, et nous avons étudié l'action du chlofibrate, face à la sécrétion gastrique. Le début de cette recherche vient du fait que nous avons une clinique d'hypertension, et nous avons une clinique des lipides à l'Hôtel-Dieu, et à l'Institut de Recherches, et à cette clinique on s'est aperçu que les patients qui prenaient du chlofibrate nécessitaient pratiquement jamais de repas barytes, alors ce qui signifiait que ils (sic) semblaient avoir un taux de maladies ulcéreuses moins élevé que les autres patients . . ."

b. L'hypertension est une maladie qui touche des millions de personnes, d'après les experts, il s'agit de l'affection la plus répandue dans le monde; elle s'attaque à l'homme, à la femme aussi bien qu'à l'adolescent. Dans la grande majorité des cas, pendant que l'hypertension prépare ses ravages sur le système cardiovasculaire, la personne atteinte ne ressent aucun malaise. C'est pourquoi, peut-être, aux Etats-Unis, où le taux d'hypertendus se situe à 25 % de la population, on l'a appelée "le tueur silencieux"."

Le sens global des informations provient, nous semble-t-il, du rapport de contiguïté établi entre les éléments du contenu. Le téléspectateur appréhende

les différences et les similarités de chaque élément par rapport à celui qui
précède (ou qui suit) sans en intégrer les contenus dans une même unité
supérieure. Il regroupe alors les notions selon un mode analogique, par "la
fausse explication obtenue à l'aide d'un mot explicatif",[25] d'un mot familier
ou de l'articulation d'un mot concret à un mot abstrait, "par cet étrange
renversement qui prétend développer la pensée en analysant un concept au
lieu d'impliquer un concept particulier dans une synthèse relationnelle"[26]
alors impossible. Le message vulgarisateur évacue l'objet même de la connaissance scientifique au profit de la reconnaissance rituelle des étapes par
lesquelles le savoir s'institue. Cependant, bien que le message retienne les
principaux moments de ce procès, il s'arrête à leur inscription matérielle. Il
ne reconduit pas l'énoncé des procédures et des stratégies à partir desquelles
la connaisance scientifique est objectivée. Le message vulgarisé est un message
largement décontextualisé. Or malgré l'éclatement qu'il impose aux contenus
scientifiques, le message vulgarisé télévisuel produit du *sens*.

Le vraisemblable narratif

L'analyse de la succession temporelle des unités verbales montre, au-delà de
la singularité de chaque segment d'informations, la constance d'un ensemble
de relations d'un segment à l'autre. Il y a là l'effet d'une structure portante
quasi narrative. La répétition de cette forme, d'un segment d'informations à
l'autre, assure la cohésion des contenus. Etant donné l'articulation étroite qui
unit le projet vulgarisateur au système mass-médiatique, les règles et procédures d'énonciation des contenus du message vulgarisé favorisent la
préséance de la fonction dramatique. Concrètement: la fonction dramatique
prime sur la fonction d'information. Qui plus est, tout élément d'information
(élément notionnel, fait, constat) est pris en charge par la fonction dramatique et y demeure assujetti.

Les émissions débutent par le constat d'un état déficient affectant un individu ou une collectivité. A ce constat succède l'amorce d'un processus
d'amélioration, entrepris délibérément par des agents (médecins, savants,
hommes de science, etc.). Patients et agents se trouvent donc liés dans l'unité
d'une même action dont le message vulgarisé décrit les péripéties. Il est intéressant de noter que la succession ordonnée des segments verbaux, analogue
au cheminement du message scientifique, recouvre les pseudo-rôles des
différents moments de la progression du procès narratif sans que jamais les
rôles narratifs que campent les sujets présents à l'écran ne soient assumés
comme tels. Ces pseudo-rôles découlent de la configuration des attributs dont
ils sont affublés.

L'émission illustre un moment d'un cycle narratif, celui de l'actualisation
du processus d'amélioration[27] et elle se clôt sans que ce processus ne s'achève,
reconduisant de facto l'amorce d'un nouveau cycle narratif. Conséquemment
le trajet informatif se résout en la description alternée de processus partiels
d'amélioration et de résidus déficients, témoignant ainsi de la présence et de

la résistance d'un obstacle (multiforme) qu'un ou plusieurs agents cherchent à éliminer progressivement. Le procès n'est jamais complet ni absolu: il n'est qu'approché. Il subsiste toujours, malgré une amélioration certaine, un résidu de l'état déficient antérieur. Chacune de ces recherches ne marque qu'un moment particulier de la connaissance scientifique: celui du temps présent. Chacune d'elles est appelée à se prolonger dans une démarche ultérieure qui franchira une nouvelle étape de la connaissance, de la même manière que chacune d'elles découle d'une démarche antérieure dont elle est le prolongement. L'information qui, somme toute, progresse au rythme de l'intrigue, repose sur l'alternance des rôles. Ceux-ci, tenants ou aboutissants de l'action entreprise, s'ordonnent par rapport à un état à conserver ou à modifier. La pseudo narrativité semble assigner comme finalité aux chercheurs la modification d'un état affectant un patient et leur donner un rôle (héros ou donateur). Celui-ci confère à leur action un sens et transforme, par conséquent, celui du message. L'alternance des échecs et des succès active le dynamisme de l'intrigue plus qu'elle ne renseigne le téléspectateur sur la validité ou la pertinence d'un geste scientifique posé. La reconnaissance du rôle assigné (patient: malade; agent: médecin, vétérinaire, biologiste, etc.) et des actions conséquentes qui lui sont dévolues, subordonne en attributs de rôle ou d'action, les résidus d'information divergents insérés dans la trame de l'énoncé et pouvant échapper à l'entendement du téléspectateur.

Le message vulgarisé structure les contenus qu'il propose au public selon une forme narrative rémanente, c'est-à-dire: une forme narrative qui se dégage de l'articulation des contenus par l'alternance des situations auxquelles ils réfèrent sans que jamais la mise en situation des agents et des patients ne soit explicite. Tout se passe comme si, du discours scientifique auquel réfère le message vulgarisateur et dont il tire sa légitimité, seule subsistait une forme vide, une forme à disposition que viennent combler des événements qui substituent à l'implication réciproque des contenus scientifiques, l'alternance des rôles narratifs. A priori une forme narrative peut véhiculer des contenus de nature scientifique, du moins rien n'interdit une telle procédure de mise en forme, si une fois complétée, elle ordonne une structuration qui contextualise les éléments d'information composant le message. Les notions, alors explicitement spécifiées par l'ensemble des faisceaux de relations qui les constituent, réfèrent aux autres notions par les corrélations qui les unissent et les codéterminent. Le message à caractère scientifique, pour satisfaire minimalement au mode de constitution, et incidemment, de désignation des objets scientifiques, doit donc rendre compte par l'organisation des contenus mis en forme, de la dialectique établie entre les notions et leur contexte. Dans cet esprit, il appert que la forme narrative supportant un contenu scientifique exerce une fonction transitaire.[28]

Nous estimons qu'il en va tout autrement lorsqu'il s'agit du message vulgarisateur. En effet, tout se passe comme si sa forme ne découlait pas d'une stratégie délibérée de présentation des contenus, mais provenait, au contraire, d'une concaténation d'informations constituant des agrégats décontextualisés puis relocalisés au sein d'une structure quasi narrative. L'opération de mise en forme effectue ainsi indirectement une recontextualisation des éléments d'informations qui composent le message. La substitution d'une trame narrative au contexte relationnel assure l'articulation et la cohérence de ces mêmes notions sans avoir à recourir à l'arsenal conceptuel qui les fonde. En fait, les informations sont subsumées par la forme narrative. Celle-ci relocalise les agrégats décontextualisés d'informations en les présentant comme événements narratifs. A l'implication réciproque des contenus scientifiques succède l'alternance des rôles narratifs. La forme narrative investit le message vulgarisateur et participe à son intelligibilité.

CONCLUSION

a) A travers l'écran le téléspectateur perçoit une image déformée du discours scientifique parée des reflets des attributs de récit. L'intelligibilité du message vulgarisé émerge de la double relation spéculaire de deux structures se réfléchissant l'une l'autre. Ni discours scientifique, ni récit véritable, le message vulgarisateur puise sa substance dans l'alternance des formes scientifiques et narratives, lesquelles se relayant, substituent constamment un discours à l'autre. Le sens du message vulgarisateur, artifice rhétorique, émergerait donc de la vraisemblance de sa forme qui reflète simultanément celles des discours scientifiques et narratifs pris comme référents.

b) Vu sous l'angle des procédures légitimées d'énonciation, la vulgarisation en parcellisant le savoir l'amoindrit: elle produit en conséquence au niveau du savoir dispensé, une société paradoxalement sous-informée aux prises avec une masse d'informations pour elle sans valeur opératoire. Le message vulgarisateur télévisuel prive le récepteur de l'acquisition d'un savoir véritable, l'illusionne par la manipulation symbolique des signes de ce savoir. Mais peut-être est-il licite d'envisager un déplacement des procédés discursifs dominants sous la poussée conjuguée du développement des formes mass-médiatiques de transmission de l'information et l'éclatement des instances traditionnelles chargées de diffuser le savoir? Il s'agirait alors moins d'une version des formes de transmission du savoir que de l'émergence d'une économie fonctionnelle de la diffusion dont les effets cognitifs sont encore insoupçonnés.

NOTES

1. Rapport du comité spécial du Sénat sur les moyens de communication de masse, sous la direction de l'Honorable Keith Davey (1970). *Bons, mauvais ou simplement inévitables*. Ottawa; Dubas, O., Martel, L. (1975). *Sciences et media*, Vol. 2 (projet de recherche sur l'information scientifique). Ottawa: Ministère d'Etat, sciences et technologie; Anonyme (1973). *Patterns of Television Viewing in Canada:* a project conducted for the President's Study of Television in the Seventies, Research Department, Canadian Broadcasting Corporation.

2. Morin, V. (1978). L'information télévisée: un discours contrarié. *Communications, 28*, p. 187.

3. Idem.

4. Insee (1968).

5. *Patterns of Television Viewing in Canada, op. cit.*

6. Singer, D. (1975). *Communications in Canadian Society.* Montréal: Copp Clark Publishing, p. 312-443.

7. Schramm, W., Chu, G. C. (1967). *Learning from Television: What the Research Says.* Washington, D.C.: National Association of Educational Broadcasters; Tichenor, P. J., Donohue, G. A., Olien, C. N. (1970). Mass Media Flow and Differential Growth in Knowledge, *Public Opinion Quarterly,* 34, p. 159-170; Maccoby, N., Markle, D. G. (1973). *Communication and Learning,* in: I. De Sola Pool et W. Schramm, Handbook of Communication. Chicago: Rand McNally College Publ. Co.

8. Gryspeerot, A. (1972). *Télévision et participation à la culture.* Bruxelles: Editions Vie ouvrière.

9. Dubas, O., Martel, L., *op. cit.*

10. Herbert, T. (1966). Réflexions sur la situation théorique des sciences sociales et, spécialement, de la psychologie sociale, in: *Cahiers pour l'analyse,* 2, p. 139-165.

11. a) La série d'émissions intitulée "Science-Réalité," retenue pour l'analyse, était diffusée le vendredi soir de 22 h. à 22 h 30 au réseau français de Radio-Canada (CBFT). Le corpus comprenait toutes les émissions diffusées durant l'automne 1976. Cette série, réalisée et produite au Canada, entendait refléter auprès du public adulte l'état actuel de la pensée scientifique et technique, dégager les axes de son développement futur et entrevoir les retombées concrètes susceptibles de transformer notre environnement quotidien. Tous les exemples cités à l'appui sont extraits de l'analyse effectuée. Schiele, B. (1978). *Incidence télévisuelle sur la diffusion des connaissances scientifiques vulgarisées (Science-Réalité: un cas particulier de vulgarisation scientifique),* Thèse, Montréal: Université de Montréal.

b) Vue sous l'angle étroit d'un certain empirisme la portée de notre conclusion peut sembler sans commune mesure avec la grandeur de notre échantillon. Nous objecterons que la constitution d'un échantillon circonscrivant les multiples variantes des émissions de vulgarisation eut permis, certes, une compréhension en extension des formes vulgarisatrices. Notre approche, en compréhension, entendait dégager un ensemble de règles, ou à défaut de régularités, permettant l'élaboration d'une grille d'analyse du procès de production du sens. Avec Popper (1973) nous pensons que cette grille se devait d'être "falsifiable" ce qui, évidemment, n'a rien à voir avec l'administration d'une preuve par le nombre (Popper, K. 1973). *La logique de la découverte scientifique.* Paris: Payot.).

12. Jacquinot, G. (1977). *Image et pédagogie.* Paris: P.U.F.

13. Schiele, B. (1980). *Transcodage et information télévisuelle:* analyse de l'organisation du système textuel du message vulgarisateur. Communication présentée au Congrès des Sociétés Savantes, Université du Québec à Montréal, mai 1980 (ronéotypé).

14. Jurdant, B. (1969). Vulgarisation scientifique et idéologie. *Communications, 14,* p. 150-161.

15. Tous les exemples sont tirés du corpus.

16. Foucault, M. (1969). *L'archéologie du savoir.* Paris: Gallimard, p. 238.

17. Moscovici, S. (1961). *La psychanalyse, son image et son public.* Paris: P.U.F.

18. Idem., p. 294-406.

19. Toutes les données citées résultent du traitement statistique effectué. Les termes "émission" et "message vulgarisateur" réfèrent à l'ensemble des émissions composant le corpus analysé.

20. "L'unité verbale" désigne "le sujet des prédicats de l'information": Morin, V., (1969). *L'écriture de presse.* Paris, La Haye: Mouton, p. 26.

21.   Par convention l'unité visuelle désigne le plan: Jacquinot, G. (1977). *Image et pédagogie*. Paris: P.U.F.

22.   Relations entre les éléments composant une image.

23.   Thibault-Laulan, A.-M. (1971). *Le langage de l'image*. Paris: Editions universitaires.

24.   Schiele, B. (1980). *Régles et procédures d'énonciation du message télévisuel de vulgarisation scientifique*. Communication présentée au Congrès de l'Association Canadienne-Française pour l'avancement des Sciences, mai 1980 (ronéotypé).

25.   Bachelard, G. (1970). *La formation de l'esprit scientifique*. Paris: Vrin, p. 21.

26.   Idem.

27.   Bremond, C. (1973). *Logique du récit*. Paris: Seuil.

28.   Que l'on ne se méprenne pas sur le sens de nos propos: nous ne nions pas que la forme narrative favorise certains types d'apprentissages. Au contraire, nous concevons fort bien qu'elle soit la seule forme vraiment utile ou efficace dans certains cas, le champ des arts par exemple. Qui plus est, c'est justement parce que la forme narrative, probablement le procédé dominant de mise en forme des contenus, induit nécessairement des profils d'apprentissage, qu'il nous paraît essentiel d'appréhender les caractères structurels d'un tel mode de diffusion des informations. Et, ce, afin de préciser ultérieurement la nature et la forme des connaissances assimilées par un sujet.

Part Two

The Role of Communication

Chapter 6

Uneven Underdevelopment and Song: Culture and Development in the Maritimes*

R. Brunton, J. Overton and J. Sacouman

It is time for the coal miners to rise up on their feet,
And crush the opposition wherever they will meet.
Too long the capitalist party has kept the miners down,
With their mansions full and plenty—on the miners they do frown.
"Arise Ye Nova Scotia Slaves," circa 1910 (Korson, 1965: 424).

Theory is too important to be left in the hands of the theoreticists.
—Editorial, *History Workshop Journal,* 1978: 6.

"U.I.C." tu me fais vivre.
On est pas Québécois. A cause nous autres
On est fait comme ça.
Dans l'Acadie vive le "U.I.C."
On fume pis on boit. Pis nous autres
Ça nous dérange pas
En Acadie vive le "U.I.C."
"U.I.C. [U]nemployment Insurance Commission" (1755, *1755*)

The conditions of existence of classes profoundly shape class cultures, less by specifying "interest" more by supplying a kind of agenda with which the cultures must deal.
—Johnson, 1979: 237

---

* This is a revised version of a paper presented to a co-sponsored session at the annual meetings of the Canadian Communication Association and the Canadian Political Science Association, University of Quebec at Montreal, June 1980. An even earlier version was presented at the annual meeting of the Atlantic Association of Sociologists and Anthropologists, College of Cape Breton, March 1980. Bob Brym and David Frand gave us concrete criticisms of the first version; Tom Regan, Liora Salter and two anonymous readers helped us revise the second version. As always, the roughage remains ours.

Le présent article aborde à la fois une question générale et une question spécifique. La thèse spécifique suggère que le sous-développement de la partie atlantique du Canada a produit et entretient une expression créatrice vivante: sa chanson, mode de communication culturel et de classe. Cette chanson a représenté un aspect intégral du développement d'une culture populaire de classe dans cette région.

La thèse générale présentée ici propose que l'analyse de la culture et de la communication populaire nécessite la situation de l'expression culturelle en question à l'interieur d'une analyse de classe éclairée des aspects sociaux, politiques et économiques du développement du capitalisme, pour que soit possible la compréhension de telles expressions.

Introduction

Like many other underdeveloped regions of the capitalist world, Atlantic Canada has long been the locus of much musical expression rooted in the experiences of the petty producer and working class, the so-called "popular" classes or the "folk."[1] It is extremely difficult, but necessary, to move towards capturing the full meaning of music for the people who create it in specific times, places and circumstances or to understand the way in which it is shaped by, and in turn shapes, experiences and struggles. Examining and placing in broad context the changing words of songs produced in Atlantic Canada can provide us with a historical and structural overview of the experiences, struggles, and ways of life of the popular classes in the region.

In general, our central argument is that all analysts of culture/communications must situate particular cultural expressions within an explicitly stated social, political and economic context that is broader than the immediate everyday context. It is precisely in order to inform the historical-dynamic analysis of specific expressions of culture in action (of culture as a viable, creative response/strategy to lived social, political and economic conditions) that the prior analysis of historical and structural conditions is appropriate. The analysts of popular culture too often have failed to recognize that much of popular culture is, in fact, popular class culture and thus is vital and important beyond, as well as within, the specific locale, occupation or performance setting.

A Workable Working Position

> The sheer surprise of a living culture is a slap to reverie. Real, bustling, startling cultures move. They exist. They are something in the world. They leave behind—empty, exposed, ugly—*ideas* of poverty, deprivation, existence and culture. Real events can save us much philosophy.[2]
>
> Willis, 1978: 1

Culture is life and movement and the very act of creation. Yet one of the main ways of looking at culture in both non-academic and academic thinking within Atlantic Canada denies life; culture is fossilized and served up as heritage. It is essential to try to understand cultural politics in the region, to criticize, and present alternative ideas and practices.

In Atlantic Canada, the dominant approach to understanding petty producer and working-class culture in general, and music in particular, stresses the traditional, rural, quaint, and folkish purity of it all along with its charming regionalism. Helen Creighton, for example, states:

> Who are the people who have kept our songs alive all these years, and where would you find them? If you searched our cities you might find a few, but it is most unlikely that they could be identified in any public place. For the most part you would have to leave the travelled highways and seek the byways that lead to secluded farms and fishing villages, where people in the old days had no outside entertainment and had to supply their own. You may find an old man beside a sheltered harbour singing to his family or closest friends, or perhaps to other fishermen as the sit mending their nets together. . . . Fishermen, farmers, lumbermen and a "scattering few" women are our main sources, and they must be sought out diligently.[3]

A St. John's merchant noted in 1927:

> In selecting our Newfoundland songs we have made a special effort to give precedence to those only that are racy of the soil and illustrate the homely joys and sorrows of our people. Most of our local poets and song writers have been true to nature in their compositions and therein lies the charm and merit of their songs.
>
> . . .
>
> [A]ll these songs are of the people and from the people of our Island Home, and are redolent of a happy past, and breathe a spirit of co-mingled freedom, independence and human sympathy that characterized the good old days of our forefathers.[4]

Until recently the above exemplified the dominant approach taken by folklore and the other human sciences and arts to analyze the culture of the people.

Such views, still lingering in many contemporary approaches to folk culture, have their roots in the Romantic movement of the late 18th and early 19th centuries. The Romantic movement was a diffuse and broadly-based reaction to the rise of industrial capitalism and the political, economic and social upheavals, such as the Enlightenment and the French Revolution, which accompanied it. Concern with social order and the overwhelming tendency to use grand models presenting simple dichotomies like Gemeinschaft-Gesellschaft, traditional-modern, folk-urban and so forth arose in this period and have influenced the structure of social science to the present day.

Romanticism expressed the uneasiness of the middle classes about the changes taking place. It expressed a nostalgia for what was seen as an older, more settled and more spiritual existence. Culture came to symbolize much of this opposition to the rapidly changing world and to represent a process of inner or spiritual development rather than external development. It represented human needs and impulses that were associated with religion, art, the family and personal life. The subjective, imaginative and emotive reigned supreme.

This anti-Enlightenment sentiment and opposition to universal values found, in turn, expression in: (a) a celebration of not one culture and civilization but many cultures (organic ways of life); (b) a strong feeling towards nature and those close to nature (the folk); and, (c) a view of inner human nature as something spontaneous and imaginative.

The range of themes is complex, and the above is only an outline. However, it is possible to identify certain issues as crucial in evaluating studies of folk culture. First, why is folklore in the English language characterized by strong anti-modernist tendencies and guilty of what A. L. Lloyd[5] calls "primitive romanticism with a vengeance"? Second, and linked with the romantic tendencies, why is the main approach to the music of the folk (in the English language) idealistic and anti-materialist and hence antithetical to Marxism?

Romanticism is expressed most clearly in the celebration of old values, tradition and purity and a concentration on the culture of peasants in isolated rural areas. At the heart of romanticism, is a simple, unilinear view of development through stages. Folk culture is considered a survival from an earlier stage of development (traditional society) which gradually is being eroded by the forces of modernization but still lingers among people isolated, geographically or otherwise, from the mainstream of society. Folk culture is often defined in terms of tradition and, mainly, oral transmission. This accounts for much of the emphasis by both amateur collectors and professional folklorists on old and unique material found in areas isolated from mainstream society and the influence of the media. The persistence of culture is thus equated with simple, sylvan backwardness and lack of growth.

Romanticism also underlies the importance ascribed to the folk culture of many regionalist/nationalist movements of the 19th and 20th centuries. In these movements the cultural component has been most often defined in terms of an opposition to a central elite or colonial culture and is seen as the esssence of the national/ethnic entity, an expression of the soul of the people. As Waller claims in a discussion of the work of Helen Creighton, "Folk songs are spontaneous expressions of a nation's soul."[6] This idealistic, almost mystical view of culture is the core of much regionalist/nationalist sentiment (a variant of "blood and soil" ideology) as can be seen in current writings on Newfoundland.[7] A culture is created through a highly selective ideological process dominated by regional elites. This construct is then held to be homogeneous and distinctive.

The construct works to some extent because many elements of folk culture are localized and because the culture is based on the common experiences and history of large sections of people in Atlantic Canada. Most often this culture is an idealized version of the way of life of the petty producer. This particular, fast-vanishing and often varied experience is elevated to the status of universal history and national culture. The diversity of cultures within the region based on ethnicity and sex, the divisions by class and within class, and the changes in all these over time are largely ignored as one culture is chosen to symbolize the nation/region. Folk culture has long since ceased to be something "for itself," if it could ever be seen that way. In many respects it is now firmly within the realm of cultural politics and as such becomes essential for people to understand, and is a focus of political struggle.

In reaction to the romantic approach, professional folklorists have pioneered alternative perspectives on folk culture in the Atlantic region of Canada in recent years. The most important of these has been the functionalist approach. This is a dynamic and contextual approach which emphasizes the setting of folk-culture production and seeks to uncover the social function of folk communication in specific contexts. Such an emphasis shifted research away from the study of archaic survivals to an examination of folklore in urban and industrial settings. This approach is apparent in much of the work done through the Department of Folklore at Memorial University.

Many of the functionalist studies are of individual creators in their social settings. Such studies often conform to another component of romanticism — the emphasis upon the unique yet typical character of each of the "true," "old time" folk artists. For instance, Ives' works all demonstrate "his insistence on the value of studying the common man among us as a typical yet unique cultural being. . . . [His works] provide a social history of the region in the late 19th and early 20th centuries that is comprehensive and yet personally moving, because they are about people as individuals, a point of value in scholarship that Ives has insisted upon for years."[8]

In works like those of Ives, social history becomes the individual's true account writ large among the common people. This counter-approach shows a ready concern and interest in ordinary people and it allows an understanding of song production, format, interpersonal context and audience, all important considerations. However, it is not and cannot be an adequate framework in the broader context of social-cultural relations that is the central concern here. Indeed, the romantic-individual approach maintains a unicultural context and glosses over class relations and the processes of class-cultural formation.[9]

The current re-emphasis in Marxism is on specifying the key interrelationships between strictly class factors and class-linked but not directly class-based social "locality" factors. These factors, ethnicity, regionalism and, in general, centre-periphery relations, take on central importance. They are treated as "real rather than ephemeral and/or vaguely illegitimate" and indeed "the simultaneity of class and centre-periphery contradictions" are to be "placed front and centre as a key factor within our analytical frame work."[10]

To understand popular culture as class culture, social locality factors must be intertwined with class factors so the fullness of lived class experience can be captured or at least allowed for within a broad Marxist framework.

To formulate an adequate Marxist approach to the question of popular culture involves starting from the basic assumption that the capitalist system is a system in which the economic, political and cultural-ideological spheres form a whole. The economic sphere is the primary one in the sense of the domination of forces and relations of production within the capitalist mode over the other spheres of activity and consciousness, but not in any simplistic, reductionist way. An adequate Marxist approach must avoid a culturalist-historicist tendency to focus primarily on experience to the neglect of relations of production, thus dealing with economic change largely through the experience of small producers and workers, and not as a shaping force.

It is necessary to appreciate class experience and understand how classes make themselves. However, human beings do not make history in the circumstances of their own choosing, and the analysis being developed here places much greater emphasis on changing relations of production and economic forces than that of the culturalists.

Within the Atlantic region, David Frank's work on the coal miners of industrial Cape Breton (1917-1926) is the best demonstration of understanding a class in a certain time, place and context. Because his project was so specific, Frank is able to analyze cultural production as a dynamic and creative process and to pinpoint variations in the cultural product in terms of performance setting and the more immediate community-level context.[11]

In comparison to Frank's process-oriented and community-level insights, any content analysis of texts, such as that in the following pages, necessarily appears ahistorical, and non-dialectical. Given that the intention here is to provide a general, less time-specific overview of song content in Atlantic Canada, such appearances are valid to a point. On the other hand, the attempt to contextualize song content in Atlantic Canada, although it encompasses less of culture than a full-fledged analysis of cultural production per se, is a broader level of analysis than the more immediate class-in-community analysis would be. As such, it is an important preliminary task in developing the Marxist analysis of popular culture.

Popular songs certainly must be understood in terms of the experiences of classes within their historical, social and geographical context. Classes form within the changing broad, yet specific, economic and political realities of capitalism. Initially, classes are defined in terms of their position within relations of production. Starting with petty producers' independence-yet-subordination in relation to capital, and the proletarian relation to capital (selling labour power to live), the common elements of class under capitalism, and hence the basis for class consciousness, in its broadest terms can be understood.

But in the cultural-ideological sphere, no pure working class (or petty producer) culture, ideology or consciousness is immediately as apparent as the expression of class position within economic relations. As capitalism develops unevenly there is great diversity within the working class and petty producers. These classes, although they have a certain homogeneity deriving from their common relation to capital, have ethnic/national/regional, religious, age and sex divisions in addition to the division of labour that has evolved under capitalism. Divisions exist on the basis of hierarchies of occupation and skill, the history of production in certain regions, etc., and all are intertwined with ethnic origin, sex, and other factors. Because the economic realities of life are different for sections of the working class and petty producers so are their experiences and their creative responses in terms of culture-ideology-consciousness. Because the economic realities of life under capitalism are the same, so to a degree are the creative responses of people. The starting point for the analysis of culture must be uneven development under capitalism, being understood in its broadest terms as uneven historically, geographically, economically, socially and so forth. The division of labour must be considered in its broadest sense, by class, geography, sex, etc. and with changes in these divisions over time.

The dynamics of capitalism in an underdeveloped region like Atlantic Canada and the changing class struggle there are apparent. However, analyzing the cultural expressions of this in terms of experience is more difficult. After all, it is only in the steel mills and educational institutions, on the sealing boats and in the decaying outports, in the bars and basement apartments, in the Canada Manpower offices and on the picket lines, in the endless afternoons before "Another World" comes on the television, at Bingo nights and in the supermarket lineups, that the contradictions and problems are lived through.[12] In these places, people's creative acts, such as song, are an attempt to understand, challenge and create meanings.

Culture is a people's creative efforts to make sense of, redefine and change the circumstances of their lives. But "cultural expressions are likely to be displaced, distorted or condensed reflections of barely understood, or misunderstood, knots of feelings, contradictions and frustrations—as well as forms of action on these things."[13] The nature of these contradictions can be discerned from an analysis of culture, from an understanding of the frustrations people face and how they attempt to resolve them. An analysis of culture also can reveal the limitations of people's struggles and point the way to more fundamental change and the betterment of peoples' lives.

Although cultural expressions may be displaced, the responses are never arbitrary. They often reveal in a startling and concrete manner the contradictions and weaknesses of capitalist society, and then have the power to transform circumstances. But they also reproduce the weaknesses, brutality and limitations of that society. This analysis is concerned with the popular classes: petty producers, petty producers in the process of becoming proletarians, and proletarians. In attempting to understand any aspect of the culture of these classes, it is vital to recognize that they are subordinated classes under capitalism. This applies as much to the cultural-ideological sphere as the political-economic sphere. The working class in Atlantic Canada has a particular subordinate position to capital through the labour market. This includes periods as a relative surplus population, as semi-proletarians oscillating between fishing, farming and factory-work, as migrant workers, and in the timeless agony and delight of life on unemployment insurance.

Popular classes have a life that is subordinate in the realm of ideas also. People accept bourgeois ideas to some extent. But, working-class ideology is not a collection of discrete falsehoods to be measured against some purely proletarian consciousness. It is a matrix of thought firmly grounded in forms of social life and organization under capitalism. It is difficult to perceive because even awareness is organized through it. Yet if bourgeois ideology appears to dominate, it is because it does appear to work. Bourgeois ideology does express something basic about the realities of life under capitalism and it does provide a basis for action. At some level bourgeois ideology makes sense.

The sphere of culture-ideology is, however, no less of an arena for class struggle than the economic or the formally political. Forms of consciousness, feelings, desires, morals, and subjectivity do not arise in some areas of life separate from production and economics and politics; they are expressed in all spheres of existence. If bourgeois ideology dominates, it does so through force. Bourgeois ideology is constantly challenged. Those who promote it constantly fight to restore their hegemony by diffusing, negating, or displacing any opposition. Working-class consciousness reflects both the domination of bourgeois ideology and the struggle of the bourgeoisie to impose it upon the everyday understandings of workers. Thus, there can be no pure working-class culture.

Song parallels the structures of feeling and the concerns of particular groups within society. Song is shaped within this framework and in turn shapes it. But cultural creation always proceeds on the foundations of past structures (class, ethnicity, locality) incorporating and modifying them. It is important therefore that, "we should start any analysis by looking for contradictions, taboos, displacements in a culture, as well as unities."[14] In this article common and persistent themes and issues in popular culture and song are pointed out as are contradictions and taboos. It is as necessary to examine the way certain issues are avoided or circumscribed as it is to examine those that are overtly expressed. Sexism, for example, is characteristic of much popular song. Women are treated stereotypically and their problems are avoided. The basis for the treatment of women as well as for male chauvinism needs to be understood as does the persistent lack of any wide concept of whole classes sharing a similar material basis and acting collectively on this. Therefore, the divisions within classes and the historical-material roots of these must be analyzed as well as efforts to overcome them. The following excerpt from a paper on music in the southern United States is indicative of the approach taken in this article:

The preserved repertoire (which, of course, excludes the more ephemeral topical songs which might well have been the most interesting) reveals not only protests against the actions of courts, sheriffs, merchants and bankers and supports for the poor against the rich, but vacillation and confusion on the subject of race, religious escapism, regional chauvinism, and so on. Southern white folk music expresses the conditions and resentments of a class, but not the politics of a revolutionary class, which was a weakness not of the musicians or the music, but of the class.[15]

An examination of the popular songs of Atlantic Canada reveals the lived experience of the people who wrote them. It provides some understanding of a class-structured society dominated by a particular social division of labour as the conditions of cultural production. Popular songs become an index of experience; the conditions for the production and reproduction of class culture become the focus of concern. A theoretically informed way of looking at the historical-material roots of culture becomes possible and teaches some important lessons for theory and practice.

Uneven Underdevelopment and Song

In Atlantic Canada, the process of capitalist underdevelopment has been and is tremendously uneven, more uneven than development in the central regions of Canada. The degree and extent of semi-proletarianization is more relevant as a socio-economic process in Atlantic Canada than in the more developed regions. Thus, capitalist accumulation in the region is more in tune with what is probably the chief form of capitalist accumulation in the world — accumulation through the exploitation and oppression of "part-life-time wage-labour households." Within Atlantic Canada, political-economic forces and relations of production have varied greatly over place and time. There has been much disparity of development by class, class-based activity and class-rooted social locality (including sub-region, sex, ethnicity/nationality, religion).

The lyrics of songs often capture and creatively express this unevenness of development. They often drive home, in more insightful and expressive ways than the most careful historical-structural accounts, the contradictory realities of living under capitalism in Atlantic Canada. Music in Atlantic Canada was and is thoroughly rooted in its broader context. Musical expressions of class-in-locality are creative analyses of the lived situation, expressing, yet simultaneously adding to and intensifying the popular class-cultural content of everyday understandings.

Many songs are part of the creative work process for small producers, small producer-proletarians and proletarians. Songs and music specifically related to work helped in learning tasks, learning rhythm and co-ordinating activities. Such songs arose directly from the co-operative process of work in certain situations. Those occupations and tasks which required co-operation and rhythm, such as hauling, making cloth and milling, most often produced this kind of song. Songs like the cloth-milling song in Gaelic from Nova Scotia ("The Black Mill") should be regarded as part of the labour process:

> Tha'm muileann dubh air thurraman
> Tha'm muileann dubh air thurraman,
> Tha'm muileann dubh air thurraman,
> 'S e togairt dol a dhannsadh.[16]

Simply to look at songs about the existence of small producers (even more recent and often more romantic ones) is to become aware of the struggle for survival in a harsh, hostile and uncertain world of natural hazards and economic insecurity. The struggle for survival, in both individual and collective terms, finds expression in different ways in the experience of petty producers. The song can be an affirmation and praise of independence and self-sufficiency as in "I'se the B'y":

> I'se the b'y that builds the boat
> And I'se the b'y that sails her!
> I'se the b'y that catches fish
> And takes 'em home to Lizer.[17]

Or, it can take the form of detailing the various struggles for subsistence (and against proletarianization). Examples of this "country cunning" are found in the songs that challenge the game laws and provide accounts of outwitting game wardens, as in the "Game Warden's Song" from Labrador which tells of salmon poaching.[18]

> Come all ye good people, goes out for law breakin',
> Don't trust de game warden whoever he be,
> For if he says no, he's only just lyin',
> For he'll do for you as he done for me.[19]

Other songs are clearly intended to promote group solidarity by providing a warning to "squealers."

> We took the moose and chopped him up and gave it all around,
> It looked just like a meat market that day on Dewey's Ground.
> The men that killed the moose, my b'ys, they would not harm a chick,
> To let that squealer inform on us we should have broke his neck.

> Our statement was all given in, everything went very well
> He said, "Five dollars is the fine or fourteen days in jail."
> And now my song is ending I'm going to propose
> It's going to pay the Squealer b'y to keep his big mouth closed.[20]

Other aspects of the struggle for subsistence and survival on the part of small producers are found in songs which oppose prohibition and taxation by the state. "Captain Shephard" provides an account of running illegal liquor and outwitting the law.

Dey searched all round the dwelling, upset de baby's crib;
Dey searched in every corner where a bottle could be hid.

So when dis bright fall opens up and all things do go well,
I hope dis brave, undaunted man will have a drop to sell.[21]

Taxation, of course, was a powerful force in proletarianization, and the
migration that it often induced in Atlantic Canada.

Dear Newfoundland have I got to leave you
To seek employment in a foreign land?
Forced from our nation by cruel taxation
I now must leave you dear Newfoundland.[22]

Insights into the economic situation and daily struggles of petty producers are provided by songs which deal with relations to local merchants, the
whole system of grading fish, and the operation of the truck system.
"Hard Times" a Newfoundland song, is worth quoting at length:

Come all ye good people, I'll sing ye a song
About the poor people, how they get along;
They fish in the spring, finish up in the fall,
And when it's all over they have nothing at all,
And it's hard, hard times.

Go out in the morning, the wind it will sing,
It's over the side you will hear the line ring,
For out flows the jigger and freeze with the cold,
And as to for starting, all gone in the hole,
And it's hard, hard times.

When you got some split and hung out to dry
Twill take all your time to brush off the flies,
To keep up with the maggots is more than you'll do,
And out comes the sun and it's all split in two,
And it's hard, hard times.

The fine side of fishing we'll have bye and bye,
Seven dollars for large and six-fifty for small.
Pick out your West Indie, you got nothing at all,
And it's hard, hard times.

The parson will tell you he'll save your poor soul,
If you stick to his books you will keep off the dole;
He'll give you his blessing or maybe a curse,
Put his hand in your pocket and walk out your purse,
And it's hard, hard times.

The best thing to do is to work with a will,
For when it's all over you're hauled on the hill,
You're hauled on the hill and laid down in the cold,
Adn when it's all over you're still in the hole,
And it's hard, hard times.[23]

This song gives a clear picture of the work of the fisherman (and the work
of his wife and family who were responsible for curing the fish), the debt bon-

dage which existed under the truck system and the importance of maintaining the quality of the product in the face of a variety of hazards, such as sun burn, salt burn, rain, and so on. The culling process was especially important as fish were graded by it. This is made clear in the following song by M. A. Devine about one woman and the government culler:

> For, she said to herself if she were nice,
> He's give her daddy a higher price.
> For the fish was damp from the weather dull,
> And might undergo a real strict cull;
> And instead of blouses and frocks for fall
> She mightn't get a new stitch at all.[24]

Women are seldom mentioned in songs except in the context of love and courtship. Few songs deal with the experiences of women in household production. One exception is "The Lovely Newfoundlander," but it presents a stereotyped image of the all-round woman, capable, versatile and firmly kept in her place.

> She can row a boat and catch the fish,
> And make a home, she runs it,
> Her garden plants, potatoes grows,
> Her work she never shuns it.
>
> She knows just when to talk a lot,
> She knows when to keep silent,
> She can sing and dance and take a chance,
> In rows she's never violent.[25]

This is clearly a class-based image of a working woman in a male-dominated petty-producer culture. At the same time, it is an idealized image of women.

The male counterpart to "The Lovely Newfoundlander" is the equally stereotyped and romanticized image of "All-Round Newfoundlanders."

> He tills the ground, erects his home, and fells the mightly tree
> From which he builds his sturdy boat that rides the raging sea;
> He's miner, sailor, farmer and mechanic all in one,
> And although his deeds are legion, yet to him they're merely fun.[26]

The "all-round Newfoundlander" semi-proletarian finds fraternal Atlantic Canadian images in the Jack-of-all-trades Bluenoser, Herring Choker, and Spud Islander. While burying in self-proclamation the toiling nature of semi-proletarian ways of living, such songs to indicate the importance of semi-proletarianization to class-cultural formations in Atlantic Canada.[27]

Small producers and semi-proletarians have struggled in individualized and fragmented ways against the economic forces which dominated them, but this was not the only method. There has been a wide variety of social movements which tried to break the hold of capitalists and improve conditions for those in fishing and farming. Some of the songs that came out of such movements were explicitly political. They were designed to mobilize people to create and maintain solidarity and to win demands. They sometimes use religious imagery to give credibility to the movement, as in the following song about the Fishermen's Protection Union in Newfoundland in the early 1900s.[28] William Coaker, their leader, is seen as the new Moses leading his people out of Egypt to a better future.

> We are coming Mr. Coaker
> Men from Green Bay's rocky shore
> Men who trod the frozen billows
> Off the shores of Labrador
> We are coming, we are waiting,
> We are forty thousand strong
> To be led by you as Moses
> Led the Israelites along.[29]

For small producers who have not been able to survive there has been proletarianization. This has not been a simple, straightforward process, given the nature of capitalist underdevelopment. For many in Atlantic Canada, work has meant hovering between existence as small producers and part-time, seasonal or temporary work locally or outside the region. For others, the process has meant unemployment and an existence on relief, welfare and/or unemployment insurance payments. Rarely has the break into proletarian status been complete.

The process of production of a relative surplus population in the region has been recorded in many songs dealing with emigration and seeking work. Songs about being uprooted and leaving home are very powerful and are found in both early and contemporary material. "Bound for Canada" and "My Dear I'm Bound for Canada," two versions of the same song, tell of a Newfoundland man forced to leave in order to find employment.

> I'm here just now in St. John's town, employment I cannot find;
> I must away, I cannot stay, I have made up my mind.[30]

One of the most poignant contemporary songs about leaving is "The Names Song" by Ron MacEachern. The verses consist of Cape Breton names, woven into a pattern. One significant aspect of this song is that it does not choose just one ethnic group from Cape Breton, but recognizes that forced emigration is a fact for most Cape Bretoners, whether Acadian, Scottish, Irish, English or any other ethnic origin.

> Go off on your way now
> And may you find better things
> Don't wait around 'till you have no fare to leave
> All the best if you're staying
> All the best if you should choose to leave
> Here's to kindness on your journey
> Here's to joy in your new home.[31]

Many songs speak of the people feeling regret in being forced to leave, of knowing there is no work back home. But still they long to return. Such songs are closely connected with those that describe going off to war and regret at leaving. One of the most popular is "Farewell to Nova Scotia." Many of these songs may express regret, but do not question war in any more critical fashion. In fact, they are often patriotic. However, one early and powerful Acadian anti-war song deals with the Acadian experience of being forced to war. "Maudite Guerre" is a powerful rallying cry for Acadians.

> Mon père est mort
> Mes frères morts
> Ma terre ruinée
> Ma belle mariée
> A cause de la maudite guerre.

For some, proletarianization has meant temporary or permanent migration out of the region. For others it has meant working locally in primary industries, such as mining, forestry, fishing, as well as in the merchant marine. There has also been some work in secondary industry and more recently in wholesaling and retailing. Many songs deal with various aspects of such work, detailing the working class experience. They must be understood as statements outlining not relations of production but the experience of relations of production. The conditions under which people work, the discipline, health and safety, time, and pay, are their experience of the relations of production. They are the specific proletarian experience, along with underemployment and unemployment.

Out of these conditions come songs about the conditions as well as songs of praise for the simple fact that people can take it and survive, songs which create humanity in inhuman conditions, and songs for relaxation. But also there are songs which are an integral part of the struggle of the working classes to unionize and secure better working conditions as well as being part of more class-conscious movements/moments in these struggles in which socialism is proclaimed, and reformism triumphs, or in which more militant stances are defeated.

One of the facts of life for working people anywhere is the danger to health and well-being experienced at work. Some occupations have, of course, been more dangerous than others. Mining, woodswork, sealing and fisheries have many dangers. It is not surprising, therefore, that a large number of songs in the region are about disasters of one kind or another. But how should disasters be described? Certainly not as simple accidents or as acts of God. To understand disasters is to understand the full impact of the underdevelopment of this region. Dire poverty and the need for a cash income have forced many people in Atlantic Canada to work in a variety of occupations, local and non-local, under virtually any conditions.

The sealing industry is a good example of the semi-proletarian experience of hardships and hazard. It was not until 1902, as a result of a major strike in Newfoundland, that the men who went to ice each spring at an extremely low rate of pay were given free berths on the sealing ship. Previously they had to pay the captain for a berth.

> Attention all ye fishermen, and read this ballad down,
> And hear about the sealers strike the other day in town,
> When full three thousand northern men did walk the streets all day,
> With cool determined faces they struck out to get fair pay
> Each steamer's crew did fall in line, while cheers out loudly sang,
> Led on by one brave Calloway, the hero of the gang.
> Free berths it was their motto, and no man would give in.
> A fight for death or glory, boys, the victory to win.[32]

The militancy of seasonal wage workers (who were fishermen most of the year) and the power of the sealers' union shows that semi-proletarians could also be working-class militants. Sealing was extremely hazardous work, but this should not be seen as a natural aspect of the type of work. The highly subordinated relation of labour to capital in an underdeveloped region is of prime importance. Extreme competition for wage work meant that companies did not have to be particularly concerned about safety, either on the ice or on the ships. Pressure to kill as many seals as possible in competition with other boats meant people worked in dangerous conditions such as bad ice and approaching storms. Many sealing songs are about these dangers.

Strict discipline always has been an overriding element of work in the merchant marine and sealing industry. The ships' captains often were tyrants, whose authority was backed by the mutiny laws. In such situations, workers had little chance of protecting their interests. The alternative to militant action (which could lead to charges of mutiny) was to mock the dangers faced, even to the extent of taking unnecessary risks. Hence, the image of the courageous, bold sealer, who, according to "A Noble Fleet of Sealers" will "Risk and dare and think it all great fun."[33]

Similar comments can be made about other aspects of work at sea. In "The Jolly Fisherman," the men are on the Grand Banks fishing for cod. They leave the mother ship in their dories and return with a good haul. The fishing is so good that despite an approaching storm the captain orders the workers back out. Subsequently, the men are trapped by the storm and spend the night in their boats. Fortunately the storm lifts and they are found next morning. Of course, many boats were caught in bad weather but often the danger was compounded by the captain or the boat owner pressuring the workers to ignore the storm. Victor Butler's accounts of his work for merchants in Placentia Bay, Newfoundland in the 1930s, clearly shows this. As captain, and against his better judgment, he was forced to risk his life and the lives of his crew by the merchants' quest for profit.

The following song about "those cruel rogues of merchants" whose "hearts are as cold as the iceberg that freezes in the North winter time" expresses the contrast between the merchants' lives of relative luxury and the workers' conditions.

When the storm it is raging tremendous
And the thunder is peeling the sky
When the whitecaps are rolling to windward
With the rain pouring down from the sky,
It is then we will roll down our mainsail
Our dories we'll have to take in
And perhaps we got poor, leaky oilskins
We're right drowned wet to the skin
And our eyelids are closing together
For the want of an hour's good rest
While those rogues are all spending your money
They are wearing and tasting the best.[34]

Other verses of the song describe the merchants at home on their pillows hugging and squeezing their darlings and having eggs for breakfast and milk in their tea. The differences were clearly perceived as was the exploitation on which merchant wealth was based. But beyond the view of merchants as rogues, there is no immediately apparent broader awareness. Individual capitalists have themselves felt the coercive nature of the laws of capital accumulation during extreme competition to survive, which is heightened during economic recessions.

The problems faced by workers on ships are outlined in the song "A Drunken Captain in a Heavy Gale."

Again we asked him to shorten sail
Or we would be lost in that heavy gale
"I'm captain here and I will not fail
For to shoot the first man who'll reef the sail."

Then up spoke one of our bully crew
Saying "There are twelve of us here in view
We'll reef her down and to sea shall go
If you interfere you'll be tied below."[35]

Such cases of workers' overt resistance to authority must, however, have been comparatively rare. Faced with the alternatives of death or mutiny there was little that could be done except appeal to "larger forces" as the song "Petty Harbour Bait Skiff" recommends. It tells of the wreck of a schooner in which all the crew but one was lost.

Now to conclude and finish
These few lines I write in pain:
Never depend out of your strength
Whilst sailing on the main
But put your trust in Providence,
Observe the Lord's command,
And he'll guard you right, both day and night,
Upon the sea and land.[36]

The hardships and dangers of being at sea, the drunken, demogogic captains, poor food and short rations are all detailed in many songs. "Homeward

Bound" tells of the pleasure of being released from the work. Such songs are often work songs for setting sails and heading home.

> All things shall be ready; all things shall be right;
> There'll be roast beef and mutton to eat day and night;
> There'll be no short allowance or rusty salt cod,
> So the hell with Starr's *Mary* and Captain Conrad.[37]

Until very recently, "independent" fishermen and seasonal fish plant workers had only narrowly united in working-class action. One of the most important of these across-class struggles against fisheries capital occurred in 1939 in Lockeport, Nova Scotia. The early part of the Lockeport lockout struggle and the unity is captured in "The Padlock on the Door."

> 'Twas in the year of '39
> Pat Sullivan came to town
> With him was Charlie Murray
> To help the man that's down.
> They organized a union
> To help the poor man out,
> And so began the initial round
> Of a most historic bout.

> Hurray for the union
> With three big cheers we roar
> To you we'll prove we can remove
> The Padlock from the Door.

> We'll starve them out say Swim Bros.
> They haven't got a cent,
> Cause the wages that we paid them
> Every week were spent.
> They'll come back again, says Swansburg
> Before a week is o'er
> A begging us upon their knees
> To take the padlock from the door.

> But union men true to their code
> Took the situation in hand
> They're working now with all their might
> And justice is their stand;
> United they stand and hand in hand
> They'll solve their problems galore
> They'll run their own Cooperative
> or take the Padlock off the Door.[38]

Despite great efforts, the solidarity was broken by the combined weight of the companies, the government, the police, and the media. Many fishermen and fish plant workers were blacklisted by the companies. In order to find work, many of those blacklisted joined the Armed Forces.

Further accounts of the way workers experienced relations of production and how they have struggled can be found in the songs dealing with lumbering and mining. Woods work meant leaving home for short periods within the region or longer periods in other parts of Canada or the United States. Lumber workers were a mobile, seasonal workforce, usually drawn from fishing and farming. They had to endure, for much of the 19th and 20th century, extremely bad conditions—low pay, poor food, poor health, injury and death. Many songs, like "In the Month of October," describe bush camp life.

> When you roll out was all you could see
> Was a darn dirty cook and lousy cookee.[39]

A similar song is the "Shantyman's Life" of Maine and New Brunswick.

> Now springtime begins and double trouble does commence
> When the waters look piercing cold
> Dripping wet is our clothes and our limbs, they are half frozen
> And our pike-poles we scarce can hold.[40]

These songs illuminate the working experiences and conditions of lumbermen, and the everyday subordination of labour capital. The difficulty of making good wages in bad stands of timber is described in "Gerry Ryan."

> Next morning we were armed with equipment,
> A buck-saw, an axe and a rod,
> With forty-nine men to make wages
> And with only spruce on a bog.
>
> It's hard for a man to make money
> When there's only scrub spruce to be found,
> And if you refuse a back chance on scale,
> The word is you got to go down.
>
> Seventy cents they would charge for a buck-saw,
> And seventy a day for your board,
> And then there's a fee for the doctor
> Out of one dollar twenty a chord.
>
> We found no complaints with this foreman,
> I think he is honest and square,
> But it fell to our lot like cattle were bought,
> And yoked to a buck-saw up there.[41]

However, the workers still resisted the actions of foremen and supervisors. Often loggers only would consent to work poor stands of timber if they were in turn given an opportunity to work good areas. Such incidents are part of the everyday struggle between workers and capital over the distribution of surplus value.

Pressure on workers to produce was no doubt the cause of many accidents. Many songs describe the dangers of woods work and the loss of life. It was hard, dangerous and poorly paid. It was work of the last resort for many small farmers and fishermen. In order to survive, they were forced to work in the woods in winter—that is, they were semi-proletarianized. They also were an ample, cheap, seasonal labour supply for the pulp and paper companies.

The close integration of fishing and lumbering in Newfoundland led to the Fishermen's Protective Union recruiting woods workers in its early phase of organizing on the northeast coast of the island. Such semi-proletarians have, in many ways, been forgotten for much of this century. The stigma attached to seasonal woods work led to their promoting a positive self-image of themselves and their occupation. The "Badger Drive" is such a song, written in 1915 by John Devine, a scaler who was fired and apparently wrote the song to persuade the company to rehire him.

> There is one class of man in this country
> That never is mentioned in song
> And now since their trade is advancing—
> They'll come out on top before long.
> They say that our sailors have danger
> And likewise our warriors bold.
> But there's none know the life of a driver
> What suffers with hardship and cold.
> With their pike-poles and peavies and bateaus and all
> And they're sure to drive out in the spring that's the time
> With the caulks in their boats as they get on the logs
> And it's hard to get over their time.[42]

In its final verse, the "Badger Drive" outlines the contradictory attitudes of workers to the companies. Although work was hard and dangerous and pay was low, it was the work available in an area of economic insecurity. Continued availability of this work depended on the "health" of the company.

> So now to conclude and to finish
> I hope that you all will agree
> In wishing success to all Badger
> And the A.N.D. Company
> And long may they live for to flourish
> And continue to chop, drive and roll
> And long may the business be managed by
> Mr. McDorothey and Mr. Cole.[43]

Loggers were especially difficult to unionize. They were seasonal workers and although they did bunk together they were often isolated and worked in small crews. In Newfoundland, a real effort was made to unionize woods workers in the late 1950s by the International Woodworkers of America. In this period, the logging sector of the pulp and paper industry was undergoing radical changes. Cutting operations were being mechanized with a consequent reduction in the labour force. This, combined with the growth awareness of the poor conditions of loggers *vis-à-vis* other workers, helped produce one of the most bitter disputes in Canadian history. Smallwood and the Liberals made a concerted effort to squash the new union and to support the Anglo-Newfoundland Development Company. The 1953 strike was a bloody one. Fishermen-strikebreakers were brought in from the coast. Legislation was passed to decertify the two legally certified locals of the IWA. Extensive government propaganda was also used to stir up local sentiment against the striking loggers. The union was presented as an outside, evil force, and this argument was used to justify the government's actions. Violence flared between strikers and supporters and the strike breakers. Union officers were attacked and during one violent incident in Badger one police constable was killed when a police detachment tried to march through a group of picketers in a narrow street. Smallwood's propaganda is conveyed in "The Loggers Plight," a song in which the strike is blamed on outside agitation.

> Before he came to our island home
> This dear old Newfoundland
> We lived in peace and harmony
> And followed the Lord's command.[44]

The "he" referred to is Landon Ladd, an organizer for the IWA who was not from Newfoundland. The song then recommends breaking the union and the creation of a new one under government-approved leadership.

> This union is a failure here,
> It never will succeed,
> So form a union of your own
> With Maxwell Lane to lead.

> With Maxwell Lane to lead the way
> The victory will be won
> You'll come to terms with A.N.D.
> Then Landon Ladd will run.

It is essential to remember that work is a creative act even though workers are exploited and oppressed in the course of it. Pride in work and the worker's courage often is expressed in songs about work. "Wabana You're a Corker" (circa 1910) from Bell Island, Newfoundland, shows workers' pride in what they do and the conditions they labour under.

> Ye men that works down in this cave,
> Your courage must be more than brave,
> To work a mine beneath the wave,
> Wabana you're a corker.

> Down in those dark and weary deeps,
> Where the drills do hum and the rats do squeak,
> Day after day, week after week,
> Wabana you're a corker.

> The boss will show you to your room,
> With a lighted lamp will show a gloom
> And perhaps those walls will be your tomb
> Wabana you're a corker.

> The driller he jacks up his bar,
> Between the rib and a loaded car,
> Where all those miss exploders are
> Wabana you're a corker.

> Come now boys and look alive
> Another pair of slices drive,

And don't come up 'till half past five,
Wabana you're a corker.

When you comes by the drain,
Who will you meet but that McLean,
Saying, "I will cut your time again,"
Wabana you're a corker.

If you're living on the Green
Every morning you'll get beans,
And at supper time again its beans,
Wabana you're a corker.[45]

The song is a detailed account of the conditions under which people lived and worked — the danger and discipline imposed by the "head kickers" (foremen) and bosses. However, this is balanced with the statement "Wabana you're a corker," meaning that the mine is viewed as a fine success.

One of the central experiences of working-class life has been the struggle to improve working conditions and wages through unions. Some comments have already been made about this in connection with sealing and logging. Like these industries, mining has been the focus of some of the most powerful union efforts in the region, especially in Cape Breton. Some of the most intense moments of class conflict have been within the mining industry. A constant threat to mine workers in specific areas has been the use of petty producers. Some mines specifically were organized to use this type of seasonal labour as these workers were prepared to accept low wages. With no shortage of workers to give the miners bargaining power, and with a large number of semi-proletarianized small producers eager for jobs, an antagonism on the part of many full-time workers to petty producers and the unemployed soon developed. These people were often employed during strikes as scab labour. The antagonism on the part of fully proletarianized and skilled "honest working men" to semi-proletarian scabs, "Newfoundlanders" and "Chezzetcookers," is reflected in "The Honest Working Man" which has been referred to as the "national anthem of Cape Breton."[46] The song was a militant, though chauvinistic, statement about the scabs who were imported into Cape Breton. It also was part of the effort to make their situation within the community untenable.

Chezzetcookers represented by the dusty black and tan;
May they never be selected, and home rule of protected
And never be connected with the honest working man.
But what raises high my dander, next door lives a Newfoundlander,
Whose wife you cannot stand her, sinch high living she began,
Along with the railroad rackers, also the codfish packers,
Who steal the cheese and crackers from the honest working man.[47]

"The Yahie Miners" is also an anti-scab song, a Cape Breton version of an English song "The Blackleg Miner," referring to rural scabs who came to work in the mines of Cape Breton. While this song also fails to identify that the companies are responsible for scabs in the first place, it is more explicitly directed against the scabs rather than at an ethnic or national community in general. Further, this song urges the workers, scabs and strikers to unite, and calls for the scabs to join the union.

> Join the Union right away
> Don't you wait until after pay
> Join the Union right away
> You dirty Yahie miners.

Songs clearly identify the economic insecurity which is the basis for much division among the working class on ethnic, sex and other lines. The often only thinly-disguised hostility towards people from Atlantic Canada in other areas of Canada and the United States must derive in part from the long history of Atlantic Canadians being used as cheap labour against the interests of the already resident and fully proletarianized working class.

Songs have played an important part in many unionizing efforts and strikes in the mining industry. During the 1973 strike by Local 5457 of the United Steelworkers at Buchans, Newfoundland, the local published a pamphlet of strike songs entitled "Come Hell or Highwater." Most of the songs call for a militant defence of the strike and for the strikers to stand together. The song "Unity Forever" states that although the strikers do not want violence, the company is starting the violence and it will be met with violence. During the strike, the president of the local, Don Head, was fined $5,000 for contempt by the Newfoundland Supreme Court because of his strike leadership. Other songs from the same pamphlet illustrate that although these songs express class consciousness and militant unity against the company, they also suggest the problem is ASARCO, a particular company, rather then capitalism.

From Cape Breton there is evidence of a more radical socialist tradition of working-class militancy building on the traditions of immigrant miners from Britain and elsewhere, as in "Arise Ye Nova Scotia Slaves." This song deals with the strike of 1909/10 when 2,500 miners in Glace Bay went on strike to force the company to recognize the union (UMWA). Six hundred soldiers were used to break up the worker's meetings and demonstrations and workers and their families were evicted from company houses. The strike was lost after 10 months.

In general, two distinct lines emerge in songs concerning the working class movement: its organization and tactics. These are not always distinct nor do they only appear in different songs. One line calls for a militant unity of workers against capital while the other either explicitly or implicitly states that co-operation should be the basis of the relationship of labour to capital, and that militancy is counterproductive. An example of this latter line is "1925 Strike Song" by Laughlin MacNeil.

> The Bolshevicky doctrine with its promise of galore
> Like many a pretty apple it is rotten at the core

Their structure built on shifting sands, their balm for human ills,
Deceive no man of common sense to accept their drastic pills.

To solve a labour problem and in order to succeed
One and all should pray to God at first and then all should heed
Not only heed but practise what our Saviour commands
When this is done the problem will be solved in every land.[48]

Radical working class movements and traditions in areas like Cape
Breton have been a persistent source of strength for subsequent struggles, but
also a source of contemporary romanticism. "Minto Miners" is one such song.

Now a Minto miner is a proud hard man
He raises his brood the best that he can
By the sweat of his brow and the pick in his hand
Loadin' our Minto coal.

Some men work and they earn their bread
When the sun is hot and high overhead
Some men's labours go on through the cool of the night
When a Minto boy becomes a man
He don't get to see much of the sun again
There ain't no sun again
at the bottom of the Minto mine.[49]

The coal miner persists as a romantic image for the working class and
middle class. The image is built on a history of militant struggles and the
dangers and hardships of the work. Such imagery has its basis in the division
of labour and differences in occupational prestige. And while it does state
something about the realities of work and existence for some workers ("you
have to be tough to survive") and perhaps a contempt for weaklings or those
who "don't make it," it can also lead men to accept poor conditions and a
work load that drives them to the limit of their endurance. Working-class
values like toughness, respectability and the virtues of the "honest working
man" are all contradictory. Respectability means being able to keep your wife
at home; toughness means being able to take it uncomplainingly; being an
honest working man means looking down on other classes of workers.

Economic insecurity and poverty is part of petty-producer, semi-
proletarian and proletarian life in Atlantic Canada. In terms of maintaining
a relative surplus population, government relief, public works and philan-
thropy have long been important. Small producers in the fisheries have been
forced to seek relief following failure of the fishery or a drop in cod prices and
the merchants' subsequent credit cut-off. Such a situation is outlined in "The
Merchant."

'Tis then he'll apply to his merchant
In hopes he will grant him relief.
But the answer he gets is a cold one
And this unto him he will say:
"You'd better apply to your member
Perhaps he'll relieve you today."[50]

For others, relief came in the form of "useful work" with the Grenfell Mission of philanthropist Dr. William Grenfell. The "Mission Song" from Labrador clearly states the resentment by some people of this form of charity.

> Come all ye poor women who work night and day,
> Making mats for the Mission for three dollars pay,
> But to tell you the truth the way it do seem,
> You'll get the milk skimmed and de relations de cream.[51]

Recently, unemployment insurance and make-work projects have become important, particularly given the current economic crisis. Unemployment is affecting a wide spectrum of people. Many songs address unemployment and the government's inadequate responses as in Jim Payne's version of "Hard, Hard Times (Revisited)".

> Well I worked out in Stephenville for a year and a half
> Till Doody cut us off and I got the shaft
> Now I'm drawing pogey and living on salt pork
> My bed-sitting room leaks and I'm looking for work
> And its' Hard, Hard Times.[52]

The chorus urges people to organize.

> Come all ye good people stand up and be strong
> We been stepped on and used for a good while too long
> Come on Newfoundlanders stand up organize
> We're fed up with promises, rip-offs and lies.
> And it's Hard, Hard Times.

Other songs outline life on unemployment insurance how it defines you. Buddy and the Boys describe what it is like in Cape Breton in the song "Hanging Around."

> Jobs are in Jeopardy
> That's a place out West
> Buddy's stuck right here
> Along with the rest
> You can tell who he is
> By the eyes in his head
> A man lives in fear
> When he fears for his bread.
>
> I have to love a fight
> Got to hate a queer
> Got to walk around downtown
> Got to guzzle all kinds of beer
> I got to buy on time
> From the Woolco store
> I got to get laid
> And I got to keep score.
>
> I'm just hangin' around
> With nothin' to do
> I'm just hangin' around

How about you
Livin' on the pogey is makin' me blue
I'm just hangin' around
With nothin' to do.

Many current songs from the Atlantic Folk Festival express a more general feeling of protest and of alienation in political, economic and social-cultural terms. For many, the work that is available is unattractive. This song, "Workin' At The Woolco (Manager Trainee Blues)," details the emptiness of a job with a large monopoly, as a meaningless cog in the works.

Taking out the garbage and sweepin' up the floor
Learnin' how to sell, what an awe-full bore
They promised a promotion but I think it's a joke
Can't wait for my lunch break to sneak out for a smoke.[53]

A powerful sense of "being caught" pervades current songs such as "I'm in Sydney and It's the Middle of Winter."

I'm in Sydney and it's the middle of winter,
You could freeze from your nose to your toes
Keep your back to the storm
And your skates at the forum
And I'll see you in June
When it's warm.
If I look kind of old
The Rockin' Saints they're my heroes
If I look kind of young
It's the disco machine
And in my final conclude
I'll shoot the drag every evening
And remember the stag line
And my chauvinist dreams.[54]

Another song by Ronnie MacEachern is concerned with the dangers of nuclear energy, specifically at Point Lepreau. "Maritime Meltdown Blues" by MacEachern is a description of potential disaster and an implicit call for people not to be apathetic about nuclear power. "Don't Fool Yourself (The Sysco Kid)" states the folly of ignoring what the Sydney Steel Corporation is doing to Sydney out of fear that jobs will be lost.

I said "The whole town's covered with shit. How can you stand to live here?"
He said "We pretend we don't see it. Besides we got lots of beer."
I said "Come on Pancho you ain't that dumb. The whole town's dull blood red."
He said "What can I say. If you take it away, we may as well be dead."[55]

These latter songs suggest a widespread dissatisfaction on the part of many people in the region. They also reveal some political awareness and elements of opposition. However, they do not suggest a way forward in any meaningful sense. Lack of such awareness in popular music is not surprising given the general lack of political organization and the weakness of a radical (socialist) movement in the region.

Much of the current wave of music is the music of revolt by working-class youth, the alienated middle classes and particular cultural groups—a revolt which is articulated culturally. In an alienating world of no work, and no future (the world of the current economic crisis), culture does offer life. Out of capitalist society, people do create, even if they also recreate many of the limitations, frustrations and contradictions of their society. The preconditions for this revolt are economic; its current expressions are largely cultural. Some cultural expressions take the form of a search for roots, for a more stable acceptable past, others are nihilistic, yet others overtly political; few see the necessity and possibility of radical social change or revolutionary transformation.

In Conclusion

Variations in the ways of living of the popular classes (petty producer, semi-proletarian, proletarian) in struggles within the popular classes, and in struggles between segments of the popular classes and capital, are experiences that find creative expression not only through overt class conflict but also through cultural mechanisms such as songs.

The overall process of uneven capitalist development, in this case uneven underdevelopment, can be linked to creative class-in-locality cultural expression of the lived situation. Presumably, the direction undertaken in this analysis will be fruitful for further insights into the larger and more crucial political and scholarly question of popular class culture in Canada. It is hoped it will also further the adequate conceptualization of the more concrete class-in-community and singer-in-context levels of analysis.

The reality of variable, contradictory class-cultural expressions in any region of the capitalist world is not a problem that can be ignored because it fits no readily available schema. It is a problem to be understood in its contextual complexity. Advancing our understanding of the lived links between capitalism as an entire system and popular class culture is no mere scholarly pursuit. It is itself a class-cultural awakening.

NOTES

1.   For a sampling of work concerning other underdeveloped regions, see Alison Acker, "The Bicycle versus the Helicopter: Cultural Resistance in Chile Today," *This Magazine* 13, nos. 5 & 6 (1979): 35-37. Gerald M. Sider, *Mumming in Outport Newfoundland* (Toronto: New Hogtown Press, 1978) gives an introductory indication of the importance of musical expression in Atlantic Canada.
2.   Paul E. Willis, *Profane Culture* (London: Routledge & Kegan Paul, 1978), p. 1.
3.   Helen Creighton, *Maritime Folksongs* (Toronto: Ryerson Press, 1961), p. vi.
4.   Gerald S. Doyle, *Old Time Songs and Poetry of Newfoundland: Songs of the People from the Days of our Forefathers* (St. John's: G.S. Doyle Ltd., 1966), p. 2.
5.   A. L. Lloyd, *Folk Song in England* (New York: International Publishers, 1967), p. 14.

6. Adrian Waller, "These are Our Songs," *Reader's Digest* 113(675): 48.

7. Theodor W. Adorno, *Introduction to the Sociology of Music* (New York: Seabury Press, 1976), pp. 154-177.

8. Richard S. Tallman, "Folklore Research in Atlantic Canada: An Overview," *Acadiensis* 8(2): 129.

9. It is worth pointing out also that these "new" approaches, especially those pioneered by Memorial University's Department of Folklore (founded as a separate entity in 1968), have played a role in the shaping of a consciousness of cultural individuality, distinctiveness and pride in Newfoundland. As such they have played a part in the growth of neonationalist sentiment in the province (see, Halpert and Rosenberg, 1974: Overton, 1979b).

10. John Saul, "The Dialectics of Class and Tribe," *Studies in Political Economy* 2(1): 36.

11. Attempts are also made by non-Marxist folklorists to place the production of music in its social, economic and historical context. Again, the work of the Folklore Department at Memorial University of Newfoundland is usually along these lines. A recent example is the work of Cynthia Lamson on the "rhetoric" of the sealing counterprotest (1979: see also Szwed, 1970). While this does go some way toward a contextualization of music production, it ultimately fails in a very serious way to transcend a "common-sense" (and therefore ideological) approach to the problem. The analysis is superficial and, where not idealistic, crudely materialistic, reducing much of the conflict to the clash of cosmologies between uninformed "urbanite ecologists" and rural Newfoundlanders' struggles to preserve a "way of life." Overton (1980a) attempts to provide a more in-depth analysis of many of the issues surrounding the seal hunt.

12. Willis, *Profane Culture*, p. 1.

13. Ibid., p. 5.

14. Richard Johnson, "Three Problematics: Elements of a Theory of Working Class Culture," in *Working Class Culture: Studies in History and Theory,* edited by J. Clark, C. Critcher and R. Johnson (London: Hutchinson, 1979), p. 235.

15. Patterson.

16. Creighton, *Maritime Folksongs*, p. 179.

17. Doyle, *Songs of the People*, p. 28.

18. For a more complete discussion of the political economy of game laws in Newfoundland, see J. Overton, "Tourism Development, Conservation and Conflict: Game Laws for Caribou Protection in Newfoundland," *Canadian Geographer* 24, (i) 1980.

19. MacEdward Leach, *Folk Ballads and Songs of the Lower Labrador Coast* (Ottawa: National Museum of Canada, 1965).

20. K. Peacock, *The Nature Songs of Newfoundland* (Ottawa: Department of Northern Affairs, Vol. 1), pp. 77-78.

21. Leach, *Folk Ballads and Songs*, pp. 214-215.

22. Peacock, *Songs of Newfoundland*, Vol. 2, p. 360.

23. Ibid., p. 21.

24. Doyle, *Songs of the People*, p. 73.

25. Peacock, *Songs of Newfoundland*, Vol. 2, pp. 370-371.

26. P. C. Mars, *The Case of Terra Nova* (London: Morris, 1924), pp. 28-34.

27. For a more complete analysis of the importance of semi-proletarianization in the Maritimes, see J. Sacouman, "Semi-protarianization and Rural Underdevelopment — the Maritimes," *Canadian Review of Sociology and Anthropology* 17 (3) 1980.

28. For details concerning the Fishermen's Protective Union, see S. J. R. Noel, *Politics in Newfoundland* (Toronto: University of Toronto Press, 1971), pp. 74-94.

29. R. W. Guy, "Muddy Hole: 1834-1866. Masgrove Harbour, 1866," in *Winnipeg Entries in Newfoundland Government Sponsored Competition for the Encouragement of Arts and Letters* (St. John's: Government of Newfoundland and Labrador, 1971), p. 45.

132   PART TWO—THE ROLE OF COMMUNICATION

30.   E. B. Greenleaf and G. Y. Mansfield, *Ballads and Sea Songs of Newfoundland* (Hatboro, PA: Folklore Associate, 1966 (1933)), pp. 314-315.
31.   MacEachern Concert, 1979.
32.   J. Murphy, *Songs Sung by Old Time Sealers of Many Years Ago* (St. John's, 1925), p. 20.
33.   Doyle, *Songs of the People*, p. 15.
34.   Ibid., p. 51.
35.   Ron MacEachern, *Songs and Stories from Deep Cove, Cape Breton as Remembered by Amby Thomas* (Sydney: College of Cape Breton Press, 1979), p. 48.
36.   Doyle, *Songs of the People*, p. 36.
37.   Helen Creighton, *Songs and Ballads from Nova Scotia* (New York: Dover Publications, 1966), pp. 232-234.
38.   Mrs. James MacKenzie, "Lockeport Union Songs" (mimeo).
39.   Creighton, *Songs and Ballads from Nova Scotia*, p. 265.
40.   Helen Creighton and D. Senior, *Traditional Songs from Nova Scotia* (Toronto: Ryerson Press, 1950), p. 274.
41.   Peacock, *Songs of Newfoundland*, Vol. 3, pp. 748-79.
42.   Doyle, *Songs of the People*, p. 18.
43.   Ibid.
44.   Peacock, *Songs of Newfoundland*, Vol. 3, pp. 775-776.
45.   Peter Neary, "Wabana You're a Corker: Two Ballads with Some Notes Towards an Understanding of Bell Island in Conception Bay," paper presented to Annual Meetings, Canadian Historical Association, 1973.
46.   Stuart McCawley, *Cape Breton "Come Ye All"* (Glace Bay: Brodie Printing Service, 1929), pp. 7-8.
47.   MacEachern, *Songs and Stories*, p. 35.
48.   For a discussion of the class struggle in Minto, New Brunswick, see Seager (1980).
49.   Steve Stevedore, *Hard, Workin' Man.* Boot Records, BOS 7102.
50.   Doyle, *Songs of the People*, pp. 51-52.
51.   Leach.
52.   Jim Payne, "Hard, Hard Times (Revisited)" (mimeo).
53.   Buddy and the Boys, *Buddy.* Shagrock Records, SAR 2019.
54.   MacEachern concert, 1979.
55.   Buddy and the Boys.

The authors thank Ron MacEachern for allowing them to use songs from an unrecorded concert.

Chapter 7

The Social Dimensions of Adult Learning

Marilyn Taylor

Les changements drastiques de vie, la redéfinition de soi, de ses valeurs sont bien des signes caractéristiques de notre époque. Non seulement commençons-nous à reconnaître aujourd'hui que l'apprentissage est l'affaire de toute une vie, mais encore nous rendons-nous compte que ce que nous avons à apprendre va beaucoup plus loin que la simple acquisition de nouvelles aptitudes et connaissances. Nous sommes souvent confrontés à la nécessité de redéfinir notre approche aux choses et d'en acquérir, pour nous-mêmes, une toute nouvelle compréhension.

L'observation que faisait Gregory Bateson que toute forme d'apprentissage est avant tout de nature communicationnelle se confirme de façon remarquable (tout au moins sur le plan de la communication interpersonnelle) dans une étude qui fut menée avec des gens qui vivaient cette expérience de l'apprentissage d'une nouvelle vision des choses. Le but de cet article est de tracer brièvement une représentation conceptuelle de ce type d'apprentissage. Cette représentation est le fruit d'une comparaison des expériences communes de huit personnes qui ont vécu ce processus et l'ont décrit à intervalles réguliers.

Ce processus d'apprentissage peut être divisé en quatre phases qui diffèrent qualitativement l'une de l'autre et constituent toutes une façon particulière d'appréhender un aspect de la réalité, une idée, un thème ou une expérience: la phase de détachement (phase au cours de laquelle idées et expériences nouvelles s'inscrivent dans une vision des choses existante); la phase de divergence (phase durant laquelle la vieille vision des choses s'effondre, donnant naissance à la confusion et la désorganisation); la phase de l'engagement (phase d'exploration intuitive qui ne se base plus sur des préjugés et donne naissance à plusieurs idées et concepts nouveaux); et la phase de convergence (phase de synthèse au cours de laquelle une nouvelle vision des choses affecte directement le comportement).

Après cette phase de convergence, l'apprentissage revient à la phase de détachement au cours de laquelle la nouvelle vision des choses est élaborée, consolidée et appliquée à toute nouvelle expérience. Le fait que ces quatre phases d'apprentissage correspondent précisement, chez la personne qui apprend, à des changements dans sa façon d'inter-agir avec les personnes auxquelles elle est associée en cours d'expérience, constitue cet aspect de l'étude qui s'apparente tout particulièrement au domaine des communications. Il existe des phases de retrait et d'engagement avec les autres qui sont inhérentes à ce processus d'apprentissage. Plus spécifiquement, il existe trois "événements communicationnels" qui semblent essentiels à l'acquisition d'une nouvelle vision des choses: (1) pour passer de la phase de la confusion (divergence) à celle de l'engagement, il doit s'établir—entre la personne qui apprend et les autres personnes qui ont de l'importance à ses yeux—un contact d'affinité (affining contact); (2) l'étape d'exploration intuitive au cours de laquelle de nouveaux concepts sont générés et accumulés est une activité de collaboration avec d'autres qui fournissent à la fois support et confrontations; (3) la synthèse finale, fruit d'une activité solitaire, n'est pas perçue par la personne qui apprend comme étant complétée avant d'avoir été partagée avec les personnes qui ont de l'importance à ses yeux.

Différentes avenues de recherche sur l'apprentissage conçu comme étant un changement de vision des choses (perspective change) suggérées par cette étude sont proposées en fin d'article: (1) chercher à comprendre de façon plus approfondie les trois "événements communicationnels"; (2) voir si ce processus d'apprentissage se retrouve dans une variété de milieux et chez différents types de personnes (si oui, comment); (3) voir si ce processus peut être relié aux changements d'environnement social (processus de groupe, changements organisationnels, etc.).

Social systems are under review and intra-generational change is prevalent in today's world. Accompanying this is a rapidly growing interest in studying how humans change and learn throughout life. Learning is an everyday feature of life, but involves much more than simply acquiring better information or a new skill. In contrast to those who lived in conditions of relative cultural stability, people now are often required to re-examine their whole approach to an issue or idea. It has become necessary to evolve an entirely new perspective, a new understanding. The development of the theory of such adult perspective change is the subject of this paper.

Gregory Bateson observes that "all forms of learning . . . must be regarded as communicational in nature."[1] This study, where learning has been explored from the vantage point of the learner, reaches a similar conclusion. Analysis of learners' descriptions of their experiences revealed a dynamic relation between "self and other" throughout the process of perspective change. The data base in this study implies an existential perspective which, as Hampden-Turner points out, has an implicit relational quality.[2] An important aspect of studying perspective change is a consideration of it as a phenomenon derived from the relation between person and context, a co-

constituted reality.[3] Nevertheless, in this study, the communication dimension of perspective change is considered in the concrete and specific terms of the relationships between the learner and other persons. The relation between "self and other" is assumed and the relation between "self and others" will be discussed.

Perspective change is a pervasively social process. While common patterns in the experiences of the learners who were observed for this study include essential periods of solitude, the data suggest that perspective change literally would not occur without specific communication events between the learner and those whom he or she perceives to be associated with the theme or issue being considered. The assumption that humans can learn independently of other people appears not only ill-founded in respect to the development of new understanding, but may also lead to initiatives that inhibit perspective change. A critical element of learning theory as related to perspective change is the need for careful, detailed attention to the social communication dimension.

The intent of this paper is, first, to present the conceptual representation of the learning process derived in this study with special attention to the social communication dimension. In addition, it suggests areas where research would lead to a theory of learning related to perspective change that takes the social reference into account.

Part I

The conceptual formulation presented here is constructed from patterns observed to be common in eight adult learners' descriptions of their experiences collected at regular intervals throughout the process.[4] Participants in the study included six women and two men who ranged in age from 24 to 50 years. These persons volunteered to be interviewed weekly throughout their association with a particularly dynamic course entitled "Basic Processes of Facilitating Adult Learning" instructed by Dr. Virginia Griffin in the Adult Education Department of the Ontario Institute for Studies in Education in Toronto. All of these people had previous training in one of the social professions and all had at least some, if not extensive, experience in their fields. The conceptualization—a cyclical sequence consisting of four phases—is a construction from the learner's point of view. The sequence, which is a pattern of human learning, is a phenomenon which would be especially apparent to the learner.

Although it is expected this sequence would be found in a similar form wherever a person is involved in a perspective change, it is important to note that the data base for this study was adult learners' experiences in association with a formal course. The perspective change or learning process was precipitated by their participation in this group in which it was assumed, as adult professional persons, they could be centrally involved in setting directions for their own learning. Since this approach to formal education contradicted their expectations from past experience, they became involved in making a fundamental change in their interpretation of the nature of knowledge and the tasks of learners and teachers.

Part II

The conceptualization of learning evolved from patterns in learners' experiences of four qualitatively different "seasons" or phases of learning. The phases occur in a consistent order, and a theme of pivotal concern emerges—in this case, the nature of knowledge, learning and teaching. The four phases—"divergence," "engagement," "convergence" and "detachment"—are represented in Figure 7-1.

The learning process is considered to begin with the divergence phase, but it is precipitated by a season of detachment which revealed a tone of anticipation. This study begins by considering the detachment phase.

During the detachment phase, the learner is observing and trying to fit his/her experiences into existing conceptual categories. At the beginning of the course, participants' expectations were discussed, and confirmed or denied: "For me the structure and organization and presentation that (the instructor) made, made sense, and was clarifying . . . [it] fit in with what I expected," commented one participant. The term "detachment" does not signify lack of interest or uninvolvement but rather that the learner relates to experience primarily through preconceived notions. The connections between the learner's interests and his/her colleagues at this point exist largely as possibilities in the mind of the learner.

The learning process begins with the collapse of the learner's frame of reference as an adequate means for understanding his/her experience. This new phase of the process has been called divergence since the learner's experience diverges or veers away from existing conceptual frameworks and expectations: there is no meaningful link between concept and experience. The key descriptor for the detachment phase was "fit." For the divergence phase "non-fitting" would be appropriate and the learners felt uncomfortable. One learner reported that "nothing was clicking" and that "the course was not going in a direction which suited me." This phase is characterized by confusion, a crisis of confidence and sometimes intense anxiety. The social pattern during this phase is one of withdrawal or distancing of self from others perceived to be associated with the source of confusion. There is "a tendency to pull back," as one learner put it. People reported communication with others and some distortion of perception. "I realized that when I'm in a bad mood I totally misinterpret what people are feeling . . . what is happening in the class," reported one person. This phase can be prolonged by denial of such confusion. When this occurred, there were instances of growing antagonism and competition in relation to others. There is a tendency to find fault with others for the discomfort and/or to blame oneself.

Figure 7-1   Four Phases in the Learning Process

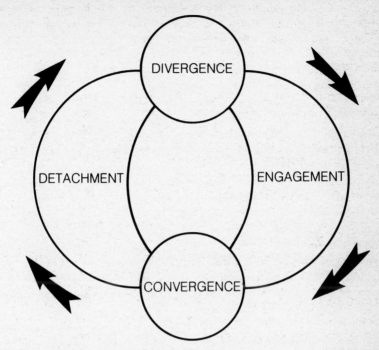

Two related and possibly simultaneous events are crucial for the learner moving out of the divergence phase. Naming the source of the confusion without feeling personally inadequate and establishing contact with others associated with that source of confusion are both essential.

The engagement phase is characterized by the learner being able to relax without having a solution to the issue. What follows is an intuitively guided exploration in which decisions are made in the face of particulars rather than in the light of a preconceived plan. At this point there is no coherent conceptual perspective which fits the experience, but the learner is prepared to go along with the experience and is able to do so without the discomfort of the divergence phase. One person described this as being able to "throw away all assumptions and presuppositions and be sort of free-floating."

An outstanding feature of the engagement phase is a series of collaborative insights or convergence episodes. There is a convergence, a coming together, of the learner with colleagues and at the same time connections are made between experience and concepts. Insights are created. One learner described it as "the head and the experience coming together." These occasions were characterized as "a combination of comfort and excitement" in relationships with others who were able to be supportive and confrontive at the same time. The importance of these occasions in the learning process was demonstrated by learners creating such a situation outside the classroom if they did not occur within. "I have to have that interpersonal bouncing of ideas to make it real," said one learner. Another reported these experiences enabled him to express what he had not been able to verbalize before. Insight and confidence derived from these episodes mounts to a point of apparent saturation, a plateau experienced by the learner in response to which he or she tends to withdraw from both activity and other persons. This signals the close of the engagement phase.

The convergence phase features a rather sudden emergence of a major insight, which gives a sense of resolution. This understanding is represented in a new conceptualization and is reflected in the novel approach adopted by the learner. The experience in this phase is of tremendous excitement and intensity. One learner noted dramatic physical reactions such as sensations of swelling in the chest. Several described a heightened consciousness such as "being aware of awareness." An extraordinary sense of clarity and perspective on issues of concern during prior phases gives the learner a strong sense of confidence and satisfaction.

The events of this convergence phase occur when the learner is withdrawn from others. The major insight or synthesis emerges out of some form of solitary reflection (such as journal writing or reviewing notes). However, learners do not seem to move out of this phase until they share their insights with those associated with the process.

This last act provides a sense of completion, and the learner returns to the stance of detachment phase. This time it is with a sense of consolidation of experience rather than the apprehension prevalent at the outset. The learner elaborates and refines the new understanding by relating it to other items and applying it to other experiences. The learner again relates to experience through a preconceived frame of reference, but this time through the new perspective. He or she no longer is directly and intensively involved with others, at least with respect to this particular theme. Relationships with others tend to be influenced by preconceived purposes. One person commented, "we all had private agendas that didn't mesh very well." He contrasted this with an earlier period (engagement phase) when "there seemed to be interweaving patterns or lines."

Part III

The learning process people experienced in the course has been described from their point of view. Each person moved through the sequence at his/her own rhythm and timing. All but one reached the engagement phase, but only three learners completed the sequence during the interviewing period. Nevertheless, the elements of the process described above were experienced by all the learners who had reached that point in the sequence. Therefore, while continuation in the process is not inevitable, this study suggests that completion of the process implies movement through certain critical points. These critical points are summarized in Figure 7-2.

Figure 7-2   Critical Points in the Learning Process

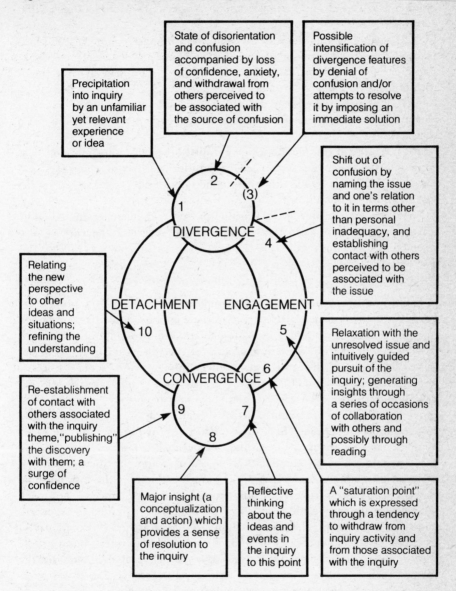

The study of these eight participants in an adult education course revealed that there is a very definite social reference for learners in three of the four phases in the sequence, precisely those phases in which change is occurring. In the group, the social reference developed through distancing to contact:

(1) The learning began in confusion with an accompanying "distance" between the learner and those whom (s)he associated with the source of that confusion.

(2) Genuine exploration of the issue was contingent upon the establishment of contact with one or several of these persons.

(3) The exploration was collaborative, that is, it implied an involvement with others who had similar concerns.

(4) The personally meaningful synthesis or resolution of the issue occurred when the learner was reflecting on past experiences and thoughts in solitude.

(5) A sense of completion which permitted the learner to "move on" was contingent upon renewed contact with significant others to whom (s)he expressed the discovery and with whom (s)he found understanding, and affirmation of intelligibility.

All of these features of the learning process take place in sequence; the learner's relationships with others is essential and integral in the learning process.

Part IV

This study attempts to describe and understand learning as a process experienced by the learner, a research approach used infrequently. More often learning is studied as outcome related to conditions or input. Learning is usually described from the vantage point of the researcher in terms of observed behaviour, although the researcher's inferences on "inner" processes are included sometimes. Undertaking a systematic comparative study that reveals patterns from the learner's point of view is an entirely new realm of inquiry that offers considerable practical benefit to learners, those who give courses and researchers. Three major directions for inquiry into the social communication dimension of learning are outlined below.

Several preliminary comments are necessary before the discussing of new research possibilities. First, it is difficult to imagine how the intrapersonal aspect of this process will ever be fully accessible for study. Since the approach is based on descriptions of experience, the data base is limited to aspects of conscious experience. The learner cannot verbalize aspects of experience of which he or she is not aware. Second, the procedure of interviewing people during an experience is a reflective activity which probably catalyzes the learner's consciousness of his/her experience, a process central to learning. The method of collecting data is a social communication that affects, indeed promotes, the phenomenon under study. However, because people who were not interviewed are able to recognize the same patterns in their learning experience, it is the contention here that interviewing is not necessary for the process to occur. What appears necessary is interaction with other people that will serve, like interviews, as a catalyst.

Part V

On an informal basis, many people have reported the usefulness of the learner-oriented analysis. However, it seems essential that more systematic studies of persons' learning experiences are undertaken to determine how widely such an approach can be applied. The method should be applied to learners preoccupied with different themes or issues.

The data base in this study is description, indeed, interpretation of experience. The formulation is constructed upon language. Cultural similarity must be presumed, to some extent, in the shared meaning of that language. The eight persons who participated in this study represented a range of ages, but they all were highly educated, Canadian social professionals interested in adult education. How would the four-phase representation of the learning process be altered if the perspective-change experience of a diverse group of people was studied? What differences among people are associated with these variations?

A second element to be considered is the setting and nature of the learning theme or issue. This conceptualization is not applicable to every experience which might be called "learning." Paul Colaizzi's study of people's retrospective descriptions of their experience of assigned learning tasks such as recitation, spelling nonsense syllables, problem-solving and perceptual-motor activity resulted in a reconstruction of experience which is entirely different from that here. He reported no pattern of attention, even in thought, to other persons. There is, however, literature in three different areas which suggests a pattern of experience similar to the conceptual formulation advanced here. One such area is literature on adult development. Adult development theorists have been preoccupied with identifying changes that occur through adult life. However, several writers have described, at least briefly, how these changes actually happen.

Roger Gould sets out a "seven-step inner dialogue"[5] that characterizes life stages between the ages of 16 and 50. His schema is derived from his experience as a psychiatrist. These steps resemble the conceptualization of the learning process formulated in this study. They begin with the need to "recognize our tension and confusion," to deal with "contradictory realities" and finally "reach an integrated, trustworthy view of a section of reality. . . ." Gould does not refer to any social communication dimension in the seven steps (perhaps assuming his own presence). But at least in describing young adults, he observes: "Group support is necessary to integrate new beliefs as part of ourselves."[6]

It is probable that process studies (collecting persons' descriptions of their experience at intervals of these adult transitions) would reveal phases and accompanying social references to those detailed in this study. Research of this nature would be useful in determining the people and the communication events that are important in life transitions.

The perspective change that occurs as people grow older is closely related to the re-orientations associated with educational settings that catalyze people to assume greater responsibility. On the basis of efforts to promote what he calls critical consciousness among peasants in Brazil, Paulo Freire[7] emphasizes the importance of "circles of culture" which enable people to "name their world" and take initiatives in community change. Although he did not systematically study how change in consciousness occurs, Freire posits the necessity of involvement with others. Jack Mezirow associates his findings from a study of college re-entry programmes for women with how Freire's work elaborates "a perspective transformation." The nine elements he suggests resemble both the process described in this study and Gould's seven-step inner dialogue. Mezirow's sequence begins with "a disorienting dilemma" and "self-examination" to "reintegration with society on conditions dictated by the new perspective."[8] Mezirow alludes to a social dimension as one of the nine elements, namely, "relating one's discontent to similar experiences of others or to a public issue recognizing one's problem is shared. . . ."[9] The laboratory and T-group training that originated with Kurt Lewin is an educational approach based on the conviction that development of new ways of relating to people and perception of self and other is achieved through group methods. Lewin's notion of attitude change as "unfreezing, changing and refreezing" and its subsequent elaboration by Schein and Bennis[10] can be compared, in general terms, to the process of learning described here. Herbert Thelen[11] and Virginia Griffin[12] have developed models of teaching (where the focus is not the relation to others *per se*) that incorporate the social communication dimension as a central feature. Careful studies of a person's descriptions of his or her experiences in educational programmes which are concerned with promoting responsibility-taking by the learner could enrich and refine the intuitions and practice of educators. Results of such studies would probably result in helpful modifications of the formulation developed in this initial study.

Finally, the literature on creative thinking and problem-solving abounds with the conceptual representation of learning described here and refers to the social communication aspect of the creative process. The importance of creative thinking and problem-solving in the technical world has led to more extensive consideration of the social in educational or adult development literature. For example, Brewster Ghiselin has formulated a scheme that refers to "commerce with disorder,"[13] and "hidden organic development" in some "long gestation period,"[14] an insight that emerges out of a "state of mind" characterized by "collectedness . . . autonomy . . . and watchfulness,"[15] and that one "tests, refines and consolidates what is attained in moments of inspiration."[16] William Gordon, a developer of the synectic group's problem-solving approach, claims "a properly operating group has advantages over the individual."[17] Comparable to the collaborative engagement phase, Gordon states that "a synectics group can compress into a few weeks the kind of semi-conscious mental ability which might take months of incubation for a single person."[18] And Morris Stein concludes, "to complete the creative process the final product . . . *needs* to be presented to and accepted by a group of significant *others* as tenable, useful and satisfying. . . ."[19]

In addition to establishing more clearly a range of applicability of this formulation and its social communication dimensions, process studies of learning in different settings would help to further clarify the connection between relationships with others and learning. For example, the literature on the creative process does not contain evidence of the divergence pattern and the need for self-affirmation. It is not clear if this is simply not discussed or arises from the fact that the problem to be solved in the creative process is more externalized than self definitive. By observing and investigating differences such as these, much could be learned about the significance of particular social communication events in learning.

Part VI

The study of perspective change could be further advanced by a detailed study of specific aspects of the learning process. In particular there are three salient and critical communication events which occur between the learner and others during the process.

The first of these occurs at the end of the divergence phase. The learner establishes an affirming contact with persons (s)he associates with the source of confusion characteristic of that phase. In this particular study, this was an event which, objectively speaking, was often obscure, but it was of significance to the learner. For one person it was the passing comment of several colleagues, who, without even mentioning his name, acknowledged the importance to them of something he had done in class. The event was a much-needed boost to the learner's self-esteem, an affirmation of self. Many aspects of such affirming contacts remain unexplored. How does the nature of the learning issue relate to this event? Are there qualities of the learners themselves, styles and orientations, which affect this part of the sequence? How do people assume this important affirming role? What is the relation of "naming the issue" and the affirming contact with others? Is one contingent upon the other? Are they simultaneous events?

An excellent example of the detailed work necessary to understand this aspect of the learning process is the study presently being conducted by Raye Kass in identifying common patterns in the experience of doctoral candidates in the initial stage of their dissertation work.[20] Kass, who regards her work as a study of "the apology stance," has identified five phases that reflect, in much greater detail than entered into here, the divergence phase and the beginning of the engagement phase. Of particular interest is her identification of patterns in the type of person to whom the learner gravitates. Kass's findings affirm and extend the patterns made evident in this study. First, there is a search for an expert, then movement toward perceived sources of recognition, followed by what she calls a discriminating involvement with significant others in a period she labels "co-construction" (roughly a parallel to the engagement phase in this study). Perhaps as a result of Kass's work, we will become accustomed to allowing for periods of disorientation in our own experience and that of others. One of the most frequently reported uses of the findings reported in this paper has been in legitimizing learners' periods of confusion.

The second form of social communication critical in this representation of the learning process occurs in the engagement phase. Supportive as well as confrontive interchanges with persons appear to have similar or complementary purposes and seem integral to the creation of connections between ideas and experience, to the generation of insights. Phrases used by learners such as "connections being made between half-formed ideas" and "drawing out thoughts" are reminiscent of Gordon's[21] identification of the catalytic effect of the group as "an efficient use of the unconscious" in creative problem solving. Phrases in learners' descriptions such as "conceptualizing on past experience" with others bears similarity to Freire's "circle of culture" that made it possible for people to "name their world."[22] Freire observed the same associated sense of confidence and satisfaction accompanying the process. Careful study of how this aspect of learning is experienced is required if more is to be learned about the connection between the nature of relationships with others and the quality of thinking possible.

Several studies from the vantage point of the learner are important contributions to an understanding of the engagement phase experience. One of these, conducted by Marge Denis, is a descriptive study of the process and dynamics of intuition in learning.[23] The intuitive plays a prominent role in the experience of the engagement and convergence phases for the eight learners who are the subject of this study. On the basis of interviews with adults who were perceived by others and/or themselves to be especially intuitive, Denis identified 18 categories of what she terms a "bipolar experience" inside and outside self. These include remaining open to the expected and the unexpected, approaching learning obliquely by focussing on the ground rather than figure, and developing an awareness of proper timing of the process and events.

Although Denis's study contributes to the understanding of the intrapersonal aspects of the process from the vantage point of the learner, Gwyn Griffith is investigating the interpersonal dynamics of inquiry. People participating in Griffith's study[24] are graduates of the Centre for Christian Studies in Toronto, most of whom are commissioned ministers in educational ministries who are attempting to evolve a collaborative relationship with people in learning groups. Griffith's work focuses on the question of authority modes in relation to the presence of collaboration in learning. The importance and qualities of defence-reducing environments in promoting collaboration in learning have been reflected in psychoeducational literature for some time. Griffith's study and others like it will provide better understanding of the relationship between the social structures of the learner's environment and the occurrence of collaborative insight occasions. One of the very exciting research possibilities in this area is based on the learner's experience *as well as* systematic observation of the environment. Through such an approach it may be possible to establish patterns of relations of the learning process to the processes of group development,[25] organizational or community change.

The final social communication event of this learning process formulation comes at the close of the convergence phase. The sense of completeness and "transportability" of the learning to other settings is provided by an occasion during which the learner shares the discovery with and finds acknowledgement from significant others. At this point, it is the discovery that is being affirmed and validated, the novel perspective, rather than the learner him/herself. Again, some people appear particularly adept in representing this wider intelligibility. Are they different from the people significant to the learner earlier in the sequence? Is there a pattern of their relation to the learning theme in the perception of the learner? Are there different modes of sharing a discovery (such as verbalized, written or demonstrated) that are especially important in giving a sense of completeness to the learning? More detailed attention to this aspect of the learner's experience is necessary for a better understanding of the importance of social communication at this point in learning.

Conclusion

> We must introduce the second person as a necessary correlative of the first and do our thinking not from the standpoint of the "I" alone, but from the standpoint of "You and I."[26]

Living and working with vitality and effectiveness demand constant reorientations in thinking and acting. The capacity to do so may only be as great as the capability to relate to others and to understand how those relationships interweave with learning.

NOTES

1.   Gregory Bateson, *Steps to an Ecology of Mind* (New York: Ballantine Books), pp. 282-283.
2.   Charles Hampden-Turner, *Radical Man: The Process of Psycho-Social Development* (Garden City, New York: Doubleday/Anchor Books, 1971).
3.   A discussion of the existential-phenomenological and hermeneutical assumptions which pertain to this study can be found in Taylor, "Adult Learning in an Emergent Group: Toward a Theory of Learning from the Learner's Perspective" (PhD dissertation, University of Toronto, 1979), pp. 13-90.

4.   The researcher did not begin the study with a conscious preconception of the process. Therefore, the interviews in this study were open-ended. People were asked to describe as much as possible of what they were thinking, doing and experiencing in relation to the setting which served as the context for the study.

5.   Roger Gould, *Transformations: Growth and Change in Adult Life* (New York: Simon & Schuster, 1959), p. 34.

6.   Ibid., pp. 62-63.

7.   Paulo Freire, *Education for Critical Consciousness* (New York: Seabury Press, 1973), p. 44.

8.   Jack Mezirow, "Perspective Transformation: Toward a Critical Theory of Adult Education," a public lecture at the University of Northern Illinois, sponsored by the Department of Leadership and Policy Studies, September 27, 1979, p. 2.

9.   Ibid.

10.   Edgar Schein and Warren Bennis, *Personal and Organizational Change Through Group Methods* (New York: John Wiley, 1965), pp. 275-276.

11.   Herbert Thelen, *Education and the Human Quest* (New York: Harper & Row), p. 85.

12.   Virginia Griffin, *Macro Processes* (Toronto: Ontario Institute for Studies in Education, 1975) (mimeo).

13.   Brewster Ghiselin, ed., *The Creative Process* (New York: Mentor Books, 1964), p. 14.

14.   Ibid., p. 26.

15.   Ibid., p. 25.

16.   Ibid., p. 30.

17.   William Gordon, *Synectics: The Development of Creative Capacity* (New York: Harper, 1961), p. 10.

18.   Ibid.

19.   Morris Stein, "Creativity as an Intra- and Interpersonal Process," in *A Source Book for Creative Thinking*, edited by S. Parnes and H. Harding (New York: Scribner, 1962), p. 90.

20.   Kass's study entitled "The Apology Stance in the Learning Process," is itself a dissertation study in the Department of Adult Education at the Ontario Institute for Studies in Education, Toronto.

21.   Gordon, *Syntectics,* p. 10.

22.   Paulo Freire, *Pedagogy of the Oppressed* (New York: Seabury Press, 1970), p. 69.

23.   Margaret Denis, "Toward the Development of a Theory of Intuitive Learning in Adults Based on a Descriptive Analysis" (EdD dissertation, University of Toronto, 1979).

24.   This is a dissertation study in progress at the Ontario Institute for Studies in Education, Department of Adult Education. The study is titled, "Images of Interdependence."

25.   An interesting parallel in the structure of the change process can be drawn between phases of the change process described in this paper and group development phases. For a comparison of Bruce Tuckman's theory of group development with this conceptual representation of perspective change, see Taylor's "Adult Learning in an Emergent Learning Group," pp. 347-349.

26.   John Macmurray, *Persons in Relation* (London: Faber & Faber, 1961), p. 38.

Chapter 8

PEACESAT—A Classic Wolf in Sheep's Clothing: Evaluating Interactive Technology in Education and Culture

Christopher M. Plant

Le but de cet article est de démontrer que l'évaluation réelle des technologies de communication interactive ne doit pas être entreprise à partir de critères économiques et techniques, mais plutôt en mettant l'accent sur les facteurs sociaux, politiques et culturels, de même que sur l'usage que font des systèmes, les populations pour lesquelles ceux-ci sont dits avoir été conçus. Une étude du projet PEACESAT (Pacific Education and Communication Experiments by Satellite), effectuée par l'auteur (Plant, 1980) servira ici d'illustration à ces propos.

Contrairement à la prétendue fonction sociale de PEACESAT et à ses objectifs de développement, son histoire révèle qu'au moment de décider de sa mise en place, les hautes instances de Washington justifiaient le projet comme allant servir à la défense des Etats-Unis dans le Pacifique et en Asie. Quant à la structure institutionnelle de PEACESAT, elle s'est avérée hiérarchisée, et hautement centralisée à Honolulu. Toutes les fonctions clés sont remplies par des caucasiens et exercées depuis les stations-métropoles (extérieures aux îles du Pacifique), tandis que les Insulaires sont exclus des organes décisionnels. Il est arrivé qu'on censure des sujets d'intérêt particulier aux Insulaires (tels les essais nucléaires en Polynésie); les directeurs des stations-métropoles et les participants caucasiens se sont alors comportés de façon paternaliste et sans considération à l'égard des habitants des îles. Une grande proportion du financement de base des bureaux de PEACESAT à Hawaii (estimé à 175,000 dollars distribué sur 5 ans, en 1975) provenait de l'Etat de Hawaii dont l'orientation militaire aura poussé PEACESAT vers plus de conservatisme.

Les résultats de cette étude corroborent des critiques déjà exprimées à l'égard de l'inefficacité, du manque de considération des besoins et des aspirations des populations des îles du Pacifique, de la dominance des métropoles sur les îles et du manque d'auto-évalution de PEACESAT. On en conclut donc qu'en conflit direct avec ses prétentions à se dégager des modèles de communication traditionnels, PEACESAT est en fait un exemple classique de domination du centre industrialisé sur la périphérie des pays moins développés et ce, dans presque tous les aspects de son organisation et de son fonctionnement—exemple classique que l'habit ne fait pas le moine. Par conséquent, l'auteur met l'accent sur la nécessité de considérer les aspects sociaux, culturels et politiques des systèmes de communication existant au Canada, de même que l'évaluation qui en est faite.

Introduction

Despite the so-called passing of the "dominant paradigm," the study of telecommunications and development is still dominated by a focus upon things, not people. Thus, the introduction of interactive technologies which make possible multi-directional, decentralized communication has been accompanied primarily by technical and economic evaluations of their performance. The effective use made of these new systems by people in rural or remote areas, especially in the long-term, has been paid only scant attention. Yet it is precisely the social, political and cultural factors—the factors that instigated technological change in the first place—that determine how a technical system is used.

The traditional focus upon things, at the expense of people has, in fact, changed very little. The mere existence of interactive technologies is not necessarily a significant contribution to rural development, to greater participation in the decision-making processes, or to equality of economic opportunity.

As an illustration of this mis-direction of focus, this paper summarizes the results of a historical and empirical study of the PEACESAT project undertaken in 1979.[1]

Background To the PEACESAT Project

PEACESAT is the longest-running experiment in the use of satellite-mediated, interactive communications technology. An acronym for Pan-Pacific Educational and Communication Experiments by Satellite, it was started at the University of Hawaii in 1971, where it was first used to link two island campuses of the University of Hawaii. Shortly afterwards, Wellington Polytechnic, in New Zealand, joined the system, making it into an international experiment. The University of the South Pacific (USP), based at Suva in Fiji, was the first Pacific Island location to join PEACESAT, seeing its usefulness primarily as a way of connecting the main Fiji campus with its extension centres scattered over the Pacific. Since then it has expanded to connect some 17 different locations in the Pacific Islands and Pacific Rim by means of a primarily audio-conference link, operating between 20 and 30 hours per week (see Figure 8-1 for map of PEACESAT ground stations).[2]

Figure 8-1   Map Showing ATS-1 Coverage and PEACESAT Terminals

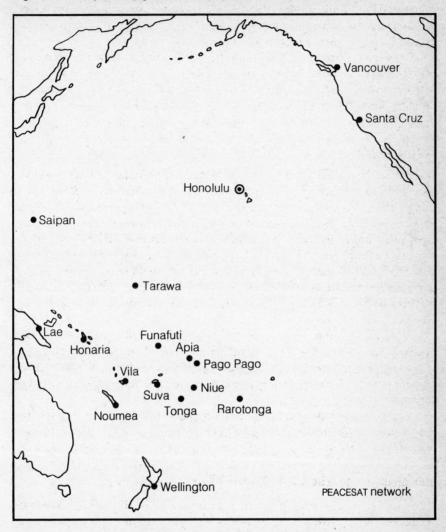

Source: PEACESAT SFU, compiled from documents from PEACESAT headquarters, Honolulu.

    Canada's entry into PEACESAT was initiated in 1975–1976 by two faculty members at Simon Fraser University's Department of Communication: Professors Pat Hindley and Gail Martin. Testing of the Vancouver station began in summer 1978. Participation in the network continued for six months until spring 1979, when the lack of funds and support forced it to close down.

    Transmissions via PEACESAT are termed "exchanges." Almost any topic can be scheduled as an exchange, provided that at least one other ground station (or "terminal") agrees to participate. Exchanges have covered a wide range of subject matter ranging from formal classes in accountancy to exchanges on oral traditions, ocean management and Boys Brigade leadership. The network has also been used for medical purposes, sometimes extensively, as in the case of occasional epidemics in the islands.

Using the ATS-1 satellite, the principal feature of the PEACESAT project has been the low cost of ground station equipment (stations have been constructed for as little as $800 U.S.) and the relative ease of operation and maintenance. The main transceiver unit at most ground stations is a taxicab unit operating on a single channel. Many stations use the push-button microphone for transmitting. The most complicated operating feature is the adjustment of the yagi antennae to track the slight shifts of position of the satellite. Most technical problems with the system have been due to a combination of inadequate tracking capability and insufficient transmission power. Corrosion of electrical equipment at sites located near the sea also has been a problem.

By virtue of its low cost, its capacity to span vast distances and its interactive nature, the PEACESAT Project has defined itself as an alternative, a departure from traditional telecommunication system models, that is specifically oriented towards the delivery of health, education and community services in less-developed areas.

Objectives of the Study

Having spent five years living and working in the South Pacific and having been employed as research assistant and acting terminal manager for Canada's PEACESAT ground station located on Simon Fraser University's campus, I suspected, in working with the system, that in many respects PEACESAT was falling far short of its stated objectives.

Consequently, the objectives of the study were: first, to examine the history and institutional structure of PEACESAT, and, second, to provide an empirical analysis of PEACESAT's actual performance in order to determine the predominant uses and users of the PEACESAT system and the relationships between them, with special reference to the use of the system by Pacific Island people.

Historical and Institutional Analysis of Project

In piecing together the history of PEACESAT from initial discussions at the University of Hawaii in 1969 to the present, it first became evident there was a serious contradiction between the project's public image and the rationale by which authorization and funds to conduct the experiment were sought. Contrary to PEACESAT's stated social service and development objectives, PEACESAT was described to NASA (the U.S. National Aeronautics and Space Administration) by Dr. John Bystrom, founder of the project, as being able to "contribute favourably to the reputation of the United States as an ad-

ministrator" in the Trust Territory of the Pacific Islands, and as serving "the
security of the free world" through tying the United States closer to its Asian
and Pacific neighbours.[3] American defence interests to be served by the increased communication capacity provided via PEACESAT are similarly
described in PEACESAT reports to NASA in 1971 and 1973.

Furthermore, Dr. Bystrom's objective from the start was to use
PEACESAT as a stepping stone to a global PEACESAT-like system which he
has termed the Extended Experiment—occasionally referred to as
WORLDSAT. With the launch of one of two additional satellites, the plan
was to extend coverage to most of Asia, at least as far as Tehran. Once more,
the contribution of the system to American foreign policy objectives is explicitly stated in a non-public document: "The geographical area covered in
the Extended Experiment is the most important in the world from the standpoint of defence." PEACESAT, therefore, could contribute to "social stability" in the area.[4]

These two fundamental constraints on PEACESAT's potential—its
orientation towards American defence interests and the U.S. drive to extend
it—constitute what, to most of the public, has been a hidden agenda held by
PEACESAT headquarters in Honolulu. Not surprisingly, this agenda has
significantly influenced other aspects of PEACESAT's institutional development.

The project's organizational structure, for example, is hierarchical,
paramount control being vested in Honolulu (see Figure 8-2). Management
meetings involving terminal managers from all locations have been conducted
irregularly over the system and have been dominated by the Honolulu and
Wellington (New Zealand) ground stations. The scheduling function has been
undertaken throughout by these same metropolitan terminals. (Metropolitan
terminals are categorized as those in the developed countries: primarily the
Honolulu, Wellington, University of California-Santa Cruz and Vancouver
terminals.) The PEACESAT Consortium Council was founded in 1973 to ad-
vise the PEACESAT project, to promote joint experiments and to act as the
major planning body for the Extended Experiment. Significantly, the council
possesses only token Pacific Islander representation, no islanders being
represented on its executive board. Consequently, most decisions affecting
PEACESAT—whether they be of a day-to-day, operational nature or those
affecting overall policy directions—have been made by non-islanders (Caucasians from metropolitan locations).

An illustration of the centralized, metropolitan control exercised within
PEACESAT is the discussion of nuclear-testing over the system by Pacific
Islanders and others in 1972. Following this discussion, which focused on
France's nuclear-testing in Polynesia, an all-Caucasian committee in
Honolulu banned all participants in the discussion from further use of
PEACESAT, and drew up "content guidelines" to prevent similar discussions
in the future. No Pacific Islanders were involved in the establishment of these

Figure 8-2   PEACESAT Organisation Chart

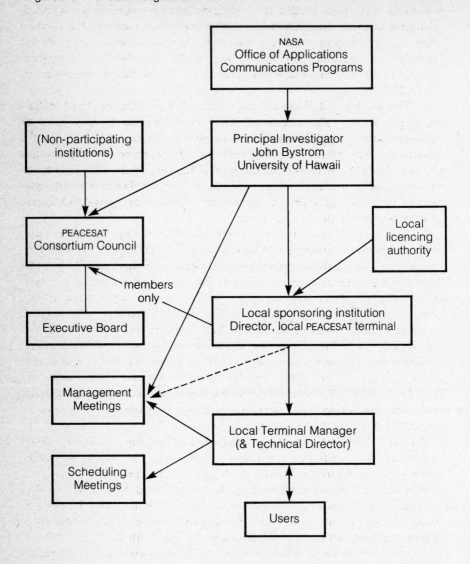

guidelines.[5] In 1979, an attempt by the Student Christian Movement in New Zealand and Hawaii to again discuss nuclear issues in the Pacific—a continuing concern of Island people—was disallowed by the Honolulu and Wellington terminal managers (exchange dated February 5, 1979).

The censorship of discussion over PEACESAT also is accompanied by a perceived insensitivity of terminal managers and some participants from the metropolitan terminals towards Pacific Islanders' needs and aspirations.[6] Caucasians often have assumed what is seen to be a patronizing attitude and doubtless offended Pacific Islanders, discouraging their further participation. In addition, the long, erudite and poorly chaired discussions between Caucasians demonstrate that PEACESAT caters primarily to metropolitan, rather than to Pacific Island, concerns. Effectively, this lack of sensitivity to Pacific Islanders and the particular development needs of the Pacific on the part of PEACESAT's key organizers has provided a third major constraint on PEACESAT.

The provision of financial support also has constrained PEACESAT's development possibilities. Although local terminals must, in most cases, be sponsored by a local institution (a notable exception is Saipan, in the American Trust Territory of the Pacific Islands, which received its terminal free of charge from Honolulu) the critical funding of the Honolulu headquarters has consistently been provided by the state of Hawaii. In 1975, costs of the entire system over five years were estimated at $350,000 US, and Hawaii provided half of this amount.[7]

In an indirect way, therefore, orientation of Hawaii's government to promoting American influence will have influenced PEACESAT's development in a conservative manner. Other financial sponsorship appears to have had a similar effect. For instance, the International Planned Parenthood Federation (IPPF) funded a conference of terminal managers in 1978. In early 1979, the situation arose where, on the same day, a natural family planning group and IPPF (both groups originating in New Zealand) each wanted to initiate an exchange series to include Pacific Island locations. The IPPF was successful at the expense of the other group. This leaves the criteria being used in determining which exchanges get scheduled open to question. Moreover, the attitude of the IPPF representative at the first of the exchanges was offensive to observers, and led to a formal complaint being made by Suva's terminal manager (exchange dated February 7, 1979).

Overall, PEACESAT has been constrained by its American foreign policy orientation, its long-term aim to expand into a world-wide system, and by the perceived insensitivity towards Pacific Islanders of key people in the project.

Not surprisingly, these constraints have influenced PEACESAT's effectiveness. This is demonstrated institutionally in PEACESAT's relations with two other institutions of major importance in the Pacific: the University of the South Pacific (USP) and Fiji's Post and Telegraphs authority. The USP's involvement with the system has been critical to its survival and development since the university has, in all, sponsored eight of the ground stations used for both the USP and PEACESAT networks. In many of these cases, participation in PEACESAT would have been impossible without the financial support of the university. In fact, six of the ground stations participate only marginally in PEACESAT, demonstrating that PEACESAT's claim to a 17-station network can be made only on the basis of the USP's commitment to satellite communication.

In 1977, three years after the USP had been granted permission to operate its own dedicated network, the Honolulu headquarters attempted to insist that stations operated by USP file their license particulars with Honolulu or be suspended from the experiment. The USP refused and as a result the operations of Honiara, Apia and Tarawa ground stations were terminated. Far from being just a bureaucratic conflict, it was a power struggle between PEACESAT and the USP over the allegiance of island stations.

The relationship between PEACESAT and Fiji's Post and Telegraphs authority (P & T) was equally bad. Prevented by the terms of its agreement with Cable & Wireless Ltd. from operating internationally in anything other than an experimental mode, Fiji's P & T duly insisted that PEACESAT exchanges in which Fiji participated be strictly experimental and educational. In the eyes of the P & T, PEACESAT repeatedly failed to co-operate in this respect, using the system more as a service, for traffic that was not experimental and that should have been carried by existing commercial services.

The alienation of these two key institutions is an occurrence which makes no sense if the authentic development of the Pacific Islands was the raison d'etre of the PEACESAT project.

In the analysis of PEACESAT's performance, two broad types of quantitative study were undertaken: an analysis of PEACESAT exchange data and a network flow analysis of the PEACESAT system.

The major objectives of the exchange data analysis were to determine the predominant categories of exchange on the system, and the predominant locations and participants, including their sex and ethnicity (Caucasian, Pacific Islander and other).[8]

The network flow analysis was concerned to measure the flow of information between and among the terminals in an attempt to determine whether any distinct relationships existed between them, especially between metropolitan and Pacific Island terminals.

The key results of the exchange data analysis can be summarized as follows:

(1) In the overall use of PEACESAT by location, metropolitan locations dominated Pacific Island locations by 64.3 per cent to 35.7 per cent of the total time, or a ratio of almost 2:1.

(2) In the amount of time-on-air used, Caucasian participants dominated Pacific Island participants by 77.8 per cent to 18.6 per cent, or a ratio of 4:1.

(3) In the initiation of exchanges, metropolitan terminals dominated Pacific Island terminals by 76.4 per cent to 23.6 per cent, or a ratio of 3.2:1. Furthermore, only 1.8 per cent of all exchanges were initiated by Pacific Island people.

(4) In the chairing of exchanges, metropolitan terminals dominated Pacific Island terminals by 82.3 per cent to 17.7 per cent, or a ratio of 4.6:1. Caucasians accounted for 91.9 per cent of all chairpersons, a ratio of metropolitan to Pacific Island dominance of 11.3:1.

(5) In regard to PEACESAT staff time-on-air, Caucasian staff dominated Pacific Island staff at the lowest with a 2.5:1 ratio, and at the highest a ratio of 5.4:1.[9]

Of the network flow analysis, the first analysis (A) measured whether a participant was: (a) asking a question, requesting information or soliciting advice (recorded as a "Q" score), or (b) providing a response, supplying information, or giving advice (recorded as an "R" score). The analysis revealed that:

(1) In regard to overall Q and R activity on the system, metropolitan terminals dominated Pacific Island terminals by 64.9 per cent to 35.1 per cent, or a ratio of 1.8:1.

(2) Regarding overall R scores, metropolitan terminals dominated Pacific Island terminals in a ratio of approximately 1.8:1 indicating a dominant flow of information from metropolitan to Pacific Island locations.

(3) Regarding overall Q scores, metropolitan dominance over Pacific Island terminals was in a ratio of 2.8:1 suggesting a predominantly passive role for the Pacific Islands, and a flow of information from Pacific Island terminals to metropolitan terminals elicited by dominant questioning activity on the part of metropolitan terminals.

Network flow analysis (B) was to ascertain the number of connections made between and among the terminals by analyzing 205 informal message periods of 12 minutes or more, amounting to almost 41 hours of air-time. Message periods occur during the first 15 to 25 minutes of each two to three hour block of exchanges as ground stations "sign on" to the system. This time is used by those stations wanting to schedule exchanges or pass a message to another station. From this study, it was evident that:

(1) In informal networking on PEACESAT, metropolitan terminals dominated Pacific Island terminals by 84.9 per cent to 15.1 per cent, or a ratio of 5.6:1. In addition, the number of messages received by Pacific Island terminals exceeded those received by metropolitan terminals by 57.6 per cent to 42.4 per cent, or a ratio of 1.4:1.

(2) The following hierarchy of networks on the system was discernible: (a) from metropolitan to Pacific Island terminals (54.1 per cent of the connections); (b) from metropolitan to metropolitan terminals (30.7 per cent of the connections); (c) from Pacific Island to metropolitan terminals (11.7 per cent of the connections); (d) from Pacific Island to Pacific Island terminals (3.4 per cent of the connections—a marginal network).[10]

Overall, the position of Pacific Island terminals relative to metropolitan terminals can at best be said to be weak, despite Pacific Island terminals outnumbering metropolitan terminals 2:1. The figure for the amount of time on air used is a crucial one, and this shows a 4:1 ratio of Caucasian dominance over Pacific Islanders. What is more disturbing is the role seen to be played by Pacific Islanders in the decision-making and administrative aspects of the system. Pacific Islanders are little more than marginal in the initiation and chairing of exchanges and the amount of time used on air by PEACESAT staff.

The results of the network flow analyses indicate a largely passive role for Pacific Island terminals receiving information from metropolitan locations. Furthermore, the marginality of Pacific Island terminals is corroborated by the insignificant networking between Pacific Island locations, and the small amount of networking from Pacific Island to metropolitan locations.

These trends are filled out by the more fine-grained results. The Honolulu and Wellington, New Zealand, terminals are overwhelmingly important, not only among the metropolitan terminals but within the system as a whole. Honolulu and Wellington combined used 54.3 per cent of all air time, initiated 67.3 per cent of the exchanges, chaired 75 per cent of exchanges and accounted for 80.5 per cent of all messages transmitted in network flow analysis.

Among participants, American nationals occupied over 40 per cent of all time on air, American males alone accounting for over 30 per cent of all time on air. The sex breakdown indicated an approximate 2:1 ratio of males over females overall, a figure repeated in the Caucasian population but not in the Pacific Islander population where the sex ratio was more balanced.

Regarding exchange categories, as specified by the University of California and used by PEACESAT, and participation within them, categories 2, 4 and 8 (decision-making conference, community development service and administrative) were overwhelmingly more important than others, making up 26.9 per cent, 24.4 per cent and 20.5 per cent respectively of the total time on air—a combined total of 71.8 per cent. Significantly, categories 2 and 4 are the least well-defined, and category 4, and category 2 to a large extent, are not concerned with topics of a more explicitly development-oriented nature.

Those categories of an overtly educational or medical value (categories 1, 3, 5 and 6: classroom instruction, professional and in-service training, research support and professional consultation) made up 20 per cent of the total time. This is low, especially when some exchanges possessed only marginal educational or medical importance. Furthermore, the role of Pacific Islanders in the latter categories is small (30 per cent of the total time on air, with only 2 per cent in category 5 and nil in category 6) while, in comparison, the figures for American nationals in the same categories are exceptionally high. American nationals occupying 86 per cent of the time in category 6, 78.8 per cent in category 5, 63.7 per cent in category 1 and 14.2 per cent in category 3.

Of particular significance is the high figure for category 8—administrative exchanges—which took 20.5 per cent of the total time. When broken down further, Caucasians made up 90 per cent of those undertaking administrative exchanges, 43.7 per cent being American nationals. This reaffirms the marginal role of Pacific Islanders in the decision-making functions of PEACESAT.

Although it is accepted that there are limitations to these analyses, mainly arising from the relatively small size of the sample and the difficulty of adequately specifying the categories of exchange, the results are significant. And they are supported by the results from a further analysis of exchanges from April 1974 undertaken in order to ensure that the main study was a representative sample.

Conclusion

Relatively little has been written about PEACESAT, and no systematic evaluations of the experiment have been undertaken. Outside of the Pacific region, PEACESAT is known about either through articles authored by those closely associated with the project, or from others who have derived their information entirely from these sources. Such information is most often descriptive and superficial in character: opinions concerning the value of PEACESAT are based on almost no empirical data. The empirical evidence that does exist is mainly technical, concerning voice levels, the reliability of the system under different weather conditions and so forth.

Regarding PEACESAT's asserted social value, there exists only anecdotal evidence concerning uses and users of the system. Examples are the use of PEACESAT by medical authorities trying to control epidemics of cholera and dengue fever in the Islands, and the real-time interviewing of a Pacific prime minister on the process of his islands' attainment of self-government. Accounts of such experiments are impressive. At the same time, they clearly are not representative.

Some significant exceptions exist to this main body of literature on PEACESAT. Both the University of the South Pacific and the University of California at Santa Cruz have complained of inefficient operating procedures, of insensitivity towards the Pacific Islanders on the part of metropolitan users, and a consequent domination of Pacific Island terminals by metropolitan terminals.[11] The first director of the Tongan terminal said: "Is PEACESAT to help big places to pontificate and dominate over smaller places? Sometimes, alas, the answer is yes" (Blundell, 1976). And the Director of the Institute of Pacific Studies at USP, after pioneering the teaching of a land tenure course in PEACESAT's early days, concludes that PEACESAT has developed into "just a de facto piece of American imperialism" (Letter from Professor R. G. Crocombe, Director, Institute of Pacific Studies, USP, to the author, September 25, 1978). UCSC entered into PEACESAT in 1977. By 1979, the director of the UCSC ground station who was initially highly enthusiastic about the university's participation in the network, commented that:

More time appears to be spent in scheduling, forward scheduling, passing messages and conducting exclusive point-to-point conferences than ever previously. First rate exchanges at any level have become fewer and fewer.
> Letter from Bryan Farrel, Director,
> Centre for South Pacific Studies, UCSC,
> to Stuart Kingan, President, PEACESAT
> Consortium Council, January 23, 1979.

PEACESAT's unclear objectives and insufficient evaluation of its own performance have also been criticized by terminal directors and NASA-contracted evaluators. One such evaluation of PEACESAT, undertaken for NASA, points out the inadequate self-evaluation task performed by the project, and speculates on the reason for this:

> Is PEACESAT an experiment, testing new communication satellite applications or frameworks, or is PEACESAT an operational service system disinterested in experimental guidelines and intent upon expansion? The Report and Evaluation material would seem to indicate the latter.
> Delbert Smith, *PEACESAT Evaluation*,
> Wisconsin: no publisher, n.d., p. 3.

The results of this study clearly support the above criticisms. Furthermore, the most striking result is that, in direct contrast to PEACESAT project claims that it represents a departure from traditional telecommunication models, PEACESAT can be seen as a classic example of the domination of the industrialized core over the less-developed periphery in almost every aspect of its organization and performance.[12]

That PEACESAT has been allowed to continue for so long without sufficient evaluation not only calls into question the extent to which PEACESAT can legitimately be described as "an experiment," but is also indicative that it has survived precisely because it has fitted in so well with the dominant values, organizational systems and policy directions of the United States.

The fact that PEACESAT has not lived up to its own rhetoric of decentralization and equality of interaction vividly illustrates that the effectiveness of a technology is primarily dependent upon its political context and its human, institutional component. PEACESAT, to its discredit, has failed to pay attention to the latter, despite every opportunity, and deserves to be labelled a wolf in sheep's clothing.

For communications in Canada, important lessons can be drawn from the PEACESAT experience. The first is that it is not sufficient to design new technological configurations, nor even to construct and operate them. It is the *quality* of communication that counts, or, as USP's Director of Extension Services said apropos PEACESAT:

> It is not enough to claim success because people talked; it is much more important to assess how and why and to what purpose.
> Peter McMechan, *PEACESAT Project*
> *Objectives: A USP Statement to the*
> *Consortium*, Suva: June 10, 1977

In efforts to provide better communications for northern, rural and native communities in Canada, the crucial question must be whether the new communication system is adapted to the particular social, cultural and political needs of the community in question. It must be determined if, in its day-to-day operations, it fosters the ability of such communities to be self-determining or, if it contributes to the diminishing of power in local hands. Significantly, the PEACESAT study demonstrates that this concern is just as relevant to interactive networks as to more traditional, one-way systems. In fact, the PEACESAT experience indicates the possibilities of producing exactly the opposite effect from that intended with communication systems that are technically and/or economically more "appropriate" than traditional ones. It is the *human* component of a communication system that must be the chief focus of attention.

This study also emphasizes that communication research must be firmly grounded in an interdisciplinary methodology. No single dimension of this analysis of PEACESAT, its history, political economy, institutional structure or operational record, would have given as full an understanding of the project as is obtained from the multi-dimensional approach. Such an approach gives great freedom to use a wide range of quantitative and qualitative methods in communications research. But that freedom is also a responsibility for the emerging discipline of communication studies. In attempting to describe the human condition more completely than the established and compartmentalized disciplines, adherents of communication studies must be flexible and wide-ranging in the methodologies used to approach the subject matter.

NOTES

1.   Christopher M. Plant, *PEACESAT and Development in the Pacific Islands* (MA Thesis, Department of Communication, Simon Fraser University, 1979).
2.   Also operating in the Pacific region are two additional ATS-1 experiments: the University of the South Pacific network, and the Department of the Interior Special Project in the Trust Territory of the Pacific Islands. My study was limited to an analysis of PEACESAT, the original experiment from which these others developed.
3.   *Pan Pacific Education and Communication Experiments by Satellite,* Request and proposal to NASA from the University of Hawaii as agent for the State of Hawaii (Honolulu: University of Hawaii, n.d., but known to be December 1970), p. 12.
4.   *PEACESAT Extended Experiment Data Sheet* (no author, publisher or date specified) and *Attachment B: The Communication Satellite Component* (no author or publisher specified, dated January 15, 1976).
5.   *PEACESAT Project Social Applications: Early Uses of International Two-way Communications by Satellite for Social Development, Report Two* (Honolulu: PEACESAT Project, 1975), pp. 66-69.
6.   Margaret Blundell, "Satellite Conferences in the Pacific Islands," *Pacific Perspective,* Vol. 5, No. 1, 1976.
7.   "PEACESAT eyes stronger 'bird,' " *Honolulu Advertiser,* December 15, 1975, p. A-3.

8. Eight categories of exchange were specified, as used by the PEACESAT system itself, and documented in Dianne Reid Ross, *Program Evaluation of the Santa Cruz PEACESAT Terminal for the period September 1, 1976 through June 30, 1977* (Santa Cruz: Center for South Pacific Studies, UCSC, October 1977), pp. 3-5:

Category 1: Classroom Instruction—including enrichment activities and both credit and non-credit courses to elementary, secondary or tertiary students;

Category 2: Decision-making Conferences—meetings involving specialists and/or administrators in the discussion of topics related to the solution of problems and the implementation of programs;

Category 3: Professional and In-service Training—exchanges enabling trained personnel to receive continuing education and to keep up with changing developments in their specialized fields;

Category 4: Community Development Service—exchanges which bring together widely separated local groups interested in improving their social environment;

Category 5: Research Support—exchanges facilitating the dissemination of discoveries and new techniques among colleagues in a rapid manner;

Category 6: Professional Consultation—exchanges assisting medical specialists in urban centres and health personnel in remote areas to exchange data on epidemics, patient referrals, and diagnostic consulting, etc.;

Category 7: Technical Development—experiments developing different technical aspects of the system, such as facsimile, teletype, and slow-scan television;

Category 8: Administrative—exchanges conducted largely by PEACESAT personnel for the administration of the PEACESAT system, such as scheduling, managment and other meetings.

9. Three different methods of calculating PEACESAT staff time-on-air were employed, providing this range of ratios.

10. The probability score for these results, using the Chi Square method, was 0.14.

11. From the USP, see: Margaret Blundell, "Satellite Conferences in the Pacific Islands," *Pacific Perspective*, Vol. 5, No. 1, 1976; Letter from James A. Maraj, Vice-Chancellor, USP, to Richard J. H. Barnes, Director, International Planning and Programs, Office of International Affairs, NASA, September 26, 1977; Peter McMechan, *PEACESAT Project Objectives: A USP Statement to the Consortium* (Suva: USP, June 10, 1977). From the UCSC, see: No author, *PEACESAT: Observations, Policy Concerns* (Santa Cruz: Center for South Pacific Studies, October 1977); and Letter from Bryan Farrell, Director, Center for South Pacific Studies, UCSC, to Stuart Kingan, President, PEACESAT Consortium Council, January 23, 1979.

12. See unpublished evaluations by: Frank W. Norwood, *ATS Experiment Proposal* (Washington, undated); and Delbert D. Smith, *PEACESAT Evaluation* (Wisconsin, undated).

Chapitre 9

Technologie de communication: démocratisation et régionalisation

Gaétan Tremblay

This work originates from an evaluation research of more than 300 hours of satellite communication experiences realized at the University of Quebec from October 1976 to February 1977.

Since the early 1960s, democratization and regionalization are two major characteristics of ideological discourse on Quebec society. The world of education is no exception. The University of Quebec—a state university—with its campus network designed for general accessibility to university services within all of Quebec, constitutes a specific area for an important study of these questions.

These two goals of democratization and regionalization are discussed from the perspective of recent developments in the technology of communication, developments which can modify the problem, the costs and the challenges in the communication systems involved.

After a brief summary of the major characteristics of interactive technology, this paper discusses three ways to state the problem of technological development: the determinist hypothesis, the voluntaristic hypothesis and the pragmatic hypothesis. *A discussion and application of the pragmatic model follows, based on a "network-structure" distinction. The major structural determinants, which affect the use of technology for democratization and regionalization, are identified.*

Je voudrais, au cours de cet exposé, reprendre cette double problématique de démocratisation et de régionalisation en rapport avec le développement de récentes technologies de communication, qui peuvent en modifier les termes, les coûts et les enjeux.[1]

Les moyens de transmission nouvellement mis au point—satellites, câbles coaxiaux à large bande, fibres optiques—la constitution d'imposantes banques de données, l'établissement de réseaux d'ordinateurs, la mise en place de réseaux téléphoniques ou vidéo, enfin bref, le développement accéléré et la mise en place d'une technologie de communication de type interactif—qu'on peut opposer à la technologie de diffusion mass-médiatique—permettent-ils d'entrevoir de nouvelles possibilités de démocratisation et de régionalisation? et à quelles conditions?

Les réflexions que je vous livre ici originent d'une recherche d'évaluation de près de 300 heures d'expériences de communication par satellite, réalisées dans le cadre du Réseau Omnibus sur satellite Hermès d'octobre '76 à février '77.[2] Elles ont également été stimulées par la mise en place du Réseau vidéo de l'Université du Québec et par des recherches en cours sur l'utilisation de l'ordinateur à des fins d'enseignement universitaire.

Les douze expériences de communication par satellite qui ont été réalisées par les diverses constituantes de l'Université du Québec[3] poursuivaient chacune des objectifs spécifiques (éducatifs, scientifiques, administratifs) mais se situaient toutes dans le cadre d'expérimentation d'un Réseau Omnibus, coordonné par le siège social de l'université qui s'était donné les buts suivants:

1. "Favoriser l'innovation en matière d'enseignement, de recherche et de gestion, afin de répondre à des besoins nouveaux (décentralisation des ressources universitaires, individualisation de l'enseignement supérieur) et à des contraintes nouvelles (limitation des ressources financières, physiques et humaines; développement du savoir; création de nouveaux programmes, etc.)

2. Déterminer le type de réseau le mieux adapté aux besoins d'une université à campus multiples et en particulier, à la vocation particulière de l'Université du Québec.

3. Mesurer l'impact de la technologie des satellites de communication sur le processus d'apprentissage au niveau universitaire.

4. Stimuler le développement des ressources techniques et le perfectionnement des ressources humaines du secteur communication de l'Université du Québec."[4]

Après avoir présenté sommairement les principales caractéristiques de la technologie de type interactif, je discuterai trois façons de poser le problème du développement technologique: l'hypothèse déterministe, l'hypothèse velléitaire et l'hypothèse pragmatique. J'essaierai d'élaborer par la suite un modèle d'analyse pragmatique fondé sur la distinction réseau-structure et identifiant les principaux déterminants structurels et culturels susceptibles d'influencer l'utilisation de la technologie dans le sens de la centralisation ou de la régionalisation.

La technologie de type interactif

Jusqu'à tout récemment, les développements les plus spectaculaires de la technologie de communication ont été réalisés dans le domaine des media de diffusion. De la transmission de la matière écrite, on est passé à la transmission de la parole, que l'on a accompagnée de l'image, puis de la couleur. . . . Durant tout ce cheminement, un même modèle de communication s'est progressivement imposé: un petit nombre de professionnels s'adressant à la masse des citoyens (tour à tour lecteurs, auditeurs ou téléspectateurs). C'est le modèle de la diffusion.

La fin du XXe siècle voit peu à peu se profiler le début d'une autre ère, où de nouveaux développements technologiques s'accompagnent de l'émergence d'un autre modèle de communication: l'interaction. Bien sûr l'interaction technologiquement médiatisée ne date pas d'aujourd'hui. Le téléphone a été inventé par Alexander Graham Bell en 1876. La lettre, qui a une histoire beaucoup plus ancienne, est un médium permettant l'interaction, même si les délais de réponse sont passablement longs. La radio amateur et le télégraphe sont également plus vieux que certains mass-media. Mais jusqu'à présent, mis à part le téléphone, aucune de ces technologies de communication n'a eu une présence et un impact aussi grands que les mass-media dans la vie quotidienne de tous et chacun. Malgré leur existence, le modèle dominant de la communication techniquement médiatisée a été et reste encore aujourd'hui celui de la diffusion.

Le satellite Hermès marque le début de la deuxième génération des satellites, caractérisés par une plus forte puissance d'émission et des antennes au sol moins gigantesques, moins coûteuses et plus mobiles. La diminution des coûts entraînera probablement une accessibilité plus large à la communication par satellite. La mobilité des antennes permettra, théoriquement du moins, de faire et de défaire les réseaux de communication au gré des besoins exprimés: la malléabilité de l'infrastructure rendra possible une plus grande souplesse dans la structuration des rapports de communication. Et la troisième génération des satellites accentuera encore davantage ces possibilités.

Les utilisations actuelles les plus fréquentes du satellite ne sont guère novatrices. On s'en sert surtout pour franchir des obstacles géographiques autrement difficiles à surmonter et acheminer ainsi dans les régions éloignées les types de communications facilement accessibles en milieu urbain (la télévision et le téléphone). Le modèle dominant étant celui de la diffusion, on utilise un nouveau médium selon les vieux schèmes de la génération précédente. Il faut avouer que les impératifs de rentabilité économique constituent d'importants facteurs de renforcement de cette stratégie d'utilisation.

Sans contester l'utilité du satellite pour la diffusion et la plus grande accessibilité aux services qu'il permet sur l'ensemble d'un vaste territoire, il faut souligner que son originalité comme médium réside fondamentalement dans ses possibilités d'interaction. Avec un satellite comme Hermès, on peut constituer des réseaux entre plusieurs points éloignés, la relation entre chacun de ces points pouvant être bidirectionnelle. Si les techniques de diffusion ont rendu le spectacle accessible dans chaque salon, les techniques de type interactif rendent possibles le travail et le dialogue à distance.

Par rapport aux mass-media, on peut relever deux caractéristiques évidentes de l'interaction techniquement médiatisée: a. il n'y a plus d'un côté un émetteur, et de l'autre, des récepteurs, mais uniquement des interlocuteurs; b. la production des messages n'est plus l'apanage des seuls professionnels de la communication, mais de tous les interlocuteurs potentiels. Les professionnels n'ont qu'un rôle de support technique.

L'utilisation généralisée des technologies de communication de type interactif a de fortes chances de modifier les attitudes de récepteurs passifs auxquelles nous ont habitués les mass-media, de bousculer l'image sociale et le rôle des professionnels de la communication et de transformer profondément nos rapports de travail.

Les quelques expériences réalisées dans le cadre du Réseau Omnibus de l'UQ—en télé-documentation—télé-transmission de données, télé-enseignement, télé-rencontres de travail—ne permettent certes pas de tirer déjà des conclusions sur toutes ces questions. Mais elles ont été suffisamment riches d'enseignement pour faire cheminer certaines problématiques, entre autres celle de l'impact du développement de réseaux interactifs sur la démocratisation et la régionalisation.

Face à l'avènement de nouvelles technologies, plusieurs adoptent un point de vue relativement déterministe. "Le médium, c'est le message," dit l'aphorisme mcluhanien. L'invention et la diffusion d'une technologie, indépendamment des usages qu'on en fait, entraîne automatiquement une série de transformations sociales, culturelles et politiques. Le développement technologique obéit à une sorte de logique interne, celle du progrès scientifique et technique qui permet une emprise de plus en plus grande sur la nature. Ce développement progressiste est inévitable. Il conditionne le devenir collectif et la seule attitude rationnelle pour les individus autant que pour les groupes est de trouver la meilleure forme d'adaptation possible. Cette indépendance de l'objet technique et son caractère contraignant pour la vie sociale s'accentuent au fur et à mesure de ce que Simondon appelle le processus de concrétisation. Si, au stade artisanal, l'objet technique possède une certaine marge d'indétermination et est susceptible de plusieurs usages se conformant à differents besoins sociaux, "au contraire, au niveau industriel, écrit Simondon, l'objet a acquis sa cohérence, et c'est le système des besoins qui est moins cohérent que le système de l'objet: les besoins se moulent sur l'objet technique industriel, qui acquiert ainsi le pouvoir de modeler une civilisation. C'est l'utilisation qui devient un ensemble taillé sur les mesures de l'objet technique. Lorsqu'une fantaisie individuelle réclame une automobile sur mesures, le constructeur ne peut faire mieux que de prendre un moteur de série, un châssis de série, et de modifier extérieurement quelques caractères, en ajoutant des détails décoratifs ou des accessoires raccordés extérieurement à l'automobile comme objet technique essentiel: ce sont les aspects inessentiels qui peuvent être faits sur mesure, parce qu'ils sont contingents."[5]

Cette hypothèse déterministe inspire deux écoles de pensée opposées:

d'une part celle des technocrates optimistes qui voient dans le développement technologique une libération progressive de l'homme, les conditions de l'avènement d'une société opulente et démocratique; et d'autre part celle des humanistes pessimistes qui considèrent toute nouvelle technologie comme aliénante, déshumanisante et qui dénoncent l'instauration accélérée d'une société programmée et robotisée. Certains d'entre eux n'hésitent pas parfois à suggérer le renoncement au progrès technologique, sinon la destruction des machines, pour retrouver les relations humaines d'un passé idéalisé.

En ce qui concerne plus spécifiquement les techniques de communication de type interactif, les pessimistes hypertrophient certains dangers par ailleurs fort réels — de violation de la vie privée, de centralisaton étatique, de dépersonnalisation des rapports humains. Par ailleurs, les chantres technocratiques optimistes proclament les effets bénéfiques qu'entraînent ces techniques de communication: avènement d'une société câblée et informatisée, démocratique et régionalisée. Promesse d'une démocratie directe et instantanée qui évoque trop le "fast food" pour ne pas être suspecte.

Pour ces déterministes optimistes, la société industrielle a jusqu'à présent été caractérisée par un processus de centralisation parce que les technologies de communication existantes ne permettaient qu'une relation univoque du centre vers la périphérie.

Figure 9-1

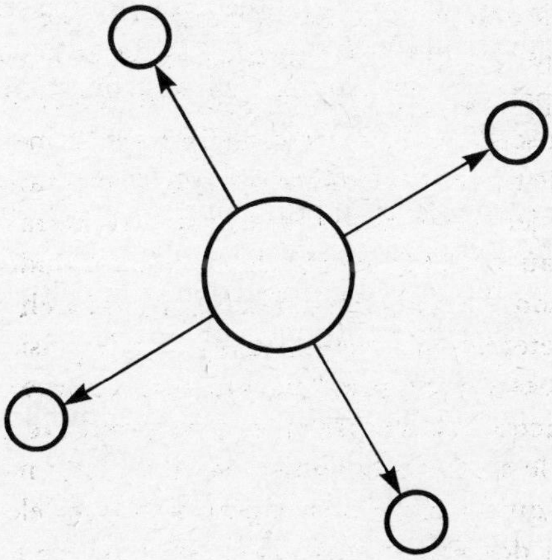

L'installation d'une technologie permettant la bidirectionalité inversera ce mouvement et instaurera nécessairement des échanges qui ne pouvaient avoir lieu auparavant, à cause de contraintes techniques.

Au lieu d'un réseau centralisé, nous accéderons à un réseau décentralisé qui stimulera les échanges interrégionaux, assurant ainsi une plus grande accessibilité aux ressources et stimulant le processus de régionalisation.

Figure 9-2

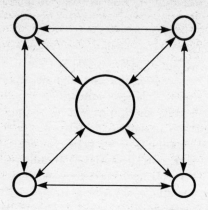

Un tel raisonnement rappelle un peu trop le simplisme d'une certaine idéologie du développement qui prétendait qu'il suffisait d'implanter une industrie lourde dans les pays sous-développés pour les mettre automatiquement sur les rails de la modernisation!

A l'opposé des idéologues de l'hypothèse déterministe, on retrouve les tenants de l'hypothèse velléitaire. Selon ces derniers, toute technologie serait neutre et ses retombées sociales, culturelles et politiques ne dépendraient que de l'usage qu'on veut bien en faire. L'objet technique n'est qu'un outil entre les mains d'un utilisateur qui peut s'en servir pour enfoncer un clou, se taper sur les doigts ou assommer son voisin. Tout est question de la volonté des usagers, de leur motivation, de leur habileté et des objectifs qu'ils poursuivent.

Cette position idéologique postule une coupure entre les conditions matérielles d'existence, la structure et les valeurs sociales, entre l'état des forces productives, les rapports de production et la culture. Elle ne tient pas compte des possibilités et des contraintes objectives qu'implique l'utilisation d'objets techniques spécifiques.

La pensée n'est libre ni des conditions socio-culturelles où elle s'exerce ni des objets qui lui servent de supports ou d'instruments. Au XIXe siecle, on avait tendance à concevoir l'univers en termes de champs de forces et de machines thermodynamiques. Au XXe siecle, on parle davantage de programmes et de systèmes d'information. Ces deux univers conceptuels ne sont pas indépendants de l'état de la technologie à l'epoque considérée.

Si l'hypothèse déterministe peut se rattacher à ce qu'Habermas appelle le modèle technocratique, l'hypothèse velléitaire relève de ce qu'il identifie comme le modèle décisionniste. L'un et l'autre, selon cet auteur, sont des constructions idéologiques qui masquent certains intérêts et s'avèrent insuffisants pour rendre compte des défis actuels:

Ni le spécialiste n'est devenu souverain par rapport aux politiciens qui, si l'on en croit le modèle technocratique, seraient en réalité rigoureusement soumis à la contrainte objective des faits et n'auraient plus qu'une possibilité de décision tout à fait fictive; ni ces derniers ne conservent en dehors des secteurs de la pratique où la rationalisation s'est imposée un domaine réservé tel que les questions pratiques continueraient à devoir y être tranchées par des actes d'arbitrage volontaire comme l'admet le modèle décisionniste.[6]

L'hypothèse velléitaire admet le développement autonome de la rationalité technique, mais elle prétend qu'il est possible d'en orienter totalement les retombées sociales et culturelles par des décisions politiques. Elle ne s'oppose donc pas à la mise en place d'une infrastructure de communication de type interactif, toute confiante qu'elle est de ses possibilités de contrôle. Les succès et les échecs ne seront imputables qu'au seul vouloir humain, individuel ou collectif.

Il n'est pas rare qu'on rencontre parmi les défenseurs d'un tel point de vue des convertis de l'hypothèse déterministe qui, confrontés aux échecs de leur modèle mécaniciste, ont résolu leurs contradictions en instaurant une coupure radicale entre le travail—"Activité rationnelle par rapport à une fin"—et l'interaction—dont la validité est celle "des normes sociales (fondées) sur la seule inter-subjectivité de la compréhension des intentions et . . . est assurée par la reconnaissance des obligations par tous."[7] Le modèle technocratique réduit l'interaction au travail, l'activité symbolique à l'efficacité rationnelle. Le modèle décisionniste les posent comme deux univers séparés, celui du calcul rationnel et celui de la décision arbitraire.

Pour poser correctement le problème de l'influence d'une technologie, Habermas propose d'adopter un modèle pragmatique:

> Dans le cadre du modèle pragmatique, la stricte séparation entre les fonctions de l'expert spécialisé d'une part et celles du politique d'autre part fait place à une interrelation critique qui ne se contente pas de retirer à l'exercice de la domination tel que le justifie l'idéologie les fondements douteux de sa légitimation mais le rend globalement accessible à une discussion menée sous l'égide de la science, y apportant ainsi des modifications substantielles. . . . C'est ainsi que d'un côté, le développement de techniques et de stratégies nouvelles se trouve orienté à partir de l'horizon explicite des besoins et des interprétations historiquement déterminées de ces besoins, c'est-à-dire en fonction de certains systèmes de valeurs: et ces intérêts sociaux dont les systèmes de valeurs sont le reflet font, de leur côté, l'objet d'un contrôle qui les confronte avec les possibilités techniques et les moyens stratégiques qu'il faut mettre en oeuvre pour les satisfaire.[8]

Pour analyser l'incidence des nouvelles technologies de communication de type interactif sur la démocratisation et la régionalisation, nous distinguerons deux niveaux, irréductibles l'un à l'autre mais en étroite interrelation: le réseau et la structure de communication. Le réseau de communication est défini par les caractéristiques de l'infrastructure communicationnelle. Il est constitué par "l'ensemble des possibilités matérielles de communication." La structure de communication, quant à elle, est déterminée par "l'ensemble des communications réellement échangées dans un groupe."[9] En d'autres termes, si le réseau est analogue à l'infrastructure routière délimitant les possibilités d'échange entre divers points, la structure est analogue aux parcours réellement effectués décrivant la fréquence, l'intensité, la direction et la valeur des échanges.

Le réseau renvoie à l'univers des objets techniques. C'est l'abstraction de leurs possibilités et contraintes d'utilisation. C'est la carte géographique des relations potentielles technologiquement médiatisées entre les acteurs sociaux.

La structure, quant à elle, renvoie à l'organisation effective des relations sociales. C'est la matrice des échanges qui se produisent dans un groupe. Elle révèle des prédilections et des interdictions qui ne peuvent s'expliquer par simple référence aux caractéristiques techniques du réseau.

Le réseau n'est pas neutre. Par les possibilités et les contraintes qu'il présente, il détermine l'éventail des possibilités structurelles. Dans un réseau centralisé, ne permettant techniquement que des relations de chacun des points de la périphérie avec le centre, il est impossible de développer une structure de communication interrégionale.

Figure 9-3

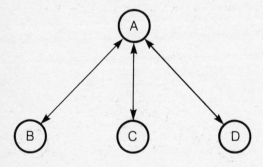

Dans un tel réseau, tout échange entre les points B, C ou D est nécessairement médiatisé par le point A. Un réseau de communication mass-médiatique uni-directionnel comme la télévision, interdit matériellement l'interaction entre les spectateurs et les diffuseurs.

Par contre, les possibilités d'un réseau ne déterminent pas automatiquement la structure de communication. Un réseau bidirectionnel multipoints—par satellite, câble ou micro-ondes—rend possible théoriquement des relations dans les deux sens entre chacun des points interreliés:

Figure 9-4

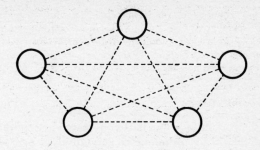

Mais l'existence d'un tel réseau n'entraîne pas nécessairement, comme le voudrait l'hypothèse déterministe, une plus grande décentralisation et une plus grande démocratisation. L'observation courante nous démontre assez facilement que, dans un petit groupe de douze personnes, même si les possibilités d'échange sont physiquement équivalentes entre chacun des individus, on retrouve un ensemble de structures variées allant de la hiérarchisation la plus stricte à la démocratie la plus ouverte. On imagine mal par quel effet magique il en irait autrement dans la communication techniquement médiatisée. Certaines routes peuvent être privilégiées et d'autres inutilisées pour instaurer à l'intérieur d'un réseau ouvert, comme celui de la Figure 4, une structure centralisée, telle que l'illustre la Figure 5.

Figure 9-5

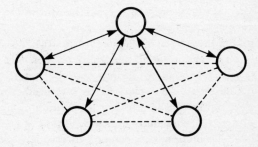

Même si toutes les constituantes de l'Université du Québec sont interreliées par satellite ou par réseau bidirectionnel vidéo, on n'assistera pas nécessairement à un mouvement de décentralisation et de régionalisation. Le réseau conditionne les possibilités structurelles, mais la structure de communication est déterminée par d'autres facteurs que les facteurs techniques. E. Rogers propose les suivants:

What is really new about communication technology is not the technology per se as much as the *social technology* of how the new communication devices are organized and used. Much of the total effect of a communication system rests on the program or software aspects, on how the audience is organized to receive and discuss the messages, and how feedback is conveyed to the communicators.[10]

Déterminants structurels:

Une structure de communication particulière est le résultat des rapports d'inter-influence entre une technique et l'organisation sociale qui constitue son contexte d'émergence et d'utilisation. Si cette structure porte la marque des "biais" techniques, elle est le produit de choix politiques, d'intérêts économiques et sociaux, de valeurs et de normes culturelles. Une structure de communication apparaît comme la résultante observée de l'utilisation effective de techniques de communication dans une société donnée. Cette utilisation ne dépend pas que des caractéristiques de l'objet technique. Elle dépend aussi et surtout de façons de voir le monde, des rapports de domination entre individus et classes sociales, des fins poursuivies, etc. La distinction réseau-structure ne recouvre pas exactement le même univers sémantique que l'opposition "déterminations techniques vs déterminations sociales." Le concept de réseau renvoie bien aux caractéristiques techniques de l'objet, à ce qu'elles rendent possibles et impossibles en terme de rapports entre les gens. Mais le concept de structure de communication ne correspond pas exclusivement aux déterminations sociales. Une structure de communication est le résultat historique, dans une société donnée, de l'interaction dialectique entre le technique et le social. Ces deux notions ne représentent d'ailleurs pas des entités discrètes. L'objet technique n'existe pas en dehors d'un ensemble technique ni d'une organisation économique et sociale, lieu de sa genèse, de son usage, de sa valeur et de son sens.

La présentation du réseau en termes de possibilités et de contraintes et de la structure comme de l'actualisation de l'un de ces possibles en fonction de facteurs sociaux peut laisser croire à une certaine antériorité logique et historique du technique sur le social. Cette interprétation ne peut être soutenue que si l'on oublie que le réseau a lui-même une histoire, qu'il est conçu, produit et mis en place dans une société donnée, qu'il est conditionné non seulement par l'évolution des connaissances mais par des intérêts économiques, des conflits sociaux et des ambitions politiques. C'est l'organisation sociale qui est préalable au fait technique et non l'inverse.

L'ensemble des rapports complexes entre le technique d'une part, le social et le culturel d'autre part, constitue un sujet beaucoup trop vaste pour être traité adéquatement dans le cadre réduit de la présente communication. Je me limiterai donc à essayer de répondre à la question suivante: une technique de communication étant adoptée (ou imposée) dans une société donnée et définissant un réseau de communication, quels sont les facteurs qui determinent primordialement l'établissement d'une structure particulière de communication? Mes observations et mes réflexions m'ont permis d'en identifier trois principaux: les ressources informationnelles, l'intérêt de l'échange et la répartition du pouvoir.

Ressources informationnelles

Les ressources informationnelles de partenaires impliqués dans un réseau de communication définissent la capacité de chacun de générer des messages intéressants, son potentiel d'émission en quelque sorte. La répartition inégale des ressources informationnelles influence la direction et l'intensité des échanges dans un réseau. Les pauvres en information deviennent facilement demandeurs et les riches pourvoyeurs. Même si l'infrastructure matérielle permet la bidirectionnalité, lorsque les ressources sont mal partagées, les communications risquent de se faire plus dans un sens que dans l'autre.

Les diverses constituantes du Réseau de l'Université du Québec, par exemple, ne possèdent pas un potentiel d'émission équivalent. Il est bien évident que l'UQAM (Université du Québec à Montréal) est un partenaire privilegié, que l'UQTR (Université du Québec à Trois-Rivières) a des ressources informationnelles plus nombreuses que l'UQAC (Université du Québec à Chicoutimi) ou l'UQAR (Université du Québec à Rimouski) même si dans certains secteurs spécifiques les petites constituantes disposent d'un savoir spécialisé de haute qualité. Si aucune autre règle ne vient pondérer le libre échange, il est fort probable que le volume et la direction des échanges seront déséquilibrés entre les diverses composantes du réseau. Loin de promouvoir la décentralisation, une telle structure ne ferait que renforcer la dépendance des régions éloignées à l'égard des grands centres urbains.

On objectera peut-être que c'est justement pour contrecarrer une telle disparité dans les ressources informationnelles qu'on met en place de meilleures infrastructures communicationnelles.[11] On espère que la technologie de communication permettra une plus grande accessibilité de tous au savoir actuellement concentré dans les grandes villes et que, dans quelques années, les régions éloignées auront augmenté leur capacité de générer de l'information. On doit admettre qu'effectivement l'installation d'un réseau de communication interactif augmentera les chances d'accès de tous aux grands réservoirs de banques de données. Mais si cet investissement technologique ne s'accompagne pas de mesures politiques précises, l'accessibilité risque fort de se traduire en une simple consommation du savoir, le potentiel de production restant concentré dans les centres urbains. La régionalisation, et même la décentralisation ne se réduisent pas à la seule accessibilité.

Il est bien évident que dans l'ensemble des possibilités, les échanges qui ont le plus de chances de se développer à l'intérieur d'un réseau sont ceux qui répondent à des intérêts réciproques des partenaires. Les cours qui se donnent sur le réseau vidéo de l'Université du Québec sont presque tous des cours qui font partie de programmes conjoints de deux ou plusieurs constituantes. Ce facteur n'est pas sans rapport avec le précédent: les constituantes plus pauvres en ressources informationnelles sont davantage motivées que les plus riches à faire appel à un système de télécommunications.

Par ailleurs, les intérêts des partenaires dans un réseau de communication peuvent être fort variés; leur expression, leur hiérarchisation et leur poursuite ne so font pas spontanément et librement. Elles se fondent sur un ensemble de valeurs sociales et sont régies par des codes normatifs précis. Suivant qu'on met l'accent sur la diffusion ou sur la production de connaissance, sur la standardisation des contenus d'enseignement ou sur l'expression des particularités locales, les intérêts des uns et des autres se présenteront de façon fort différente. Ils seront également influencés par les normes qui définissent la pertinence, la valeur et l'utilité des messages ainsi que des modalités d'interaction. Enfin, l'intérêt de l'échange sera pondéré par son coût, économique et social.

La notion d'intérêt de l'échange déborde le strict cadre communicationnel et renvoie au contexte social et culturel global. Bien sûr, on n'échange qu'entre partenaires physiquement interreliés et, de ce point de vue, le développement des systèmes de communication, tout en nous libérant des lois de la proxémique, peut favoriser l'émergence d'intérêts communs nouveaux entre des interlocuteurs qui s'ignoraient. Mais la constitution de telle ou telle structure de communication, en fonction des intérêts de chacun, dépendra de la politique d'utilisation du réseau, qui en fixera les objectifs prioritaires et les règles d'usage.

La répartition du pouvoir

Le pouvoir peut être sommairement défini comme la capacité socialement reconnue, fondée sur la force, la richesse, la loi ou la connaissance, de prendre des décisions et d'en contrôler l'application. Certains auteurs affirment que le fondement du pouvoir dans la société contemporaine réside dans la connaissance et l'information. C'est un point de vue relativement réducteur, qui neglige le poids des facteurs économiques et légaux, mais on peut difficilement nier que l'information soit devenue l'une des composantes importantes de l'exercice du pouvoir, et que le pouvoir s'exprime fortement dans les structures de communication. Dans le domaine communicationnel comme dans d'autres, le pouvoir se traduit en termes de contrôle:

• accessibilité à l'information
• possibilité de stocker l'information
• capacité de rétention et de manipulation de l'information
• habileté à utiliser l'information au moment opportun.

La question dès lors se pose: le développment des nouvelles technologies de communication de type interactif enclenchera-t-il un processus de plus grande répartition du pouvoir? Oui, répondent les apôtres de la technologie, parce que les nouveaux réseaux amélioreront les possibilités de feedback. Ils vont même parfois jusqu'à rêver d'une nouvelle forme de démocratie directe. Mais qui aura accès à quoi, et à quelle conditions? Jusqu'à présent, cette extension de l'accessibilité semble avoir surtout profité aux banques, aux institutions de crédit et aux organes gouvernementaux pour leur permettre de constituer de meilleurs fichiers de renseignements, et présente souvent les allures d'une intrusion dans la vie privée des citoyens. Dans le domaine de l'éducation, on peut espérer que ces nouvelles facilités de communication se traduiront de façon plus positive par un accès plus facile de tous à des sources variées et étendues de connaissances. Mais acessibilité à l'information d'égale pas pouvoir. Elle n'en constitue tout au plus qu'une composante.

Quant aux possibilites de feedback, elles sont effectivement très grandes dans un réseau bidirectionnel. Mais on confond trop facilement feedback, participation et partage du pouvoir. Le feedback est avant tout un mécanisme de contrôle qui permet à un système-machine, individu ou groupe de recueillir des informations pour ajuster son comportement et poursuivre plus facilement les objectifs qu'il s'est fixés. Ceux qui fournissent leurs réactions n'ont qu'une participation bien mince dans ce processus. Ils permettent même au pouvoir de raffermir son contrôle en lui donnant l'information qui le rend plus efficace. Le mécanisme de feedback n'entretient qu'un leurre de participation.

Un réseau multi-points de communication bidirectionnelle n'entraîne donc pas nécessairement la décentralisation et le partage du pouvoir. Il peut même servir de support à un mouvement tout à fait inverse en rendant le pouvoir central plus efficace, sous couverture d'une participation illusoire.

Le pouvoir ne réside pas dans les mécanismes d'ajustement du comportement par rapport à des objectifs—feedback—mais plutôt dans le processus qui conduit à la discussion et à la détermination de ces objectifs. Un réseau de type interactif permet les deux. Mais le partage du pouvoir n'est pas un effet miraculeux de la technologie. Il relève d'un vouloir politique. Et faute de mesures précises visant à redistribuer les champs de responsabilités et de contrôle on peut redouter que la nouvelle technologie de communication ne serve qu'à renforcer le statu quo. Le discours sur l'accessibilité et la régionalisation qui entoure ce développement technologique n'aurait à cet égard qu'une fonction de masquage idéologique.

À l'intérieur même des réseaux interactifs, le pouvoir trouve de nouveaux lieux d'exercice, subtils mais non moins réels. Qu'on pense seulement au fait que la gestion d'un réseau constitué de plusieurs points interreliés implique une importante fonction d'aiguillage. Qui contrôlera cette gestion?

Facteurs culturels:

Il existe une distinction classique en sociologie entre l'organisation sociale et la culture. L'organisation sociale renvoie aux rapports d'intérêt et de pouvoir entre les divers acteurs sociaux, la culture aux façons de percevoir, de sentir et de penser définies par les normes et les valeurs communément partagées par un groupe social donné. La praxis sociale est fonction et de l'organisation sociale et de la culture du groupe.

Si le processus de régionalisation et de démocratisation est conditionné par des déterminants sociaux, il est aussi fonction de facteurs culturels.

Notre recherche ne nous a pas permis de faire un inventaire systématique de ces facteurs et d'évaluer leur poids respectif sur les expériences réalisées. Il nous semble quand même qu'un modèle général d'analyse de l'influence et la technologie dans un processus de régionalisation devrait comporter une dimension culturelle. Dans le domaine de l'éducation, des facteurs comme la conception de l'apprentissage et du rôle respectif de chacun des acteurs, les attitudes face à la technologie, les représentations des objectifs et des finalités de la communication exercent une influence certaine sur toute tentative de régionalisation et de démocratisation.

Conclusion: De la centralisation à la régionalisation

Comment passer d'une sociéte bureaucratique centralisée à une société régionalisée, si cette dernière apparaît comme un objectif souhaitable en ce qu'elle rend le pouvoir plus attentif aux particularités locales, le rapproche des citoyens et augmente leur pouvoir de contrôle? Comment régionaliser le système d'éducation québécois? Comment régionaliser sans balkaniser, répartir le pouvoir sans provoquer son émiettement?

Le discours sur la régionalisation est encore fort ambigu. Pour les uns, elle se limite à une accessibilité generalisée aux ressources et aux services; pour d'autres, elle se confond avec une simple déconcentration géographique des services gouvernementaux et une décentralisation administrative. Pour certains autres enfin, elle est synonyme de partage effectif du pouvoir politique.

La technologie de communication de type interactif est riche de nouvelles possibilités d'échange entre les partenaires sociaux. Mais je pense avoir démontré que les structures réelles de communication ne sont pas entièrement déterminées par les caractéristiques du réseau où elles s'inscrivent. Une structure décentralisée ne verra le jour qu'en fonction d'un certain nombre de choix collectifs en ce qui concerne les ressources informationnelles, les valeurs sociales qui régissent les motivations et la répartition du pouvoir.

> Le développement technologique n'obéit pas qu'à la seule logique du progrès scientifique. Il est déterminé par des intérêts économiques et politiques autant qu'il les détermine. Les récentes techniques de communication ne seront facteurs de libération plutôt que d'asservissement qu'à la condition que se manifeste un vouloir politique *à travers ce qu'Habermas appelle une libération de la communication,* (i.e.) une discussion publique, sans entrave et exempte de domination, portant sur le caractère approprié et souhaitable des principes et normes orientant l'action, à la lumière des répercussions socio-culturelles des sous-systèmes d'activités rationnelles par rapport à une fin qui sont en train de se développer.

Mais cette libération de la communication apparaît pour l'instant comme bien utopique. Quelles sont les contradictions de la société actuelle qui rendront son émergence possible? Voilà une question qui demeure encore sans réponse satisfaisante.

Il importe cependant de poursuivre la recherche pour connaître les retombées socio-culturelles des nouvelles technologies, explorer les différentes possibilités d'utilisation et mettre à jour les stratégies du pouvoir en place. La diffusion la plus large possible de telles informations apparaît comme un préalable à toute discussion publique et à toute décision politique véritablement démocratique.

NOTES

1.   Rodgers, Everett M. (1976), Communication and Development, The Passing of the Dominant Paradigm, *Communication and Development Critical Perspectives,* SAGE Publications, Beverly Hills, London, pp. 130-132.

2.   Tremblay, G., *Evaluation du Réseau Omnibus, Participation de l'Université du Québec au programme Hermès,* tome V, Québec, juin 1978.

3.   *Description des expériences évaluées.*

Les diverses constituantes de l'Université du Québec ont réalisé, d'octobre '76 à février '77, un ensemble d'expériences de communication par satellite, dans le cadre de ce qui se voulait un "réseau Omnibus." Douze expériences différentes ont été menées à bien dans des domaines aussi variés que le télé-enseignement, la télé-transmission de données, la télé-documentation et les télé-conférences de type scientifique, administratif ou socio-culturel, pour un total de près de 300 heures. En voici une brève description:

Microscopie électronique

Télé-travail de type scientifique entre des chercheurs de l'Institut Armand-Frappier à Montréal, de l'INRS-océanographie à Rimouski, de l'Université Laval à Québec et de l'UQTR à Trois Rivières. Liaison unidirectionnelle vidéo et bidirectionnelle audio, du 21 octobre 1976 au 9 novembre 1976. Discussion sur des analyses au microscope électronique diffusées à partir de l'Institut Armand Frappier.

Amicis (analyse des modalités de l'interaction en situation de communication instantanée par satellite)

Expérience d'encadrement éducatif d'enseignants en exercice organisée par le Centre de Développement en Environnement Scolaire de Trois-Rivières en collaboration avec des enseignants de l'Ile d'Orléans, près de Québec. Du 26 octobre 1976 au 30 novembre 1976. Une partie de l'expérience a été realisée en audio bidirectionnel et l'autre avec en plus une liaison unidirectionnelle vidéo. La discussion portait sur le rôle de l'enseignant et de l'environnement à l'occasion d'un projet pédagogique impliquant la participation active des élèves.

Télé-référence UQTR-UQAR

Expérience de documentation à distance impliquant des bibliothécaires de Trois-Rivières et des clients de l'Université du Québec à Rimouski. Du 28 octobre 1976 au 2 décembre 1976. Entrevues de documentation. Une partie de l'expérience a été réalisée en audio bidirectionnel et l'autre avec en plus une liaison vidéo unidirectionnelle.

Télé-documentation

Expérience de documentation à distance, similaire à la précédente à la difference que la recherche documentaire ne se faisait pas en présence du client. Liaison bidirectionnelle audio entre des bibliothécaires de Rimouski et des clients du Bas du fleuve et de la Gaspésie. Du 27 octobre 1976 au 25 novembre 1976.

Maîtrise en administration publique

Expérience de télé-enseignement organisée par des professeurs de l'Ecole Nationale d'Administration Publique. Cours en analyse de système donné à Quebec à un groupe d'étudiants et retransmis par satellite à des étudiants de Hull et à un groupe témoin de Québec. Du 9 décembre 1976 au 16 décembre 1976. Liaison unidirectionnelle vidéo et bidirectionnelle audio.

CEUOQ

Le Centre d'Etudes Universitaires dans l'Ouest québécois a été à lui seul le lieu d'une série d'expériences en télé-enseignement et en télé-conférence entre les villes de Rouyn, Hull, Val d'Or, Chibougamau et La Sarre. Les deux plus importantes ont été un cours sur l'histoire du syndicalisme et une télé-conférence entre des agents de liaison dans plusieurs sous-centres de la CEUOQ. La liaison entre Hull et Rouyn était bidirectionnelle vidéo. Les autres villes disposaient d'antennes de 2M (Chibougamau et Val d'Or). Du 2 février 1977 au 25 février 1977.

Intercom

Expérience organisée par le Département des Communications de l'UQAM impliquant les télévisions communautaires de deux petites villes, Buckingham et St-Raymond de Portneuf. Les citoyens des deux villes ont échangé sur une foule de sujets. Liaison bidirectionnelle vidéo. Du 14 février 1977 au 23 février 1977.

INRS — Océanographie

L'INRS-Océanographie de Rimouski a organisé une expérience visant à mesurer l'efficacité de la télé-transmission de données par satellite en reliant un houlographe de type Data-Well Waverider à une antenne de 1M située à Métis-sur-Mer. Du 27 octobre 1976 au 25 novembre 1976.

Radio-Orbital

Le Département des Communications de l'UQAM a réalisé une expérience de communication ethnologique entre trois communautés de Madelinots: celle des Iles-de-la-Madeleine, celle de Verdun et celle d'Arvida. L'expérience, conçue pour la transmission audio sur antenne d'un mètre, touchait aux multiples facettes de la vie de ces trois groupes. Seules deux émissions diffusées par Radio-Canada ont cependant pu être réalisées. Le reste de l'expérience a été compromis par les difficultés techniques. Décembre 1976 et janvier 1977.

4.   Université du Québec, *Réseau Omnibus, Plan d'expérience*, 1976, p. 11.
5.   Simondon, Gilbert, *Du mode d'existence des objets techniques*, Aubier, Editions Montaigne, Paris, 1969.
6.   Habermas, Jurgen, *La technique et la science comme idéologie*, Gallimard, Paris, 1973, pp. 106-107.
7.   Ibid., p. 22.
8.   Ibid., pp. 106-107.
9.   Flament, C., *Réseaux de communication et structures de groupes*, Dunod, Paris, 1965, p. 4.
10.   Rogers, E. M. (1976), op. cit., p. 143.

11. "L'objectif primordial de l'Université du Québec est d'assurer une plus grande accessibilité de tous à l'enseignement universitaire au Québec. La distribution géographique de ses unités d'enseignement, de ses centres et sous-centres d'apprentissage, détermine un (campus) de 800 milles de longueur. Toutefois, comme les ressources humaines et physiques sont limitées, l'Université du Québec doit tirer le meilleur parti possible de la technologie des communications." (Université du Québec, *Réseau Omnibus, Plan d'expérience*, 1976, p. 9).

12. Habermas, op. cit., pp. 67-68.

Chapter 10

The Information Economy in Late Capitalism

G. Warskett

Des études empiriques démontrent qu'un changement structural s'est produit à l'intérieur des économies des sociétés capitalistes avancées amplifiant leur caractère informationnel. Cette tendance logique-historique s'explique par l'importance des unités individuelles du capital industriel. La concentration du capital moderne requiert l'assurance d'un vaste flot de profits futurs, présentant le moins d'incertitude possible. Dans le but de susciter les conditions favorables à la continuité et à la sécurité de leurs opérations, les entreprises ont adopté une forme de compétition que j'appellerai "cybernetic competition." L'entreprise moderne constitue donc un système de cybernétique sur les marchés, fonction ancillaire qui requiert une quantité d'information énorme et soutenue. Exercée manuellement à l'origine, la manipulation de l'information tend de plus en plus à s'automatiser de sorte que la main-d'oeuvre peu spécialisée diminuera en nombre pour ensuite adopter la tendance inverse. Corrélativement, l'état a pris en charge un grand nombre de fonctions liées à l'information, destinées à modérer les contradictions inhérentes à la "compétition cybernétique."

Cette analyse vise aussi à souligner que les développements de la technologie informatico-communicationnelle ne sont pas spontanés mais proviennent de demandes des planificateurs du secteur privé à ceux du secteur public.

Section 1

The principal idea being explored in this paper is the underdeveloped notion that the "information age" has its roots in the economy of late capitalism. The expression *information age,* or *post-industrial society,* as it was coined by Daniel Bell,[1] signifies the onset of a structural development from the predominantly industrial society towards one where services become the key sector of the economy, and communication concerns shape the economic, social and perhaps political structures of the new society.[2]

The concept of late capitalism developed by the contemporary Marxist

Ernest Mandel[3] conveys the sense of society and the state being shaped by the imperatives of "monopoly capitalism," a later stage of capitalist development distinct from the antecedent competitive form. Other economists, not working within the Marxian tradition, including Galbraith,[4] and Baran and Sweezy,[5] also have documented the same events. They analyze the phenomenon from the viewpoint of the sphere of circulation, or markets, describing it in terms of large corporations ruling over the markets of mature industrialized economies both nationally and internationally.

This paper argues that large corporations, as forms of highly centralized and concentrated capital, are responsible for the transformation of the economy in the phase of late capitalism into an information-based economy.[6] Concentrated forms of capital must monitor and control their economic environment, that is, take on the attributes of a cybernetic system in addition to their normal production activities.

The policy position taken in this paper is the obvious one that remedial public action, even if practical and allowed within the institutional and power structure of the state, cannot be either formulated or implemented without knowledge of the causes behind these changes. The subject of this paper is the causes of (business related) information growth in the modern economy, but its ultimate concern lies in the formulation of a viable public communications policy for the "information age."

The performance of a national economy is customarily measured by the familiar Gross National Product index of economic production, the indicator of the market value of all goods and services produced in each period of production (quarterly, annually, etc.). In the instance of modern industrialized societies, the long list of component commodities that constitutes expenditures on consumption goods and on investment goods gives us a glimpse of a complex and diversified system of production. This production system consists of an extended network of industries numbering in the thousands, with some industries producing finished products for sale as final consumption goods, some turning out producer (capital) goods, some producing and selling commodities in various stages of processing, fabrication and assembly, and some industries participating in several or all of these activities. In addition, a wide division of labour has evolved with the expansion of production that took place over the history of industrial capitalism. It has led to a massive structure of skills and work functions, placed in a matrix of horizontal and vertical relationships,[7] that in total fulfill the "function of the collective worker."[8] Behind this production structure lies an equally impressive infrastructure of wholesale and retail trade, financial and banking operations, etc.

Somehow, this medley of economic activity has to be organized and coordinated into an entity with some degree of coherence. In a capitalist economy this coherence is supposed to arise automatically through the price mechanism. Commodity exchange is mediated through markets ruled over by the price system and the law of supply and demand. The allocation of resources (including labour) and produced commodities is organized through a complex of interconnected markets—the real or conceptual meeting point for buyers and sellers in a commodity. The fact that the GNP is espoused as an adequate indicator of economic performance reflects the widespread agreement on the *cybernetic* adequacy of the market system. This is a view which this paper does not share, for it fails, among other things, to explain the rise in information activities in the economy and more fundamentally, it is a position which is inconsistent with the production of information.

The price mechanism alone cannot satisfy the cybernetic needs of con-centrated and centralized capital (the quintessence of which is, of course, the giant and often multinational corporations). While the price mechanism is important, its allocative function and competitive strategic role is secondary as far as large corporations are concerned. Primacy is invested in the discre-tionary intelligence operations carried out within private bureaucracies.

It is exactly these key operations which remain unrecognized in the GNP and National Income Accounts estimates, leaving disguised the fact that con-siderable economic resources have been diverted from the production of goods and services having use-value to activities which have no use-value, and here are termed informally *information* activities. The information activities are the labour, capital and material resources assigned to the function of co-ordination and control of markets (thus making prices secondary) and to the overall management of the economy by the public sector. These operations will be described later, but it should be emphasized here that the attainment of individual and global cybernetic control over the chaotic processes of pro-duction, consumption and decentralized economic decisions, is ultimately unrealistic as a goal, and efforts to attain such control only feed the demands for further investment in information.

On the other hand, the decennial census can provide us with estimates of the size and extent of the structural change visited upon the economy by the demands for information activities. However, it affords only rough estimates and although this source is used here to obtain employment estimates by oc-cupation in the information sector, the reader should be forewarned of the impossibility, through these estimates, of separating two principal functions of information work that are conceptually distinct. These functions are cybernetic work,[9] that is, labour related to the cybernetic functions of monopoly capitalism, and the global functions of capital,[10] these being the supervisory and management roles. The cybernetic work category lies within the "function of the collective worker," representing the work performed in aid of completing the circuits of capital.

It is thus imperative to complete the capital circuits that give cause to the need for cybernetic work. As seen from the perspective of Marxian economic theory, the surplus value extracted in the work process by management from productive workers must constantly be realized in the capital form useful on commodity markets: money profits. Otherwise no exchange takes place in the commodities needed in the next period of production, no investment goods are purchased, and the accumulation process is interrupted. Modern corporations thus create within their particular private bureaucracy the "unproductive"[11] cybernetic work required by the logic of cybernetic competition,[12] a competition between large capital entities for individual longevity and security against contingencies (created by rivals and fickle markets) harmful to the steady realization of profits. These aspects will be developed in Section 3.

Section 2

The U.S. census estimates that more American workers are engaged in producing symbols than things.[13] In Canada, the proportion of the workforce involved in information activities is second only to the United States. It stands at 40 per cent, and is still growing.[14] Given the lack of congruence between the definition used here of information functions and census classification of occupations, as well as the desire to make international comparisons, the following broad occupational groups are useful but imperfect. They do, however, give a rough impression of the extent of information work being done.

The information workforce, as defined by the Canadian census, is divided into four main occupational groups: information processors (administrative and managerial, supervisory and clerical workers); information producers (scientific and technical, brokers, insurance agents, surveyors and consulting occupations such as architects, systems analysts, etc.); information distributors (educators and communication skills such as journalists and broadcasters); and information infrastructure (postal and telecommunication workers, information machine workers). All categories except for the information infrastructure occupations have shown relative growth in every decennial census year since 1931, and without exception all have grown absolutely. The size composition of the information workforce for 1971 can be seen from Figure 10-1.

A specific and revealing instance considers manufacturing, the heartland of industry. The invasion of information work into this sector had taken 36 per cent of manufacturing employment by 1971. Growth patterns also are revealing. Using a different set of data, on identifying nonproduction activities with information, information hours of work grew nearly 250 per cent between 1948 and 1973. In contrast, production hours of work increased in the same period only 128 per cent (Table 10-1). What is also significant is the growth in manufacturing capital in this period, divided between plant and building construction, and machinery and equipment, as well as the parallel growth in output. The plant and building construction in manufacturing increased at about the same speed as information work, but the growth of machinery and equipment—capital at the shop floor—grew at the tremendous rate of nearly 450 per cent over 25 years.

Figure 10-1   Information Occupations as a % of the Canadian Labour Force, 1971

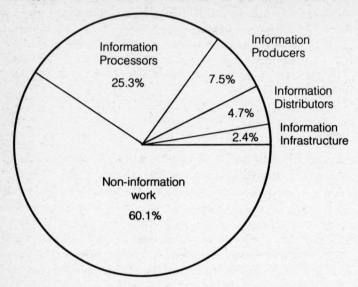

Source: Derived from decennial census statistics, 1971.

The above statistics are significant because they act as crude indicators of the labour intensity in the two spheres, production and information, and of their productivity. Construction appears to have grown with the manufacturing workforce generally, wherein the bulk of the growth occurred in information activities, but the rapid formation of machinery and equipment at the shop-floor level is clearly responsible for the slow increase in production work during a period of large output growth. In other words, rapid advances in production work productivity have been made, but the same cannot be said for information work. A continuation of such a trend, it is widely feared, would see manufacturing swamped by information workers to the degree that productivity gain on the shop floor will be more than offset by information employment.

Section 3

Early industrial technology can be characterized by its chief function of harnessing, transmitting and controlling power latent in nature for the purpose of production. Steam power was conveyed to mechanical levers which operated cutting and pressing tools. At that stage there was little commercial need in industry for data processing, monitoring, co-ordinating and control functions.[15] These generalized cybernetic functions were felt in the 20th century with particular force, leading to the rise of information work and later to knowledge-intensive technology based on electricity. But why should the

Table 10-1: Quantity Indexes of Inputs in Canadian Manufacturing
1948-1973

| Year | Hours of Work | | Construction | Machinery & Equipment |
	Information	Non-information		
1948	1.00000	1.00000	1.00000	1.00000
1949	1.12275	0.99286	1.02637	1.09312
1950	1.17292	0.99522	1.03967	1.15825
1951	1.26148	1.04821	1.06723	1.26376
1952	1.34235	1.06157	1.12438	1.40397
1953	1.40188	1.08670	1.18645	1.55635
1954	1.42698	1.02868	1.23687	1.67446
1955	1.47244	1.04858	1.28876	1.76889
1956	1.54626	1.08534	1.36794	1.91537
1957	1.56931	1.07057	1.46626	2.10312
1958	1.54049	1.01364	1.54239	2.22891
1959	1.53301	1.02865	1.59472	2.30423
1960	1.55998	1.01285	1.64180	2.39053
1961	2.14814	0.98351	1.67600	2.46640
1962	2.15869	1.01538	1.71193	2.53736
1963	2.19513	1.04185	1.75750	2.62183
1964	2.25953	1.09055	1.81374	2.75007
1965	2.37162	1.14291	1.90131	2.94527
1966	2.47318	1.19372	2.02615	3.20179
1967	2.53360	1.18991	2.14789	3.45290
1968	2.52242	1.18241	2.24451	3.61498
1969	2.54049	1.20875	2.34537	3.75001
1970	2.45607	1.18849	2.47387	3.94075
1971	2.40581	1.18916	2.59626	4.13529
1972	2.41847	1.22931	2.68524	4.28773
1973	2.48407	1.28471	2.77272	4.46585

Source: G. Warskett, *The Role of Information Activities in Total Canadian Manufacturing*, Report for the Department of Communications, Ottawa.

business need for intangible information grow so strongly within the sphere of industrial capital in this century and not earlier? Why did the corporations undertake to divert a larger and larger segment of the workforce away from the production of material goods and services and put them to work in offices on an intangible product yielding, so it seems, no profits?

The answers must be sought in the changing form of capital itself, especially in terms of scale, as well as the stages of transformation that competition undergoes. Indeed, to understand the rise of information production in late capitalism we have to consider and understand alternative modes of economic organization and co-ordination in a complex system of industrial production. In an economic system geared to self-interest and the profit motive, where there is no centralized agency of co-ordination and no binding social obligation to produce according to planning quotas or feudal prescription, there nonetheless has to be some principle that calls forth supply to meet the demand for commodities. Needs defined in terms of use-value cannot suffice as a method of organization where the profit motive is concerned, but one such principle is based on relative commodity prices, as we noted in the introduction. The organizing principle based on relative prices is, of course, the famous law of supply and demand, a principle which brings order to markets yet requires the least amount of information to be processed by buyers and sellers (the market agents). In principle, these market agents, functioning in accordance with the maximization of satisfaction, each play a small and passive role in the system of cybernetic organization of markets. Each agent is relatively unimportant to the operation of the overall system of market pricing, an unimportance usually attained through smallness. Insignificance and passivity are the reason the total system can function with very little cybernetic knowledge; in this case market prices themselves constitute full knowledge![16]

Such a cybernetic system works well only under conditions of perfect competition. Smallness implies small capital units for production purposes. This means that no single industrial concern can be so vast as to command a large share of the market or be able to create ripples in the stockmarkets because of impending bankruptcy. Neither could the failure of a manufacturer cause repercussions upstream and downstream in the chain of industry independency. Nothing of the magnitude of the Chrysler crisis is conceivable, with its serious ramifications for employment and the numerous suppliers dependent on it.

In the actual historical circumstances of early capitalism, the cybernetic requirements of industrial entrepreneurs were very modest, and scarcely any expenditure went into information gathering and processing. This fact was reflected at the analytic level by Adam Smith's theory of the "invisible hand" which made clear that market prices constituted all the necessary information for harmonious economic action.[17] The invisible hand was designed to mediate the affairs of small business and tradesmen whose unimportant investments demanded very little in the way of information. A similar view was taken by other early writers, including Ricardo[18] and Marx (who also studied the development of monopoly and attached great importance to it).

But the cybernetics of price-competition is not the only organizing principle that constructs order out of chaos in a "free-enterprise" economy. In fact, this simple picture of decentralized economic decision-making based entirely on current market prices is completely at odds with the modern form of large industrial capital. The emergence of capitalism from its competitive stage to modern monopoly development is characterized by the tremendous concentration of capital that has taken place and the penchant for private and public planning. Some of the most outstanding features in the modern economy are a high capital-labour ratio, changing products and production techniques, durability of leading firms in industry, absence of price competition and the great extent of non-production employment in the private sector.[19] In modern capitalism, "unimportance" is becoming less and less prevalent, and no longer is it a virtue. There is an important technological dimension to being large, and a small company often is a technological laggard. New techniques of production and work structures ("Fordism" or assembly-line production being the best known example), in order to be translated into unprecedented productivity gains, generally require capital indivisibility. These large, capital-intensive plants entail heavy investment and tremendous risks, and the unpredictability and short average business life characteristic of competition is no longer consistent with capital formation under monopoly capitalism. Markets must be secured and sustained over the relatively long life of fixed working capital required to justify the initial heavy investment. Entry into the industry by potential competitors must be discouraged by high barriers so that established businesses are enabled to protect their expensive investments. Novel demands arise for instruments of risk avoidance and its sharing.

Market prices are cybernetically inadequate as signalling devices and message carriers in an economy dominated by large corporate capital units. Competition still exists, but it is largely of a non-price variety. At the abstract level this form of competition here is termed cybernetic competition. One concrete manifestation of this competitive form is oligopolistic competition which largely eschews the price mechanism as a system of market signalling.

The actual structure of oligopolistic industrial organization blunts the use of pricing as a signalling medium. Under oligopoly, prices are disinclined to move with an imbalance in market forces. Much trading takes place under contracts, secret tender, confidential pricing arrangements,[20] or between establishments vertically integrated under one company, as with Bell Canada and Northern Telecom. Much more reliance is placed in non-price competition and hence upon information about consumer demand elasticities, rivals, and potential entrants into the industry. In this way the leading modern corporation is induced to undertake the production of information itself or to purchase it from consultants, advertising agencies, market research firms, etc.

The modern petro-chemical industry is a good example. Even before production can start up in a new plant a considerable amount of intelligence work must be financed. Much of it relates to considerations of survival under cybernetic competition. Investment planning and the evaluation of markets must be undertaken; assured access to feedstocks for the chemical process must be secured, through long-term contracts and/or extensive government lobbying, and most important, the huge financial capital has to be raised and co-ordinated. This capital is raised not only from the retained earnings of a consortium of firms within the industry, but from chartered banks and various venture-capital sources, both domestic and foreign. Capital must be mobilized on a scale unknown in early capitalism. Finally, the actions and long-run plans of foreign and domestic potential rivals in the same target markets must be known as fully as possible, since the operation could never recover if its market share were decimated before these tremendous outlays were replenished through sales. Another aspect which makes any petro-chemical plant so unlike a competitive enterprise is that for the former, because of the heavy debt charges and the sunk cost in planning and co-ordination, the overall cost of production rises rapidly if there is any cutback in demand. The competitive firm reduces output, lays off (unorganized) workers, reduces material inputs, and in this way holds down costs propor-tionately. A competitive firm can do this since it operates under constant returns to scale. The large petro-chemical concern, operating under increas-ing returns to scale, cannot tolerate so easily short-falls in demand. Thus the early pre-production planning and intrigue must be all the more comprehen-sive.

This example only begins to show the investment involved in intelligence operations. But it also indicates the vital problem endemic to large units of capital, at the conceptual level identified as uncertainty and risk. Uncertainty in this context denotes a lack of vital knowledge needed to reduce risk. It only can be alleviated at a cost, through investment in information or in controll-ing the circumstances which create uncertainty in the first instance. The ob-jective is to minimize the risk of taking a profit penalty on existing capital or when planning the pattern and direction of new investments. In principle once the technology is chosen, then the labour and materials content of the commodity, and hence its cost of production, is known. However, the pro-fitability of the production undertaking is uncertain and subject to com-petitive marketing conditions (that is, the completion of the capital circuit, following Marxian terminology). Various non-price competitive tactics are mounted by individual corporations with the overall strategic purpose of cap-turing a secure share of the market over the life-time of the product or even the company name. The urgency of delivering markets to the corporations is even greater as production technology gives single plants, operating at full capacity, the capability of supplying a large fraction of world demand (under the existing international distribution of income).[21]

The other important area of uncertainty is rising operational costs, not only the rising cost of labour and materials, as shortages produced by widen-ing industrialization put pressures on wages and resource prices, but also the unpredictable costs of interest charges on borrowed capital, a factor that in-creases in importance as capital units and industrial technology grow in scale. The only secure protection against these large and damaging uncertainties is a powerful hold over markets with a strong consumer-loyalty to the corpora-tion's products. Under such ideal conditions, capacity production can be sus-tained even when increased operating costs are passed on to consumers as higher prices. But security has to be won, and won by the development of in-formation workers.

Figure 10-2 shows the modern corporation as a cybernetic system of con-trol designed to manipulate and maintain markets, both for input requirements and in its products. The corporation surrounds itself with a series of information channels through which markets are monitored, and feedback control loops for adjusting its response to changing demand conditions, actions by rivals, and cost charges. In this schematic (static) view of the typical large corporation, the process of production, beginning at the factor input markets and ending in sales to final buyers (in this case the consumer market), is subject to several control loops. The exogeneous elements, such as external economic conditions, the actions of rivals and of trade unions, are shown on the far left of the figure as perturbing the stability of input markets. As the backward loops (2 through 5) suggest, the corporation endeavours to neutralize the uncertainties to which these important markets are subjected. The corporate headquarters is the controlling intelligence in a hierarchical system of cybernetic control. Operating in conjunction with subordinate elements of control, it manages the entire production process through its occupation of the most important nodal point in the complex of corporation information channels. From that informationally strategic location, headquarter's control can be near or distant (both organizationally and geographically) as considered necessary, and the centres of subordinate control can function with relative autonomy inside their alloted sphere of influence. Thus advertising exerts its particular influence over consumer markets. Similarly, sales and market research respectively appraise and respond to developments in the final market as well as in distribution. Personnel and the research and development departments also carry out their particular cybernetic functions. Conflicts of goals constantly arise within the corporate structure, these having to be managed and resolved at the top level of headquarter's command through its autonomy and nodal control over information and instruction channels.

We can see how these complex demands on the cybernetic system for information translate into information production by treating the cybernetic aspects of oligopolistic competition in more detail. This competition takes place at many levels, the major ones as we saw in Figure 10-2 being changing production techniques, product variety and modifications, and the creation of loyal customers.[22]

The bulk of research and development activities is directed towards reducing production costs, particularly the cost of a unionized workforce, by developing and refining labour-saving production technology and by exploiting scale economies. This form of research and development investment is difficult to separate from expenditures applied to product differentiation and development, the second of the three competitive methods mentioned above. This also requires many highly qualified information workers, all engaged in the task of capturing a larger market share or in maintaining the existing one, and not to be counted as engaged in the work solely associated with production. To these goals of research and development investment should be added a further purpose that is of equal importance to oligopolistic competition, namely the raising of entry costs to potential rivals. The number

Figure 10-2   The Corporation as a Cybernetic System of Control: Private Planning Economy

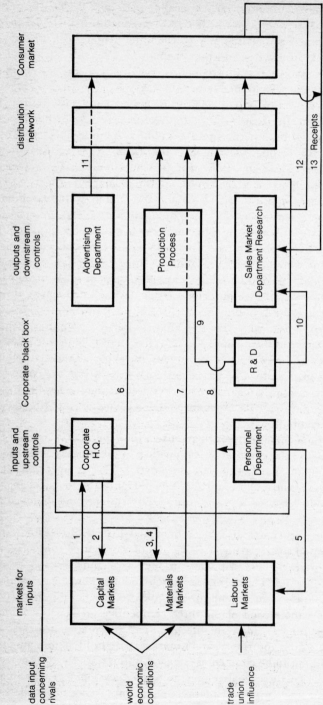

1. Borrowings.
2. Capital market monitoring and search for funds on favourable terms.
3. Acquisitions or amalgamation with producers of materials and resources, for sake of control and to deny direct access to rivals.
4. Long term contracts, for the same reasons.
5. Monitoring labour situation.
6. Control over middlemen and upstream acquisitions.
7. Materials input flows.
8. Labour flows, conditioned by and constantly under surveillance by personnel.
9. Changes in the production process.
10. Changes in product.
11. Manipulation of buyers.
12. Monitoring final demand.

of competitors in an industry characterized by large capital and steady profits is kept very small by several factors, including the need to match the research and development investment that is maintained by leading firms in the industry, and the high cost of advertising.

Heavy advertising expenditures have become one of the leading characteristics of oligopolistic industries, and advertising itself has become an important industry. This is not the place to analyze advertising, but some observations are worth making. Without committing advertising expenditures, market entry is now virtually impossible, except in the less important competitive markets where many small establishments are competing and retail price information helps determine sales. Because of the saturation advertising which takes place under oligopoly, advertising is essential to create awareness among buyers of the presence of products in the market.

In the case of durable goods the latter competitive goal can be achieved through high quality follow-up repair and service, but inevitably more faith is placed in the strategy of locking customers into a never-ending chain of product improvement. New facilities are offered either as add-ons to existing facilities or replacements in the process of upgrading. The prime example of this sales technique is IBM computer systems. They have been shaped as much by market strategy as by any purely technological development. As can be imagined, a successful sales technique of this high order requires a small army of information workers—market researchers, development engineers, product cosmetic engineers, sales force, cost accountants, advertisers, etc.

Finally, it is essential to diversify in order to spread investment risk with the objective of realizing profits when and where markets are favourable, and to cross-subsidize those operations temporarily encountering bad market conditions. This last precaution is another instance of the multifold consequences flowing from the vast size and fixity of modern industrial capital.

In summary, the large size of capital that goes hand in hand with oligopolistic competition requires considerable foresight and planning for stability and longevity. These information demands are compounded by the additional necessity to monitor and control, (a) relevant markets for the supply of materials, (b) labour supplies and the workforce on the shop floor, (c) distributors, and (d) consumers. Furthermore, information work is required to mount and sustain non-price competitive action, to out-fox rivals by generating new products, new process techniques, and new markets.

Section 4

By conceptualizing the corporation as a cybernetic system of control the rise of unproductive, information-work functions in private bureaucracies is explained. Information directed to achieving security and continuity for modern production capital is also produced and processed in public bureaucracies.

Much of the corporate cybernetic operations constitutes a form of private planning, as opposed to market allocation through the free play of supply and demand. However, the individual plans are not co-ordinated and indeed are keenly competitive, offering no basis for overall economic stability. In an important sense it can be argued that cybernetic rivalry between corporations creates a self-defeating struggle for individual security. The constant anxiety to preserve and maintain the value of production capital, always undermined by externally caused shortfalls in demand and by competition, produces a social over-investment in information production. One only has to think of advertising expenditures and product differentiation efforts to be convinced of this. Not so obvious is the fact that the state by means of some facets of its public bureaucracy directly bears some of these information costs designed to moderate business risk and uncertainty. A key example of this role is given by Keynesian-type stabilization policies, implemented through deficit financing and income transfers, which are designed to sustain aggregate demand and to dampen cyclical tendencies in the economy; in other words, to reduce uncertainty concerning expected future developments of national income.[23] This function requires the maintenance of a central statistical bureau in the form of Statistics Canada, and the provision of additional information and administration services in government departments—Industry, Trade and Commerce, Finance, Treasury Board—as well as in other government institutions such as the Bank of Canada. In these and other ways, the private economic plans of corporations are supplemented by the public planning actions of the state in late capitalism, and the public bears the risk and control of future uncertainty.[24]

Incidentally, it is no small irony that the growth of the public sector should have caught the imagination of the neo-conservatives so vividly. For them, the principal cause behind the economic ills throughout the advanced capitalist world is the fact that the non-market sector, particularly the government sector, is cramping market production by absorbing economic resources wastefully.[25] This viewpoint exhibits a failure to acknowledge the importance of the public bureaucracy to the successful operation of the private sector ruled by the concerns of risk and uncertainty. It also fails to recognize that many information activities of the kind discussed here cannot be privatized. Even the private corporations find it rational to carry out the bulk of their information production within the boundaries of the corporation, and not contract-out to other firms and buy information as a market commodity.

Section 5

We see therefore that the rise of the information-based economy has in turn given rise to extensive information-employment growth within enlarged private and public bureaucracies. But the demand for information, for cybernetic purposes alone, appears limitless, and clearly the simple paper-based technology for information gathering, processing, distribution and storage has become prohibitively expensive. There remains a key dimension to information which has not yet been discussed — the factor of speed.

The swiftness of information processing becomes a paramount factor when large volumes of data are being processed within a time frame suitable for decision-making. Late information is worthless, and the manual handling of symbols on paper cannot generally keep pace with modern requirements of cybernetic competition. Timely action informed by sufficient information has high commercial value. It also has high military value, and consequently much of the high-speed computer-communication technology which pervades information activities today was first developed within the military (and not within the private sector). Even the theory and application of cybernetics arose in the military context. In a civil context this demand for timeliness of information, because of a standing statutory deadline, emerged with great urgency for the American 1951 census. This was the first instance of the non-military use of an electronic computer. The modern census is typically a very large-scale, customized, information-processing activity, that is marked not only by massive volume but by the need for many consistency checks and adjustments and by the complexity of a multiplicity of cross-tabulations. Such an activity normally takes years to complete and has since outrun the capability of a human workforce. Only computer technology makes timely, relatively error-free results possible. This example represents the technical concerns of information processing that underlie the subsequent change which has taken place in all parts of the economy,[26] where information-processing work was too slow and getting to be increasingly expensive.

Today, computer-communication technology, especially under the strong commercial inducement of rapidly falling costs, has assumed a position of importance throughout the entire economy, and not only in information activities. Computers are becoming part of production processes, entering the office and slowly gaining a foot-hold in the home. The trend of rising information employment is already in the process of being turned around, as the labour-intensive administrative and information-processing jobs are becoming increasingly subject to displacement by information machines. Lower-level white collar employment is threatened particularly by such developments as electronic fund transfer systems in banking, electronic mail and the use of machines in the retail trades. But the impact of the technology reaches into the very manufacturing process itself. Production workers increasingly are worried by the insertion of computers in process control, and in the extension of plant automation, developments which it is widely envisioned will cause layoffs and the destruction of labour unions based on trade skills. Another development looming is robots undertaking fabrication as well as assembly work. Significantly, these computer-assisted manufacturing developments, embodying re-programmable flexibilities, likely will become economical for shorter production runs leading to widespread applications, and ultimately, to the fully-automated factory. Such trends will manifest themselves at the employment level as a reduction in production jobs accompanied by an increase in highly-skilled information jobs, including programmers, systems engineers, etc.

The telecommunications half of the new information technology functions in the dimension of co-ordination and control — of machines, by machines and of people and machines by those higher in the chain of authority. It holds the electronic highways of the two-way data flows between authority and vassals. Technology has removed the prohibitive expense of distant, wide-channel communications and opened the way for corporate centres to monitor, and be informed of, developments in the far-off markets of its operations. The technology also paves the way for corporations to exercise managerial authority through commands undistorted by the brevity or coding which normally gave room for local discretion in making marketing and other decisions. The reins of corporate authority thus draw tighter through the new information technology.

Section 6

Every corporation exists in the dimensions of space and time. The falling cost of computer-communications is increasing the capability of corporate headquarters to extend tight control over more regions of the globe and to reach further afield into new product markets. Consequently, the arena of corporate collision is ever widening. Along the time dimension, the quest by corporate entities for continuity and duration is aided by the same advances in computer-communications technology that are responsible for widening the extensive dimensions.

However, the two dimensions must collide. They collide because the sought-after security of future returns to current investment is directly in conflict with the capability of other corporations to intrude into market territories presumed to be one corporation's private domain. Computer-communications technology helps a particular business to increase future certainty on the one hand, but undermines it with the other. These contradictions also enter into the public policy of planning income and growth. It was essentially an informational policy of public risk-bearing and stabilizing future economic development, made possible through large information-type activities. But these good intentions are contradicted by the instabilities and uncertainties created through the extra mobility better communication gives to capital crossing national boundaries. Thus the ends of state economic administration can be sorely frustrated by unintended capital flows, causing a poor balance of trade performance or a sagging currency.

Particular social costs brought about by the bias in communication technology are inevitable, not because of any intrinsic element in technology but because of the power relations which the technology reflects. It is not difficult to argue that the strongest bias in information technology is one that favours the business community, while the benefits to citizens are only incidental. For example, while Bell Canada, other provincial telephone companies and CN-CP communication show tremendous eagerness to push ahead with developments that will establish a nation-wide broad-band communication network for business use, it is only the regulatory powers of the Canadian Radio-television and Telecommunications Commission (CRTC) over Bell Canada that guarantees residential telephones installed on demand.

The key to fresh profits and growth under conditions of limited material resources appears to be held by the dynamic computer-communications sector, and the accent is on productivity increases through information technology. But although these productivity increases could mean lower inflation in the price of goods and services, the gains probably will be at the expense of information and other workers who suffer job loss or job reclassification. The actions of labour unions may help to spread the cost more equitably, but the impact on specific groups may worsen their economic positions, such as that of women workers whose occupations are mainly in information and services and whose average pay is 40 per cent below that of men in Canada.[27] The quality of working life also could suffer, a process already visible as office typists and secretaries are herded into the factory setting of word processing centres, and inside postal workers are put on the letter-sorting assembly line.

Higher information productivity conceivably could benefit no one apart from the information industry. This seemingly paradoxical situation could well arise as the opportunities offered by lower communication costs are wasted on yet more advertising and other forms of oligopolistic competition. More centralizing tendencies could devastate particular communities and further deepen regional underdevelopment. Concurrently, the constant, heavy, socially unnecessary investment in information technology assures the growth and wealth of the information-technology industry.

Section 7

The main objective in this paper is to show that information developments are rooted in the oligopolistic nature of modern capital. This factor will influence the effectiveness of public communication policy. A cataclysmic policy based on the notion that the market price mechanism be restored is certainly not the answer, for such an action is wholly infeasible both because no institution possesses the power to see it through and because the imperatives of modern capital could not permit it. Although some minor policy initiative could be taken with respect to the use of technology for various ends and means, such as "new home services," broadcasting satellites, Telidon, etc., the major issues will remain to be resolved by the combatants in the battleground itself — the corporations in struggle with each other — and with a force that increasingly has to be reckoned with, the unions. The unions likely will fight with both a rear-guard action on layoffs and a new initiative for a shorter work week and work year. This is exemplified by the collective bargaining fight of the Canadian Union of Postal Workers for a shorter work week (which was won) and demanded by the Federal government clerks (which was lost).

The government will be caught up in a regulatory imbroglio regarding the future of cable services and the interface between computers and telecommunications. But the room for manoeuvres in public policy is severely circumscribed for, of course, the state is part of the problem.

NOTES

1. D. Bell, *The Coming of Post-Industrial Society* (New York: Basic Books, 1973). See also his article by the same title in *Dialogue*, 11(2), 1978.

2. Most authors are either fascinated by the technology or deeply concerned about the social impacts. Apart from questions of ownership and control in communications the economic issue rarely emerges. See M. P. Hindley, G. M. Martin and J. McNulty, *The Tangled Net* (Vancouver: J. J. Douglas Ltd., 1971); F. Webster and K. Robins, "Mass Communications and 'Information Technology' ", R. Miliband and J. Saville (eds.), *The Socialist Register*. London: The Merlin Press, 1979: E. B. Parker, "Social Implications of Computer/Telecoms System", *Telecommunications Policy*, December 1976.

3. E. Mandel, *Late Capitalism* (London: New Left Books, 1975).

4. J. K. Galbraith, *The New Industrial State* (London: Deutsch, 1969).

5. P. Baran and P. Sweezy, *Monopoly Capital* (New York: Monthly Review Press, 1966).

6. I use the term information in this context in a specific sense. I am referring to the minimal knowledge required for rational economic decision-making. In the standard economic theory of price competition, the prices themselves convey sufficient information for this purpose. See my "Information, Competition and Cybernetic Work," *Studies in Political Economy*, 5, 1981. Thus, for example, I am not referring to the cultural aspects of communications.

7. The Canadian Dictionary of Occupations (CCDO) describes and lists some 10,000 occupations.

8. G. Carchedi, "On the Economic Identification of the New Middle Class," *Economy and Society* 4 (1976): 1-86.

9. G. Warskett, op. cit., 1981. While the helmsman function denoted by the word "cybernetic" implies the action of control, I feel justified in making the link with information, since control requires the gathering and ingestion of information if it is to be rational and directed.

10. Carchedi, op. cit.

11. The terms "productive" and "unproductive" are used in the sense of Marx, where productive labour is identified as the *only* source of surplus value.

12. The concepts of cybernetic work and cybernetic competition are developed more fully in Warskett, 1981.

13. M. V. Porat, *The Information Economy* (Stanford: Center for Interdisciplinary Research, 1976).

14. Forthcoming OECD publication on the Information Economy.

15. C. Babbage in early 1800s invented a marvellous calculating machine thus making computation technology available. Lack of interest doomed it to obscurity. An example of early automation is the Jac loom in France in 1793.

16. See for example, O. Lange and F. M. Taylor, edited by B. E. Lippencott, *On the Economy Theory of Socialism* (New York, 1938).

17. This is an old debate as to whether state planning could reproduce the waste-free allocation function of the "free market" price system without itself making too great a call on resources. Lang and Taylor thought yes while von Hayek and others said no. In fact both sides admired the price system owing to its alleged capacity for effective market signalling with the least amount of data or messages to be transmitted. But this capacity was predicated upon small capital or perfectly competitive circumstances.

18. The Ricardo-Sraffa paradigm, if applied to the problem of economic organization, would include the rate of return on capital outlay along with prices as a complete system of market signals.

19. Report of the Royal Commission on Corporate Concentration, March 1978, Ottawa.

20. Inco, for example, being the leader in the nickel markets has traditionally maintained secrecy over its pricing contracts.

21. Ethylene plants under construction in Alberta are dubbed "world-scale" in recognition of this fact. Consider also steel production overcapacity, shipbuilding, drug manufacturing, even farm implements, all of which suffer drastic profit loss if markets do not hold up under pressure from rivals or during a recession.

22. The same points are also made in my paper to appear in *Studies in Political Economy*.

23. Keynes in the *General Theory* showed a tremendous concern for uncertainty and its adverse effects on investment, but this important aspect has received little attention since. The view of Keynesian economics as a cybernetic system has been developed in my "Information, Competition and Cybernetic Work."

24. My discussion regarding the role of the public sector is exceedingly brief and clearly needs further attention. There are several theories of "capitalist planning," one which sees it as arising in *response* to the contradictions created by Keynesianism (see Bill Warren, "Capitalist Planning and the State," *New Left Review*, 72, 1972). My analysis does not disagree with the thrust of such arguments though it does emphasize other reasons for "economic co-operation" between state and capital. However the following quote from Warren exemplifies the general awareness of the importance of uncertainty in this regard:

> It is no argument against the feasibility of national capitalist planning that it takes place in the context of the uncertainties of the world markets. Such a view is based on a failure to understand the nature of such planning: it is a method of reacting to uncertainty and dealing with it in a systematic and rational way (p. 24).

25. "The marketed output measure . . . shows the largest increase in the ratio of government claims where resources are actually transferred from the market sector, and the prime reason why it has shown non-market sector claims taking so much extra marketed output in Britain on a pretax basis is that the actual transfer of resources from the market sector to the non-market sector has been exceptionally great. Much of the increase in spending therefore has the dual effect of increasing claims on resources by *non-producers* and reducing their supply at the same time." (Bacon and Eltis, *Britain's Economic Problem: Too Few Producers*, Macmillan, 1976, p. 95; emphasis mine. The identical analysis is applied to Canada and the United States elsewhere in the book.)

26. For some interesting details see F. Webster and K. Robins, op. cit.

27. L. MacDonald, "Wages of Work," in *Women in Canada*, edited by M. Stephenson (Toronto: General Publishing, 1977).

Part Three

Methodology for Communication Analysis

Chapter 11

The Communication of Bias and the Bias of Communication

D. J. Crowley

Le concept de biais structurel revêt un aspect problématique. Cet aspect est lié à notre façon de comprendre le rôle social des technologies de communication, à ce que Harold Innis appelait la capacité à la fois d'atteindre un plus grand réalisme et de créer davantage de possibilités d'illusion, ce qui va de pair avec la mise au point des technologies en question. Aussi, l'intérêt social et scientifique envers l'analyse du biais structurel a-t-il été étroitement rattaché aux stratégies institutionnelles de lutte contre ce phénomène surtout de la part des medias de nouvelles et d'information. En même temps, le concept de biais s'est transformé en une notion éminemment subjective qui a perdu sa puissance analytique.

Pour récupérer le concept de biais structurel en tant que concept analytique utile, nous estimons qu'il faut en comprendre les trois formes principales: la forme perceptuelle, la forme interactionnelle et la forme représentationnelle. Cette distinction analytique peut être confirmée par une foule d'études sur les communications tant empiriques que théoriques; elle peut nous aider à saisir davantage le rôle du biais structurel dans le processus de communication.

Enfin, nous affirmons que la récupération d'un concept de biais moins biaisé s'impose si nous voulons préserver l'intention critique des études en communication. Un concept critique du biais nous permettrait d'approfondir davantage les réalités des communications afin d'établir une distinction plus nette entre les limites structurelles empiriques nécessaires et inutiles de nos jugements et de nos actions.

Part I

The concept of bias has attained a deeply politicized status. Even in the social sciences, where one expects a more disinterested attitude, the term has come to label three sorts of phenomena — prejudice, stereotyping and, less frequently, errors arising from research techniques. In the latter case, the concept of bias refers to the familiar and enduring problems encountered in statistical analysis, but in general the term now is pejorative. As a concept, bias has become judgmental, censorious and proscriptive, something to be studied but also to be avoided.

The question raised, then, is whether a concept that has become so judgmental has any analytic value left. Or more to the point, what role can such a concept play in public life, a public life supposedly served by the discourse of the social sciences, and, in any case, now suffused with the language and influence of these disciplines.

The pioneer communications scholar Harold Innis issued an early warning about the tangle that arises from proscriptive use of the concept. The concept of bias, still a key to his work on communications, was a dominant concern in his last years.

Innis's struggles with the social dimension of technologies and the manipulative dimension of the formation of opinion led him to suspect that "as modern developments in communication have made for greater realism they have made for greater possibilities of delusion."[1] This double-edged insight led Innis away from the idea that bias resembled a reflex, a type of systematic thoughtlessness in other peoples' response patterns. Nor did he believe bias could be prevented by combining practical recipes and a sustained critique of practices. Innis did not anticipate nor did he expect an end to bias. Instead, he incorporated its ambiguous status more and more deeply into his thinking as he strove to see its interwoven meaning at various levels in our social interactions.

Bias establishes privilege — privilege of position and conceptual privilege, states Innis. It bestows the power, if not the right, to define reality, to set its agenda, and thereby name its preoccupations. As a social scientist Innis recognized that bias animates every aspect of the subject matter and the way it compounds the task of the scientist. Since Heisenberg's comments on the effects of observation in physics or Hawthorne's remarks about the impact of experiments on the performance of workers, the scientist must deal with the complexity of his own influence on the subject matter being studied. Social scientists face disturbing questions about the growing affinity of social research with media, stock exchange and bureaucracy.

In retrospect, Innis raised far more questions about the concept of bias than he answered. However, he did propose that a concept of bias, to be exhaustive, must invoke matters of culture, social structure and history. The question of bias is a question about how shared cultural frames of reference, which result from and orient patterns of social interaction, relate to the values inherent in those preferred channels of communication laid down by historical circumstance.

It is time to look for a more complete conceptual framework and a less judgmental concept of bias.

Part II

The prevailing study of bias approaches it as something to be avoided. This is accomplished in part by using the term phenomena: biased reporting, sampling bias, biasing the audience and mobilization of bias. The latter is perhaps the most encompassing current usage of the term. Mobilization of bias refers to a process in which "the dominant values and the political myths, rituals, and institutional practices . . . favor the vested interests of one or more groups . . . and by means of which contrary ideas and issues are suffocated, kept covert, or killed before they gain access to the relevant decision-making arena."[2] Claus Mueller points out the bias in the political process "rarely becomes evident because the nature of public controversy is shaped in advance by the elites."[3]

The political analysis of bias is the focus of the more detailed studies done on its communicational aspects. Two recent books on journalism in the United States, Gaye Tuchman's *Making News* and Michael Schudson's *Discovering the News*, contrast bias with prevailing notions of objectivity and neutrality. Tuchman identifies bias with ideology as a "means not to know" and a strategy for maintenance of the status quo.[4]

Schudson and Tuchman pointedly remind us of the historical context in which bias represents the other side of the guiding methodological concepts of objectivity and neutrality in modern journalistic practice. Bias is seen as that which is to be avoided. The legacy of this is, they argue, the petrification of the concepts of objectivity and neutrality. The concept of objectivity dogmatically assumes that objectival knowledge represents the world, independent of the human knower and his intentions. In the world view that results, a scientific method is assumed to be the means for truly reflecting the reality "out there" without distortion. In much the same way, neutrality becomes dogmatic when it fails to question its own limits, preferring instead to believe that a scientific method in conjunction with a neutral stance is capable in principle of answering all meaningful questions, and therefore, capable of expanding its truth-discerning function throughout all matters in a culture. Such views fail to discern the ways in which any scientific method is internally limitless but externally bound. Moreover, in substituting a pseudo-methodism for the complexity of social phenomena, such strategies overlook what Fernando Flores calls the ontological nature of understanding, which refuses to be subject to a mere methodology.[5]

An examination of the concept of bias involves considering the authority of scientific discourse. That authority ought to come only from the explicit efforts to produce unconstrained agreement.[6] To this extent, an interest in particular logics and methods is valid so long as those logics and methods do not degenerate into strategies which are non-contextual, non-historical and without reference to the purpose of their explanations. And to this extent, when social scientists promote a view of bias as something to be avoided but something which cannot be analyzed independently of that conclusion, a false doctrine may well be at work. It certainly is a prejudicial doctrine and one that has lost much of its claim to scientific authority. Given this, how analytically useful can such a concept be?

However, the widespread persistence of and public support for strategies to control bias in such practices as news and reporting, as well as the continuing critique of bias in science, can be recorded. Furthermore, much of the initial conceptual-theoretical framework can be provided by communication studies.[7]

Part III

Communication studies on bias can be divided in several ways. For simplicity, the analytical, not empirical, distinction of bias into perceptual, interactional, and representational forms is used here. These three forms are in reality tangled, confused and intermingled, but they can help recover the concept of bias.

Many communication studies implicitly draw upon a model prevailing in the social sciences that identifies man in terms of limited rationality, social uncertainty, and the strategies he develops to compensate for this state of affairs. To different degrees, they underscore the mutually reinforcing relationship between man and his social environment, a relationship often characterized by interdependencies and incongruities. In one variant, man uses his senses to interpret his relationship to his reality; in another variant his senses are seen more as a means of interacting with it. On the one hand, man is the product and the producer of his socially and culturally bound biases; on the other, he is the prisoner struggling to escape the distortions and deceptions contained within them.[8]

This way of looking at things is not new. Its antecedents are part of the 20th-century obsession with understanding the limitations of human perspective or point of view. Walter Lippmann provided one of the earliest formulations in media studies: "For the most part we do not first see, and then define. We define first and then see." Communication analysts generally have accepted the distinction between a first order awareness, in which reality, much like the model proposed by the sense-data empiricists, is imposed upon the senses and a second-order awareness in which perceptions in the form of meanings and values are essentially imposed upon reality. All societies, it is argued, emphasize certain attitudes towards behaviour and belief—and the same pressures that produce conformity within a society are responsible for the differences between societies.

Such broad differentiation in perspectives constitutes the defining limits of a perceptual bias. All this is well known; perceptual bias refers not to personal preference but to the sense in which second-order awareness constitutes a shared set of codes and values.

Controversy always has surrounded the psychological dimension of this thought, but on the whole its significance and influence has been in lessening the simplistic view about how and what we experience in our encounters with various linguistic-symbolic media, gestures, paintings, films, commercial photographs, and classification systems. Empty gasoline drums, Whorf noted, were more dangerous than full ones not only because the fumes they contained were more explosive but because people habitually perceived the empty ones as less dangerous.

The hypothesis that humans share patterns of awareness which in turn guide behaviour is a significant one. Unfortunately, most studies based on such a hypothesis are more descriptions of a state of affairs than explanations of the dynamics of the process.

Moreover, this conception of perceptual bias places actions and judgments within empirical enclosures. Thus it explains misunderstanding between cultures (the blundering American businessman abroad in Hall's description of dilemmas arising from the different meanings that different cultures give to the use of distance in interaction); the shaping of pathologies through interaction (in Birdwhistell's detailed descriptions of how incongruities between what we say and what our gestures reveal produce severe cognitive impasses in relationships); the influence on visual description (in Gombrich's demonstration of how Albrecht Durer's woodcut of the rhinoceros in 1515 still constrained stylistically the products of graphic artists working with the real thing in the African bush two centuries later); or the limiting of opinion (in Berger's analysis of how the visual imagery of media publicity serves, despite its volume, to narrow rather than broaden the choice between what is desirable and what is not).[9] However, it is not clear how perceptual bias would account for creativity, for the generation of alternative judgments and actions, or the acceptance of counter-interpretations. In other words, it does not account for all those processes of dislocation and change where social consensus and commitment must be continuously refashioned in the absence of, for example, the mechanisms of those democratic institutions that we count upon, if erratically, in the West.

The concept of interactional bias begins from a more elaborate psychology. It adds a stronger sense of the social dynamics to the stabilizing and de-stabilizing of a second-order awareness. Social codes and conventions, our most general schemata, result from the ways in which we experience. Given that there is both interpretation of and interaction with social realities, actual patterns of social interaction will only ideally be without distortion, disburbance, or maladjustment. More important, perhaps, is the assertion that such difficulties are the rule, not the exception, and that the incongruities and uncertainties that arise from social interaction describe the overall pattern of the modern social condition.

Bias, then, is one of the responses to this uncertainty. It is a systematic response, a pattern of interactions which has more reality than the isolated interactions themselves. Systematic biases provide a way out of incongruous circumstances. Given that these patterns of interaction are relatively few in number and distributed over a wide range of social roles in society, they can be considered the defining patterns of orientation among members of a given social order. Though the analysis of such orientations has been associated with a variety of therapeutic efforts to correct them, the concept of international bias is a genuine attempt to explain how the anticipation and prejudice that guide human interaction have a basis in the patterns of interaction itself.

Most often these explanations deal with the incongruities and uncertainties arising from actual patterns of interaction. Gregory Bateson, for example, has used the concept of calibration to explain how the self-corrective process by which order is imposed on reality, provides a bias to the system at the same time it provides a meaning and value to experience. This exposes the perceptual bias in common frames of references that is maintained by, and in turn helps orient, interactional patterns.

In addition, this argument could be related to the habitual values placed upon preferred channels of communication. Politicians, it could be argued, have these values placed upon preferred channels of communication in common with other politicians, as do judges with other judges, or brokers with other brokers, because in complex societies shared frames of reference and social orientations depend upon communication communities which are demarcated with respect to time and with respect to space, or distance. The temporal biasing of such communication communities (political, judicial, commercial) devolves into progressive and regular patterns which Bateson describes as complementary modes (emphasizing cohesiveness, dependency, mutuality), and symmetrical modes (emphasizing competitiveness, equivalency, rivalry).

At the same time, modern technological societies add complex technological features to these modes (technologies referring here to the general sense of organization and not simply to the machinery involved). The organizing influence of communication technologies, Innis has argued, augments the spatial biasing of interaction. He divided this influence into social orientations growing out of direct personal propinquity (a preponderance of indigenous relationships, local forms of persuasion, insularity, and parochialism) and orientations growing out of technological mediations over distance (as in constituencies of professional, political, or other special interest groups, with a preponderance of exogenous relationships).

In modern societies, Innis recognized, it is increasingly necessary to recognize the knowledge and new forceful modes of intervention or access that such technologically mediated orientations give. Thus, in addition to the technology, the intervenor could be viewed as a source for explaining the biasing of interaction. At the interpersonal level he or she might take the form of a therapist; with government, a regulator, planner, or social animator; in business, a developer; academically, a critic. In all these instances, the advocacy function of intervenors seems to carry clear advantage for the democratic process in that it serves to propose changes and openly identify with alternatives.

At this point begin the difficulties of the concept of interactional bias and the interactionist perspective on which it depends. The attempt to understand the consequences of interventions (in the case of new technologies such as interactive media or therapies or any other similar social strategy or policy) occurs at precisely the point where the theoretical rigour of the interactionist position breaks down. Faced with this, interactionists become unconvincing and, at times, offer little more than thinly veiled preferences and alliances in support of the very subjects and processes they should be examining critically. The recent passion in communication studies for defending indigenous oral cultures in the face of crushing modernization may be laudable by most standards. It even may be helpful to announce one's own personal or political affinities at such moments as academics and researchers have been doing with embarrassing regularity in the past decade. However, just as more information has no proven relationship to increased knowledge, forthrightness in admitting one's beliefs does not compensate for conceptual inadequacies. Announcing one's position is a demonstration of the social scientist's willingness to provide a context for his or her work and purpose for its examination. Although they may reveal their own biases, social scientists are unlikely to evade for long the broader conceptual-theoretical enigma they have unearthed.

Part IV

One reason why the concept of interactional bias runs into problems is that social scientists have failed to either abandon or re-think the classical model of communication—that of the sender-receiver. At present, however, there is no convincing alternative.

Traditional definitions of the communication process employ terms such as source, sender, message, channel, noise, receiver, destination, and feedback. These terms are used as much to label phenomena as to establish anything significant about them. The conceptions are borrowed from computational engineering, where they have precise and useful technical applications. As a basis for explaining the process of human communication they are inadequate, being too simple to capture the process. These shortcomings are not surprising, since the model has given little attention to the symbolic interactive features of the process.

Given the problems with the interactional perspective, the attempt to view communication as a process by which ideas are transferred from a source to a receiver "with the intention of changing his or her behaviour" produces significant problems.[10] It has been wryly noted that the founding of communication on something like a Platonic notion of "idea" betrays a certain arrogance in light of the fact that, despite its use in common language, "idea" is one of the most disputed concepts in western thought. Serving as the starting point for a discourse, the concept of idea, as message, almost certainly would lead to more problems than it solves.

To accept such a definition of communication requires that meaning is viewed in an unrealistic way. In contradiction to the implicit atomism contained in such formulations, for a full half-century now the various semantic schools of language and behaviour (the Morrisian semantics, degenerative schools of artificial intelligence, French structuralist semantics and semiotics, to mention only the most widely known) have proposed that universal meaning inside a culture is a correspondence between utterance and behaviour. Such approaches explicitly include the fact that human understanding is always realized in the medium of language.[11]

Definitions of communication that exclude the complexity of the symbolic mediations in social interactions are inadequate. Consider the example furnished by the famous newsphoto stills of Patty Hearst, machine gun in hand, during the robbery of a San Francisco bank (the stills were reproduced from the security camera film). This set of photographs provoked wide-ranging and different interpretations from commentators and the public at large. The Hearst photos were seen both as the image of a hardened revolutionary and that of a terrified and helpless victim.

Media analysts and communication researchers tend to approach the question of meaning entailed in such representations by examining the uses of pictures, captions, and text by the media and, in this way, provide an account of their consequences. For several decades now, more critical analysts have emphasized the distortive impact of such contents and their deceptive or misleading labelling through captions or voice-over narration, especially the consequences of identifying people with words such as "terrorist," "kidnap victim," and so on. More ideologically explicit researchers have raised parallel doubts about the motives behind the style and selection criteria of press coverage.[12]

Thus, on the one hand, media studies have described the rhetoric of media coverage as simplistic, misleading and pre-judgmental. On the other hand, the press and the electronic media have been faulted for ignoring arguments in favour of slogans and for turning occurrences that reflect significant responses to underlying social and economic conditions into spectacles that resist insight; or condemned for allowing unrepresentative elements in society to use the media to titillate the public into cantankerous rages and irrational opinions.

These studies do not take into account other people's cognitive processes. Their capacity for representing the negative effects of media messages on everyone in general and no one in particular is indefatigable (except perhaps those startling cases where children are claimed to have re-enacted television crimes). These studies represent not the conclusion of a sceptical science doing its job but the result of what has been called a flattened view of the entire symbolic action. The meaning of the messages is reduced to what the social scientist is able to attribute to them. Given the apparent lack of a serious concern for symbolic-interactive dimensions of the communication process in the theoretical predispositions of most experts, the referential and condensational power of symbols is lost by viewing messages as somehow evoking such narrowed (which is to say prejudicial and stereotypical) responses, confined largely to an emotive scale and, apparently, manipulative. A sense of the substantial complexity of this symbolic interactive process is lost through such analyses. There is little appreciation of how the power of metaphor and imagery arises through the very contrariness and opacity of the relationship between utterance and behaviour.[13] Where social scientists ought to be moving more cautiously through the social interactional dynamics of meanings, especially the richness of its attribute dimensions, many find themselves further down the road, voicing doubts about its neurotic and ideological effects in the form of implicit and not so implicit comments on other people's thought processes.[14]

An understanding of the multiplicity of matters bound up in the study of bias depends significantly upon how the communication process is conceived. The concept of interactional bias goes a long way towards recovering bias as a useful concept, one that recognizes bias as something to be understood rather than simply something to be identified and avoided. However, the concept of interactional bias currently rests within a larger circumstance, where social scientists do not recognize that their ideas about representation generally are problematic. In failing to acknowledge the complexities that characterize the relation of utterance and behaviour within the communication process being examined, they have weakened the concept of interaction at precisely the point where attention to its symbolic dimensions would have granted strength.

The mistaken belief that what the observer gets out of an event, especially the trained observer, can be attributed directly to the reasoning process of the participants in those events is commonly pointed to as an example of representational fallacy. Representational fallacies, much in the spirit of the preceding argument, imply that adequate accounts of the social interaction cannot overlook the status of the observer. Studies of the social meanings produced by media, notably in France and the United Kingdom, have underscored the connotative function of language. The criticisms of Roland Barthes and Stuart Hall, in line with some practices of the new journalism, have helped indicate ways in which the presentational forms of journalism are a significant part of the subject matter reported.[15] At the same time the communicative function extends well beyond the range of these studies of meaning, production and consumption to include the permanent tension in every speech act between what is said and what is not said (but may be otherwise implied). Making the presentational forms more transparent, by exposing their ideological intentions, for instance, only begins to account for the different ways in which symbols relate simultaneously to a person's conceptions and to his or her actions. Many studies still cling to vestiges of a communication model in which the correspondence between utterance and behaviour can be realized independently of the actual conceptions and actions of the social actors.

For some time, the extent to which representation enters into our deliberations on other people's judgments and actions has been accorded varying importance. Representational bias refers to these problems inherent in strategies of observation, and it confronts scientific observation which does not escape these problems by virtue of its status, but rather intrudes more deeply into them.

Representational bias shows that the problem cannot be isolated as that of a methodological weakness in handling symbolic-linguistic features. Nor can public admission of the so-called bias of the social scientist avert the problem.

It is widely observed that all routine judgments and actions are dominated by a belief in their local representativeness. Experimental evidence for this nearly universal experience is instructive. Amos Tversky, in studies where he asked people to judge, for instance, whether a large hospital with many births or a small hospital with far fewer births would be more likely to have days on which the rate of boy births exceeded the average (which is 50 per cent), found that people thought the likelihood to be the same for both hospitals despite the fundamental statistical truism that a larger sample is less likely than a small sample to stray from the average. Humans commonly believe, it seems, that such averages occur equally in all samples regardless of their size. Gamblers act on another version of this belief when, after witnessing a long run of red at the same roulette wheel, they place their bets on black. The fallacy in the heuristic formula in both cases involves viewing chance as a self-corrective process, one might even say a moral one, where it is expected that the global characteristics of chance (in roulette the equal occurrence of red and black; in births the equal occurrence of girls and boys) will be demonstrated in each local case, that is at each gaming table and in each hospital. And it is not only ordinary people and gamblers who rely on such intuitive schemes; when local representativeness creates the illusion of validity it can be difficult to correct the impression on the part of experts as well.[16]

The schemes for testing the truth of a hypothesis, a nearly universal experience in some parts of social science these days, occasionally can systematically conceal its falseness. Recently this was demonstrated in the teaching of sign language to chimps. In a stunning reinterpretation of evidence, Herbert Terrace, who devoted several years to teaching a single chimpanzee to use sign language, described his reluctant but progressive disenchantment with what he and his researchers thought was positive evidence of the chimp's language-learning ability when they began to review the extensive videotapes of their own experiments. Contrary to their own observed data, this meta-data of the experimenter interacting with his subject revealed that fully 90 per cent of the signing behaviour on the part of the chimp came in response to similar gestures by his trainers. Half of these responses were imitations of signs used in the questions asked by the trainers, while many others seemed to be imitations of signs the trainers had unconsciously started but not completed.[17]

When Terrace re-examined the now famous science documentary on another chimp, "The First Signs of Washoe," he found that the documentarist had consistently edited the episodes so that this initial prompting of the trainers was not seen. The uncut version of these same episodes disclosed that all the more complicated displays of signing by Washoe came in imitation of similar signs by the trainers themselves. It may be true to say that such documentaries often mimic the various forms of science they report on, but unlike the social scientist who sets out to teach chimps verbal skills and ends up with a serendipitous demonstration of their non-verbal ones, the documentarist who substitutes dramatic results for the tedious but more meaningful process of research, like scientists who permit this, confounds a public reasoning process both are there to serve.

If there are consequences to social scientists' failure to recognize the way all our gestures, not just the ones we intend, can become signs to chimpanzees, it is a variant of this problem that social scientists encounter when failing to grasp the obverse of this process in which judgments and actions taken within the social scientific community are transformed in transmission outside it. The scientist who reports that 90 per cent of the scientists who ever lived are alive today may have a very clear sense of what he or she intends by such an assertion. He or she may, for instance, be stressing the continuing role of the scientific community in our lives by underscoring its importance as a political constituency. However, when a reporter or a teacher repeats this while neglecting to point out that statistically this fact was as true 50, 100, or even 150 years ago as it is today, a sense of disproportion may be unwittingly created. And considering the vast quantities of "information" that today pass over frontiers defining epistemic communities whose differences and distinctiveness we only dimly understand, the problem is significant.

Some communication scholars have disseminated cold comfort in recent years with the statement that social science always contains these paradoxes of representation. They identify a ritual function where the representations *of* reality become also representations *for* reality. Social science, by this account, constructs social reality as it produces social meaning. But this is an unsatisfactory statement describing an unsatisfactory state of affairs.[18] The distinction between representations *of* and representations *for* is critical. As such representations pass through increasingly dense networks of communication channels, the incongruities and uncertainties multiply. If the distinction between representations *of* and representations *for* reality is lost, social science in essence loses its critical function. Then it is possible to conclude that social sciences' explanations are relatively subtle ways of promoting the very realities they describe, and social science would have no choice but to promote one side or another. The precariousness of the critical position and the difficulty social scientists experience in relating to it, emphasizes not the falseness of communicational bias but its existence as the problem that must be addressed.

The concept of bias can become a source of critical insight when, as in the present argument—admittedly a derivative one—it becomes possible to see in the distinction of perceptual, interactional and representational aspects, an indication of how communication studies can recover. It is a modest proposal, but it conceals a warning. Social scientists should not expect to remain indefinitely at large if we allow the critical function in the concept of bias to be lost, while continuing to traffic in the authority of the discourse by saying, in effect, "that is my bias."

NOTES

1. H. A. Innis, *The Bias of Communication* (Toronto: University of Toronto Press, 1951), p. 82.
2. Peter Bachrach and M. S. Baratz, *Power and Poverty* (New York: Oxford, 1970), p. 11.
3. Claus Mueller, *The Politics of Communication* (New York: Oxford, 1973).
4. Gaye Tuchman, *Making News* (New York: The Free Press, 1978); Michael Schudson, *Discovering the News* (New York: Basic Books, 1978).
5. Richard Bernstein, *The Restructuring of Social and Political Theory* (New York: Harcourt Brace Jovanovich, 1976).
6. In making this argument, I am following closely the case made by Jurgen Habermas, *Knowledge and Human Interests* (Boston: Beacon, 1971) and *Theory and Practice* (Boston: Beacon, 1973). Fernando Flores, a former member of Allende's cabinet in Chile, has published little to date in English, but his discussions, notes, and criticisms have been an important contribution to the discussions here.
7. Alvin Gouldner, *The Dialectic of Technology and Ideology* (New York: Seabury, 1976); Jerome Ravetz, *Scientific Knowledge and Its Social Problems* (New York: Oxford, 1971); Roland Barthes, *Elements of Semiology* (London: Cape, 1967); Michel Foucault, *The Order of Things* (New York: Pantheon, 1970); Erving Goffman, *Frame Analysis* (Philadelphia: University of Pennsylvania Press, 1974).
8. Simon Herbert, *Models of Man* (New York: Wiley, 1957), *Sciences of the Artificial* (Cambridge, Mass.: MIT Press, 1969); Karl Deutsch, *Nerves of Government* (New York: Free Press, 1963); Kenneth Arrow, *The Limits of Organization* (New York: Norton, 1974), in the decisionist literature; Paul Watzlawick, *Pragmatics of Human Communication* (New York: Norton, 1967); Orin Klapp *Opening and Closing* (New York: Cambridge, 1978) in the interactional literature.
9. Carroll, John B., ed., *Language, Thought and Reality: Selected Writings of Benjamin Lee Whorf* (New York: Wiley, 1956); Sol Worth and John Adair, "Navajo Film-Makers," *American Anthropologist*, Vol. 72, 1970; Edward Hall, *The Hidden Dimension* (Garden City, New York: Doubleday, 1966); Ray Birdwhistell, *Kinesics and Context* (New York: Ballantine, 1970); E. H. Gombrich, *Art and Illusion* (New York: Pantheon, 1965); John Berger, *Ways of Seeing* (London: BBC, 1972).
10. Everett Rogers and Rekha Agarwala-Rogers, *Communication in Organizations* (New York: Free Press, 1976).

11. Fernando Flores, unpublished manuscript; see also, Hans-Georg Tadamer, *Truth and Method* (New York: Seabury, 1975).

12. See, for instance, the anthology by James Curran, *Mass Communication and Society* (London: Arnold, 1977).

13. In the matter of the Hearst photo, for example, I knew about the photograph before I actually saw it. I saw it first as a still and later as a television film, each time in the context of different people, mindful of the constellation of beliefs, judgments and actions that such events seemed to implicate.

14. This argument has been made by others, notably by Kenneth Burke, *Language as Symbolic Action* (Berkeley: University of California Press, 1966); and more recently by Clifford Geertz, *The Interpretation of Culture* (New York: Basic Books, 1973). The work of Murray Edelman remains a model of integrity in these matters, especially *Politics as Symbolic Action* (Chicago: Markham, 1971).

15. Roland Barthes, *Elements of Semiology* (London: Cape, 1967); but also a different position in S/Z (Paris: Editions du Seuil, 1970); Stewart Hall, "The Determinations of News Photographs," in Curran, op. cit.

16. Amos Tversky and Daniel Kahneman, "Judgement under Uncertainty: Heuristics and Biases," *Science,* Vol. 185, September 1974.

17. Herbert Terrace, *Nim: A Chimpanzee who Learned Sign Language* (New York: Knopf, 1979).

18. Nor do the major authors of this argument contend that we should remain satisfied. See, for instance, James Carey, *Sociology and Public Affairs: The Chicago School* (Beverly Hills: Sage, 1975).

Chapter 12

Cultural Indicators Research: Canadian Prospects

Douglas Baer

*Le présent article discute du rôle possible dans l'étude des mass medias cana-
diens, de la recherche par les indicateurs culturels, telle que créée par l'École
américaine de communication d'Annenberg. On y évalue brièvement les
recherches réalisées précédemment dans le cadre du projet tout en faisant une
critique se rapportant tout particulièrement au débat sur l'hypothèse du
"mean world" (mauvais monde). Certaines des implications du débat quant
aux perspectives futures de la recherche canadienne sont ici examinées à la
lumière, en particulier, des préoccupations soulevées par l'école d'Annenberg
et de celles perçues comme devant être explorées par les chercheurs canadiens
dans le contexte de la société canadienne. Il est ici suggéré que ceux-ci ne
devraient pas uniquement transférer la recherche américaine au Canada,
mais plutôt se préoccuper des problèmes particuliers à la société canadienne;
quelques suggestions sont apportées en ce sens.*

*L'auteur propose ici que les chercheurs canadiens devraient s'intéresser à
la question des différences de valeurs entre le Canada et les Etats-Unis et propose brièvement des hypothèses de recherche dans cette direction. Certaines
valeurs, en particulier, devraient être explorées (ainsi, la séquence
"achievement-ascription" (réussite-attribution) dans laquelle s'inscrivent des
différences entre les valeurs canadiennes et américaines) plutôt que de tenter
l'analyse exhaustive d'un champ dont les limites n'ont pas été correctement
définies, tel que dans les écrits découlant des travaux de Milton Rokeach.
Toujours dans le contexte des différences de valeurs canadiennes et américaines, l'article suggère que les recherches devraient s'orienter vers l'évaluation des institutions publiques plutôt que privées. Des propositions de recherche quant au rôle de l'idéologie dominante dans les mass medias canadiens
sont aussi mentionnées, de même que des suggestions d'indices d'évaluation.*

*En résumé, l'auteur soutient qu'étant donné que la recherche par les in-
dicateurs culturels s'est limitée à l'évaluation globale des sociétés, le potentiel
des efforts énormes produits dans cette direction en vue de fournir des informations utiles sur les effets des programmes et types des programmes est resté
inutilisé. Cependant, il n'y a rien dans les mécanismes de mesure existants qui*

en interdise l'usage à de telles fins, comme le suggère le présent article. Enfin, à cause des problèmes de déduction dus à l'imputation aux medias d'effets découlant de leur contenu, les recherches canadiennes par les indicateurs culturels devraient à l'avenir faire une vaste utilisation des sondages.

The cultural indicators project at the University of Pennsylvania has been in operation for more than a decade.[1] The project's research focus continues to be the assessment of levels of violence on American network television, but there has been an attempt to diversify and move into new areas of study, including the portrayal on television of women, minority groups, older people and human sexual relationships.

From the perspective of the study of the mass media in Canadian society, it is important to consider whether Canadian researchers should embark upon a massive project paralleling the work of the Cultural Indicators Project in the United States. It can be argued that a major content analysis project for entertainment television warrants the attention of Canadian researchers. But a thorough and critical examination of the purposes and potentials of the "cultural indicators" methodology must be made to ensure that Canadian researchers do not simply transplant a coding instrument, which in itself has a limited usefulness, for the continuing concerns of Canadian media research. It can also be argued that the use of content analysis would be enhanced greatly by the concomitant implementation of other, parallel research projects employing other methodologies (viz., survey research). In addition, with respect to current cultural indicators research in the United States, there is an adequate linkage between the content analysis of mass media content on one hand and the assessment of effects on the other.

In Berlin in 1977 and again in Philadelphia in 1979, George Gerbner and the members of the cultural indicators project at the Annenberg School of Communications at the University of Pennsylvania invited representatives of various universities and media institutions around the world to participate in an international version of the study. The proposal involved the cross-national replication of the American project, with some provision for researchers in the respective countries to "add on" areas of study appropriate to their individual needs and research objectives.

The intention of these meetings was to develop a coding instrument for each country in conjunction with the Annenberg school and train coders through a process that would enable cross-national comparison of data. Training tapes distributed from Annenberg would be a way of facilitating this.

In some ways the unit of analysis of the cultural indicators project is not the individual television programme or the individual viewer but rather society (or societies) taken as a whole, and so cross-national replication is of considerable importance to the Pennsylvania project. For in this instance, measurements from different societies became the only source of variation, excepting perhaps measurements at different points in time, as the entire message system is conceived as unitary and the results of the entire exercise of the measurement of prime-time television in any given year is said to produce one single measurement.

The cultural indicators project has two basic components: (a) message system analysis, and (b) cultivation analysis. The former involves an extensive content analysis of prime time network television dramas (all entertainment programming, excluding commercials), usually focusing on one selected week of television programming with additional measurements taken over a longer period of time for verification. From the standpoint of the amount of effort put into the project, it would appear that most of the resources dedicated to the cultural indicators project are channeled into this aspect of the research.

Message-system analysis deals with the content of the medium, whereas cultivation analysis deals with the effects of television viewing. From the results of the message system analysis (or analyses), certain media effects are established, and then further tested through cultivation analysis.

The best known hypothesis derived from the Annenberg research is that violent television causes individuals to experience heightened levels of anxiety about being attacked themselves. Integrally related to the perception of an increased probability of violence is a higher level of distrust of other people. This is sometimes referred to as the "mean world syndrome."[2] Television characters after all have a much higher probability of being involved in violence than do people in everyday life.

It is useful to examine briefly the connection between cultivation analysis and message-system analysis. For example, using the "mean world" hypothesis, it is possible, on the basis of message-system analysis, to draw a distinction between a "television answer" and a "real world answer" to the question, "How much violence is there in society?" If the message-system analysis indicates there is a high proportion of violence within the realm of television dramas, the television conception of reality is that violence is pervasive. If the actual risk of an individual being subjected to violence in a given community or neighbourhood is 1:10,000, but the television risk ratio (risk ratio for television characters) is 1:5, persons who, when asked to estimate their personal likelihood of being victimized, respond with an answer closer to the 1:5 ratio than the 1:10,000 ratio, are said to have given the television answer to the question. If those who watch the most television have a greater tendency to give the television answer, then it is reasonable to conclude that television has an impact upon the perceptions of the level of violence in everyday life.

In terms of the ultimate utility of the Annenberg approach, there is nothing inherent in the technique which would preclude its application to content areas beyond the narrow focus of research undertaken thus far, with a few important caveats discussed below. One might, for example, wish to ascertain whether women or minorities are portrayed in dominant versus subordinate positions in work situations and how the proportion of women portrayed in superior positions corresponds with workforce statistics. From this, the impact torsion on the actual beliefs of viewing audiences could be evaluated.

Assumptions in the Original Cultural Indicators Project

Virtually any social research method carries some form of normative baggage with it. Theoretical orientations do not operate independently of the societies from which they arise, and the popularity of a particular approach often can be traced to structural factors within the society. The danger for any Canadian research thus is clear: in the field of mass communication, the problematic(s) faced by Canadian researchers may, in some instances, be different from that faced by their American counterparts.

Take, for example, the supposition that the mass media may be seen as reflecting social values, at least at the institutional level, in a given society. The cultural definition of society provided by the mass media, especially television, in the United States may indeed reflect social values (at the institutional level) within that society. But the situation in Canada may be different: given the domination of Canadian television by American programmes, the same sort of inference, that of the mass media reflecting in some senses the cultural values of certain dominant institutions if not society at large, may not be appropriate. Content analysis thus would not provide the same sorts of clues about social values in Canada as it would in the United States.

In some senses, the cultural indicators project represents an anomaly in the research tradition of American media scholarship. Rather than being a "within system" criticism as routinely appears in the pages of academic mass communication journals such as *Journal of Broadcasting*, Gerbner's approach appears to be an "of system" critique. However, instead of attacking the institutions per se, the cultural indicators critique is aimed at the message produced by these institutions. First, television is seen as a conservative medium providing resistance to meaningful social change. In Gerbner's words:

> Today television is, for all practical purposes, the common culture. Culture is the system of messages that cultivates the images fitting the established structure of social relations. As such, the main function of culture is to cultivate *resistance to change*. It functions to make people accept life as good and society as just no matter how things really are.[3] (emphasis added)

In addition to considering television a conservative element by resisting change, Gerbner regards it as an agent of standardization. It "mainly standardizes, ritualizes, streamlines and spreads assembly-line symbol mass production into the lifespan of an otherwise heterogeneous public."[4]

Linked to this basic set of assumptions, all viewers are regarded as receiving similar messages, and similarities (both in terms of content and effect) are more important than differences. In the words of Horace Newcomb, "The implications are that all viewers are 'getting' similar messages and that they get certain messages rather than others."[5] The rationale adopted to support this contention stems from the observation that television viewing is non-selective.

The modus operandi of cultural indicators research begins to be apparent. First, cultural indicators research takes as its unit of analysis society as a whole, rather than seeking to evaluate individual variations within that society. "Cultivation analysis," as used in Gerbner's approach, seeks to measure the effects of television through a rather unsophisticated measure of television usage (self-reported exposure to television in general) rather than attempting to evaluate the impact of a particular type of programme content. As far as cultural indicators research is concerned, individual programmes are merely indicators of a broader construct—the cultural system of television. While ironically, Gerbner et al. have been criticized for unreasonably disaggregating television programmes into "incidents of violence,"[6] in other senses they do quite the opposite by refusing to deal with media (television) programming in anything other than an aggregate sense.

This type of analysis remains within the parameters of traditional quantitative analysis and provides little more than a descriptive discussion of the levels of violence on television. As mentioned previously, the only comparisons made within the United States are comparisons between different time periods. Gerbner et al. even appear to be reticent about making comparisons between networks in any sense other than treating each network as an indicator of a larger social (media) system. Because cross-national research offers the opportunity for researchers to step beyond the descriptive and into a comparative frame of analysis, within the presumptions of the Gerbner approach this type of research becomes very important to the project.

Without attempting to deny the utility of cross-national research, it will be argued that the tendency of Gerbner and other researchers at the Annenberg School of Communications to deal with the message system solely at the aggregate level unnecessarily restricts the scope of the project and places severe constraints on the use of the extensive content analysis data which have been painstakingly collected.

Cultivation Analysis: An Examination of Findings

The Annenberg team's assumption of undifferentiated impact also gives rise to a particular style of measuring the impact of the cultural system of television. While message-system analysis works predominantly at the aggregate level, cultivation analysis reaches into an individual level of analysis by measuring the impact of television viewing on viewer conceptions of social reality.

A logical extension of the Annenberg team's assumptions discussed thus far may be that television operates uniformly on all viewers, to a large extent independent of the actual extent of exposure or type of exposure experienced by any individual. It might plausibly be argued that television is successful in creating a homogeneous, uniform, standardized view of the world even among those individuals whose exposure is minimal. This interpretation would be in line with Gerbner's main argument, and implies that the only appropriate measurement one could make would be *between* societies, and not between individuals within a society. The Annenberg researchers, however, do not appear to adopt this extreme version of the claim that analysis should take place only at the aggregate level. Rather, they argue that differential impacts of television viewing correspond with exposure to the medium; hence, cultivation analysis seeks to identify the impact of television by comparing heavy television viewers with light television viewers.

The cultural indicators approach to the problem may provide a crude test of the general notion of television effects. That is, without denying that different types of content will have different effects, the argument of the cultural indicators project might be that a strong test of the "violence effects" (or "mean world") hypothesis would be to measure television use in general as an indicator of exposure.

Gerbner et al. report findings consistent with the postulated impact of television viewing on the "mean world" syndrome and on perceptions of the extent of violence in society. Unfortunately, the cultivation analysis portion of the cultural indicators project has not been the subject of as intensive a level of original research as the message-system analysis. Data for cultivation analysis appear to have been obtained from two sources: (a) small, ad hoc surveys conducted within local areas such as Philadelphia in the United States, and (b) the secondary analysis of existing surveys. One might be inclined, nonetheless, to accept the results of the cultivation analysis were it not for the recent publication of other studies, by Doob and MacDonald, for example, which apparently fail to replicate the "mean world" effects imputed by the cultural indicators researchers.[7]

The major criticism of the cultural indicators team research is that its unsophisticated use of bivariate relationships to attempt to impute causality is inappropriate. Certainly, the fallacy of this approach is evident to any researcher familiar with multivariate research methods: one should not confuse covariation with causality. At a minimum, the Annenberg researchers should have employed a number of statistical controls to eliminate multiple, sometimes contradictory explanations for the television-effects hypothesis. Doob and MacDonald suggest, in fact, that the effect of television violence is contingent upon certain environmental factors. Many of these factors are not controlled in the cultural indicators reports. The Doob and MacDonald study is unable to find a significant relationship between television usage and an increased assessment of the likelihood of crime in one's neighbourhood. This may be damaging to the "mean world" hypothesis. At this point, however, it cannot be said that the study refuted the findings of Gerbner et al. since there were methodological problems.[8]

Perhaps the most damaging attack on the "mean world" hypothesis and its concomitants has been in the recent article by Michael Hughes. Hughes uses the same data employed by the Annenberg researchers in their earlier secondary analysis (National Opinion Research Centre, General Social Surveys for 1975 and 1977) but applies a greater variety of statistical controls (using the same dependent variables) in a multiple classification analysis. Hughes finds that "only one of the five relationships claimed by Gerbner et al. holds up after controls." He concludes that "statistical analysis . . . suggests strongly that when one controls for relevant social and socio-economic variables, the claims made by Gerbner and his associates . . . do not hold up."[9]

However, Hughes's re-analysis is beset with some problems. First, he employs an "ordinary least square" methodology which most practitioners would consider inappropriate given the nature of the variables he included in the analysis. It would have been far more appropriate to have used a more statistically justified approach such as log-linear analysis.[10] Secondly, he fails to give the reader the necessary evidence that "interactions" and "multicollinearities" do not pose a threat to the validity of his findings. Despite the many problems of his re-analysis of the original Annenberg research, Hughes's work raises serious doubts about the "mean world" hypothesis.

Hughes argues that one is unlikely to obtain significant or conclusive findings because television's impact may indeed be pervasive, affecting even those who are not heavy television viewers. However, there is a considerable amount of criticism originating from the opposite perspective—that television viewing cannot be treated as a unidimensional phenomenon. Salomon and Cohen state, "The meanings of 'viewing' are derived from the theoretical conceptions of what it is in television that may have one or another effect when viewed."[11] One need not dispute the claim of Gerbner et al. that television as a whole depicts society as violent and imbues fear, in order to object to the measurement of television viewing in the cultivation analysis portion of their research. However, if one is attempting to infer that the *violent* content of television programming causes certain effects, the viewing of violent content should be measured—not total viewing per se. Of course, the message analysis portion of the project provides precisely the data needed to ascertain the degree of violence within particular programmes.

The fundamental problem is that measuring exposure to individual types of television programming may be incompatible with the overall assumptions of the Annenberg cultural indicators study. Still, there is nothing inherent in the methodology employed in the study (in its cultivation-effects analysis) to preclude a more detailed analysis within content types, or a better connection between findings of the content analysis on the one hand and findings of "effects analysis" on the other. Indeed, working within the cultivation effects tradition, Hawkins and Pingree assess the different effects of various types of television viewing by Australian children with the assumption that "stronger cultivation effects at one age might simply reflect greater exposure to a particularly affecting program type."[12]

Measuring television exposure as a unidimensional phenomenon severely restricts the utility of cultivation effects research. It precludes the development of interesting and important hypotheses regarding the interaction between the type of viewing and the effects of that viewing. Inasmuch as the "normative baggage" created by the world view of the cultural indicators researchers at the Annenberg school may have hampered them from doing further work on the differential effects of television programmes of different types, it would be appropriate for subsequent researchers to travel with a lighter load.

Content Analysis Measurement in the Canadian Context

One common criticism of the cultural indicators instrument for message analysis is that it is too narrow in focus. The actual coding instrument is, of course, immense. A recent version of the form involved 60 basic measurements for each programme, 15 measurements for each major and minor character, 15 measurements for each "violent action," and 12 measurements for each "close personal relationship" in each programme. It is possible that within a single half-hour or hour television drama more than 500 separate measurements might be taken.

The size of the Annenberg-developed instrument poses a two-fold problem for Canadian researchers:

(1) If the problems which are chosen in a Canadian study replicate those chosen in American studies, the American results (i.e., the Annenberg team's work) can be used to measure American programmes aired in Canada, leaving only a small amount of uniquely Canadian programming to be coded. This would save a considerable amount of research effort, and enable a cultural indicators project to proceed in Canada with a relatively modest budget.

(2) If a wider focus is adopted, it may be necessary to code all programmes available in Canada, both of Canadian and American origin. This would be an enormous task given the large number of television networks in Canada.

The development of a number of specialized, minority entertainment services in Canada also could pose problems for a content analysis project. Certainly, the task of a message-system analysis would have been much easier in the 1950s when Canada operated under a single-station television policy (the CBC was the only television network allowed to operate in Canada prior to 1960). At issue in the present situation is which networks or broadcasting stations should be included in the analysis. Should minority language broadcasting stations such as multicultural television stations operating primarily in a language other than English or French be included? Or should the analysis be restricted to the television networks? With the development of the UHF television spectrum in Canada, an increasing proportion of entertainment viewing consists of independent (non-network) television stations instead of network viewing. The appropriateness of the strategy of only selecting network television would be under question, and will be exacerbated by the future development of special programming systems such as pay television on cable systems.

The problem of defining which types of television networks or stations warrant inclusion in an analysis is not unique to Canada. But unless considerable energy is diverted from the coding of all Canadian prime-time programming by the simple use of the results of the Annenberg analysis for all American programmes carried in Canada, Canadian researchers will face a task more immense than that of their American counterparts.

This practical consideration might augur strongly against the simple transplant of the American instrument into Canada. It is unlikely, for example, that Canadian researchers could match the level of financial support available to such a project in the United States, given the smaller parameters within which Canadian funding agencies operate. Yet, if indeed a Canadian study could operate within a theoretical vacuum, adoption of the American instrument would be an excellent strategy. But it will be argued below that there are unique yet important problems germane to the Canadian situation that have not been considered within the research foci of the Annenberg researchers and may be more deserving of attention than, for example, the issue of media violence.

The question of which programming to include in a message system analysis cannot be answered in any definitive sense at this point. The resolution of this problem can occur only with some knowledge of the availability of research resources. A criterion such as audience size could be considered to ascertain which programmes should be examined (on the presumption that those programmes with greater audiences have a greater impact, within certain limits). Certainly this also would reflect systemic properties: the nature (and size) of the technical delivery system, cost (if any) to the viewer, and the time of day at which the programme is aired. Such a criterion would, however, imply certain dangers to the validity of some hypotheses which might be constructed: by reducing the extremes (i.e., minority audience programming), the variability in programming content is decreased. If then one wishes to make inferences about how different types of programmes have differential influences on audiences, the findings may be unduly affected by the increased homogeneity in the programme content being analyzed. The "audience size" criterion would also, in all likelihood, eliminate non-official language programming which can have a special socializing role in the lives of ethnic minorities in the country.

Still another possibility would be the sampling of programmes; that is, not selecting all available programmes but selecting a sample. The cultural indicators research does this to a limited extent: while every programme available on prime-time television is usually analyzed, the one week of programming (in some cases, more than one week) is selected as representative of the entire season. It is assumed that any given week will provide a reasonably representative sample and that programming on, say, week seven, will not systematically be either more or less violent than programming on week three. However, sampling programmes out of a week's schedule, rather than choosing the entire schedule as a sample, may entail serious inferential problems. Different strata involving different programme *types* could be established and each stratum could be sampled to ensure representativeness. Yet even this strategy could go awry if the definition of the stratum does not correspond well to the theoretical focus within which the work is completed (or within which later analysts try to undertake secondary analysis with the data).

There are, then, pragmatic issues which must be resolved before a major content analysis project can be undertaken in Canada. But these issues are far less critical than the substantive issues which underlie, or should underlie, the analysis in the first place.

The Definition of Canadian Problems

Canadian researchers have been studying television violence and related issues, such as the "mean world" hypothesis; however, it is questionable if this is the right focus. The publication of a massive, seven-volume report on violence in the mass communication industry in Ontario may be seen as signalling an interest, at least at the governmental level, on this issue. But the Report of the Royal Commission on Violence in the Communications Industry did little more than draw on existing media research in its assessment of the impact of violent television, and given this, reference to original sources in the area of violence-effects may be more profitable. More importantly, the field may have been overworked relative to other research areas in Canada which have received scanty attention in comparison.

There should be a different Canadian "sense" by which problems in mass media studies are defined. Canada's situation is structurally dissimilar to the United States. For example, cultural domination is not an issue in the United States. In the treatment of minority groups in the United States, there is no analogue to the official status accorded the French language in Canada. Even between comparable English-speaking communities in Canada and the United States, it can be argued there are deep-rooted historical and institutional differences. In the area of race and ethnic relations, too, there is a long-standing belief on the part of many scholars that Canadian society differs from American society.[13] How are these differences reflected (or mitigated) in the mass media? To what extent do the mass media serve to override long-standing differences between Canada and the United States? These questions are important from the standpoint of the scholarly analysis of cultural forces in Canadian society.

Canada–United States Value Differences

The discussion of the Canada-United States value differences has formed part of a major debate in Canadian social science scholarship. While empirical analyses bearing on the formulations of these authors are few, there have been some cross-national studies which have demonstrated the existence of value differences between Canadians and Americans.[14]

How long can Canadians be expected to hold different cultural values in the face of a constant bombardment of American television programming? Porter states:

> In sharing common mass media, Canadians and Americans share a common exposure to advertising and hence common standards of taste and common items of consumption. If the Canadian item is not an exact replica produced by a Canadian subsidiary, it is not unlike the United States prototype. There is no real evidence to suggest that economic integration and cultural inundation are resented or resisted by the vast majority of Canadians.[15]

Porter's comment that the mass media determine "standards of taste and common items of consumption" is reminiscent of the comments of Michael Hughes, cited earlier. Both argue that the cultural system, taken as a whole, affects people regardless of individual variations in exposure.

If the mass communication subsystem is indeed monolithic in terms of the production of a uniform culture across all of North America, then perhaps no further analysis is warranted. For, under this conception, Canadian programme producers can do little more than produce entertainment programming that will ultimately promulgate the same cultural values as the American programming it presumably borrows from. It is true that the majority of television viewing in Canada consists of American-produced programming. But what are researchers to make of the Canadian programmes which are available? Are they to be regarded as fundamentally similar, or can we look for differences which may signal differences in audience orientations and effects?

Minimally major differences between Canadian and American entertainment programming could be expected given the differences in levels of funding and, more importantly, differences in institutional constraints. Although recent CRTC criticisms say the CBC is too commercially oriented, the CBC is not under the same institutional pressures as the American commercial broadcasters. The influence of American production values (presumably carrying with them other sorts of values) on Canadian producers, many of whom may aspire towards employment outside of Canada, cannot be denied. Still, it is reasonable to expect some variation in programme content and implied social values, and it is this variation which should be the subject of closer scrutiny by Canadian media researchers.

Although Porter's observation that Canadians do not "resent or resist" the extent of American involvement in Canadian culture and the Canadian economy may in some ways be valid, there is a considerable level of support in

Canada for measures designed to limit the inflow of American television programming. In a recent (1980) Gallup poll, 67 per cent of respondents indicated they approved of a Canadian content regulation requiring a minimum of 50 per cent Canadian content during prime time. Only 24 per cent of those sampled indicated that they disapproved of the measure.[16] This finding is consistent with research examining the level of support respondents indicated for Canadian content rules in general (without the actual 50 per cent level specified) and in terms of general attempts by the country to repatriate ownership of the economy, based on a 1977 study.[17] In addition, work by Lambert and Curtis suggests the level of concern regarding American cultural influence has increased over the past decade.

The majority support for a Canadian content rule in the late 1970s also can be contrasted with the earlier findings of Sigler and Goresky (based on a 1970 poll) in which there was not majority support for such a measure.[18]

Determining what societal values, as portrayed by the mass media, should be evaluated and measured and how this measurement takes place raises many problems. There is not sufficient space here to detail the potential difficulties but a brief review of how Canada-United States value differences could be evaluated within the context of cultural indicators research is useful.

One of the best-known attempts to measure human values at the individual level is the work of Milton Rokeach, whose work might form a basis for a discussion of Canada-United States value differences. Rokeach's "value inventory" involves two types of values — the instrumental and the terminal.[19] He uses a rank-ordered measurement system and claims that the 36 values he has derived constitute an irreducible set which, while varying in magnitude between individuals and societies, are present in all societies. This latter claim is based on the results of a factor analysis undertaken on data involving the various value items he originally conceived. Yet Rokeach's work is open to criticism on several levels:

(1) The definition of the "values" is sometimes obscure, and likely to have different connotations for different respondents. Especially problematic are "values" such as "inner harmony."

(2) There is no indication that Rokeach's "values" are at all salient to individuals in a general population. In fact, some studies have suggested the contrary.[20]

(3) As a sampling of a hypothetical domain of items representing a universe of all possible value orientations, Rokeach's list appears, if anything, limiting. For example, the 18 "instrumental" values were drawn, almost arbitrarily, from a list of over 555 traits found elsewhere in psychological literature.

These criticisms, and others, are outlined by Jones et al.[21] Rokeach's items may not adequately cover the domain of content implied (i.e., all possible personal values). In addition, Rokeach's claim that his 36 items constitute an irreducible set is based on the interpretation of a methodologically inappropriate use of the factor analysis technique.[22]

From the standpoint of the study of the mass media and Canadian society, it would be useful for researchers to aspire towards more limited immediate objectives involving comparisons of particular types of values thought to differ between American and Canadian society.

The idea of taking a limited number of value-dimensions and attempting to define them more rigorously, circumvents one of the major problems inherent in the measurement of a large number of social value dimensions in a given study, that is, the ability of researchers to obtain reliable (consistent) measurements. To code television programmes in terms of a large number of values, a researcher might be compelled to simply ask coders to rate programmes (on the basis of coder perception) in terms of the degree to which the programmes display given values (e.g., coders could be asked to rate a certain programme on a scale of 1 to 5 for each of a large number of values, without being given detailed instructions as to how this might be done or what criteria might be applied). If responses to this type of coding practice are not idiosyncratic, there might at least be systematic forms of error: coders with different social backgrounds will likely provide radically different ratings (hence, low reliabilities in measurement). By focusing on a small number of values, more reliable and valid indices are possible, involving specific attributes rather then an intuitive interpretation of the values implicit in a programme.

One possible area for study is that of the degree of traditionalism in Canadian society. It can be predicted from Lipset's thesis that Canadians are more ascriptive and traditional. But findings from the study by Crawford and Curtis suggest the opposite — in the realm of social conservatism, Canadians are more liberal in terms of support for premarital sex, for example. The implications of attempting to evaluate the content of television programming along a traditionalism/non-traditionalism dimension are relatively straightforward. A number of programme (content analysis) indicators could be formulated to measure, for example, the extent and nature of sexual portrayal on television. How frequently are sexual encounters portrayed or implied? In what detail? To what degree are non-traditional sexual practices such as homosexuality implied or portrayed? To what extent are these practices depicted in the context of some normative pronouncement, either explicit or implied?

Canadian Values and Social Institutions

Another related area is suggested by Herschel Hardin in his book, *A Nation Unaware*. Hardin discusses at length the existence in Canada of a "public enterprise" culture which differentiates Canada from the United States. For various reasons, Canada has, at the institutional level, opted for a greater level of government involvement in the economy. While a perfect translation from institutional values to individuals (en masse) is not possible (that is, values implicit in certain forms of institutional development and/or values held on the part of elites responsible for political institutions), at the mass level it can be expected that Canadians are less attached to the dominant values legitimizing free-enterprise capitalism.

Hardin argues that a distinctively Canadian culture — one which is less related to the ideology of private enterprise and laissez-faire capitalism — is threatened by what he calls American culture in Canada. American cultural institutions are seen as responsible for promulgating private enterprise culture in contradistinction to a Canadian public enterprise culture. The issue of the legitimacy of Canadian economic and political institutions, and the role of the mass media in legitimizing or de-legitimizing such institutions, is an important one within the context of the Canadian mass media. Certainly, one would expect most media effects in this regard to operate outside the context of entertainment programming (most influence would be expected to occur through news and public affairs programming) but political institutions are routinely portrayed in entertainment programming, implying that certain values and attitudes *may* be transmitted via such programming. Of considerable concern to Canadian researchers is the recent finding that public institutions are treated with less approval by the press than are private institutions; even when institutions are similar in nature (a Crown corporation in comparison with a private corporation operating in the same economic sector), Winter and Frizzle found that private institutions were discussed more favourably.[23] Is it possible that this process might extend to portrayals within *entertainment* programmes? To what degree are certain institutions simply not portrayed, leaving Canadians, for example, to assume that all economic activity of any importance occurs in the private sector?

The Mass Media and Dominant Ideology

Related to the issue of private versus public development is the extent to which the mass media foster the promulgation of a dominant ideology regarding the distribution of wealth and economic activity in society. Dominant ideology in this context refers to belief systems that make palatable the inequalities in the distribution of power and wealth that prevail in society. A dominant ideology seeks to explain, justify and even impute justice to social inequality.

Gerbner et al. come tantalizingly close to dealing with dominant ideology in their research. They discuss how television has a legitimizing influence and how it makes people accept social outcomes as good and just. However, they largely ignore the degree to which certain beliefs and attitudes attendant to a dominant ideology are transmitted through the mass media. Previous research in Canadian society has examined the impact of educational institutions on beliefs related to dominant ideologies,[24] following earlier work in Canada and the United States dealing with the impact of such attributes as social class position on acceptance of beliefs that legitimize differential distributions in wealth. Certainly, the inattention paid to the mass media is symptomatic of the general tendency of researchers dealing with the socializing impact of various institutions to ignore the mass media as either: (a) unimportant; (b) homogeneous in impact; or (c) impossible to measure. This situation is, to say the least, unfortunate.

It needs to be determined how researchers can analyze the role of the mass media in terms of dominant ideology. First, some of the components of a dominant ideology supporting the accumulation of private wealth and the unequal distribution of wealth in society must be derived. It should be noted that at the level of individuals, some people may subscribe to isolated propositions (taken from those outlined below) about the nature of the social world while others might subscribe to the entire set of logically interrelated propositions. Of importance here is the possibility that an individual may subscribe to one or more of the propositions, but not all of them, despite the logical connection of these propositions within the context of the legitimization of inequality. While programming is expected to display more consistent implicit ideologies, there is nothing suggesting that if one particular conception of the world is dominant, related conceptions must also be made available. A partial list of propositions, which could be subsumed under the notion of dominant ideology, follows:

(1) Ascribing to personal character (motivation, hard work, laziness, ambition) rather than systematic or institutional factors the ultimate responsibility for worldly success or failure.

(2) A belief that social welfare measures have already gone too far and now penalize ambition and industry and reward sloth and dependence.

(3) A belief that private industry should be allowed to operate in the economic sphere without government interference, and that it is largely through government involvement in the economy that economic difficulties prevail.

To pursue the analysis of the role of the mass media in terms of dominant ideology, the relative importance of situational versus individual factors in determining outcomes of television dramas must be assessed, even if these outcomes are not directly related to economic rewards. The connection here is that certain types of programmes may place a strong emphasis on individual achievement while others attribute some if not most of the outcome to situational factors (including "accidents") beyond the control of characters in the drama. This distinction can be analyzed both in terms of the outcome of any particular programme in a series and in terms of the context of the programme. Clearly, characters in continuing series do not change rapidly in terms of economic or social position, but observers should look for clues as to what factors enable them to occupy their current position in the first place.

Related to this is the manner in which characters from different social classes are depicted. Aside from the general observation that television characters tend to be predominantly middle class, differences between the personalities of upper class as opposed to lower class characters should be looked for. Are the latter portrayed as lazy and/or indifferent? Are upper class characters portrayed as more aggressive, more ambitious, and so on? These distinctions may be especially important if they are distinctions made *within* any given programme as opposed to differences between programmes which might focus on different social levels.

The portrayal of social mobility on television also is an important and related area of study. It is unlikely that any one individual character will be seen to exhibit either upward or downward social mobility within the context of a given programme — although undoubtedly some exceptions occur. But there are other clues about mobility chances which are provided within the context of the lives of characters on television dramas. Are blue-collar (lower-class) individuals portrayed as being locked in by external circumstances? Or are they seen as operating fundamentally within the context of free will? In terms of social mobility process, status inconsistents also play an important role. The dominant ideology asserts that individuals who have achieved through hard work and effort high educational qualifications will be rewarded for their perseverence and their willingness to defer economic gratification.

In addition to the outcomes of social dramas on television, the more direct ideological pronouncements made by the characters should be observed. Although it is unlikely that either supportive or non-supportive statements of dominant ideology appear in themselves in most television programmes, there may be occasions in which characters themselves make statements like, "Everyone who gets somewhere in this world gets there because he works hard." The context in which these statements are made is important. Are they made by "good" characters or "bad" characters? How serious are the characters when they make the statements? Do the statements correlate with actions occurring within the context of the drama?

Some Research Directions

An attempt has been made in this article to argue that Canadian researchers should pay attention to certain problems that have not received an adequate amount of analysis within the context of American media scholarship. Some of these issues, because they impinge more on the nature and existence of Canadian society, are unlikely ever to receive much attention in the United States. Other issues may be given inadequate attention because of particular biases or predilections common in the discipline in the United States.

Some suggestions have been made with respect to particular areas that could be studied within the context of content analysis. But earlier, the objection was raised that content analysis, in itself, is of very limited utility unless coupled with some other form of research designed to disentangle media effects. It is, of course, inappropriate for researchers to attempt to make inferences regarding effects solely on the basis of the *content* of communication systems, and hence one must turn to other research methods. In Canada, very few systematic surveys dealing with the mass media have been undertaken. Those studies which have been done have frequently suffered from problems of inadequate conceptualization and/or poor item design. Furthermore, the best source of data for researchers dealing with the mass media in Canadian society frequently is to be found in surveys aimed at other, non-media issues such as certain voter studies and studies of attitudes toward crime.

The need for adequate survey research dealing with the mass media in Canada is related to the development of cultural indicators (i.e., message analysis) research in this country in two senses. First, some of the efforts of a message system analysis would be wasted if researchers found themselves unable to launch a concomitant survey to assess attitudinal correlates of mass-media viewing patterns. Secondly, media scholars should be careful to ensure that the development of a cultural indicators project does not lead to over-reliance upon the content analysis method.

Canadian media researchers are becoming increasingly sophisticated in their use of content analysis, independent of the development of the Annenberg coding instrument. The method has been applied, for example, to news coverage in federal elections[25] and to the coverage given to different language groups in the country. These developments are to be encouraged, but ultimately researchers should move to marry the data obtained through content analysis to effects/audience attitude pattern data obtained through survey research. It is to be hoped the latter would involve some form of measurement of the viewing of individual programmes or at least programme types. An objection could be raised that such survey measurement would be costly, given the need for respondents to fill out media diaries, and that the measurement of media viewership might contaminate the measurement of social attitudes and values (unless measurement of each occurs on separate occasions). These objections are worthy of note. However, given the exploratory nature of research in this area, virtually any form of adequately conceptualized and pre-tested survey research would undoubtedly represent a marked improvement over that which has previously been available.

In addition, it may be possible at the preliminary level for media-relevant variables to be measured in conjunction with existing surveys designed for other purposes. For example, in the area of news coverage of federal elections, researchers in the field would have been aided immensely if the survey research being done in the area had included some measure asking respondents which television networks they watched when they watched television news (a number of recent national surveys have, however, asked respondents to indicate the frequency with which they watch television news). While such crude measures would likely be subject to some measurement error, they would at least permit researchers to go beyond describing media content into the realm of assessing the relationship between the medium and its audience.

The same consideration applies to entertainment programming. In survey research, respondents can be asked a number of questions the answers to which can be used as indicators of exposure. For example, is the respondent familiar with a given programme? Did the respondent watch this programme during the current (or previous) week? How frequently can the respondent recall watching the programme (i.e., with what frequency is the programme usually viewed)? While Canadian researchers should aspire ultimately toward the implementation of survey research which is not only longitudinal in nature but also involves the use of media diaries as measurement devices, there are a number of less costly alternatives which may be feasible in the interim.

A critical difficulty with respect to effects research in the mass media is that of properly imputing causality. Programme "X" may be identified as containing a higher level of a given attribute (violence, particular social values, etc.), but this does not imply that individuals who watch the programme are necessarily affected even if they display higher levels of some related attribute, such as fear of violence, than non-viewers. Stated baldly, in media research, selection as an alternative explanation for correlational findings can rarely be ruled out, especially in the context of cross-sectional research.

The development of a longitudinal survey instrument for the assessment of mass media effects, undertaken over a period of time deemed appropriate for the measurement of causal processes related to media use, is long overdue. Given the nature of the socialization process of prime-time television, the survey should attempt to include special samples of adolescents in such surveys rather than arbitrarily interviewing only those over the age of 18, and it should attempt to develop special measurement instruments to assess the effects of television on children.

It is hoped the field will reach a sufficient level of maturity in the near future to execute such a project, of which cultural indicators research could form an important part.

NOTES

1. Cf., George Gerbner, Larry Gross, M. Eleey, M. Jackson-Beeck, S. Jeffries-Fox and N. Signorielli, "Television Violence Profile No. 8," *Journal of Communication* 27 (1977): 171-180; George Gerbner, "The Dynamics of Cultural Resistance," in Gaye Tuchman, A. Daniels and James Benet, eds., *Hearth and Home: Images of Women in the Mass Media* (New York: Oxford University Press, 1978), pp. 46-50; George Gerbner and Larry Gross, "Violence Profile No. 6: Trends in Network Television Drama and Viewer Conceptions of Social Reality 1967-1978" (Mimeo, Annenberg School of Communication, University of Pennsylvania, 1976).

2. This "distrust of people" may refer to people in general, or it may refer to political elites (inasmuch as cultivation analysis uses traditional survey items designed to measure "political efficacy"). For a discussion of the survey items used by Gerbner and his associates in cultivation analysis, cf., Michael Hughes, "The Fruits of Cultivation

Analysis: A Re-examination of Some Effects of Television Watching," *Public Opinion Quarterly*, 44:294-295 (1980).

3.   George Gerbner, "The Dynamics of Cultural Resistance," p. 47.

4.   George Gerbner, "A Reply to Newcomb's Critique," *Communication Research* 6 (1977): 228.

5.   Horace Newcomb, "Assessing the Violence Profile of Gerbner and Gross," *Communication Research* 5 (1978): 264-282.

6.   Cf., Paul Hirsch, "Production and Distribution Roles Among Cultural Organizations," *Social Research* 45: (1978): 315-330.

7.   Cf., Anthony Doob and Glenn Macdonald, "Television Viewing and Fear of Victimization: Is the Relationship Causal?" *Journal of Personality and Social Psychology*, 37 (1978): 170-179; also, Hughes, *op. cit.*

8.   Doob and MacDonald used a sample size of only 290. And one of the critical F-ratios used by these researchers to *discount* the television effects hypothesis was close to significance at a level of 0.10 (Doob and MacDonald, Table 5), which is hardly sufficient evidence for a strong claim of null findings.

9.   Hughes, pp. 295-296.

10.   Hughes' use of "dummy variables" as dependent variables in Ordinary Least Square analysis (of which multiple classification analysis is one type) violates two important assumptions: that of an unrestricted range for the dependent variable and the assumption of homoskedasticity of error terms. For a discussion of the implications of this problem, cf., Michael Gillespie, "Log Linear Techniques and the Regression Analysis of Dummy Dependent Variables," *Sociological Methods and Research* 6 (1977): 116 and Leo Goodman, "How Not to Analyze Nonrecursive Systems pertaining to Qualitative Variables," *Political Methodology* 4 (1977): 23-24. For a discussion of the alternative, more justified log-linear techniques which should have been used, cf., Michael Swafford, "Three Parametric Techniques for Contingency Table Analysis: A Nontechnical Commentary," *American Sociological Review* 45 (1980): 664-690.

11.   See also Garriel Salomon and Akiba Cohen, "On the Meaning of and Validity of Television Viewing," *Human Communication Research*, 5 (1978): 264-282; Jack McLeod and Garrett O'Keefe, Jr., "The Socialization Perspective and Communication Behaviour," in F. Kline and P. Tichenor, eds., *Current Perspectives in Mass Communication Research*, Vol. 1, Sage Annual Reviews of Communication (Beverly Hills: Sage Publications, 1972), pp. 121-168; Robert Hawkins and Suzanne Pingree, "Some Processes in the Cultivation Effect," *Communication Research* 7 (1980): 193-226.

12.   Hawkins and Pingree, p. 197; emphasis added.

13.   Cf., Seymour Martin Lipset, *Revolution and Counterrevolution*, 2nd ed. (London: Heineman, 1970); John Porter, "Canadian Character in the 20th Century," in *The Measure of Canadian Society* (Toronto: Gage, 1979), pp. 89-101.

14.   Cf., Craig Crawford and James Curtis, "Canadian-American Differences in Value Orientations," *Studies in Comparative International Development* (forthcoming, 1980).

15.   Porter, "Canadian Character in the 20th Century," p. 98.

16.   Canadian Institute for Public Opinion, "Gallup Report," July 26, 1980.

17.   Unpublished analysis undertaken by the author on data provided from the 1977 Quality of Life study by the York University Institute for Behavioural Research. In this study, 72 per cent of the sample supported a Canadian content regulation, while 13 per cent disapproved. (The author assumes full responsibility for these interpretations and acknowledges that the Institute for Behavioural Research as the source of the data used in the analysis bears no responsibility for these interpretations.)

18.   Cf., Ronald Lambert and James Curtis, "Social Stratification and Canadians' Reactions to American Cultural Influence: Theoretical Problems and Trend Analyses," *International Journal of Comparative Sociology* 20 (1979).

19. Milton Rokeach, *The Nature of Human Values* (New York: Free Press, 1973). For a more recent update involving work done using Rokeach's "value inventory," cf., Milton Rokeach, *Understanding Human Values* (New York: Free Press, 1979).

20. Russell Jones, John Sensenig and Richard Ashmore, "Systems of Values and Their Multidimensional Representation," *Multivariate Behavioural Research*, 13 (1978): 225-270.

21. As reported by Jones et al., op. cit., p. 253.

22. Rokeach uses rank-ordered data which can be expected to produce a singular correlation matrix; while many computer programs might be expected to simply fail to yield results (and print an error message), it appears as if Rokeach obtained results on the basis of computer rounding error—hardly the basis for a major conclusion regarding the dimensionality of human values! Cf., Rokeach, "Change and Stability," pp. 146-147.

23. James Winter and Alan Frizzel, "The Treatment of State-owned versus Private Corporations in English Canadian Dailies," *Canadian Journal of Communication* 6 (1979).

24. Douglas Baer and Ronald Lambert, "Education and Support for Dominant Ideology," paper submitted to the Annual Meeting of the Canadian Sociology and Anthropology Association, Montreal, 1980, p. 2.

25. CRTC Committee of Inquiry into the National Broadcasting Service, "A Content Analysis: The Canadian Broadcasting Corporation: Similarities and Differences of English and French News," report prepared by Arthur Siegel for the Canadian Radio-television and Telecommunications Commission, July 1977.

Chapter 13

On the Implications of Content and Structural Analyses

*John Jackson**

Le mérite de l'une ou l'autre des analyses de contenu et de structure pour le produit culturel est envisagé ici en tant que question de méthodologie. L'objectif visé est de retrouver le rapport entre certaines techniques d'analyse, leurs racines théorétiques et les conséquences d'en adopter une plutôt qu'une autre au niveau empirique. Le débat est fondé sur une étude en cours dans laquelle la relation est faite entre des pièces radiophoniques en langue anglaise de la CBC et leur milieu social.

On examine les hypothèses courantes se rapportant à l'analyse de contenu et de structure, pour arriver à une décision sur la combinaison la plus appropriée, basée sur ces hypothèses et leur relation avec le cadre théorique adopté pour l'étude. En particulier, le travail de deux experts des secteurs sociologiques de la connaissance et de la culture, Lucien Goldmann et Karl Mannheim, est examiné afin de situer chaque technique dans sa propre problématique.

Un texte radiophonique de la CBC a été choisi pour illustrer les implications d'adopter l'une ou l'autre technique. On observe que chacune expose la pièce à des interprétations très différentes, l'une fondée sur l'idée d'identification du contenu entre l'ouvrage et son contexte social; l'autre sur une homologie de structures entre la structure de la pièce et celle des systèmes d'idées de groupes sociaux.

Perhaps this essay should be titled "Content Analysis: Once More Around." Anyone working in communication studies, the sociology of culture, the sociology of knowledge or related fields is familiar with the issues surrounding the long-standing debate on the nature and effectiveness of content analysis.

---

* The author wishes to acknowledge the contribution of his colleagues working on the Concordia University Radio-Drama Project: Professor H. Fink, Mr. Greg Nielsen and Ms. Rosalind Zinman.

Most reviews raise at least two points around which the arguments revolve: the quantitative/qualitative and the manifest/latent content issues.[1] On occasion these two, in turn, are subsumed under the broader topics of form and content and the relations between the two, or the relative advantages and disadvantages of content and structural analyses as techniques.[2]

Other issues, no less important, tend to find their way into the debate. To name but two: insofar as content analysis is associated with the social sciences, the impasse between the subjectivity of literary analysis and the objectivity of science will focus on content analysis and, within the social sciences, content analysis is at times central to clashes between empiricists and anti-empiricists.[3] Needless to say, the list is much longer.

In this essay, the debate is entered with a specific objective in mind. The objective is to seek the relationship between particular techniques of analysis, their theoretical roots and the consequences of adopting one or another at the empirical level. To put it another way, when a researcher is faced with an array of empirical materials, a technique of analysis is adopted as a means of sorting and understanding. In so doing, the theoretical base from which the selected technique was developed also is adopted. Indeed, few researchers would deny that techniques of data gathering and analysis are epistemologically and ontologically neutral, that is, any technique designed for data manipulation presupposes answers to questions about the nature of knowledge and reality. Unfortunately, some researchers are not very explicit about the assumptions underlying their techniques of analysis and, therefore, about the implications of adopting one or another technique.

It is the purpose of this essay to report on an experience in which, faced with a set of radio-drama plays to be understood in relation to their social milieu, decisions had to be made regarding techniques of analysis. A review of the assumptions underlying content and structural analyses was undertaken and decisions were made based on the relations between these assumptions and the theoretical framework initially adopted for the study. In the course of this essay, content and structural analyses will be contrasted by locating each in a particular problematic.

Relating each mode of analysis to a problematic means to link each thought structure of a particular set of epistermological, theoretical and methodological assumptions to a related subject matter. Only in this manner is it possible to assign each to its proper place and to better comprehend the implications of each in the research process. It is not intended to imply that content or structural analyses are inexorably tied to a particular problematic. Modifications are possible when it is understood what is to be modified.

This essay begins with a look at each mode of analysis, reviews familiar arguments, and seeks to understand the objectives of each. This is followed by the attempt to link each mode of analysis with a particular problematic. The works of the two scholars in the fields of the sociology of culture and knowledge, Lucien Goldmann and Karl Mannheim, are taken as representative of two contrasting problematics of thought structures with respect to the analysis of cultural materials.[4] Finally, on the empirical level, one mode is contrasted with the other in application using a selected radio-drama for illustration.

Before proceeding further, it should be noted that the overall interest here is in radio-drama as a cultural product and in uncovering the relations between the structures of these works and idea-systems associated with social groups in English-Canadian society. Radio-drama, especially CBC productions prior to the onset of television, was selected not because it was popular culture (though many would so define it) nor because it was part of the so-called great tradition (few would so classify it), but because in English Canada it was the principal training ground for the development of English Canadian theatre: literary creation, acting, directing and production. For three decades, CBC radio-drama was not only popular entertainment but also the major vehicle through which indigenously produced materials could be made public.[5] These productions were indeed a part of English Canada's invisible culture, invisible in the shadow of American and British literature, drama, and entertainment and, therefore, receiving little critical attention.

Content and Structural Analyses

At first glance what appears to distinguish content analysis from structural analysis is neither the quantitative/qualitative nor the manifest/latent distinctions, but the type of questions addressed to cultural products and whether the investigation remains rooted in the empiricist tradition or crosses over to literary criticism. Some examples will help to illustrate the different approaches.

On the side of content analysis:

(1) In a study of daytime radio serials in the 1940s, Rudolf Arnheim asked, "Do radio serials choose the large centres of modern life as settings . . . or do they prefer small towns or the village? . . . What are the social backgrounds of the people presented in the radio serials?"[6]

(2) In a study of popular songs in the 1960s, the investigator noted that, "attention was paid to four selected topics, chosen not only because of their currency but because of their relevance to the youth subculture . . . love-sex . . . religion . . . violence . . . social protest. . . ."[7]

(3) A study of newspaper advertising in Montreal asked, "What procedures do department stores follow and what adaptations do they make in preparing advertising for a bilingual and bicultural setting? . . . How does the bicultural milieu offset management's advertising decisions?"[8]

(4) In a study of French–English reactions to the October Crisis, "the media portrayal of these two solitudes provides a unique opportunity for explaining in greater detail how English and French Canadians conceive of their alternate realities."[9]

The following are examples from the side of structural analysis:

(1) On the sociology of film: ". . . pourquoi a tel moment historique y a-t-il tel cinema? Pourquoi le neo-realisme en Italie dans les années d'aprés-guerre et non pas en Allemagne ou en France?"[10]

(2) In a study of the American western film: "[what] historical changes in the structure of myth correspond to the changes in the structure of . . . dominant [social institutions]?"[11]

(3) On the sociology of the novel: "The basic hypothesis [is] precisely that the collective character of literary creation derives from the fact that the structures of the world of the work are homologous with the mental structures of certain social groups. . . ."[12]

(4) In a study of the English Canadian novel: "Our . . . intention [is] to show the ways in which the idea of class has found expression in English Canadian novels . . . [to reveal] the ideological matrices in which the idea of class has been embodied . . . [and] suggesting how the ideological configurations underlying the novel might be related to more general ideological principles in society."[13]

The contrast is interesting. One set of questions, those associated with content analysis, concentrate on a moment of time and ask if certain selected categories of content (the background characteristics of characters in plays, negative or positive responses to political candidates, types of behaviour, etc.) of the observed items match those in the society at large or some segment of the society. The relationship is one of identity of content.

The set of questions associated with structural analysis is more inclined to capture totalities and ask if the structures of observed items correspond to the structures of idea-systems within the society. The relationship is one of corresponding or homologous structures rather than one of identity of the content of coding categories.

To extend the comparison further, content analysis leads to descriptions of the "isolated elements which enter into the totality"[14] of the cultural product(s) and matches these with similar isolated elements observed in the world external to the product.

In contrast, structural analysis places the emphasis not on the elements per se, but on the relations among them or the ways in which they are combined. The link between cultural products and their external worlds, then, is not an identity of content but a correspondence between modes of combination of elements.

In the first set of questions, the "facts" seem to speak for themselves, while in the second set the "facts" are the observed effects of "bundles of relations." In this respect, the following comments are revealing:

> Direct observation does reveal to us that human beings are connected by a complex network of social relations. I use the term "social structure" to denote this framework of actually existing relations.[15]

> When we describe structure we are already dealing with general principles far removed from the complicated skein of behaviour, feelings, beliefs, etc. that

constitutes the basis of actual social life. We are, as it were, in the realm of grammar and syntax, not of the spoken word.[16]

Content analysis is compatible with the first statement and structural analysis with the second. The two modes of analysis are embedded in different problematics or thought structures.

Problematic Sources

At the most general level of theoretical assumptions, a review of related literature[17] reveals two axes around which these two modes of analysis appear to revolve. Particular studies may focus on the individual or the collectivity, following the (XY) axis in Figure 13-I, or on the creative or consumption process, following the (AB) axis in Figure 13-I.

Figure 13-1

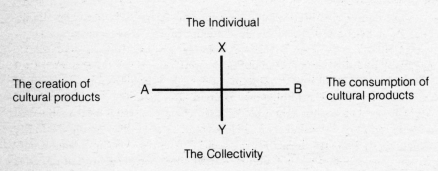

The Individual

X

The creation of   A ——————————+—————————— B   The consumption of
cultural products   cultural products

Y

The Collectivity

In combination, which is the case for most studies in the field, the (XB) cell emphasizes the individual as consumer or recipient of communications while the (BY) cell emphasizes the functions of particular creations relative to idea-systems within the society as a whole. The (AX) cell employs a psychological analysis of the creative process while the (AY) cell generally employs a sociological analysis. Work based on the theoretical assumptions located above the (AB) axis, that is, (AX) and (XB) combinations, tends to assume an atomistic or aggregate conceptualization of society in which the individual is the focus of observation and analysis. At one level, the individual is conceptualized as the consumer of culture and knowledge, as for example, in a study which reported on the "behaviour of adolescents . . . as active agents in the selection of media and integration of materials within media."[18] Manifest behaviour is the locus of both observation and analysis.

At another level, the individual elements are conceptualized as the discrete elements (usually quantifiable but not necessarily) which together somehow or other make up the product consumed.[19] It is here that content analysis combined with attitude and opinion research, is likely to be found.

The cultural object is reduced to its quantifiable elements by content analysis, the participants are reduced to their socio-economic categories or ranged along various axes of sociological variables by such techniques as audience research, and the activities are reduced to clinically isolated simple communication flow models. . . ."[20]

In contrast, work based on the theoretical assumptions located below the (AB) axis, that is, (AY) and (YB) combinations, assume either an emergent or a relational conceptualization of society in which the collectivity is the force of analysis. An emergent conceptualization assumes an integrated and harmonious whole. A relational conceptualization assumes a complex of elements which are at once complementary and contradictory, and the focus of analysis is on these relations.[21] It is here that structural analysis is found.

Wright's 1975 study of the American western film did not use categories to draw out discrete items of information from his sample of film. It did not seek the attitudes and opinions of members of an audience nor categorize audiences according to socio-economic attributes. The interest was in the structure of myth underlying the content and the correspondence of these structures with the structures of dominant institutions.

Similarly, Goldmann directs his work on the novel towards the question of the relation between the structures of creative works and the structures of idea-systems of certain social groups, especially social classes.

At the extremes, content and structural analyses as techniques are embedded in opposing problematics. The use of one or the other without modification carries along a set of assumptions about the social and cultural world. Each limits the questions posed and structures the empirical world in a manner consistent with their theoretical assumptions.

The Sociology of Knowledge and Genetic Structuralism

In the radio-drama project, both techniques of analysis are used to answer different questions, and being cognizant of the above problem the problematic implications of each have been made as explicit as possible. For the moment at least, a combination of the sociology of knowledge problematic of Karl Mannheim and the genetic-structuralist problematic of Lucien Goldmann is used here for analysis.[22] This was decided through a study of various problematics addressed to questions concerning the relations between culture and social structure, an assessment of the appropriateness of the radio-drama data to each, and an exploration of particular techniques relative to each problematic.

The problematics of Mannheim and Goldmann share a common thread. Both are historicist in overall orientation. Mannheim draws from both Weber and Marx but emphasizes the historicism of the former. Goldmann draws from Lukacs, Marx and Piaget, and his historicism is rooted in the work of Lukacs. Both address the production of cultural goods and both emphasize the collectivity, Mannheim less so than Goldmann. Content analysis flows relatively easily from Mannheim's problematic while structural analysis is the defining characteristic of Goldmann's work.[23]

Though Mannheim's work is derived from both Weber and Marx, Weber's thinking had the far greater influence.[24] In contrast, Goldmann's work in the sociology of literature was clearly Marxian in orientation.[25]

Both Mannheim and Goldmann addressed themselves to the production of cultural materials (as opposed to effects), adopted a social determinism and rejected empiricism as valid for the human sciences. They part company where Mannheim's epistemological question leads him to define knowledge as partial and relative and to assign the search for "truth" to the detached intellectual. In contrast, Goldmann, basing his epistemology on Lukacs's notion of practice, chose to stress totalities and to assign the search to social classes and, thus, to the relations of production.

The implications of this departure are two-fold. First, each conceptualizes social class in a different way. While both accept the base/superstructure metaphor, it receives only brief and vague attention from Mannheim, moving as he does, to a Weberian conceptualization of class as stratification. Goldmann, though arguing that social groups are not always related to social classes, locates his theoretical emphasis in social classes and class struggle. This is obviously tied to his acceptance of practice as the criteria of knowledge combined with a structuralist orientation.

Secondly, this stance of Goldmann is consistent with his holistic position, a position which does not allow him to take cultural products as discrete items which reflect (in the sense of a mirror image) the ideologies of social groups or the more general social context. Rather, cultural products are themselves elements of social structures, the products of social groups *as subjects*.[26]

For Goldmann, the analytical task first is to penetrate and depict the structure of the world of a cultural product (such as a radio-drama), to show the relations or combinations of elements within the product, elements being symbolic materials structured into interrelated themes. This first step yields an understanding of the product. Its re-insertion into the broader social structure, the level of *explanation*, requires a search for homologous structures located in the world visions of significant social groups. In other words, "analysis is directed towards instances of formal or structural homology between a social order, its ideology, and its cultural forms."[27] The process is less dependent on the immediately observed than on a structural and historical analysis "in which general form has become apparent, and specific instances of this form can be discovered, not so much or even at all in content, but in specific and autonomous but finally related forms."[28]

Mannheim takes a different route. His relativism, combined with the notion of partial knowledge and the methodology of detachment (as opposed to practice), leads to a view of cultural objects or knowledge as discrete items reflecting the ideologies and utopias of social groups. In this framework a cultural product carries three levels of meaning: (a) an immediate objective meaning, (b) an expressive meaning which directs analysis to the individual author or creator, and (c) a documentary meaning which is the essential character of the product and, as such, a meaning not necessarily available to the individual creator.

The documentary meaning is close but not identical to Goldmann's structural world vision. The difference is that Mannheim calls for an ideal-typical rather than a structural analysis in order to extract the meanings at each level. The process adopted by Mannheim is one in which single expressions (i.e., constructed as ideal-types) and records of thought are traced back to specific world views also described in ideal-typical terms.

Thus Mannheim's statements, if his problematic is carried to the empirical level, describe an identity of content between specific world views and cultural products. Goldmann's search for homologous structures between the world of specific cultural objects and the world visions of social classes takes quite a different direction. With this established, a partial and illustrative analysis of a selected radio-drama follows below.

The Radio-Drama: A Synopsis[29]

A brief synopsis of the play will help orient the reader to the analysis which follows.[30] The main characters in the drama are Roy and Jean Manley. Among the others are two women who work in a flower shop, Roy's secretary Ruth, Jean's mother, Paul Chasik the cabinet-maker and his wife Judy, Jean's Uncle Harry who is a minister, and Roy's business associates, Ballard and Peter.

The action takes place over the months from Mothers' Day in May to the following Christmas Eve. Music and sound effects create the visual counterpart for scene, tone and mood. Music with a college football flavour signals Roy's presence. Jean's musical theme—she is at times very lonely and troubled—is distinct in itself. Musical changes and sound effects also bridge and indicate shifts of scene including the flower shop, the Manley home, the business office, stag party and restaurant.

On one occasion, Jean goes to visit her mother who lives in the small town of Wilbury, a quiet and peaceful place where people are "never too busy to stop and talk. . . . There's no hurry, you know."[31] The language and characterizations of the drama are modern and realistic.

Using the drama of motherhood, the author heightens the tension of the play. Jean decides to leave her husband Roy, after eight years of marriage, and shortly after she learns that she is pregnant with her first child.

The author makes use of a modern-day parable told by Jean to her uncle. We are born at the edge of a wood and life's passage or living is finding our "way through the wood." On the way, there are many distractions—beautiful glades, inviting and comfortable clearings, mossy banks where the warm sun filters through.

These distractions entice and seduce, and most people do not make it through the wood. They stop at the comfortable clearings, unwilling to venture beyond the darkness into the unknown. The lesson of the parable is that it is possible to pass through the wood and pass up what is seemingly comfortable. There is a light beyond, a light of truth. The journey to the light is a searching one: by probing, searching and questioning, the individual matures, and finds strength, independence and freedom.

Jean is the character in the play who articulates the parable and is prepared to go through life seeking and questioning. With human life stirring within her, Jean's dissatisfactions surface. She is not willing to settle for the material comforts of her home and safety of marriage. Her questioning stance brings forth the illusions, the half-truths and the stereotypes her husband cherishes.

Jean's values are reflected in her attitude towards mothering and her own mother. It is not the physical conditions of the home that matter to Jean.

> I don't think of the home as a dear little thatched cottage set in a clearing in the wood . . . or a ten-room mansion with a four-car garage. To me a home should be a place where the warmth comes from the parents' love and understanding, and where the children's hours are lighted by the glimpses of the truth which their parents show them. . . . Parents *can* do so much harm, Uncle Harry.[32]

Jean cherishes close personal relations. She is searching for truth, based on experience. She questions her uncle, a minister, on the meaning of faith and belief, especially in her world of the 1950s, when "moral standards all seem to be changing."[33] For Jean, religion means one's own personal faith and belief, not merely church-going. She stresses the value of the well-being and happiness of the individual, putting a high mark on feeling as opposed to rationalism. She believes that behaviour is caused and can be changed and perfected. Jean is cast as the character of high ideals who is willing to risk the safety and comforts of her married life to face the unknown. She is sure that the way through the wood is the way to truth, emancipation and growth.

Roy Manley, Jean's husband, is a character whose traits and values oppose Jean's. But, "Roy is a good man. He is a respected man. . . . He is a type of Canadian man in whom much of the strength of the country lies."[34]

Roy's response to the news of his wife's pregnancy is one of great pleasure. There is pleasure too at the thought of having a son. "It's got to be a son," he says.[35] As his surname symbolically suggests, the meaning of having a child for Roy is closely tied to his sense of manliness. Roy sees his son as an extension of himself. One of his first actions was to go out and buy a pair of boxing gloves "just made for baby's hands."[36] Of course, Roy would initiate his son in the "Manley" way: boxing gloves and stag parties. "I want him [my son] to be a man, to believe in the right things. . . . We're going to be pals, my boy and I."[37]

Roy is sure about his beliefs.

> The basic things—the fundamentals. First, the family, the home. Destroy the family and you destroy the nation. Second, religion—faith in God. Going to

church is an old Canadian custom. See where I'm getting to now? The fundamentals.[38]

He sees no contradiction in tying his fundamental beliefs to the commodity he
is selling. He is preoccupied with his business—Domestic Fuels—and a pend-
ing advertising campaign.

> I want our advertisements to express our belief in these things—sell that belief.
> As a matter of fact, it's an idea that ties in very well with our product Domestic
> Fuels—we sell to the home. And we're going to picture the home, the family, as
> a fortress against Communism.[39]

As Jean notes, he has a "blind faith in things—motherhood, the Canadian people, things like that."[40] Anyone or anything else, such as Communism, is suspect. Roy is filled with half-truths, stereotypes of agnosticism,
Canadianism, Communism, foreigners, women, mothers and children.

Roy is obviously distressed at his wife's decision to leave him. He is left
momentarily confused and powerless, retreating into boyhood dreams of success, fights and stag parties. However, it does not take Roy long to reconsider.
He asserts,

> To hell with clever women. Instinct, Ruthie—that's what it is. Instinct. Some
> women understand men . . . some don't know what makes 'em tick. . . . You
> know what a man is, Ruthie?. . .[41]

Roy finds comfort in Ruth, his secretary, who is so kind, so humble.

> You're comfortable—no, that isn't right . . . comforting. . . . I hadn't noticed
> it before—but you got that instinct to comfort a man—when he needs it.[42]

The questions that confront Jean and Roy Manley go beyond their lives.
The author directs the parable to all Canadians—after all, Jean and Roy are
"typical." The probing light reaches beyond the surface of Canadian society
to the institutions of family and church, the market economy, home and
motherhood: husband-wife relations, male-female roles, and beliefs. Jean
challenges all.

The Analysis

Content and structural analyses each require an identical point of entry insofar as each must, at the level of observation, deal with what is given, that is,
the surface content. The cutting-up of the play according to a set of
categories (ideal-types as per Mannheim) or to thematic elements (as per
Goldmann) requires a definition of coding units.

A content analysis would tend to adopt units based on the speeches of individual characters and/or the role content of the actions of characters, that
is, units which are amenable to quantification. Since the major interest here is
in structural analysis where themes are the basic elements and the relations
between themes take priority over the frequency of appearance of any single

one, what are best described as "units of dialogue" are used here. For the moment, it is sufficient to note that a unit of dialogue is an exchange of statements made in an interaction situation in which an exchange of propositions is completed.

The following example, extracted from the play, will serve to illustrate these units. Each unit is numbered, the numbers referring to the structural analysis that follows.

Each unit is coded indicating the scene (first two digits), the sequence (next three digits), and the theme (last two digits).

Extract from "The Way Through the Wood" [43]

Music: Up and out

GIRL: (Assistant in flower shop) Will that be all then, Mr. Manley?

ROY: Yes—I think so. Two dozen red roses. Mother likes them. Funny how all women go for red roses, isn't it?

GIRL: Do they?

ROY: Sure they do. Every time. I sometimes wonder how you florists have enough red roses to go around every Mother's Day.

O1001-11

GIRL: Oh, we manage. Shall I send the bill to your office?

ROY: Yes, do that. (Going) Try and see that they get there first thing in the morning, eh?

GIRL: We'll do our best, Mr. Manley.

ROY: Okay. Good-bye.

GIRL: Good-bye.

01002-11

GIRL: Well, he's done his duty for the year.

GIRL 2: (Slightly off) What's that, Mary?

GIRL: I say he's done his duty for the year. I'd like to know if he ever does anything for his mother in between. And I bet he'd even forget Mother's Day if his secretary didn't remind him.

GIRL 2: You sound bitter, dear.

GIRL: I'm always bitter on Mother's Day. Did you hear him? "Funny how *all* women go for red roses." How does he know?

01003-25

GIRL 2: That's just one of those handy things men make up for themselves. Saves a lot of trouble—and keeps the price of red roses up.

GIRL: And helps to pay our wages. Oh, here's another. This one's yours.

GIRL 2: Okay.

Sound: At "our wages" above the traffic noise swells as a customer enters.

GIRL 2: Yes, sir — can I help you?

MAN: (Slight fade in) Yes . . . er . . . I'd like a couple of dozen red roses.

01004-14

* * *

Content Analysis

As noted above, Mannheim's schema draws attention to three levels of meaning: the objective, expressive and documentary meanings. The expressive level, which leads us directly to a consideration of the author's and producer's "intended" meanings, is a problematic rejected in this essay. In so doing, Mannheim's concept of the worldview of a cultural object is altered.

The objective meaning is the meaning of the observed or objective content arrived at through an ideal-typical analysis. Simultaneously, the documentary meaning can be discerned either through the construction of the ideal-types (the categories of analysis), from observations of the society at large or through the matching of such observations with ideal types constructed from a reading of the play, in much the same way in which sociologists place specific communities along a rural-urban continuum. The point is, at the level of documentary meanings, the result is an identity of content.

A selected reading of the play points to any number of types which could be constructed around definitions of male-female roles: husband/wife, son/mother, daughter/mother, son/father, daughter/father, male dominant/female dominant attitudes towards male-female roles in the family, and in the work setting, attitudes towards specific social institutions, and so on. Even a cursory reading of the play points to the utility of any set of categories which depicts some aspect of male/female relations with an emphasis on the problem of women in society.

A careful analysis based on some such set of categories would reveal the struggle of a woman to liberate herself from the intellectual and moral tyranny of a male-dominated social setting, a setting acutely present in Jean's relations with her husband and the actions of their respective supporting characters. The resolution reveals the continuity of a male-dominated society, with extreme loneliness, if not ostracism, awaiting Jean. These results, in turn and by imputation, may be taken as related to (in the sense of an identity of content) the attitudes of and conflicts in the suburban middle classes of the 1940s and 1950s over the role of women.

Structural Analysis

A structural analysis proceeds from a different set of questions. Following Goldmann, the interest here is in structural homologies. The *relation* between the cultural object and the social world of which it is a part in and of itself (not a mirror image) is the focus of analysis.

Referring back to the extract from the play, the first step is a simple coding of all units of dialogue by scene and sequence as recorded in the first five digits. The next step, which involves the reconstruction of the themes, is at the level of analysis. At this point each unit of dialogue is placed on an index card. The cards are then sorted into themes. This requires a judgment which only can be made through a constant shifting between the content of the play and a knowledge of the social world in which the play is rooted. The resulting themes are no longer observational units or samples of manifest content but clusters of relations among these units.

Theme 11 (the last two digits) is a combination of units which expresses a particular set of values with some coherence running through the work. Theme 25 expresses another such set. The themes do not, of course, appear in sequence. The units of each are scattered throughout the play. In the case of the illustration, the first and second units are linked together as part of theme 11, the third unit is a member of another theme, and the fourth of yet another. The relations among the units within each theme are simply relations of identity of meaning.

Two major themes interact in a specific manner throughout the play. Theme 11, identified with Roy, is a value set which in the popular social science of the day was characterized as "1950s suburban middle class," most often associated with mobile white-collar, professional and managerial occupations.

It is a set which places a high priority on a romantic idealization of family and community, an idealization which contained specific prescriptions regarding the respective behaviours of males and females, based on male dominance and aggressiveness. The emphasis on family and community contained an exclusiveness which encouraged negative attitudes towards "outgroup" members. The values tended to be politically conservative as opposed to liberal. Male aggressiveness was a psychological correlate of free enterprise and competition.

Theme 25, identified with Jean, though nonetheless "middle class," was characterized as influenced by existentialism but more concretely expressed in an empiricism (one believes only what one sees) and individualism. It is anticonformist and skeptical of values surrounding family, community and nation. In this sense it is more open and tolerant. It tends to be politically liberal to left-liberal. Little value is placed on collectivities, while considerable value is placed on the individual. The individual here is not the aggressive free-enterpriser but the open, feeling individual who seeks solutions to social problems in perfecting interpersonal relations.

The remaining themes are sub-themes of one or the other value sets. Two of these characterize, at the concrete level, the personifications of the two major themes primarily through the characters of Roy and Jean. An additional three refer to the sources and institutional supports of the basic themes; e.g., Roy's theme finds its source in the United States media and Jean's in Europe via immigration. Roy's themes, the church and the economy, are mutually reinforcing.

The next and final step is concerned with the relations among the themes. It is this level of analysis which yields the structures that can be examined in relation to structures of idea-systems within the larger society. The procedure is to place the units of dialogue sequentially along a horizontal axis while at the same time organize them thematically along a vertical axis.[44] For purposes of illustration, eight themes, numbered from 1 to 8 are used. The resulting simulation of the play would look something like the diagram below:

```
1 . . 4 . . . .
1 2 . . . . . .
. 2 . . . 6 . .
. 2 . . . 6 . .
. . . 4 . . . 8
1 . . 4 . . . .
. 2 . 4 . . 7 .
etc.
```

By reading from left to right, the manifest content or story line is obtained. By reading from top to bottom, the thematic content is revealed, but one step removed from observation insofar as the themes consist of the units of dialogue ordered not in sequence but by theme. The way in which the themes are related is arrived at by examining the interaction between 1, 2, 4, via the story line.

The two major themes stand in opposition to each other, with Roy's theme in a dominant position and Jean's in a subordinate position. There is no resolution to the tension in the sense of a new thesis. The play concludes with Roy's theme in a dominant position, though in the middle sequences Jean's gains a temporary ascendency.

This article begins the first set of "successive approximations" as called for by Goldmann. This first approximation must now interact, as it were, with approximations of appropriate social structures, such as social groups. As a final note, however, a hypothesis is advanced with respect to this operation.

The hypothesis is that the structure of the play as revealed in its first approximation is homologous with the mental structures of particular factions of social classes in the same time frame insofar as the manner in which these factions are related to each other. The relationship between the two major themes corresponds to the relationship between the ideologies adhered to by two factions of the middle class during the 1940s and 1950s. This is the tension between the old middle class (rural and urban independent commodity producers and merchants) and the new middle class (professional and managerial personnel). The latter category is objectively a part of the proletariat but subjectively identifies with the capitalist class.[45]

Evidence suggests that the former faction was beginning to lose its dominant position to the latter after 1940. The ideology of the former grouping, though frequently associated in the popular social science literature with the organization man, corresponds to that described as theme 11. The relationship between theme 11 and theme 25 corresponds to the relations between these two factions. This hypothesis would guide further inquiries, inquiries which would require a structural analysis of these ideologies.

Recapitulation

It appears that content and structural analyses lead in different directions. A content analysis is inclined to portray the play as a discussion of the role of women in society and the futility of assuming a resolution other than a continuation of the status quo. A structural analysis leads to a set of interrelated themes structured in a fashion homologous to the ideologies of particular factions of particular social classes. In this analysis the play does not reflect a particular aspect of class struggle, it is itself a part of that struggle expressing a correspondence in origin and development between its combination of themes and the combination of themes within the ideologies of the competing factions.

Content analysis leads to positing a relation between a cultural product and the social world which is best described as an identity of content. In contrast, structural analysis leads to probing relationships between the two which are best described as structural homologies. It is implied here that "a cultural phenomenon acquires its full significance only when it is seen as a form of general social processes or structure."[46] The underlying assumption is that a cultural product is not ephemeral as in a mirror image but is itself a reality. In contrast, Mannheim's relativism and concept of partial knowledge emphasizes social context, a context which knowledge or culture somehow represents or reflects.

Furthermore, Goldmann's problematic, in which the criteria for knowledge are to be found in practice and class struggle, defines the social group, not the individual, as the *subject*. Mannheim's problematic locates the criteria for knowledge in the detached intellectual shifting the emphasis to the individual as subject, leaving the social group as *context*.

The objective of this essay was to contrast content analysis with structural analysis by locating each in a particular problematic and to follow through with an illustrative analysis of one item. It was, however, the intention to use both modes of analysis. The selection of Mannheim's sociology of knowledge thesis permits the adoption of a content analysis without entirely violating the Goldmann problematic upon which this work is based. This is possible because of the similarities found in the two.

However, content analysis is adopted in a very limited way and as a means for initially sorting the volume of scripts on hand. The scripts will be sorted by time period, author and producer. Within each of these categories they will be submitted to a content analysis based on an ideal-typical mode, consistent with Mannheim. This will yield the "objective meanings" of the works and serve to guide the formulation of a subsequent structural analysis. It will be from this latter phase that conclusions are drawn about the relations between the materials and the society at large.

NOTES

1.   For example, see: O. R. Holsti, *Content Analysis for the Social Sciences and Humanities* (Don Mills: Addison-Wesley, 1969); George H. Lewis, "The Sociology of Popular Culture," *Current Sociology* 26 (3) 1978.
2.   For example, see: Ibid., pp. 26-31, Hugh D. Duncan, *Symbols in Society* (New York: Oxford University Press, 1978), pp. 3-15; Lucien Goldmann, *Toward a Sociology of the Novel* (London: Tavistock Publications, 1975), pp. 158-160.
3.   For example, see: Robert E. Spiller, "Value and Method in American Studies," *Jahrbuch fur Amerikastudien*, Band 4, 1959, p. 18, as cited in Duncan, op. cit., and John Shepherd, "Music and Social Control," *Catalyst* 13 (1959): 37-46.
4.   Goldmann, op. cit.; Karl Mannheim, *Ideology and Utopia* (New York: Harcourt Brace Jovanovich, 1955).
5.   The Concordia University Radio-Drama Archives provide the data base for the project. The archives contain two sets of materials: CBC English language radio-drama scripts produced between 1933 and 1961 and ancillary materials composed of administrative and production correspondence, memoranda, notations, etc. from the CBC central registries in Halifax, Montreal, Ottawa, Toronto and Vancouver. The script material is indexed and stored on computer tapes permitting ready access to the materials according to title, producer, original author, date and location of production, and a content description. The Archives are open to interested scholars. Information may be obtained by writing Professor Howard Fink, Radio-Drama Project, Concordia University, Sir George Williams Campus, 1455 Maisonneuve Boulevard West, Montreal, Quebec, Canada, H3G 1M8.
6.   Rudolf Arnheim, "The World of the Daytime Serial," *Mass Communications*, edited by Wilbur Schramm (2nd edition, Urbana: University of Illinois Press, 1960), pp. 392-393.
7.   Richard R. Cole, "Top Songs in the Sixties: A Content Analysis of Popular Lyrics," *Mass Communications and Youth: Some Current Perspectives*, edited by F. G. Kline and Peter Clarke (London: Sage Publications, 1971), p. 89.
8.   F. Elkin and M. B. Hill, "Bicultural and Bilingual Adaptations in French Canada: The Example of Retail Advertising," *Canadian Review of Sociology and Anthropology* 2 (May 1965): 135.
9.   Gertrude J. Robinson, "The Politics of Information and Culture during Canada's October Crisis," *Studies in Canadian Communications*, edited by G. J. Robinson and D. Theall (Montreal: McGill University Press, 1975), p. 142.
10.   A. Goldmann, "Quelques problemes de sociologie du cinema," *Sociologie et Societes* 8 (1976): 72.
11.   W. Wright, *Six Guns and Society: A Structural Study of the Western* (Berkeley: University of California Press, 1975), p. 14.
12.   Lucien Goldmann, op. cit., p. 159.
13.   J. Paul Grayson and L. M. Grayson, "Class and Ideologies of Class in the English

Canadian Novel," *Canadian Review of Sociology and Anthropology* 15 (1978): 279-280.

14.   Claude Lévi-Strauss, "The Structural Study of Myth," *The Structuralists from Marx to Lévi-Strauss,* edited by R. de George and F. de George (Garden City, New York: Doubleday & Company, 1972), p. 174.

15.   A. R. Radcliffe-Brown, *Structure and Function in Primitive Society* (London: Cohen & West, 1952), p. 190.

16.   Meyer Fortes, *Time and Social Structure and Other Essays* (New York: Humanities Press, Inc., 1970), p. 3.

17.   Lewis, op. cit. James Carey, "Communications and Culture," *Communications Research* 2 (1975): 176-189. James Anderson, "Mass Communications Theory and Research: An Overview," *Communications Yearbook I,* edited by Brent D. Ruben (New Brunswick, New Jersey: Transaction Books, 1977), pp. 279-289. Paul Cappon, ed., *In Our Own House: Social Perspectives on Canadian Literature* (Toronto: McClelland & Stewart, Ltd., 1978). Mikel Dufrenne et al., eds., "Aesthetics and the Sciences of Art," *Main Trends of Research in the Social and Human Sciences* (Part 2, Vol. 1, Paris: Mouton & UNESCO, 1978).

18.   Serena E. Wade, "Adolescents, Creativity and Media: An Exploratory Study," Mass Communications and Youth, pp. 39-50.

19.   Arnheim, op. cit.

20.   Bryn Jones, "The Politics of Popular Culture," *Working Papers on Cultural Studies,* No. 6, p. 25, as cited in Shepherd, op. cit.

21.   Jean Piaget, *Structuralism* (New York: Harper & Row, 1970), pp. 6-10. L. Goldmann, op. cit., pp. 157-158.

22.   We have also attempted to incorporate a modified version of Northrop Frye's archetypal literary criticism. See Howard Fink et al., "Literary and Sociological Approaches to the Analysis of CBC English Language Radio-Drama," paper presented at the Annual Meetings of the Canadian Ethnological Society, Montreal, March 1980.

23.   This section is based on Greg Nielsen, "Problematics for a Sociology of Cultural Products," unpublished MA Thesis, Department of Sociology and Anthropology, Concordia University, 1980.

24.   Peter Hamilton, *Knowledge and Social Structure* (London: Routledge & Kegan Paul, 1974), p. 121.

25.   Raymond Williams, *Marxism and Literature* (Oxford: Oxford University Press, 1977), pp. 138. Terry Eagleton, *Marxism and Literary Criticism* (London: Methuen & Co., Ltd., 1976), pp. 32-34.

26.   L. Goldmann, op. cit., pp. 159-160.

27.   Williams, op. cit., p. 106.

28.   Ibid., p. 105 (emphasis added).

29.   The synopsis was contributed by Rosalind Zinman in Fink et al.

30.   "The Way Through the Wood," CBC broadcast, December 9, 1951. Written by Alan King, produced and directed by Peter McDonald. Music composed by Lucio Agostini and directed by Samuel Hersenboren.

31.   Ibid., p. 24.

32.   Ibid., p. 11.

33.   Ibid., p. 10.

34.   Ibid., p. 12.

35.   Ibid., p. 4.

36.   Ibid., p. 13.

37.   Ibid., p. 18.

38.   Ibid., p. 7.

39.   Ibid., p. 8.

40.   Ibid., p. 11.

41.   Ibid., p. 44.

42.   Ibid., p. 45.

43.   Ibid., pp. 1-2.

44.   See, for example: Lévi-Strauss, op. cit.

45.   See, for example: Carl J. Cuneo, "A Class Perspective on Regionalism," *Modernization and the Canadian State,* edited by D. Glenday et al. (Toronto: Macmillan of Canada, 1978), pp. 132-156.

46.   Williams, op. cit., p. 105.

Chapter 14

L'élection du Parti québécois en novembre 1976: axiologie du discours de presse

Michel de Repentigny

In the following paper, the author describes a linguistic method for analyzing newspaper content, an approach to content analysis which he devised by adapting the theory and methodology of functional syntax to the needs of treating objectively and coherently the semantic content of a large number of newspaper articles. His main objective is to analyze the content of political discourse in newspapers as a linguistically structured object, with the sentence as the basic formal and linguistic unit.

The subject treated is the election of the Parti québécois in November 1976 as it was perceived by the political and social actors whose reactions to this event were reported by the seven newspapers selected for the study. These actors fall into two groups of antagonists: Pequistes and Non Pequistes, the latter group being made up, for the most part, of members of the federal or provincial political parties and, to a lesser extent, by non-political social agents coming from different fields of endeavour, but principally, to no one's surprise, from the economic and industrial sectors.

The first task assigned to this study was that of drawing up a lexicon conceived as a closed list of actors and political concepts or "stakes," such as Quebec, Sovereignty-Association, Language, etc. which were hypothetically taken to be sufficiently recurrent in the ensuing political discourse as to adequately circumscribe what it was that most retained the attention of those who held such discourse, and which, to them, thus represented the major aspects of the news event in question.

The sentences in the newspapers which contain, either explicitly or implicitly, an item of this lexicon, constitute the corpus of this research project. They are subsequently divided, in accordance with the objective criteria of functional syntax, into three logical (i.e., non-linguistic) categories: Actors, Actions and Propositions. The purpose of this division is two-fold: to identify the actors, actions and propositions relevant to the subject matter, and to draw up a complete inventory of syntactic associations of the terms of the lexi-

con with one another as well as with contextual linguistic segments or terms which are indeterminate and undeterminable outside a corpus of actual use.

Once the complete inventory of term or segment associations is established, the final procedure consists of describing the semantic nature and make-up of these syntactic associations (or in the wording of this study: their axiological content): a procedure which implies that the content analysis of such a corpus must indicate whether a given association in the inventory of term X with term Y is direct or indirect; and if direct, that the semantic content of those terms which function as linguistic intermediaries between the two be examined, and the axiological information they supply in regard to lexicon items be given.

The results of this undertaking, as they are given in this paper, are strictly preliminary: they reflect the possibilities of this method to proceed from the traditional standpoint of content analysis, which is to measure the content of a corpus according to pre-determined hypotheses and categories, while indicating by the same token how an axiological study of these results can be carried out.

Cette communication est le fruit d'une application concrète de procédés méthodologiques pour l'analyse d'un contenu de presse qui, à l'époque où fut faite cette communication, étaient encore en gestation et où les principes théoriques qui les sous-tendent n'avaient pas encore fait l'objet d'une mise au point bien arrêtée. Par conséquent, le lecteur est prié de garder présent à l'esprit le fait qu'il s'agit ici de la présentation d'une approche encore tâtonnante. Tel quel, donc, cet article tient beaucoup plus du domaine des intentions de recherche que de la description triomphante de résultats assurés. Ce n'est cependant que partie remise car au moment où paraîtra cet article la thèse de doctorat, dont tout ce qui suit représente l'objet, aura été achevée.

OBJECTIF

Le but que nous poursuivons c'est de tenter de cerner puis de décrire le discours politique de presse québécois et canadien en tant qu'objet linguistique.

Notre propos n'est pas de faire double emploi avec tout ce qui s'est fait depuis plusieurs décennies — notamment aux Etats-Unis et en France — en matière et en manières d'analyse de "contenu" chez les uns ou de "discours" chez les autres: nos ambitions sont trop modestes pour que nous pretendions ici doubler ces recherches-là en les prenant de vitesse sur le plan théorique. Il n'entre donc pas dans les intentions de ce travail de montrer comment les pratiques de l'analyse de discours ou du "content analysis" pourraient s'asseoir sur de plus solides assises théoriques; ni même d'identifier les lacunes de telle ou telle étude qui a été faite (et dont la réalisation est en soi méritoire étant donné le contexte de la grande confusion théorique qui règne dans ce domaine des sciences humaines) en suggérant les moyens de les combler d'une façon adéquate ou jusqu'ici insoupçonnée.

Notre seule prétention, et elle est bien modeste, sera de faire valoir la possibilité très réelle d'étudier un contenu de communication de telle manière que soient respectés les principes d'une théorie stable et éprouvée — celle de la linguistique fonctionnelle — et d'indiquer la possibilité éminemment souhaitable d'entr'ouvrir une porte par où nous souhaiterions entrer en contact avec des chercheurs d'autres disciplines que la linguistique, et à qui nous laisserions le soin de s'occuper des questions non-linguistiques que n'aura pas soulevées cette thèse ou qu'elle n'aura pas su traiter de façon satisfaisante.

Nous estimerons avoir atteint notre objectif si, en fin de parcours, cette thèse apportait une meilleure connaissance, d'abord des rapports fonctionnels entre la structuration syntaxique d'un discours et les significations qu'il communique, et ensuite des comportements discursifs de nos quotidiens lorsqu'ils traitent de ce qu'il est convenu d'appeler "la question nationale" au Québec.

L'intitulé de notre recherche implique que nous avons *analysé* un discours de presse et plus précisément un *contenu*. Cette double implication rend indispensable que nous situions notre recherche par rapport aux vastes champs de l'analyse de contenu, entendue au sens du *content analysis* américain et de l'analyse de discours telle qu'elle se pratique en France.

CONTEXTE THÉORIQUE

Le "content analysis" américain

Telle que nous la connaissons aujourd'hui, l'analyse de contenu a pris son point de départ dans les services d'intelligence américains lors de la Deuxième Guerre, s'est raffinée à son emploi par des politicologues qui s'en sont servi pour appuyer prédictions et orientations en politique étrangère et de défense par le gouvernement américain, et d'une façon générale, depuis le *Content Analysis in Communication Research* (1952) de Bernard Berelson, par les sociologues nord-américains qui se sont intéressés aux communications de masse et qui ont multiplié les programmes et les centres d'études ou de recherches en journalisme-communication aux Etats-Unis d'abord, au Canada ensuite et depuis peu, en France.[1]

L'analyse de contenu a donc été, pour des raisons historiques, l'affaire des sociologues qui, comme les historiens, ont vite éprouvé le besoin de soumettre textes et documents écrits à des analyses plus rigoureuses (ou plus expéditives) que celles que pouvait représenter une lecture attentive ou une connaissance "intime" de ces écrits.

L'empirisme et l'attitude mécaniste caractérisent la pratique nord-américaine de l'analyse de contenu où l'on n'est vraiment jamais très loin de "réalités palpables." Dans cette optique, un journal c'est très souvent ou à tout le moins d'abord, un objet matériel bien concret avant que d'être l'objet des considérations plus mentalistes auxquelles son contenu, l'ensemble de ses sens ou ses structurations proprement sémantiques et idéologiques invitent, par ailleurs, d'autres approches d'analyse.[2]

La nature ou l'identité du contenu qu'on se fixe pour objectif de rendre explicite n'entrent pas ou peu dans les considérations théoriques ou méthodologiques préalables de l'analyse de contenu. Dans la plupart des cas, les questions relatives aux unités d'un contenu ne se posent pas: c'est l'article (en analyse de presse) considéré comme un tout qui est "codé" selon les catégories de l'analyste et selon son orientation générale en termes d'un "contenu" positif, neutre ou négatif; ce dernier aspect du codage étant le resultat d'une perception consensuelle de l'orientation de l'article qui se dégage de sa lecture par plusieurs encodeurs.

Ce que "contenu" recouvre ou peut recouvrir est tenu pour une chose acquise. Tout se passe comme si analyste et lecteur s'entendaient pour comprendre, naïvement, qu'il s'agit là du "sens" d'un discours, de son "orientation," de ses "points de vue" sur les êtres et les choses, de ses "parti-pris," etc. Ainsi, les unités discursives ne font pas toujours l'objet de définitions préalables ou rigoureusement opératoires: lorsque le corpus se compose de textes de presse, par exemple, l'unité n'est ni le mot, ni la phrase, ni l'alinéa. Ce que l'analyste retient dans tel article peut être n'importe laquelle de ces divisions discursives. Mais il ne retient pas telle phrase, tel alinéa ou telle "idée" pour la raison qu'il s'agit là d'unités discursives mais plus simplement parce que le journal y parle du sujet de son étude.

De telle sorte qu'en définitive et pour l'essentiel, le contenu n'est pas, strictement parlant, celui des messages mais bien plutôt celui que l'analyste a lui-même retenu au départ et qu'il appelle "sujets" ou "catégories" ou même "hypothèses": en d'autres termes, c'est l'ensemble des propositions que formule l'analyste pour définir ou identifier les sujets (thèmes), les catégories (contenu logique) et ses hypothèses qui constituent le contenu.

Une des principales conséquences d'une telle pratique de l'analyse de contenu, c'est que l'appareil méthodologique donne une place considérable aux données quantitatives. Au fait, l'essence même de l'étude s'y trouve car son objectif consiste précisément à *mesurer* un objet qu'on met en rapport avec des éléments de contenu qui transcendent l'objet. Les compilations, les distributions, les relations et corrélations des éléments de contenu fixés au départ servent ici à caractériser l'objet et à le comparer soit à un autre objet de même nature, soit à des données modèles.

L'analyse du (de) discours

Nous regroupons sous l'appellation "analyse du (de) discours" la pratique, abondante, variée et souvent complexe, de l'analyse de "textes" selon des modèles structuraux-linguistiques.

L'analyse du discours s'est constituée en champ de recherche surtout au cours des dix dernières années[3], en France, et ses principales manifestations ont émané de centres de recherche qui se sont inspirés de théories linguistiques, allant du formalisme russe au transformationalisme en passant par le distributionnalisme, pour poser la problématique du discours, c'est-à-dire d'unités textuelles qui, par définition, dépassent les limites de la phrase.

L'analyse de discours fait le pont en quelque sorte entre la linguistique et le *content analysis*. Les premières étapes de sa méthodologie lui font faire l'analyse linguistique d'un discours en vue de dépasser la stricte structuration linguistique du discours tel que le définissent les linguistes et d'accéder à un domaine de considérations où points de vue et réflexions sur les choses ne sont plus guère inspirés par la linguistique mais relèvent plutôt de la sociologie, de la psychologie sociale, de l'étude de "formations sociales", de la sémiotique, etc. En nous contentant ici de schématiser les voies qu'emprunte l'analyse de discours pour dégager les caractères structuraux immanents d'un corpus, nous pouvons les ramener aux deux approches qui se sont avérées jusqu'à maintenant les plus abondantes en travaux de recherches et en publications: analyses lexicologiques (lexicométrie et champs sémantiques) et analyses syn- taxiques (approches distributionnalistes et transformationnalistes).

On voit d'emblée que l'analyse de discours se situe aux limites du champ de la linguistique *stricto sensu*: aux limites en ce sens qu'elle ne peut pas, pour le moment du moins, quitter des yeux ce champ auquel elle emprunte des concepts et des méthodes dans l'espoir de les articuler et de les intégrer dans une théorie du discours, c'est-à-dire d'ensembles signifiants qui participent de la communication par signes linguistiques mais dont les structurations ne sont pas que linguistiques. Qu'elle passe pour une "linguistique du discours" suggère déjà l'ambivalence de son statut théorique: une linguistique encore "balbutiante"[4] parce qu'elle prend pour objet autre chose que la langue ou encore parce que ses objectifs lui font dépasser ceux d'une description stricte- ment linguistique — ce qu'elle est aussi — et l'amènent sur un terrain qu'elle partage avec d'autres sciences humaines.

Malgré des dissemblances criantes, surtout en ce qui regarde le postulat de l'immédiateté ou non du sens ou de son uni (équi-) vocité, l'analyse de con- tenu et celle du discours ont en commun un point de vue sur le corpus-objet qui donne tout son poids au principe fondamental de la linguistique fonction- nelle, à savoir que "parler, c'est communiquer." Elles tiennent compte en ef- fet des situations de communication, c'est-à-dire des facteurs ou des com- posantes non-linguistiques qui sont présupposés par l'acte du discours, tels que les statuts respectifs du sujet parlant et du récepteur, les rôles que jouent formations sociales ou conditions de production dans le processus d'énoncia- tion, etc. Toutes choses dont l'analyse linguistique, même fonctionnelle, n'in- clut guère dans ses objectifs, les ayant toujours considérées comme hors de son champ d'étude, "comme réservoir des complexités difficiles à ordonner et lieu où pouvaient se développer la subjectivité du locuteur, mais plus encore celle du chercheur."[5]

Pour les analystes de discours, et contrairement à ceux du *content analysis*, la structure linguistique d'un texte n'est pas transparente. Ces deux pratiques de textes considèrent bien le texte comme un objet social au même titre que n'importe quelle autre manifestation de comportements sociaux, mais seule l'analyse de discours se préoccupe, dans un premier temps, des caractères structuraux immanents d'un texte dont la substance linguistique n'est pas perçue comme "innocente": les attributs structuraux-linguistiques du discours renvoient à des présupposés et à des implications transtextuelles de production de "messages."

On peut entrevoir les grandeurs et les servitudes de l'analyse de discours. Il est indéniable qu'elle est beaucoup mieux appareillée que la traditionnelle analyse de contenu pour envisager et traiter des questions relatives au contenu d'un discours entendu au sens strict d'un ensemble linguistique structuré de sens et de significations. S'il est vrai qu'un discours, de quelque genre qu'il soit, n'est pas qu'objet linguistique et qu'à le considérer tel n'est pas une raison suffisante pour qu'on l'analyse linguistiquement—l'histoire, par exemple, étant aussi apte à rendre compte des *Serments de Strasbourg* que la philologie ou la linguistique moderne—il n'en demeure pas moins que son énonciation et sa communication passent par la langue, et sans doute d'une manière encore plus contraignante dans le cas d'un discours qui prend la forme écrite, où les éléments de la situation non-linguistique de communication d'un message oral doivent être pris en charge, énoncés linguistiquement, par le texte. Or, il nous semble que l'analyse d'inspiration linguistique du discours tente, en gros, de répondre à la question de savoir comment le discours ou tel type de discours passent ou ne passent pas par la langue. Nos pensées et nos points de vue sur les choses ne sont pas forcément linguistiques de nature: cependant, la structuration linguistique demeure une condition nécessaire à leur communication écrite, qu'il s'agisse d'une dissertation, d'un article sur un fait divers ou d'une liste d'épicerie.

En conséquence, l'entreprise à laquelle se livre l'analyse de discours apparaît immense: et, du fait de son ampleur, toujours fragmentaire si on compare les travaux et les réflexions qu'elle a apportés jusqu'à ce jour à une hypothétique théorie générale du discours. Maingueneau conclut: "Notre parcours, au lieu de nous faire rencontrer des méthodes s'exerçant mécaniquement dans des domaines constitués, n'a guère suscité que des interrogations, sans même nous permettre de circonscrire exactement le champ de l'analyse du discours."[6]

Avant lui, Régine Robin, après avoir montré le caractère fondamental de l'apport de la linguistique à l'analyse du discours, doutait qu'une telle analyse puisse rester intra-linguistique et "posait dès l'abord que les discours sont gouvernés par des formations idéologiques", d'où la nécessité bien sentie d'élaborer une théorie qui un jour, articulerait d'une façon adéquate le discours "entité linguistique" et le discours "formations sociales." Mais une telle théorie n'existe pas; "il faudra maintenant trouver des solutions."[7]

Mais en attendant, on assiste à une espèce de bricolage méthodologique, à des pratiques *ad hoc* de l'analyse de corpus, qui, pour prolifiques et valables qu'elles soient, ne constituent pas pour autant, toutes ensemble, une "linguistique du discours."

L'analyse linguistique

L'analyse de contenu, l'exégèse ou l'étude thématique en littérature ont su étudier un corpus sans pour autant le soumettre aux exigences d'une analyse linguistique comme telle. Du reste, et dans la vaste majorité des cas, cette question ne se posait même pas puisqu'on n'aurait guère su à quelle contribution mettre les résultats d'une analyse phonologique, lexicale ou grammaticale. Un chercheur, pour intéressé qu'il soit par les contributions possibles à ses recherches à lui de telle méthode ou de telle théorie, a toujours le loisir de les considérer comme autant de cadeaux encombrants si on insiste pour qu'il les mette à profit.

"Bien loin que l'objet précède le point de vue, on dirait que c'est le point de vue qui crée l'objet."[8] Un même objet-dans-le-monde peut ainsi se multiplier lorsqu'on entreprend de l'objectiver. Cela étant, une analyse du discours, de presse par exemple, une analyse linguistique du papou, une analyse sémiotique d'un vaudeville ou un *content analysis* des *Nixon Tapes* ne reproduisent pas des objets-dans-le-monde: ils en recréent de nouveaux, chacun selon son point de vue. "All of the sciences of man signify and arise from the fracturing of an organic whole . . .: all substitute a spurious analytic totality for holistic unity."[9] Or une des questions que soulève cette objectivation d'un objet-dans-le-monde, question dont l'incidence sur la conception et la confection d'une méthode d'analyse nous paraît fondamentale, c'est le degré d'écart ou d'adéquation entre l'objet réel originel et la re-création qu'en produit un point de vue objectivant. Pour citer à nouveau Tyler: ". . . the rise of that objectifying consciousness which takes itself as its own object, creating for itself a vision of the past and a premonition of the future which it first naively takes to be objectively real and only later comes to doubt as the project of its own subjectivity."[10]

La morale de cette histoire peut se résumer aux deux points suivants:

a) une recherche se doit, non pas de tenter de coller le plus possible à la réalité d'un contexte global—ce qui bien entendu, rendrait impossible l'objectivation requise par la science—mais d'être *ouverte* à la réalité multiple et complexe de l'objet en contexte réel; il est en effet difficile pour un chercheur de prétendre que ses théories décrivent ou expliquent le monde si son métalangage n'a pas de rapports évidents avec les faits;

b) le choix d'une approche théorique et la construction d'un appareil méthodologique, que ce dernier soit très, peu ou pas du tout formel, peuvent légitimement être évalués en termes du degré de facilité avec laquelle on peut s'en servir pour observer et décrire les faits (pragmatisme), du degré de convergence des résultats que peuvent obtenir plusieurs usagers de la méthode (fiabilité) et du degré de correspondance entre ces résultats et les faits observables dans la réalité quotidienne (et non pas entre les résultats obtenus et l'application de la méthode qui les a produits) (pertinence).

Des trois modes d'analyse que nous passons ici en revue, c'est celui de la linguistique fonctionnelle qui nous a semblé le mieux répondre aux exigences d'une heuristique comme celle que nous venons de décrire.

La linguistique fonctionnelle apporte en effet un minimum de garanties quant à la rigueur — pour ne pas dire l'objectivité — avec laquelle on peut vouloir mener une recherche sur le contenu d'un corpus (fiabilité de l'appareil); et tout aussi important, sinon davantage, elle permet d'objectiver un discours de telle manière que soient respectés les faits observables relatifs à l'acte de parole en tant qu'acte de communication et en tant que représentation en contexte d'expériences humaines (pertinence des résultats).

Nous pouvons maintenant tenter de répondre à la question sous-jacente dans ces pages et que Jean-Claude Gardin a déjà posée aux analystes de discours: pourquoi appliquer telle méthode à un corpus?[11]

a) Comme il entre dans les objectifs de cette recherche de montrer comment on peut appréhender les éléments d'un lexique politique en en relevant les valeurs contextuelles (axiologiques) à l'intérieur d'un corpus donné, il est nécessaire de recourir à une méthode qui ne postule pas au départ un contenu hypothétique mais qui le cherche au contraire dans l'objet auquel elle est appliquée; d'où l'inutilité pour nous de recourir à une batterie de catégories para-linguistiques ou de propositions para-textuelles[12] comme le font les analyses de contenu traditionnelles.[13] C'est pourquoi nous avons refusé de faire pareille analyse d'un lexique sans d'abord passer par une analyse syntaxique. Une analyse fonctionnelle de la syntaxe d'un corpus d'article de presse étant adéquate pour atteindre cet objectif en ce sens qu'elle permet:

(1) d'identifier des unités formelles avec une relative facilité;

(2) de segmenter uniformement et dans l'ordre toutes les composantes énonciatrices d'un texte ou d'un ensemble de textes;

(3) de délimiter toutes les données contextuelles d'un lexique préalable et, partant, de rendre opératoire et efficiente une axiologie linguistique.

b) Un article de presse est le produit d'un acte de communication qui compte parmi toutes les caractéristiques qui le spécifient en tant qu'acte journalistique et qu'il a en commun avec d'autres actes de communication, celle de communiquer par signes linguistiques. Cela revient à dire que le produit (nous ne disons pas toute la démarche) de l'activité journalistique est une activité sur le langage: il nous paraît dès lors fondé qu'on fasse l'étude de cette activité au moyen d'une méthode dont les principes théoriques ainsi que les procédés d'analyse ont été conçus et formulés afin d'étudier l'acte de communication en tant qu'actualisation de système linguistique.[14]

Fondé et non pas suffisant ou impératif en soi, mais assurément indispensable pour répondre à la question: comment les journaux, dans le contexte d'une actualité donnée, définissent-ils les éléments du lexique politique de cette actualité? Ou en d'autres termes: quelles valeurs, axiologiques de sens (valeurs que prennent des signifiés lexicaux en contexte effectif d'énonciation) l'information de presse attribue-t-elle, par la structuration linguistique qu'elle donne à une expérience sociale, aux "mots" dont elle-même et/ou ses récepteurs se servent pour indexer cette expérience?

MÉTHODOLOGIE

Le corpus

Constituer un corpus d'articles de presse sur un sujet donné n'est jamais une mince affaire. En raison, notamment, de l'abondance de la matière rédactionnelle (combien d'articles? sur quelle période de temps?), et des difficultés que pose la tâche de définir d'une façon opératoire des notions telles que "sujets d'actualité" (comment découper l'actualité? en quelles catégories classer les événements couverts par la presse?) et "genres journalistiques" (quels sont-ils? article -vs- éditorial -vs- chronique -vs- dossier -vs- reportage?). La question se pose également de savoir quels journaux on va retenir pour un sujet donné et selon quels critères.

a) Le sujet du corpus

Pour parer à ces difficultés, et comme nous étions de toute manière libre de choisir notre corpus, nous avons choisi pour sujet l'élection du Parti québécois le 15 novembre 1976; plus précisement, les réactions à cette election, de la presse et des acteurs publics ("politiques" ou non).[15]

À vrai dire, il est sans intérêt de savoir si ce sujet d'actualité a été retenu par goût ou pour les besoins de la cause méthodologique. En l'occurrence, l'un et l'autre se confondent ici. Il serait sans doute assez facile de succomber à la tentation de persuader le lecteur qu'il s'agit d'un événement historique de la première importance dans l'évolution politique du Québec, et que, partant, il est tout indiqué qu'on en étudie les manifestations dans la presse de l'époque, etc. Nous y résisterons: d'abord parce que nous serions le premier étonné de révéler, quant aux résultats généraux qui se dégageront du contenu événementiel de ce corpus, des choses qui n'aient pas été tout au moins pressenties par n'importe quel lecteur attentif de cette presse et que, du reste, il n'a pas nécessairement oubliées depuis.

Ensuite, parce qu'il nous paraît plus important de faire valoir les avantages pratiques, c'est-à-dire méthodologiques, d'un tel sujet. Lorsque cette actualité s'est produite, elle a en effet créé la situation journalistique suivante:

(1) tous les quotidiens, tant francophones qu'anglophones, tant du Québec que du reste du Canada, ont traité de cet événement. Cette lapalissade n'en est une qu'en apparence: elle ne doit pas cacher l'intérêt que cela représente, au niveau de la constitution d'un corpus, que d'être assuré que tous les journaux qui y figurent ont couvert tel événement.[16]

(2) tous les quotidiens l'ont couvert d'une façon égale, à toutes fins pratiques—c'est-à-dire qu'ils ont publié des textes sur cet événement en nombre

presque égal; ce qui signifie que très peu de nouvelles relatives à cette actualité n'ont pas été rapportées par chacun des quotidiens en question. Cela facilite une étude comparative aussi bien par sous-événements qu'au niveau général de l'actualité ainsi ponctuée;

(3) comme il s'agissait d'une actualité de nature provinciale et nationale, tous les quotidiens, même les plus démunis à cet égard, y ont assigné leurs propres journalistes plutôt que de s'en remettre exclusivement aux dépêches d'agences de presse;

(4) enfin, la désignation stricte de ce sujet d'actualité (réactions à l'élection du P.Q.) et l'ampleur de la couverture nous ont semblé rendre légitime le choix d'une période de temps qui va du 16 novembre 1976 (lendemain du scrutin) au 29 novembre inclusivement. Fait inusité, les journaux ont traité de ce même événement, à la une, tous les jours, pendant ces deux semaines. Il faudra attendre au printemps suivant alors que le ministre d'Etat au développement culturel, Camille Laurin, rendra public son projet d'une charte de la langue française au Québec, pour que l'actualité reliée à l'élection du Parti québécois "garde" la une pendant plusieurs semaines.

b) Le choix des journaux

La sélection des journaux de ce corpus s'est faite selon les paramètres suivants:

(1) *langue*: journal francophone -vs- journal anglophone;

(2) *géographie*: (a) grande ville -vs- petite ville; (b) Québec -vs- Canada;

(3) *type rédactionnel*: (a) "ordinaire" -vs- de "prestige"; (b) grand format -vs- tabloïd.

Tableau 14-1: Sélection des journaux selon les paramètres de langue, de géographie et de type rédactionnel

	Francophone		Anglophone	
	Québécois	Canadien	Québécois	Canadien
grand format/ grande ville	Le Soleil (Québec)	Le Droit (Ottawa)	The Montreal Star (Montréal)	
grand format/ petite ville	La Tribune (Sherbrooke)			
"de prestige"	Le Devoir (Montréal)			The Globe and Mail (Toronto)
tabloid	Le Journal de Montréal			

Lexique politique et signes-cibles

Ce que nous avons voulu déterminer par l'analyse linguistique d'un tel corpus, c'est la nature axiologique qu'il attribue à un lexique conçu comme un ensemble fermé et pré-établi de notions courantes dans le débat politique sur les options constitutionnelles des partis politiques canadiens et québécois.

Les éléments de ce lexique sont les signes-cibles du corpus: ils représentent autant de signifiés qui prennent par l'emploi spécifique qu'en fait le discours de presse, des valeurs sémantiques particulières; autrement dit, l'analyse que nous avons faite du "contenu" d'un corpus de presse a consisté à identifier les sens que ce corpus attribue en l'associant par son énonciation même à tel autre lexique, indéterminé et indéterminable en dehors du contexte linguistique de ses énoncés.

Sur le plan de notre méthodologie, ce lexique politique représente par conséquent une première étape dans l'analyse du contenu linguistique d'un corpus de presse comme celui que nous venons de décrire. Étape qui en est

Tableau 14–2:   Lexique politique: signes-cibles et champs lexicaux

Acteurs		Positions Politiques			
		Constitutionnelles		Ethno-Linguistiques	
Parti Québécois (A)*	personne politique gouvernement Québec (capitale)†	Québec (1)	État province Québécois pays population	Langue (5)	français anglais francophone anglophone unilinguisme bilinguisme
Non-Parti Québécois Fédéral (B1)	personne politique parti politique Ottawa	Canada (2)	État province(s) Canadiens pays population	Minorité (6)	– au Québec – au Canada groupe ethnique
Non-Parti Québécois et non-fédéral (B2)	personne politique provinciale agent social non-politique	Souveraineté (3)	indépendance séparatisme nationalisme souv.-assoc. référendum		
		Unité Canadienne (4)	fédéralisme constitution canadienne AANB‡ reine confédération		

* La lettre ou le chiffre entre parenthèses servent à noter les occurrences des signes-cibles dans les fiches de segmentation. Voir *infra* p.
† Les champs lexicaux ne sont pas donnés comme exhaustifs dans ce tableau.
‡ Acte de l'Amérique du Nord Britannique.

une de transition entre la pertinence d'un texte[17] et sa segmentation par la syntaxe dont nous traiterons plus loin. Au chapitre de la pertinence, c'est en effet la présence ou l'absence d'un des lexèmes de ce lexique qui soulevait à nouveau la question de la pertinence, mais au niveau de la phrase cette fois.

Aussi, cette étape méthodologique nous permet de délimiter, à l'intérieur du contenu linguistique, des éléments de contenu dont nous nous sommes fixé pour tâche d'expliciter l'organisation axiologique. Ce lexique représente dès lors le véritable objet de notre analyse.

La segmentation du corpus

Ainsi que nous l'avons annoncé dans l'introduction, le but de cette thèse, c'est de décrire le discours politique de presse en tant qu'objet linguistique. À la lumière de ce qui précède, nous pouvons maintenant définir le *discours politique de presse* comme suit: l'ensemble des énoncés de personnes politiques ou d'agents sociaux, médiatisés par ceux d'un journaliste ou d'un journal, et qui expriment un point de vue sur un ou plusieurs éléments d'un lexique politique.

Sur un plan très général, nous voulons savoir ce que recouvrent effectivement—c'est-à-dire dans la réalité même du discours de presse les différents signes-cibles d'un lexique politique. Ce qui revient à dire que le *contenu* de ce discours sera celui des sens dont des *Acteurs* et des journaux investissent ce lexique politique, lesquels sens ces discours se trouvent à proposer comme une interprétation de l'actualité. Insistons ici sur le fait que notre méthodologie ne définit pas au départ et de son propre cru les éléments de ce lexique: elle en laisse pour ainsi dire le soin aux usagers des termes de ce lexique qui eux, en tant qu'usagers, ne s'en servent assurément pas comme signes-cibles mais en contexte linguistique et discursif.

Dans cette optique, il faut pouvoir non seulement juger de l'importance quantitative d'un concept, "souveraineté" par exemple—ce que nous permet de faire un simple relevé des occurrences de ce concept ou de ses équivalents lexicaux—mais aussi et surtout en savoir les co-occurrences, c'est-à-dire les occurrences des signes ou suites de signes auxquels les articles de presse l'associent et qui en bloc constituent le champ axiologique de ce concept. Pour ce faire, c'est par la segmentation du corpus selon une procédure d'analyse syntaxique fonctionnelle que nous avons relevé les associations signes pour ensuite établir les champs axiologiques qui en déterminent le sens, et voir comment ceux-ci se comparent entre acteurs et entre journaux, de même qu'avec ceux qui sont constitués dans le discours de presse pour les autres signes-cibles de notre lexique politique.

Il y a donc lieu de distinguer deux parties dans un travail de ce genre: une analyse syntaxique suivie d'une analyse axiologique qui s'appuie sur la description du corpus apportée par la première.

Le point de départ théorique de cette méthodologie pour une analyse linguistique d'un contenu a été donné par Conrad Bureau dans *Linguistique*

Tableau 14-3: Fiche d'inventaire des associations aux signes-cibles

Page Ph #	Acteurs PQ	Non-PQ	Autres	Actions	Propositions Éléments associés	Signes-cibles	Éléments associés	ASS #	S-C	MOD	DRC	RPT
35-01		Trudeau		"réagira" encore demain		à l'élection du PQ		01	B1-A	a	0	II
54-02	René Lévesque			répète de façon solennel-le		tous ses engagements		02	A-A	a	+	IV
03		Trudeau		rencontre		les h. d'affaires		03	B1-B2	a	0	V
04			Bronfman	urges		businessmen	to save "our be- loved country"	04	B2✓	a	+	V
								05	B2-2	a	+	V
05	Neuf députés péquistes					"fidèles" à la Reine		06	A-4	a	0	I
06		Le g. fédéral		ne serait pas lié		par les résultats de référendums		07	B1-3	h	–	II
07			Royal Trust	is staying put				08	B2-∅	a	+	II
55-08		[Ottawa official]	Quebec	[says] doesn't have authority		to opt out.		09	B1✓	a	↑	II
								10	1-3	a	–	IV

fonctionnelle et stylistique objective. Cet ouvrage montre une voie à suivre pour faire l'étude stylistique d'un auteur (écrivain ou écrivant, artiste ou artisan) de telle manière qu'elle puisse s'appuyer sur une analyse linguistique préalable—c'est-à-dire sur un ensemble de principes et de définitions assorti de critères et de procédures qui permettent une démonstration par les faits. C'est en ce sens qu'une stylistique peut être objective.

Bien qu'il ne s'agisse pas pour nous de caractériser la syntaxe du discours de presse, nous considérons, comme Bureau, l'analyse syntaxique comme une démarche méthodologique préalable: non pas pour décrire un style journalistique mais pour caractériser des perceptions de concepts. L'analyse de la syntaxe du corpus sert ainsi celle des valeurs de sens que prennent, en contexte d'énoncés, les signes-cibles.

> L'étude de l'organisation sémantique elle-même d'un texte est tributaire de l'analyse syntaxique: l'analyse sémantique, en effet, ne peut se réduire à un pur index du vocabulaire et des fréquences, établi sans tenir compte du contexte, car un tel index, même assorti du calcul des écarts et du X2, ne renvoie qu'aux signifiés de la langue, même pas aux sens des signes dans l'oeuvre (. . .)
> La syntaxe est condition d'émergence du sens contingent, particulier et concret d'un signe, de sa valeur singulière dans tel énoncé. (p. 148)

L'analyse syntaxique

Nous avons signalé plus haut le parti qu'on peut tirer d'une analyse fonctionnelle de la syntaxe d'un corpus pour l'étude d'un contenu linguistique: identification d'unités formelles: segmentation uniforme et dans l'ordre; délimitation de données contextuelles. Le produit de cette segmentation par l'analyse syntaxique est d'abord réparti en catégories logiques pré-établies pour permettre ensuite de relever toutes les associations de segments—directes et indirectes—qui sont faites par le texte à un signe-cible.

Comme l'indique la fiche[18] qui a servi à relever les associations de signes aux signes-cibles, nous distinguons trois catégories logiques principales où nous avons inscrit les segments syntaxiques d'énoncés selon la nature des trois données de base auxquelles correspondent ces catégories, à savoir: (a) un personnage politique ou public *(Acteur)* (b) qui agit ou qui parle ou que le journal fait agir ou parler *(Action)* et (c) ce que l'énoncé propose au sujet de l'acteur ou de l'action *(Proposition)*. Ces catégories[19] recensent tous les segments d'énoncés en reprenant, de façon simplifiée, les "figures politiques", et l'"acte politique" de la *Grammaire du journal politique* de Jacques Rivet.[20]

Cette catégorisation du discours journalistique exprime un point de vue préalable sur une façon de faire journalistique qui consiste, pour l'essentiel, à attribuer ou à distribuer des responsabilités pour ce qui arrive *dans* une collectivité ou *à* une collectivité sociale.

Les critères pour la répartition des segments dans ces trois catégories sont strictement syntaxiques. Les deux premières recensent des segments d'énoncés—terme ou groupe de termes—qui remplissent les fonctions syntaxiques de sujet primaire ou de prédicat nominal: c'est la catégorie *Acteurs*;

dans la catégorie *Actions*, le prédicat verbal de l'énoncé; la troisième catégorie *(Propositions)* regroupe des expansions syntaxiques ou bien des *Acteurs* ou bien des *Actions*. Lorsque l'énoncé ne comporte pas d'*Acteur* défini ici comme un sujet primaire humain, la *Proposition* comprend dans ce cas tout l'énoncé.[21]

L'analyse axiologique

La fiche de segmentation permet de relever dans les énoncés pertinents d'un texte, quatre types d'associations possibles à un signe-cible, selon le découpage de l'énoncé en catégories logiques. A savoir:

a) *Acteur* ↔ *Action*:
Royal Trust ↔ is staying put

b) *Acteur* ↔ Elément propositionnel (associé ou signe-cible)
Neuf députés péquistes ↔ "fidèles" à la Reine

c) *Acteur* ↔ *Action* ↔ Elément propositionnel
"René Lévesque ↔ répète de façon solennelle ↔ tous ses engagements

d) Élément propositionnel ↔ Signe-cible propositionnel
Bronfman urges businessmen ↔ to save "our beloved country"

Formulée d'une façon générale, l'analyse axiologique a pour but de décrire le sens qu'une association syntaxique (c'est-à-dire en contexte effectif d'une phrase) confère à un signe donné en examinant les termes de cette relation avec d'autres signes.

La démarche de cette analyse consiste à reprendre les données de la segmentation syntaxique et l'information contextuelle sur les phrases que fournissent nos inventaires Signes-Cibles, Direction et Rapport pour encadrer l'examen des valeurs axiologiques et en indiquer les étapes.

En procédant ainsi, nous nous trouvons à envisager deux grandes catégories de résultats qui peuvent être extraits des fiches d'inventaire:

a) *des résultats strictement quantitatifs* comme on en présente dans n'importe quelle analyse de contenu traditionnelle. Il s'agit, bien sûr, d'établir les récurrences de différents types d'*Acteurs*, des signes-cibles, des associations de S-C, des directions, etc.

Ces récurrences, si elles peuvent nous renseigner sur des types de structurations syntaxiques du discours de presse de même que sur certaines fréquences relatives à l'objet, au propos ou au thème de ce discours, ne nous disent que peu de choses sur la perception de l'actualité politique en question et que communique le discours de presse, celui du journal ou celui des *Acteurs* qui s'y expriment. En un mot, elles ne font qu'indiquer ce sur quoi portent ces discours et avec quelle régularité; à la limite, elles ne peuvent servir que *d'index*.

Un index *spécialisé* toutefois, et c'est son intérêt: il peut servir, en effet, une analyse plus approfondie d'un corpus ou d'un discours quelconque.[22]

b) *Des résultats apportés par l'analyse axiologique:* Cela étant, et comme nous l'avons dit plus haut, nos résultats quantitatifs servent de point de départ pour l'analyse interne des associations de signes par la syntaxe. Des résultats quantitatifs préliminaires nous ont vite montré que des divers signes-cibles du lexique, ceux qui désignent des *Acteurs* étaient de loin les plus fréquents.[23] En conséquence, le déroulement de l'analyse axiologique empruntera celui qu'indiquent les résultats quantitatifs: nous irons, dans un premier temps, des *Acteurs* aux autres signes, cibles ou non, auxquels ils sont associés dans l'inventaire S-C des fiches; puis, dans un deuxième temps, aux paires de signes-cibles de ce même inventaire, où n'apparaît pas d'*Acteur*. Soit:

Figure 14-1   Possibilités d'associations de signes: Acteurs, cibles ou non signes-cibles

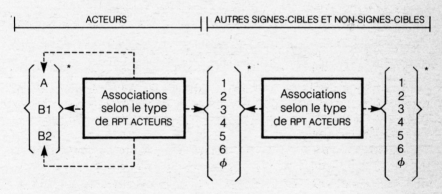

* Selon l'ordre des indices de récurrences des associations S-C.

Cette démarche tiendra également compte des résultats quantitatifs de l'inventaire des rapports entre *Acteurs* (comme l'indique la Figure 4) qui sous-catégoriseront, en même temps qu'ils les marqueront sémantiquement, les différentes associations d'un *Acteur* donné avec un signe-cible. Ainsi, pour l'*Acteur* A, nous aurons:

$$A \dashrightarrow \begin{Bmatrix} \text{RPT I} \\ \text{RPT III} \end{Bmatrix} \dashrightarrow \begin{Bmatrix} \text{S-C B1} \\ \text{B2} \\ 2 \\ 4 \\ 5a \\ 6 \\ \emptyset \end{Bmatrix}{}^{[24]} \qquad A \dashrightarrow \text{RPT IV} \rightarrow \begin{Bmatrix} A \\ 1 \\ 3 \\ 5f \\ 6 \\ \emptyset \end{Bmatrix}{}^{[24]}$$

et/ou le déroulement de cette analyse correspond à une séquence qui n'est pas celle de la numérotation des signes-cibles du lexique mais plutôt de l'importance fréquentielle (indices de récurrences) de chaque association.

RÉSULTATS PRÉLIMINAIRES

Les résultats qui suivent proviennent d'une analyse sommaire[25] d'une partie du corpus francophone, c'est-à-dire 16% des textes du *Devoir* et du *Droit*, et 29% de ceux du *Soleil* et de la *Tribune*. En tout, cela représente 126 articles ou 23% de l'ensemble de ces quatre journaux. Les données quantitatives de cette analyse ont trait à ce corpus partiel.

Pour ce qui regarde l'analyse sémantique, elle ne traitera que des *titres* de ces 126 articles.

Analyse quantitative: textes et titres

Les faits saillants de l'analyse quantitative des textes et de leurs titres sont les suivants:

a) les dix associations de Signes-cibles les plus fréquentes—et qui représentent 50% des 2369 associations de Signes-cibles de ce corpus partiel—sont:

Tableau 14-4:   Dix associations de signes-cibles les plus fréquentes: 1190 associations sur 2369

1. A ↔ B1: 264 (22.2)*	6. B1 ↔ B1: 92 (7.8)	
2. A ↔ 3: 162 (13.6)	7. B1 ↔ $\emptyset$: 91 (7.8)	
3. A ↔ $\emptyset$: 146 (12.3)	8. B1 ↔ 4: 85 (7.1)	
4. A ↔ 1: 107 (9.0)	9. 1 ↔ 3: 77 (6.5)	
5. B1 ↔ 1: 93 (7.8)	10. B1 ↔ 3: 73 (6.1)	

* Ces pourcentages sont petits, mais il faut savoir qu'avec 10 signes, il y a 54 combinaisons possibles de ces signes.

On notera que les associations d'un signe-cible avec des non-signes-cibles ne représentent que 20% de cet ensemble. Ce qui peut signifier que dans nos quatre journaux il y aurait une tendance assez nette à faire signifier les termes courants d'une actualité politique les uns par rapport aux autres. On n'en déduira pas pour autant, toutefois, que le discours de presse n'explique pas l'actualité à laquelle renvoie notre lexique politique de signes-cibles, ni qu'il ne fait que la redire dans les termes d'un lexique fermé et au moyen d'une phraséologie facilement prévisible. Il importe en effet, que l'on considère les deux aspects suivants de notre inventaire d'associations de signes-cibles:

(1) il indique toujours une association signe-cible à signe-cible *lorsque la phrase en comprend plus d'un*;

(2) *il n'épuise pas le contenu* de l'association: il ne fait que l'indiquer.

Le premier point exige par conséquent que l'on revoie les phrases en cause afin d'établir s'il existe ou non une relation syntaxique directe entre deux signes-cibles; en d'autres termes, d'établir s'il y a ou non dans telle phrase des segments *intermédiaires* entre deux signes-cibles. Le deuxième point évoque la nécessité d'une analyse axiologique à laquelle il appartient d'identifier et d'interpréter la nature et le contenu sémantique d'une association de même que de préciser les manières dont des segments intermédiaires ou des non signes-cibles informent sur le rapport associatif entre deux signes-cibles.

Compte tenu de ces réserves, le fait que 80% des phrases de ce corpus partiel comportent une association S-C ↔ S-C suggère tout au moins que la presse tient un discours où l'actualité politique est représentée linguistiquement de telle manière que, non seulement les termes d'un lexique fermé sont récurrents, pris isolément, (ce qui n'aurait rien d'étonnant dans l'optique des critères que nous nous sommes donnés pour juger de la pertinence d'un texte pour la constitution du corpus) mais que soient, en plus, très récurrentes les phrases qui énoncent *deux* termes d'un lexique qui ne compte que neuf champs lexicaux.

Ainsi, dans notre corpus, le Parti québécois se retrouve dans un contexte syntaxique qui l'associe, directement ou indirectement, à des termes qui désignent l'un ou l'autre des deux signes-cibles B1 *(Acteurs Politiques Fédéraux)* ou 3 *(Souveraineté)* trois fois plus souvent qu'à des non-signes-cibles (0). Phénomène qui n'est pas banal dans le contexte d'une élection *provinciale*: élection qui, selon l'interprétation à laquelle invitent ces résultats, se serait jouée avec des *Acteurs* fédéraux actifs dans les coulisses et qui, une fois le Parti québécois élu, sont mis en rapport avec ce dernier par la presse, ou qui se mettent eux-mêmes en rapport avec le Parti québécois en prenant l'initiative du discours politique de la presse; dans le contexte d'une élection, aussi, où la stratégie du Parti québécois durant toute la compagne avait consisté très précisément à *mettre en veilleuse* son option constitutionnelle.[26]

On observera, d'autre part, la fréquence assez importante de l'association B1 ↔ B1, la cinquième plus fréquente association de ce Tableau. Les *Acteurs* fédéraux ont beaucoup parlé — ou fait parler — d'eux dans les deux semaines qui ont suivi l'élection du Parti québécois. Cette fréquence concorde aussi avec les résultats de l'analyse des *Acteurs* que nous dégagerons plus loin.

b) Fréquence d'occurrence d'un signe-cible.[27] Si on considère maintenant la fréquence d'occurrence d'un signe-cible dans quelque association que ce soit, c'est-à-dire une association avec un terme de son propre champ lexical, avec un autre signe-cible ou avec un non-signe-cible, le signe-cible le plus récurrent est B1: il a, en moyenne, pour les quatre journaux, une fréquence d'occurrence de 23%. Cela signifie, qu'en moyenne toujours, pour chaque deux associations de signes, soit

$$k \leftrightarrow 1$$
$$x \leftrightarrow y$$

un de ces quatre signes sera le signe-cible B1. Des quatre journaux, c'est le *Devoir* qui a la plus forte occurrence de B1 (28.8%); sa récurrence dans la *Tribune* est celle de la moyenne (23%); le *Soleil* et le *Droit* sont en-dessous avec 20% chacun.

Le troisième signe-cible le plus fréquent est *Souveraineté*.

Figure 14-2   Fréquence d'occurrence de chaque signe-cible: textes et titres
(corpus partiel).

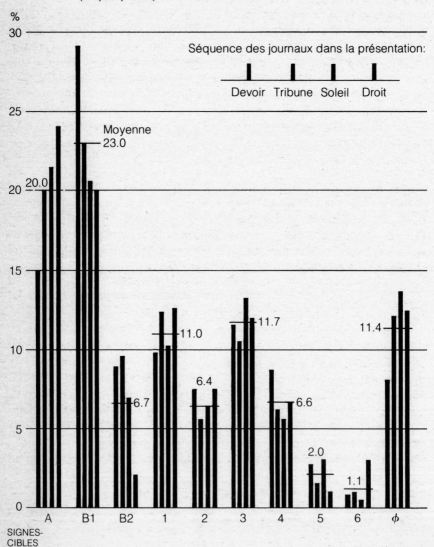

Ces données sur la fréquence d'occurrence du signe-cible concordent avec celles que nous venons de voir au sujet des associations les plus fréquentes, où effectivement les signes-cibles B1, A et 3 sont ceux qui reviennent le plus souvent dans la formation d'une association.

Une dernière observation sur la récurrence des signes-cibles: si on examine les écarts entre les quatre quotidiens pour ce qui concerne ces récurrences, on peut noter:

(1) ce qu'on vient de constater au sujet de l'écart prononcé entre le *Devoir* et les trois autres journaux en regard de la récurrence de B1;

(2) que le *Droit* s'est peu intéressé au signe-cible B2 (*Acteurs* politiques provinciaux non-Parti Québécois et *Acteurs* sociaux non-politiques): 2% contre une moyenne de 6.7%; mais qu'il donne, par contre, une récurrence beaucoup plus marquée au signe-cible 6 *(Minorités)* que les autres journaux: on s'y serait attendu de la part d'un journal francophone hors Québec et dont une partie des lecteurs sont Franco-Ontariens;

(3) qu'à l'exception de ces deux cas-là, il y a une similitude assez frappante dans les fréquences d'occurrence de *cinq* des dix signes-cibles pour les quatre journaux de même que pour n'importe quelle combinaison de *trois* journaux dans le cas des cinq autres signes-cibles.

Analyse quantitative des titres seulement

Tant pour ce qui a trait à la fréquence des associations de signes-cibles qu'à celle de chaque signe-cible, l'analyse quantitative des titres seulement révèle des résultats sinon identiques, du moins très semblables à ceux que nous venons de dégager pour l'ensemble des textes et titres.

C'est dire qu'ici aussi les associations les plus fréquentes sont A ↔ B1, B1 ↔ B1, A ↔ 3, etc., avec de légères modifications dans les cinq premiers rangs de notre Tableau 3 des dix plus fréquentes.

De même, les moyennes de récurrences de chaque signe-cible pour les titres produisent un graphique qui est très ressemblant à celui qu'on obtient pour le corpus textes et titres.[28]

Nous n'insisterons donc pas sur ces données quantitatives brutes relatives aux titres seulement.

Il faudrait cependant souligner avant de passer à la deuxième étape de cette analyse, que dans ce cas précis de l'avènement du PQ au pouvoir, les responsables des titres au journal n'ont guère pris de libertés par rapport aux textes-journalistes, du moins en ce qui concerne les associations et les récurrences de signes-cibles.

Analyse sémantique des titres

Si d'abord on examine la nature ou l'identité des signes-cibles A, B1, B2 en position syntaxique d'*Acteurs*, on peut constater

a) une très faible occurrence du S-C A (16 fois sur 84 énoncés, ou 19%), les référents *René Lévesque* et *PQ* représentant respectivement 9 et 6 de ces 16 occurrences de A en position *Acteurs*;

b) en contrepartie, le S-C B1 compte pour 39% des *Acteurs* et B2 pour 42%. Or si on départage dans ces deux dernières classes sémantiques, les hommes politiques des acteurs sociaux non-politiques, on obtient 44 acteurs politiques sur 84 (52%) qui, s'ils ne sont pas fédéraux, sont tous fédéralistes. On retrouve Trudeau et ses Libéraux fédéraux en position *Acteurs* 10 et 18 fois respectivement.

Figure 14-3   Moyennes de la fréquence des occurrences de chaque cigne-cible: textes et titres: ———; titres seulement: ------.

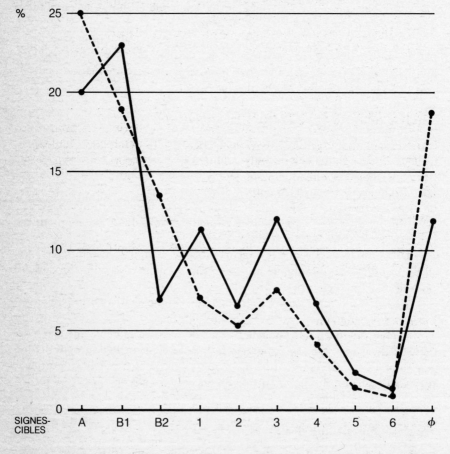

Note: L'écart et/ou les changements de direction des lignes des signes-cibles A, B1 et B2 s'expliquent en bonne partie par une re-désignation des Acteurs non-fédéraux en B2 dans la segmentation des titres seulement: dans celle qui avait été faite antérieurement des textes et des titres, on ne distinguait pas entre B1 et B2.

Un examen de ces mêmes signes-cibles en position *Propositions* révèle au contraire une récurrence égale de ces deux types d'*Acteurs*, A, B1/B2.

A la lumière de ces données, on pourrait prétendre que ce sont les hommes politiques fédéraux ou fédéralistes *qui prennent l'initiative* de l'action discursive au lendemain de l'élection du Parti québécois; ou, pour dire les choses autrement, que les journaux se sont davantage intéressés à diffuser ce qu'ont dit, pensé ou voulu faire *les adversaires du PQ* qu'à recueillir les commentaires des artisans de la victoire électorale du PQ.

Un simple coup d'oeil sur la composition lexicale des segments syntaxiques qui désignent nos *Acteurs* et les *Actions* avec lesquelles (en tant que sujets syntaxiques) ils sont en implication réciproque, ne peut manquer de voir une caractéristique sémantique dominante de ces réactions à la victoire du PQ: à savoir le *négatif*.

En effet, le négatif marque l'énonciation d'une réaction dans 71% des segments: soit d'une façon grammaticale:

Le PQ *n'*est *pas* mandaté pour obtenir l'indépendance.

La victoire du PQ *ne* signifie *pas* que Trudeau doive démissionner, etc.: soit d'une façon lexicale:

Trudeau *refuse* de discuter

Trudeau va nous mener au *désastre*

Les Québécois *mécontents,* etc.

Dans les 126 titres ici considérés, la très grande majorité, c'est-à-dire tous les titres sauf 13, du genre "Marchand avait prévu sa défaite" ou "L'élection du PQ vue par les hebdos français"—la très grande majorité donc, peuvent être classés selon une thématique à trois volets. Soit:

a) *Changements*

Exemples: Ça va ébranler beaucoup de monde;
Les Québécois n'accepteront plus l'intolérance des anglophones.
Ce volet regroupe 50% des énoncés.

b) *Statu quo*

Exemples: Personne ne va déménager du Québec;
Trudeau s'en tient au statu quo.
Ce volet regroupe 32% des énoncés.

c) *Problématique:*

Exemple: Période de réflexion pour 350,000 Acadiens.
Ce volet regroupe 18% des énoncés.

On voit sans peine que ces réactions à l'élection du PQ associent cette élection à une source de *changements* à venir et peut-être à craindre—Lévesque est un homme *dangereux*, dit Mackasey;

Consternation aux Communes—

mais pour lesquels changements on peut se préparer en discutant de la *pro-blématique* qu'ils soulèvent—

Faire face au PQ en déclenchant des élections—

en y réfléchissant sur la place publique; ou bien encore que l'on peut toujours carrément *nier:*

Le PQ a été mandaté pour gouverner et non pour séparer le Québec;

L'élection du PQ ne représente pas une défaite pour le Canada.

Le dernier point à indiquer, c'est que l'association syntaxique de nos trois signes-cibles A, B1, B2, à chacun des trois volets de cette thématique indique

a) que les acteurs fédéraux sont *sur-représentés* dans les énoncés classés sous le volet "Statu quo" (48% contre 41% pour B2 et 11% pour A);

b) que le Signe-cible B2 s'associe à 50% au thème "Changements";

c) et que la problématique politique rendue explicite par l'élection du PQ est évoquée à parts égales (40%) par les S-C B1 et B2.

CONCLUSION

Après avoir vanté sans mesure, pendant un certain temps, les possibilités de la linguistique pour toutes sortes d'analyses, après avoir tenté allègrement de jouer de la "performance", du "syntagmatique" et des "traits pertinents", on a trop vite qualifié la linguistique de "science pilote" pour l'étude des comportements individuels ou sociaux de l'homme. L'engouement s'est estompé lorsqu'on s'aperçut que ce n'était là qu'artifices de méta-langage sans rapport véritable avec l'objet sur lequel on les appliquait, que le structuralisme, auquel la linguistique (et notamment la phonologie) avait donné un tel essor, semblait donner toute liberté pour improviser n'importe quelle méthode, pour rendre compte de n'importe quoi, qu'on ne se posait même pas la question, par exemple, de savoir si tel "système de communication humaine" pouvait raisonnablement être étudié avec des concepts empruntés à l'analyse de systèmes phonologiques. La polysémie du terme même de communication, qui fait qu'aujourd'hui encore il peut recouvrir des choses allant d'une vieille paire de bottines aux *Fleurs du Mal* en passant par le thermostat qui règle mon calorifère, allait, d'autre part, engendrer deux sémiologies opposées sur le plan théorique: une dite de communication et l'autre de signification. De telle sorte qu'après avoir cru que la linguistique avait son mot à dire en tout et sur tout, on est arrivé à douter qu'elle l'ait à dire sur quoi que ce soit.

Il est de mise aujourd'hui de douter de la compétence des linguistes en matière d'étude d'objets à valeur sociale: on fait valoir, par exemple, que les différentes espèces de messages que les gens reçoivent quotidiennement ne sont pas que linguistiques de nature. Soit. Qui peut nier qu'une annonce publicitaire est autant commerciale que linguistique ou sémiologique de nature? Quant à affirmer qu'elle est plus l'une que l'autre, autant affirmer qu'un mot est plus signifié que signifiant ou vice-versa. Enfin, l'extrême complexité du langage, à tous les niveaux et partout où il se manifeste, exige des méthodologies qui ne sont pas toujours faites pour retenir l'attention de ceux qui veulent faire les choses rondement. . . .

Au terme de cette présentation, à vrai dire trop sommaire, d'une méthodologie pour l'analyse axiologique du discours de presse, nous voudrions souligner, au cas où cela n'aurait pas été fait avec suffisamment de clarté dans les pages qui précèdent, la contribution de la syntaxe fonctionnelle à l'analyse d'un contenu de presse.

Sur un plan théorique général, la contribution de la linguistique fonctionnelle à l'analyse de contenu nous paraît non seulement valable, mais importante. Cette approche tient compte, en effet, de ce qui est indéniablement la première caractéristique formelle d'un tel contenu: à savoir qu'il est fait de langue, qu'il communique des expériences humaines au moyen d'une représentation linguistique dont le propre est d'être linéaire. Une fois admis ce truisme, on reconnaîtra l'utilité d'une analyse qui se fixe pour objectif de montrer ce qui est dit par ce contenu, d'en identifier les sens et les significations par l'examen de la structuration syntaxique des phrases qui le créent et dont la première fonction dans un énoncé consiste précisément à surmonter l'obstacle de la linéarité de la chaîne linguistique en marquant les relations entre les éléments de l'expérience.

On aura toujours le loisir, bien entendu, de discuter des pré-supposés idéologiques du discours journalistique, de l'"inter-texte" d'un éditorial, de structures de surface et profondes, du statut problématique du Sujet, des conditions de production de la presse marchande, bref, de tout ce qu'il est possible pour un article ou un bulletin de nouvelles de manifester ou de cacher en tant que discours social. Toutes choses passionnantes, assurément, mais qui ne nous semblent pas rendre caduque ou hors de propos la question de savoir, d'abord, *comment est dite l'actualité*, puis ensuite, de savoir par quels procédés d'analyse, rationnels et objectifs autant que faire se peut en sciences humaines, on peut l'apprendre.

Pour terminer, deux points, plus techniques, que nous souhaitons mettre en evidence: la définition de la phrase selon la linguistique fonctionnelle[29], en plus d'être opératoire, représente vraisemblablement ce qu'il y a de plus rigoureux en la matière.

Etant donné la nécessité pour toute espèce d'analyse de contenu de segmenter d'une façon ou d'une autre un corpus en éléments de contenu, on n'insistera jamais assez sur la valeur d'une segmentation qui opère à l'aide de critères efficaces, c'est-à-dire systématiques et conformes aux faits observables: cela ne nous paraît pas être le cas pour les critères selon lesquels on découpe des segments "entre deux blancs sémantiques" ou entre des signes de ponctuation dite "forte". Un titre de journal comme le suivant — et qui n'a rien d'exceptionnel pour un titre — *Bankers lying low, "no need for alarm"* (*Montreal Star*, 20 11 76, p. A3) comprend-il un "blanc sémantique" entre les deux syntagmes *Bankers lying low* et *"no need for alarm"* et si oui, à quoi le sait-on; en suivant le critère que la virgule n'est pas signe de ponctuation forte, n'y a-t-il là qu'une seule phrase? Si, enfin, on estime qu'il manque "quelque chose" à cet énoncé, on serait bien étonné que les éléments manquants se retrouvent dans la tête de l'analyste.

Ce même titre montre aussi l'apport d'une définition linguistique de la phrase pour distinguer, dans un corpus d'articles de presse, entre le discours que tiennent d'une part, journal et journaliste: *Bankers lying low*, et celui que tiennent, d'autre part, les personnages publics auxquels le journal passe "le micro" pour qu'ils s'y expriment directement: *"no need for alarm"*.

NOTES

1.   Voir Y. de la Haye et B. Miege, "Les sciences de la communication: un phénomène de dépendance culturelle?", dans *Communication et Information*, II-3, automne 1978, p. 7-23.

2.   Voir à titre d'exemple: Marlene Cuthbert, "Canadian Newspaper Treatment of a Developing Country. The Case of Jamaica," dans *Canadian Journal of Communication*, Summer 1980, p. 16-31. Ses catégories sont: "placement in the paper," "dateline," "column inches," etc. pour l'aspect couverture des événements, et "Tourism," "Cold War," "Development," etc. pour l'aspect sujet de l'actualité.

3.   Bien que le *Discourse Analysis* de Z.S. Harris date de la même année que le *Content Analysis* de Berelson, 1952, les tentatives en France d'applications méthodologiques à l'analyse du discours de cet ouvrage n'ont pas été immédiates, comme ce fut le cas aux Etats-Unis pour le *Content Analysis*. *Discourse Analysis* n'a été traduit en France qu'en 1969.

4.   Le mot est de Dominique Maingueneau, *Initiation aux méthodes d'analyse du discours*, Paris, Hachette Université, (Langue-Linguistique-Communication), 1976, p. 21.

5.   Régine Robin, *Histoire et Linguistique*, Paris, Colin (Linguistique), 1973, p. 20.

6.   Maingueneau, p. 183.

7.   Robin, pp. 96-97, 117.

8.   Ferdinand de Saussure, *Cours de linguistique générale*, Paris, Payot, 1976, p. 23.

9.   Stephen Tyler, *The Said and the Unsaid. Mind, Meaning and Culture*, Academic Press (Language, Thought and Culture: Advances in the Study of Cognition), 1978, p. 3.

10.   Tyler, p. 17.

11.   Jean-Claude Gardin, *Les analyses de discours*, Neuchâtel, Delachaux et Niestlé, 1974.

12.   Voir à titre d'exemple: Daniel Latouche, "Le traitement de l'information en période électorale, I: Le contenu de l'information" dans *Communication et Information*, Hiver 1977, Vol. II, no. 1, p. 1-30.

13.   Sur cette question, voir L. Guespin, "Problématique des travaux sur le discours politique," dans *Langages*, Sept. 1971, no. 23, p. 13ss.

14.   On aura compris qu'il faut entendre ici par "analyse linguistique" celle que définit Conrad Bureau dans *Linguistique fonctionnelle et stylistique objective*, Paris, P.U.F., 1976, p. 50, "non pas au sens de: qui a rapport au langage ou de: qui porte sur le langage, mais avec le sens suivant: selon les méthodes de la linguistique."

15.   Ces réactions ont été abondantes au point où une semaine plus tard, le *Soleil* donnait à lire ce titre étonnant de lassitude: *Trudeau "réagira" encore demain à l'élection du PQ* (S 23 11 76 B1).

16.   Nous le savons d'expérience, ayant fait pour l'UNESCO, en 1979, une étude sur la perception des pays en développement dans la presse québécoise où la couverture

d'événements ponctuels relatifs à ce sujet d'étude est très inégale. Comme le *Journal de Montréal,* par exemple, y accorde beaucoup moins de place que le *Devoir,* l'analyse obtient des résultats quantitatifs d'une valeur parfois douteuse à cause de l'insuffisance des données et doit constamment pondérer ses résultats pour tenir compte de ces absences d'information dans un ou plusieurs des journaux du corpus. Et en définitive, une des conclusions les plus importantes qu'on peut tirer d'une telle situation, c'est que tel journal n'informe pas ou peu ses lecteurs sur l'actualité en question: or une telle constatation n'exige guère une analyse détaillée de textes de presse. Voir Michel de Repentigny, "Perceptions des pays en développement dans trois journaux québécois," dans *Communication et Information,* Vol. III, no. 2, Hiver 1980, p. 165-197.

17. Envisagée en termes d'une dichotomie entre Parti Québécois (A) et Non-Parti Québécois (B): action, réaction et contre-réaction manifestée par l'un ou l'autre au sujet de lui-même ou de l'autre. Ce qui crée cinq types de rapports possibles A−B: (I) PQ−NON-PQ; (II) NON-PQ−PQ; (III) PQ−NON-PQ; (IV) PQ−PQ: (V) NON-PQ−NON-PQ.

18. Voir page suivante.

19. Dont les désignations, on le voit, ne doivent pas être prises dans leurs acceptions grammaticales. Insistons sur le fait qu'il s'agit bien de catégories logiques et *non pas linguistiques.*

20. Jacques Rivet, *Grammaire du journal politique à travers Le Devoir et Le Jour,* Montréal, Cahiers du Québec/Hurtubise HMH (Collection Communications), 1979, Chapitres VII et VIII.

21. Toute notre terminologie en matière de syntaxe et d'analyse syntaxique est empruntée à Bureau, op. cit.

22. L'objectif d'une étude précise peut ne pas l'entraîner au-delà de cette tâche qui établit des résultats quantitatifs: c'est l'objectif usuel de l'analyse de contenu. De cette quantification des données, l'analyste passe ensuite directement à leur interprétation.

23. Voir ci-après.

24. Le signe-cible 5a désigne Langue anglaise; 5f Langue française.

25. Au moment où ces résultats furent livrés dans notre communication auprès de l'Association Canadienne de Communication en juin 1980, la partie de notre thèse qui traite d'analyse axiologique n'avait pas encore été pleinement conceptualisée: ces résultats sont donc essentiellement quantitatifs de nature.

26. Rappelons pour l'intelligence de ces lignes que le Parti québécois choisit en 1976 de mettre l'accent sur la nécessité pour les électeurs québécois de changer de gouvernement après six ans de "mauvaise administration" par le Parti libéral, et de minimiser, pendant cette campagne électorale, l'importance que l'électorat devait accorder aux options constitutionnelles du Parti québécois (notamment celle de la "souveraineté-association"), options qu'il avait fait valoir aux élections de 1970 et de 1973 et où il n'avait réussi à faire élire que sept et six députés.

27. Voir Figure 2.

28. Voir Figure 3.

29. Voir celle de Conrad Bureau: "une construction linguistique syntaxiquement auto-suffisante et où les éléments constitutifs, monèmes et/ou syntagmes, sont en relation d'implication, directe ou indirecte, par rapport à un seul prédicat ou à plusieurs prédicats coordonnés." op. cit., p. 65.

Chapitre 15

Le contenu comme miroir de la communication: l'école européenne de sémiotique

Manar Hammad

The European tradition of semiotics, referring to the works of Ferdinand de Saussure and Louis Hjelmslev, has seen recently new developments with the discourse analysis undertaken by A. J. Greimas and his followers. The main aim of this school today is to reveal the articulations of discourse, constituting the latter as an object of knowledge, recognizable by formal criteria.

The different levels of description, as well as the structures that are manifested therein, lead to what can be called, by comparison, a grammar of discourse, having a syntagmatic dimension and a paradigmatic dimension.

At the surface level, where the actantial structure plays the role of reference skeleton, the recognition of actantial shiftings allows the pointing out of the traces of the speaking subjects as well as of the subjects in the speech. Furthermore, the analysis of the circulation of descriptive and model values leads to a portrayal of subjects and the characterization of their direct or indirect action.

In other terms, the discourse appears as a device reflecting as a whole the speaker, the audience, and the relation posited between these two. Far from being restricted to the analysis of the "message's content," as Lasswell thought it did, the analysis of discourse reveals an organization of the entire set of phenomena and instances related to a communication act as a whole. In this sense, it presents itself as a theory of communication.

This theoretical point is illustrated by the description of some examples taken from the Referendum Campaign (Quebec, 1980).

Propos:

La tradition européenne de sémiotique, se réclamant des travaux de F. de Saussure et de L. Hjelmslev, s'est développée récemment avec les analyses discursives menées par A. J. Greimas et ses disciples. L'objectif principal qu'elle se donne aujourd'hui est de mettre à jour les articulations du discours, constituant ce dernier en tant qu'objet de savoir reconnaissable grâce à des critères formels.

Les différents niveaux de la description, ainsi que les structures qui s'y manifestent, conduisent à ce qu'on pourrait appeler, par comparaison, une grammaire du discours, pourvue d'une dimension syntagmatique et d'une dimension paradigmatique.

Au niveau de la grammaire de surface, où la structure actantielle sert d'ossature de référence, la reconnaissance des débrayages actantiels permet de repérer les traces des sujets énonciateur et énonciataire. D'autre part, l'analyse de la circulation des valeurs descriptives et modales permet de dresser un "portrait" des dits sujets, ainsi que de leur action directe ou indirecte.

En d'autres termes, le discours se révèle être un dispositif réfléchissant à la fois celui qui l'énonce, celui à qui il est destiné, ainsi que la relation posée entre ces deux instances. Loin de se restreindre au "contenu du message" comme le suggérait Lasswell, l'analyse du discours met au jour une organisation de l'ensemble des phénomènes et des instances attachés à un acte de communication. En ce sens, elle se présente comme une théorie de la communication.

Nous illustrerons notre propos théorique par la description-analyse de quelques exemples tirés de la campagne référendaire.

Dire aujourd'hui qu'un objet porte la trace de ses conditions de production est un lieu commun largement diffusé. Cependant, l'ensemble de ces traces est rarement interrogé, et encore moins analysé en tant que système: la recherche d'inspiration sociologique se contente souvent de décrire le milieu de production et d'affirmer son influence sur l'objet produit. Au mieux, elle donne des exemples de cette influence. Ce que nous nous proposons de montrer ici, c'est que la méthode sémiotique permet une description fine de l'image que le destinateur donne de lui-même et de son destinataire à l'intérieur même du message. Alors que le schéma de Lasswell pose le message comme une entité isolée circulant entre le destinateur et le destinataire, nous montrerons que ce message porte l'inscription de ces deux instances qui lui sont "extérieures," de même qu'il reflète leurs programmes d'action. En somme, nous serions en mesure de voir *dans* le message ce que l'approche traditionnelle en communication recherche *hors* du message (dans son contexte sociologique). Formulée autrement et de façon plus imagée, cette proposition devient: le message fonctionne comme un miroir de son contexte communicationnel.

L'expression "miroir" est plus qu'une image commode. En effet, la description syntaxique[1] du contenu permet de voir que la structure qui sert à décrire l'organisation des unités de l'énoncé (les actants et les fonctions de faire ou les fonctions d'état qui les relient) permet de décrire aussi l'organisation des instances de l'énonciation telles qu'elles sont inscrites dans l'énoncé. Un examen rapide permet de constater que l'investissement actoriel[2] des instances actantielles n'est pas nécessairement le même aux deux niveaux (énonciatif et énoncif) mais la grammaire sous-jacente est identique.

Un développement abstrait sur ce point deviendrait vite incompréhensible pour toute personne non familiarisée avec l'approche greimasienne. Il convient donc de donner ici quelques exemples d'analyse portant sur des messages relativement brefs, et de revenir au propos théorique pour conclure.

Premier exemple: fragment de publicité pour le Oui au référendum.[3]

> Ceux qui disent qu'on est bien comme ça sont les mêmes qui disaient on est né pour un petit pain. Ce n'est pas vrai. On *peut* avoir un meilleur contrat avec le reste du Canada.

Jean Duceppe énonce posément ces paroles à l'écran de télévision, avec toute la conviction dont il est capable. Il est donc possible de l'identifier comme énonciateur du message. Cependant, la publicité contient un autre fragment inscrivant la signature (écrite) du Comité National pour le Oui. Par conséquent, le Comité National pour le Oui[4] s'énonce comme énonciateur ultime du message, posant dès lors J. Duceppe[5] dans le rôle d'énonciateur délégué. Cette hiérarchisation des énonciateurs installe une relation de pouvoir entre le CNO et J.D. (déléguant et délégué) de même qu'une relation de manipulation: le CNO fait jouer à J.D. un rôle. Par conséquent, le CNO est à l'origine du vouloir-faire de J.D., instaurant ce dernier comme sujet de l'énonciation. En cela, le CNO apparaît comme une instance transcendante, source des modalités qui définissent la compétence du sujet énonciateur délégué.

Ainsi, nous voyons que le "destinateur" du schéma de Lasswell n'est pas une "boîte vide", ou une "boîte noire" incompréhensible et inconnaissable de laquelle sort le message. Elle commence à s'articuler comme une instance dotée d'une compétence modale (vouloir-faire, pouvoir-faire). La suite du message nous permettra d'en préciser l'articulation. Notons ici cependant que l'instance du destinataire, investie par le téléspectateur, n'est pas encore articulée à ce stade.

"Ceux qui disent. . . ." "Ceux" est posé comme sujet dans l'énoncé. Il s'agit d'une instance définie comme non-personne, comme le dit E. Benveniste dans son analyse des pronoms[6] (in *Problèmes de linguistique générale*, pp. 225 à 266), en ceci qu'ils sont exclus de la relation que l'énonciateur pose entre lui (je) et son énonciataire (tu). Cette non-personne sera par la suite disqualifiée puisque son discours sera invalidé, (cf. "ce n'est pas vrai"). Donc, elle dit faux. Son propos est trompeur. Elle induirait l'énonciataire dans l'erreur. Disant cela, J.D. s'oppose à elle et lui dénie la possibilité de conseiller l'énonciataire. En d'autres termes, si J.D. est un énonciateur (délégué), la non-personne du "ceux" apparaît comme un énonciateur opposé, un anti-énonciateur inscrit dans l'énoncé. L'énonciataire (= spectateur) est donc pris entre deux énonciateurs qui entretiennent entre eux une relation polémique. Comme c'est J.D. qui a la parole, il termine la lutte à son avantage et disqualifie son adversaire. La procédure de disqualification repose sur l'assimilation d'un énoncé (on est bien comme ça) à un autre énoncé (on est né pour un petit pain) lequel est proprement inacceptable du point de vue de l'énonciataire. Mais ceci importe peu à notre propos, et nous ne rentrerons pas dans le détail du procédé ici. Plus important est le statut de l'énonciataire, pris entre deux instances rivales, et qui n'est toujours pas défini dans le discours. Cependant, il est frappant de voir qu'en une phrase, il est déjà situé entre les "bons" et les "mauvais" qui cherchent à se l'arracher, comme il est ballotté dans le "monde naturel" en dehors de l'univers du discours publicitaire qui nous intéresse ici.

"On peut. . . ." Qui est "on"? C'est un "nous" atténué, regroupant le "je" énonciateur, le "tu" énonciataire, et peut-être d'autres qui sont laissés dans l'ombre. Mais ce qui est essentiel, c'est que "moi" et "toi", unis, nous avons le *pouvoir* de faire quelque chose. Ce pouvoir, sur lequel J.D. appuie fortement en prononçant *"peut,"* est justement disponible parce que "je" et "tu" sont unis. Du même coup, le "tu" énonciataire se trouve doté d'une compétence modale: il *peut.* Et son pouvoir provient de son union avec son énonciateur.

Non seulement l'énonciataire n'est plus une case vide, puisqu'il est investi de pouvoir, mais de plus, il est doté d'un programme présupposé: il veut avoir un meilleur contrat avec le reste du Canada. Ainsi reconnu, ce programme présuppose que le contrat actuel de l'énonciataire n'est pas satisfaisant, laquelle insatisfaction fonde le désir du changement. L'énonciataire est donc un actant doté d'une compétence analysable en *vouloir* et *pouvoir* faire, lesquels vont lui permettre d'accomplir son faire programmatique. Ce programme s'énonce comme l'acquisition (on peut *avoir*) d'un objet de valeur qui lui est actuellement refusé. Et qui possède cet objet de valeur au moment de l'énonciation? Le message précise que c'est le reste du Canada. En d'autres termes, l'énonciataire est posé comme un sujet dont le programme est d'arracher à un anti-sujet identifié, l'objet de valeur qui lui est actuellement refusé.

Ce discours de trois lignes est donc peuplé de cinq actants que nous venons de voir (il y en a un sixième que nous verrons tout de suite):
—un actant destinateur, manifesté par les acteurs énonciateurs CNO et J.D. Cet actant se qualifie en invalidant
—l'actant anti-destinateur, manifesté par "ceux" qui détournent le sujet du veritable objet de valeur (le meilleur contrat) et le persuadent de se satisfaire d'un faux objet de valeur (le sixième actant) manifesté par le "petit pain" du "on est bien comme ça";
—l'actant posé comme sujet par le destinateur. Cet actant-sujet est virtuellement dans tout énonciataire du discours acceptant le contrat fiduciaire (de confiance) proposé par J.D. quand ce dernier identifie le vrai et le faux;
—l'actant posé comme anti-sujet dans un programme non-polémique,

puisqu'il s'agit de *contrat*. Cette relation est à distinguer de celle que le destinateur pose entre lui-même et son anti-destinateur, laquelle est une relation polémique plus dure. Ainsi, la lutte a lieu entre le destinateur et le "mal," alors que le sujet n'a affaire qu'à une négociation de contrat, c'est-à-dire à une lutte atténuée.

En trois lignes, l'énonciateur convoque dans son discours une instance qui se veut destinatrice, il la disqualifie, la domine, et s'installe en son lieu et place comme unique destinateur véridique. Puis, d'un énonciataire case vide, il fait un sujet compétent auquel il assigne une tâche qui consiste en une quête d'objet-valeur par une négociation contractuelle. Le raccourci est saisissant, et le portrait de la situation politique est fidèle, même s'il n'est que partiel. D'autres messages publicitaires viennent le compléter.

Deuxième exemple: fragment de la même publicité pour le Oui:

> Ça fait quand même des années qu'on essaie et qu'on tourne en rond. Si on dit non, ça va continuer. Si on dit oui, c'est le déblocage et le début de vraies négociations.

Ici aussi, l'énonciateur ultime est le CNO qui reconnaît en J.P. Lallier un énonciateur délégué. Tout comme J.D., il ne parle pas à la première personne et effectue en débrayage, posant "on" comme sujet de l'énoncé. Qui est "on"? Conformément à ce que nous avons vu dans le 1er exemple, "on" recouvre au moins le "je" de l'énonciateur et le "tu" de l'énonciataire. Mais comme J.P.L. est un ancien ministre, ce "on" peut recouvrir aussi les autres ministres, et le gouvernement, ou tout au moins un ancien gouvernement. Il subsiste un certain flou sur ce point, mais ce n'est guère important pour l'articulation du discours: je et tu, et peut-être d'autres instances, essaient depuis des années. Qu'essaient-ils? Nous, les énonciataires, nous l'inférons du fragment précédent:[7] ils essaient d'obtenir un meilleur contrat. Mais nous pouvons le trouver dans le fragment même, dans le dernier syntagme: "de vraies négociations". Voici donc définies deux instances liées par une relation du désir: "je" et "tu" comme sujets désireux (puisqu'ils essaient) d'obtenir un objet de valeur (des négociations). L'énonciateur (je) et l'énonciataire (tu) sont des sujets dotés de la modalité du *vouloir* fondatrice de leur compétence.

"[Et] . . . on tourne en rond." Cette compétence est insuffisante: le sujet virtuel ne parvient pas à s'actualiser. Il est bloqué, et il lui faut quelque chose pour débloquer la situation. Quelle peut être cette chose?

"Si on dit non, ça va continuer. Si on dit oui, c'est le déblocage. . . ." C'est le "oui." Et que veut dire le "oui"? Du point de vue sémiotique, c'est ce qui accorde au sujet la compétence actualisante, et la théorie nous dit que cela peut être soit un "savoir-faire", soit un "pouvoir-faire." Or le retour à la question posée par le référendum[8] montre clairement qu'il s'agit de "pouvoir." Le gouvernement qui pose la question demande à la population de le rendre compétent en lui déléguant le pouvoir expressément pour cette négociation.

Le programme posé par ce fragment est donc celui de la négociation. Le discours ne se propose plus, comme dans le premier exemple, de définir la tâche, l'objet-valeur, et le destinateur. Ici, l'énonciateur et l'énonciataire font partie du même sujet qui négocie son nouveau contrat. C'est déjà un sujet instauré dès les premiers mots. Cependant, il s'aperçoit qu'il ne suffit pas de vouloir: il faut pouvoir. Et ce sujet sait, par énonciateur interposé, quel est le moyen d'acquérir le pouvoir: il suffit de dire oui. Donc, au moment de l'énonciation, l'actant sujet (manifesté par les acteurs énonciateur et énonciataire) veut renégocier son contrat et sait ce qui va lui permettre d'acquérir le pouvoir de négociation: ce savoir est programmatique, définissant ce que le sujet aura à faire lors du référendum.

Le cumul des deux fragments nous fournit l'organisation suivante:

Troisième exemple: fragment de la même publicité pour le Oui,

parce qu'ensemble on veut l'égalité, tout bien réfléchi, c'est oui.

L'énonciateur délégué est un coeur féminin qui parle en disant, lui aussi, "on." Comme c'est un collectif, il est identifiable déjà comme un nous. En s'adressant à l'énonciataire par "on", il s'englobe avec "tu" et précise même "ensemble." Énonciateur et énonciataire sont donc sujet de l'énoncé, et ce sujet *sait* ce qu'il *veut*; c'est l'égalité; ce qui présuppose un autre actant (anti-sujet) qui n'est pas identifié comme l'égal du sujet. Voici donc la définition du meilleur contrat des fragments précédents: il s'agit de l'égalité S/S et de l'élimination de la domination actuelle. Le programme tracé est donc le message d'une situation polémique de domination à une situation contractuelle d'égalité. Selon ce discours, cela fait "quand même des années" que le Canada connaît la mésentente d'une situation polémique, et il définit l'objectif, les moyens, et les acteurs qui vont changer cet état de choses pour établir une entente entre les deux parties opposées.

Dans ce dernier fragment, le sujet est défini non seulement comme *voulant* et conscient de son vouloir, mais il est de plus un sujet qui *réfléchit*. C'est donc un sujet cognitif aussi et non point seulement un sujet pragmatique qui se propose d'effectuer la transformation pragmatique.

Nous voici donc, au bout de 30 secondes, avec l'image d'un sujet constitué, doté d'un programme, d'une compétence cognitive et d'une compétence pragmatique, prêt à accomplir sa tâche. Ceci dans l'univers du discours. Or il se trouve que l'énonciataire du monde naturel n'a pas accompli cette tâche (victoire du Non). Il n'a donc pas cru en cette image de lui-même qu'on lui proposait. Par conséquent, face à ce discours persuasif, il a effectué un faire interprétatif et il n'a pas entériné comme *véridique* ce portrait qu'on lui a fait. Pourquoi cela? Qu'est-ce qui a affecté son *croire* en la vérité de ce qu'affirmait J.D. (lequel se posait comme possesseur du Dire Vrai?) Ne serait-ce pas un croire antérieur, résultat d'une autre persuasion? Ce n'est pas l'analyse de ce discours qui pourra nous le dire. Il nous faudra analyser d'autres discours, dont certains devront être *réduits* par celui qui est énonciataire ici et qui sera devenu énonciateur. Nous aurons alors des éléments de réponse.

Cependant, sans cela, nous savons déjà que l'énonciateur, l'énonciataire, et d'autres instances discursives sont des lieux pleins, dotés de compétence et de programmes. . . .

Quatrième exemple: publicité pour le Non au référendum.

> Think about it. The PQ has been planning separation for a long time, that's what the referendum is all about. Because no matter how you slice it, sovereignty means separation. A YES vote will cut Quebec out of the rest of Canada, and who knows if that cut will ever end. Think about it. Vote positively "NO."

À la télévision, l'énonciateur délégué n'apparaît pas à son énonciataire. Seul l'énonciateur ultime se nomme, et son délégué reste invisible, alors que sa voix se fait entendre à la manière de celle qui interpela Moïse sur la Montagne. Un premier effet de véridiction réside là, dans cette oblitération de l'image de l'énonciateur. La voix qui parle, c'est celle de la vérité. D'ailleurs, elle va développer une activité cognitive exemplaire: elle va réflechir, analyser, découper (slice). Et l'image viendra simuler les opérations verbales pour obtenir, par la conjonction de deux discours (le verbe corroboré par l'"objectivité" de l'image où l'on découpe le Québec à l'aide de ciseaux) un effet de vérité construite. Nous avons donc là deux procédures persuasives de véridiction:

— l'utilisation du vrai absolu, par la voix posée et calme d'un énonciateur invisible inscrivant sa certitude dans le ton et le débit;

— l'obtention d'un vrai construit par la confrontation de deux discours conformes.

L'énonciateur s'adresse directement à son énonciataire et le pose d'emblée comme un sujet cognitif: "Think about it." Le premier mot fait de l'énonciataire un sujet pensant. Puis on lui assigne un objet de reflexion; "it." La suite dira ce que ce "it" représente par cataphore: il s'agit du référendum et de ce qu'il prépare. Le référendum n'est pas une chose en soi, ce n'est qu'un paraître, dit le discours, puisqu'il en révèle l'être véridique: le PQ programme la séparation. Le PQ est posé comme sujet de l'énoncé, et son activité sépare. Que sépare-t-elle? Elle séparera en deux ce qui est aujourd'hui un: "A yes vote will cut Québec out of the rest of Canada. . . ." C'est donc une action contre ce Un, duquel le PQ va extraire, exciser, une partie pour en faire un *autre*. Cet autre pourra se dresser un jour contre cet un, mais ce n'est pas dit. Ce qui est posé, c'est:

1. l'agression programmée du PQ contre le Canada, dans une polémique Sujet/Anti-Sujet;

2. l'arrachement d'un objet de valeur (le Québec) actuellement conjoint au Canada, et qui en sera disjoint par l'action du PQ;

3. maintenant, le statut est celui d'une entente présupposée, puisque le Québec et le Canada ne font qu'un. Après un Oui au référendum, il y aura

mésentente, puisque le *un* sera *deux*. Il est pertinent de noter ici le renversement de l'affirmation du discours pour le Oui (cf. le 3eme ex.) qui transposait[9] les deux termes de la proposition: maintenant, il y a mésentente puisqu'il y a domination, et par le nouveau contrat il y aura entente puisqu'il y aura égalité. Les deux discours se disent vrais et construisent leur procédure persuasive. Lequel sera-t-il cru par l'énonciataire? Nous émettons l'hypothèse (banale) que le faire interprétatif de ce dernier sera largement dépendant des vérités qu'il aura posées comme premières antérieurement à la réception des systèmes développés par les discours qui nous concernent. Il s'agirait donc de ses croyances pré-discursifs, et tout discours persuasif devrait en tenir compte et ne pas poser l'énonciataire comme une instance vide que le discours se chargera de remplir, ou de construire ex-nihilo. L'analyse et la confrontation des discours nous amènent donc à definir une image complexe de l'énonciataire, fondée sur les fragments observés et non pas sur une connaissance intuitive préalable.

"A yes vote will cut Québec out of the rest of Canada. . . ." Le Oui est posé ici comme l'adjuvant du PQ puisqu'il lui permettra de réaliser son programme. C'est lui qui conférera donc au PQ la compétence qui lui manque, et c'est bien le seul point sur lequel les deux discours sont d'accord: le Oui est constitutif de la compétence du gouvernement péquiste, et cette compétence est selon le pouvoir, puisqu'il sera pratiquement impossible (= ne pas pouvoir faire) de rebrousser chemin: "Who knows if that cut will ever end."

"Vote positively No." L'injonction est claire. L'énonciateur s'adresse à son énonciataire comme un actant destinateur s'adresse à l'actant sujet qu'il manipule. Il lui dit ce qu'il faut faire et valide *positivement* l'acte recommandé. La structure actantielle serait donc:

La conjonction avec 0 (Québec) constitue la performance principale et le vote (Non) constitue la performance qualifiante qui actualisera la victoire de S (énonciataire) sur S̄ (PQ). En d'autres termes, le Non est un objet négatif qui, donné au PQ en réponse à la *question* référendaire, attribuera à ce dernier une compétence négative (non pouvoir) qui l'empêchera d'accomplir son programme pragmatique identifié comme mauvais (la division).

Cette injonction de vote est précédée d'un "Think about it" qui répète celui du début du message. Il insiste sur le statut cognitif de l'énonciataire-sujet, alors qu'on lui demande une performance pragmatique (voter). Pour l'énonciateur, il est donc important de donner à l'énonciataire une image "complète" de lui-même: il a les deux dimensions essentielles du sujet, la dimension cognitive et la dimension pragmatique.

La comparaison avec le discours pour le Oui permet de mettre en relief une difference essentielle à notre avis: l'énonciateur du Non ne cherche pas à persuader son énonciataire que ce dernier *peut* changer le cours des choses. Dans son discours, cela va de soi. L'énonciataire est présupposé conjoint avec la modalité du pouvoir, et c'est le PQ à qui elle manque. De même, l'énonciateur du message pour le Non ne cherche pas à montrer à son énonciataire que ce dernier veut quelque chose. Pas du tout. Cet énonciataire n'a pas d'autre programme que de persévérer dans son être, et c'est le PQ qui vient le menacer de dol. Sa réaction est donc de légitime défense. Il *devra* donc dire Non pour ne pas être lésé. Ainsi, le sujet énonciataire du discours pour le Non est un sujet doté *a priori* du *pouvoir*; le discours vient le *poser* en tant que sujet de raison, sujet cognitif, pour lui fournir un *savoir* qui, une fois évalué, aboutit à l'installation de la modalité du *devoir*. La compétence modale posée est donc syntaxiquement la suivante: *pouvoir, savoir, devoir* faire une performance immédiate (voter Non) pour actualiser un programme de base (sauvegarder l'entente de la mésentente programmée par S). Rappelons que le discours du Oui construisait un sujet-énonciataire en le *persuadant* qu'il peut, lui *apprenant* qu'il veut, et lui définissant un programme global (l'entente après la mésentente) actualisable par un programme immédiat (voter Oui). La suite modale syntaxique est donc *pouvoir, savoir, vouloir,* et la différence ne porte pas uniquement sur le dernier terme (devoir voter Non/vouloir voter Oui) mais aussi sur l'acquisition des deux précédents (présupposés pour le Non, posés pour le Oui).

Nous en conclurons que ces deux discours ne s'adressaient pas aux mêmes auditeurs, ou, en d'autres termes, que leur énonciataire ne peut pas se manifester par les mêmes acteurs. *Par construction*, ces discours s'adressent à des sujets différents, définis par des compétences modales différentes. L'analyse sémiotique nous apprend donc que les comités nationaux pour le Oui et pour le Non ne s'adressaient pas à la même population. Leurs discours opèrent, sur la population québécoise, un découpage a priori, et il leur était impossible de persuader les mêmes personnes. Il ne s'agit donc pas d'une campagne nationale dirigée vers l'ensemble de la population.

Nous retrouvons aussi par là une image des énonciateurs, les uns établissant un contrat avec ceux qui croient détenir le pouvoir (Comité National pour le Non) et les autres établissant le leur avec ceux qui ne croient pas le détenir (Comité National pour le Oui).

Ainsi, l'analyse sémiotique de ces deux énoncés relativement courts (30 secondes chacun) permet de donner une image de la situation politique à travers son inscription dans les messages. L'effet de miroir est illustré, et nous espérons qu'il est démontré, dans la mesure où notre discours aura été suffisamment persuasif.

Les notions qui ont été le plus sollicitées sont les suivantes:

— la distinction énonciation/énoncé;
— le concept de programme sémio-narratif;
— la structure actantielle définissant les rapports S/S̄, Dr/Dr̄, S/0. . .
— le concept de compétence modale des actants;
— l'acquisition ordonnée des modalités.

La structure actantielle a été utilisée aussi bien pour la description des instances de l'énoncé que pour la description des instances de l'énonciation, et c'est justement là que réside l'effet de miroir.

Tableau 15-1

1er fragment:
Programme = OBTENTION D'UN NOUVEAU CONTRAT

Actants:	Dr	S	O	$\bar{O}$	$\underline{S}$	$\overline{Dr}$
Acteurs:	CNO, JD	Er, Ere	meilleur contrat	contrat actuel	reste du Canada	Ceux

Compétence du Sujet: Posée par Dr selon le Vouloir et le Pouvoir;
Dr donne à S un savoir sur cette compétence.

2eme fragment:
Programme = ACQUISITION DU POUVOIR-NEGOCIER

Actants:	Dr	S	O	$\bar{O}$	$\underline{S}$	$\overline{Dr}$
Acteurs:	CNO, JPL	Er, Ere	OUI	NON	reste du Canada	$\emptyset$

Compétence du Sujet: Posée par Dr selon le Vouloir et le Non-Pouvoir-Négocier
préalable; La conjonction aved le OUI assure l'acquisition du
Pouvoir.

Intégration des deux fragments:
Programme de base = *NEGOCIATION* D'UN NOUVEAU CONTRAT

Actants:	Dr	S	O	$\bar{O}$	$\underline{S}$	$\overline{Dr}$
Acteurs:	CNO, JD, JPL	Er, Ere	meilleur contrat	contrat actuel	reste du Canada	Ceux

Compétence du Sujet: Reconnue par Dr selon le Vouloir;
Donnée par Dr selon le savoir (Savoir la Vérité, Savoir prévoir
la suite); Sera acquise selon le Pouvoir quand S accomplira le
programme secondaire.

Programme secondaire = *OBTENTION* DU POUVOIR-NEGOCIER

Actants:	Dr	S	O	$\bar{O}$	$\underline{S}$	$\overline{Dr}$
Acteurs:	CNO, JD, JPL	Er, Ere	OUI	NON	reste du Canada	$\emptyset$

Actants: Instances de la grammaire sémio-narratice de surface;
Acteurs: Instances discursives manifestant les rôles actantiels;

Dr	= Destinateur	$\overline{Dr}$	= Anti-Destinateur	Er	= Enonciateur
S	= Sujet	$\underline{S}$	= Anti-Sujet	Ere	= Enonciataire
O	= Objet-Valeur	$\bar{O}$	= Objet-Valeur négatif		

NOTES

1. A la suite de Hjelmslev et Greimas, nous parlerons d'une syntaxe du contenu. Ch.S. Peirce réserve le terme syntaxe à la combinatoire de ce qu'il appelle des signes (lesquels correspondent à des éléments de l'expression chez Hjelmslev), tout en négligeant la possibilité de développer une syntaxe propre au niveau du contenu.

2. Les "actants" de la structure superficielle se manifestent par des "acteurs" dans le discours, sans que la correspondance soit biunivoque: à un actant peuvent correspondre plusieurs acteurs, et inversement. Ex: "l'opposition parlementaire a posé une motion de censure . . ." nous propose deux actants (i.e., l'opposition et le gouvernement) manifestés chacun par plusieurs acteurs (des députés d'un côté, des ministres de l'autre).

3. Je tiens à remercier M. Jocelyn Laberge, journaliste à Radio-Canada, qui m'a demandé de lui analyser ces quelques fragments qui servent à illustrer mon propos ici.

4.   Note CNO, ci-après.

5.   Note J.D., ci-après.

6.   Emile Benveniste, *Problèmes de linguistique générale,* Paris, NRF, 1966, pp. 225 à 266.

7.   Par cette opération, nous admettons que les différents fragments de la publicité que nous analysons ne sont que les parties d'un même discours, lequel est reconnaissable provisoirement par les marques du dispositif publicitaire (30 secondes insérées dans d'autres émissions avec images initiales et terminales caractérisées). Nous pouvons poser ultérieurement la question de l'unité de tous les messages d'une même campagne.

8.   Le Oui et le Non inscrits dans ce fragment fonctionnent comme des anaphorisants qui rattachent le fragment analysé à l'instance initiatrice de la campagne référendaire: la Question à laquelle il faudra répondre par Oui ou par Non. Le contexte de la campagne référendaire est donc "appelé" par le jeu anaphorique inscrit dans le message.

9.   En logique, la transposée de p q est q p.

Chapitre 16

L'imagination sociale de la télévision

Serge Proulx

From the point of view of critical sociology, the author puts forward a reflection on the phenomenon of television within the present context of society's crisis. Mass television casts images, significations and models through which groups, collectivities or social classes appropriate for themselves a process of self-identification and of self-construction of the social fiction. Thus one can speak of a cultural effect of television upon society.

After having given the main characteristics of the history of social and television development, the author suggests three particular axes in constructing the sense of image and reality of television viewers: psycho-sexual, socio-political and cosmic-ecological. In the present crisis of the capitalist economy, television is involved in the creation of the social demand for goods' consumption and destruction. Moreover, this new crisis brings about the setting up of new sophisticated systems integrating computers and telecommunications, systems which could greatly change the market and uses of television. A new social demand is structuring itself around the "need for self-supervision."

With society being in crisis, the social fiction seems more and more fragmented. The excessive "explosive" use of television increases the confusion between reality and fiction in the imagination of the viewer. Mass television thus is involved in the widespread social movement for breaking up the social relations and the fiction of these relations. Alternatives for television that aim to shift the present social and technological development are described.

Introduction

En avril 1980, à l'occasion de la conférence de fondation de l'Association québécoise pour la recherche en communication, le sociologue Guy Rocher a parlé de la nécessité d'orienter des recherches dans la voie d'une épistémologie de la télévision. Cette piste de recherche m'apparaît très féconde et j'aimerais vous livrer le fruit de certaines réflexions et lectures personnelles dont l'orientation vise à contribuer à une épistémologie critique de la télévision.

Comme le souligne bien Guy Rocher, les épistémologues ont cantonné pendant trop longtemps leur étude critique à la stricte connaissance scientifique. Il est temps de questionner la connaissance quotidienne, nous rappeler les travaux de Berger et Luckmann. Or, la connaissance quotidienne dans la vie privée de millions de Nord-Américains téléspectateurs de tous âges, sexes, races, classes ou croyances, à l'heure actuelle, se structure de manière prédominante, en étroite relation avec la télévision. La télévision agit pour eux comme "synthétiseur de réalité."[1]

Il n'y a pas seulement les contenus du petit écran, mais aussi la forme télévisuelle elle-même qui influent dans le processus de construction psychique de la réalité par le téléspectateur. Il y a également le micro-contexte de la réception (familiale, de voisinage, de loisirs, etc.) qui est transformé par ce nouvel usage social qui consiste à "regarder" et "écouter" ce nouvel objet technique. Ces trois niveaux de l'interaction entre le téléviseur et l'usager rejoignent assez bien ce que W. Weaver avait désigné comme les trois niveaux de la problématique d'analyse de la communication: sémantique, technique et pragmatique.

Une épistémologie de la télévision procédera ainsi à l'étude critique de la connaissance humaine produite par l'interaction avec cet objet technique aux niveaux sémantique, technique et pragmatique. En même temps, il s'agirait de croiser cette première dimension de "communication" avec une seconde dimension concernant les niveaux de contexte humain de décodage de la connaissance ainsi produite. On pourrait ainsi distinguer successivement le niveau psycho-physiologique (au sens d'une biologie de la connaissance), le niveau socio-politique (mise en évidence des cadres sociaux de la connaissance) et le niveau cosmique-écologique (élaboration implicite et explicite d'une conscience du temps et de l'espace, et des rapports des individus et des sociétés à la nature). Ce croisement des dimensions "communication" et "connaissance" ouvre sur les premiers éléments d'un paradigme pour une épistémologie de la télévision. Pour chacune des neuf cases de cette typologie à deux dimensions, il s'agirait de procéder au repérage des "distorsions systématiques", au sens d'Habermas, dans la construction de la connaissance, et à l'expérimentation des possibilités de création de nouvelles formes de connaissance.

Mon propos d'aujourd'hui n'est pas de procéder à une présentation systématique et exhaustive de cette problématique. Je voudrais simplement réfléchir sur le phénomène de la télévision dans le contexte actuel de crise de société à partir d'un concept privilégié pour une épistémologie critique: celui d'*imaginaire social*. Notre discours (sociologique) se situera donc plutôt au niveau socio-politique, avec quelques allusions à des ponts possibles avec les autres niveaux d'analyse.

J'emploie le concept "d'imaginaire social" en suivant les traces théoriques de C. Castoriadis et M. Rioux. Plutôt que d'utiliser le concept d'*imaginaire* dans son premier sens marxiste (la dimension idéologique qui fausse la réalité et la fait apparaître "sens dessus dessous"); ces auteurs préfèrent insister davantage sur l'aspect "transformateur" que comportent les notions d'imagination et d'imaginaire.

Le point de vue que nous adoptons est celui d'une sociologie critique. C'est une démarche qui cherche à se distinguer à la fois du point de vue fonctionnaliste et du point de vue marxiste économiste. La perspective fonctionnaliste se centre sur la découverte des fonctions sociales que remplit le phénomène étudié. La télévision sera ainsi considérée comme instrument de contrôle social, contribuant à la reproduction idéologique et économique d'une société de plus en plus urbaine et de plus en plus industrialisée.

La perspective marxiste économiste définira la télévision comme instrument idéologique, politique et économique appartenant à la classe dominante qui la contrôle. Dans la société capitaliste en crise, la télévision apparaît ici comme une institution sociale secondaire qui contribue à reproduire la forme marchande des rapports sociaux. Ce qui est sous-entendu ici, c'est une relative neutralité de la technique télévisuelle; le contrôle économique changeant de mains, la télévision deviendrait un instrument au service du socialisme.

Le point de vue de la sociologie critique considère que le fonctionnalisme tout autant que l'économisme marxiste réduisent les effets sociaux de la télévision à une trop simple expression. L'impact social de la télévision est complexe: d'une part, ce n'est pas une technique neutre puisque sa forme même empêche l'échange et la communication; d'autre part, des signifiés multiples, contradictoires, sont diffusés et échappent en partie au contrôle de ceux qui possèdent les medias. Il existe un pouvoir culturel et symbolique relativement autonome de la télévision, en partie indépendant du pouvoir de ceux qui en contrôlent la propriété. Même s'il est vrai que la télévision a jusqu'ici contribué à accroître l'efficacité de l'ordre dominant, elle constitue une formidable force technologique et symbolique dont certains effets dans l'imaginaire des téléspectateurs peuvent contribuer à une transformation des consciences.

Comme le dit Marcel Rioux, pour qu'advienne une autre forme de société, il faut dépasser le strict niveau de la critique des conditions de domination et d'exploitation: il devient nécessaire de se contraindre à imaginer et inventer une autre façon d'être en société. Une sociologie de l'imaginaire social tentera alors de saisir le processus et les formes culturelles dans lesquelles les individus, les groupes, les classes, les générations et les collectivités nationales créent et auto-construisent leur avenir social.

La face cachée d'une sociologie de l'imaginaire social consiste à explorer des pratiques de rupture symbolique avec l'imaginaire qui prédomine et assure, par sa vision de bonne société, la reproduction de l'ordre social. L'épistémologie critique de la télévision pourrait ainsi se compléter par une expérimentation du côté des usages alternatifs du médium, qui ouvrent vers la création de nouvelles formes, de nouveaux contenus, de nouveaux contextes.

Mes réflexions ne sont encore que des ébauches: aussi, appellent-elles confrontations et fécondations avec la pensée et la pratique du lecteur.

L'imaginaire social et la télévision: quelques repères historiques

Le sociologue Pierre Ansart a bien souligné l'ambiguité de la pensée de Marx dans son emploi de la notion d'imaginaire social. Parfois, l'imaginaire va "faire écran" entre la réalité sociale du travail et la connaissance; l'imaginaire devient ainsi "fallacieux" dans le mode de production capitaliste en apparaissant sous la forme du fétichisme de la marchandise. Par contre, Marx va insister ailleurs sur le fait que l'imaginaire est partie constituante de la pratique sociale. C'est cette seconde définition qu'il nous intérese de reprendre ici: l'imaginaire social n'est pas que le reflet des pratiques concrètes, il en est partie constituante et active.

En ce sens, on peut parler d'une action culturelle de la télévision dans la société; la télévision de masse projette des images, des signifiés, des valeurs, des modèles que pourront s'approprier des groupes, des collectivités, des classes ou des nations dans leur processus d'auto-identification et d'auto-conscientisation.

Tout en évitant une *réification* du phénomène de télévision qui constituerait celui-ci en force technologique et symbolique autonome, nous postulons une action symbolique spécifique de l'industrie culturelle des medias dans l'imaginaire de la société. Dans ce contexte, nous offrirons ici quelques repères historiques mettant en parallèle l'histoire de la télévision et celle de la société nord-américaine (et plus particulièrement québécoise).

La généralisation de l'achat d'un récepteur de télévision dans les foyers nord-américains se produit au coeur de la décennie des années '50. Dès 1956, par exemple, 60% des ménages québécois possèdent un téléviseur. En 1960, ce pourcentage dépassera 80%. Je pense que l'imaginaire social de l'après-guerre a été marqué de manière décisive par l'avènement de la télévision.

Jusqu'en 1961, la société d'état Radio-Canada (C.B.C.) aura le monopole de la production télévisuelle canadienne. Pendant ce premier âge de la television, certaines couches populaires de la société québécoise, peu familières avec le domaine "artistique", deviennent par la force du petit écran consommatrices d'objets culturels qui appartenaient jusque-là à l'univers de la "culture cultivée." Pensons par exemple à diverses émissions littéraires, aux représentations de ballet classique ou de théâtre de boulevard français, ou à certaines émissions de réflexion sur l'information internationale. . . . La télévision de masse exerce ici une action culturelle de socialisation des couches populaires à la culture des humanités classiques, culture jusque-là diffusée de manière élitiste par les "collèges classiques."

Bien sûr, la télévision de la décennie '50 ne sera jamais une véritable voie de remplacement des "collèges classiques" dans l'apprentissage des humanités. La télévision a ici fonction de "leurre": elle ne donne que l'illusion aux couches populaires qu'elles peuvent accéder à quelque chose d'autre que leur culture quotidienne de pauvreté. Cette télévision participe toutefois à une socialisation et à un élargissement des "visions du monde" de cette première génération de téléspectateurs.

Cette période est marquée par l'idéologie de la croissance économique et par celle de la "fin des idéologies." Dans cette société où les mots d'ordre sont "productivité, organisation et consommation," l'industrie de la télévision, par sa liaison étroite avec la publicité, devient le mécanisme par excellence d'amplification de la consommation de masse. On connaît une élévation généralisée du niveau de vie matérielle et la télévision contribue à l'affermissement de l'*American Dream*. Les citoyens devenus "téléspectateurs," intériorisent le mythe de la croissance illimitée et celui du bonheur humain dans la consommation des objets matériels.

L'année 1961 marque l'entrée en opération des premières stations privées de télévision. C'est le début d'une seconde période significative de l'histoire de la télévision; c'est l'ère d'une nouvelle concurrence entre l'industrie privée et la société d'Etat. Les "cotes d'écoute" deviennent un paramètre décisif dans les stratégies de programmation. L'industrie de la publicité prend de plus en plus d'importance: les messages intéressent moins que les audiences. Ce mouvement de commercialisation de la télévision va favoriser à la longue une diminution de la variété des contenus et une standardisation des messages pouvant susciter le meilleur taux d'écoute.

Contradictoirement, l'imaginaire social et les pratiques socio-politiques vont connaître dans la décennie '60 une radicalisation progressive marquée par les contestations des institutions dominantes. Au travers de la contestation de la guerre américaine au Vietnam, au travers de la prise de conscience des noirs américains, puis de celle des étudiants un peu partout à l'intérieur du monde industrialisé, une nouvelle conscience politique radicale apparaît.

La télévision impose ici à l'imaginaire social une action culturelle paradoxale. D'un côté, ses images sont marqueés par les porteurs de cette nouvelle conscience. La télévision de masse de la décennie '60 va ainsi jouer un rôle important dans la dissémination d'informations concernant les inégalités et les oppositions idéologiques, dans les différentes couches sociales. Mais en même temps qu'ils sont ainsi amplifiés et largement dissémines, les signes et les codes de la contestation sociale sont par ailleurs recupérés par la forme télévisuelle elle-même. La télévision "aplatit" ces nouveaux signes, les neutralise dans la mosaïque des messages à circulation autoritaire et unidirectionnelle. La contestation sociale est récupéree par le format télévisuel élaboré pour répondre avant tout aux besoins de l'industrie publicitaire et à la logique du profit.

La décennie '70 marque la mort progressive des illusions révolutionnaires dans l'imaginaire social. Du côté des idéologies révolutionnaires dans les sociétés fortement industrialisées, c'est le désenchantement. Dans les régimes de droite comme de gauche, ce sont les Etats et les appareils militaro-industriel-scientifiques qui triomphent. Partout, les collectivités s'enfoncent dans l'aliénation; ce sont les appareils de contrôle technocratique des territoires qui gagnent chaque jour plus de pouvoir. Les déséquilibres et les inégalités dans le développement économique international se font de plus en plus criants. Et puis, il y a l'affaire du prix du pétrole. L'économie capitaliste mondiale entre dans la troisième crise de son histoire.

Pour E. Enriquez[2], les collectivités réagissent principalement de quatre manières à la crise: elles procèdent à des innovations limitées et plutôt communautaires; les individus valorisent un repliement complet ("narcissique") sur eux-mêmes; les vieilles croyances ressurgissent; des groupes choisissent l'accentuation du pourrissement (des *punk* aux terroristes). Du côté des appareils de contrôle social, la crise permet de stopper la contestation et de mettre en place un *système de surveillance* de la société. Les nouvelles technologies informationnelles (particulèrement la télématique) deviendront un moyen privilégié pour assurer cette fonction de surveillance.

La deuxième moitié de la décennie '70 et le début de la décennie '80 sont donc marqués par l'accroissement de l'anomie sociale. Les individus perdent leur confiance dans l'Etat, détenteur privilegié du pouvoir social. Le pouvoir d'Etat a de plus en plus de difficulté à se légitimer dans l'imaginaire social des collectivités. La télévision, par son pouvoir d'action culturelle et idéologique, devient un instrument privilégié pour assurer le consensus social. Dans cette société de crise du sens social, un mouvement de privatisation s'amplifie et la gouverne politique devient de plus en plus une affaire de media. Alors que plusieurs chercheurs suggèrent la fin du règne des "communications de masse" qui seraient remplacées par des systèmes de consommation fortement individualisés, nous croyons que plus que jamais, la société de crise devient société de masse. La télévision participe ainsi à un mouvement de dé-structuration des relations sociales organiques: suite à l'intensification de cet individualisme consommationniste, les individus deviennent isolés, fragmentés, incapables de se penser effectivement comme groupes, classes ou collectivités.

La décennie '80 risque ainsi de voir une intensification du processus déjà amorcé d'informatisation de la société.

C'est dans ce contexte de crise du sens dans la société et de sortie télématique de crise qu'il me paraît intéressant de réfléchir critiquement sur le phénomène de la télévision. S'il y a une "crise de la télévision conventionnelle", c'est d'abord parce que l'imaginaire social et la société elle-même sont en crise.

L'identité imaginaire du téléspectateur

Certains critiques parlent d'une "crise de la télévision": après une période de relative abondance, la télévision conventionnelle (radiodiffusion) se sentirait menacée économiquement par l'arrivée de nouveaux diffuseurs. Pensons en particulier à la télédistribution et à la télévision à péage, à l'élargissement de la gamme des possibilités de choix qu'elles suscitent pour les téléspectateurs, auxquelles se combinent des offres de nouveaux services commerciaux cherchant à produire, et ensuite assouvir, des besoins d'auto-surveillance, d'auto-information et d'auto-entretien chez les consommateurs.

Il faudrait peut-être parler d'une transformation appréhendée de l'usage social de la télévision. Le petit écran risque de jouer un rôle encore plus grand dans la vie quotidienne des foyers des années '90. Déjà, la télévision des années '60 aura joué un rôle d'amplification socio-culturelle de la transformation objective des réseaux familiaux. Mais le téléviseur n'a pas fait que rapprocher physiquement de lui les téléspectateurs et contribuer ainsi à les faire s'isoler psychologiquement les uns des autres.

La quantité, la qualité, le débit des images visuelles, des sons et des mots fournis par le téléviseur, concourent au processus par lequel le téléspectateur se construit des images mentales de la réalité et donne du sens à sa propre vie. Ces images mentales pourraient se distribuer selon trois axes privilégiés de construction de l'identité du téléspectateur.

Le premier axe est celui de l'identité psycho-sexuelle. On considère généralement que la télévision a contribué jusqu'ici au maintien des stéréotypes de rôles sexuels. La plupart des téléromans — malgré des exceptions notables — ont propagé une vision traditionnelle de la division sexuelle de la société. Les images de télévision ont joué un rôle important dans l'identification aux figures d'autorité: par exemple, l'image du père, "figure de production," est mise en concurrence avec les images des "idoles de divertissement" du petit écran.[3]

Ici, la télévision amplifie la crise identitaire de la figure paternelle dans la cellule familiale, et contribue au mouvement déjà observé par certains philosophes de l'école de Francfort, à savoir une fuite de la responsabilité que l'individu transfère à des autorités collectives, extérieures à son experience.

Le second axe de construction mentale de la réalité est celui de l'identité socio-politique du téléspectateur. La télévision est un moyen privilégié de construction de la réalité politique. Dans la société industrielle et urbaine, il est devenu impossible qu'une majorité de citoyens contactent le pouvoir social et politique dans une expérience directe et immédiate. Plus généralement, la télévision encourage et amplifie le processus d'éloignement des téléspectateurs de leur propre experience.[4] L'écoute de la télévision devient un alibi pour les téléspectateurs qui s'éloignent d'autres activités demandant une implication physique et mentale plus importante. Les possibilités de création sont atrophiées au profit d'un usage de la télévision qui donne l'illusion de la liberté et celle de la participation politique. La télévision a contribué à une déstructuration des réseaux communicationnels de voisinages et de communautés locales. Elle n'a pas jusqu'ici réussi à faire s'accroître significativement les solidarités régionales et la conscience de classe. La télévision offre les images des rapports sociaux qu'une société choisit de se donner, à travers la sélection qu'effectuent les micro-milieux des artisans, des cadres, des propriétaires et des entreprises-annonceurs de la télévision.

Il y a contribution à l'individualisation de l'imaginaire social des téléspectateurs. Le "comportement d'écoute" constitue un retrait par rapport aux possibilités de vivre des expériences. Le reportage sur l'événement, la scène de fiction, l'imaginaire publicitaire se substituent progressivement à l'expérience directe et immédiate qui consisterait à participer à l'événement lui-même. Le téléspectateur peut rester chez lui inactif et bien au chaud; les images selectionnées par les fabricants de messages lui donneront l'illusion de participer à la réalité extérieure et au pouvoir social. Je voudrais distinguer ici la participation psychique (dont parle souvent McLuhan) et la participation motrice qui implique l'action. Il ne faudrait pas confondre le niveau psychotechnique de reconstruction psychique d'une image constituée de points lumineux qui balaient l'écran sur 525 lignes et y laissent toujours beaucoup de blanc, avec le niveau proprement sémantique par lequel le téléspectateur donne du sens aux signaux du petit écran. Ce sont ces significations, en plus du contexte spécifique de réception, qui peuvent éloigner ou non le téléspectateur de l'action.

Devant l'immobilité corporelle, la non-sélectivité mentale et la passivité socio-politique que semble provoquer l'usage immodéré de la télévision, force nous est de conclure que le village global électronique serait celui d'une majorité plutôt silencieuse et muette.

Le téléviseur est devenu agent de socialisation aux valeurs urbaines et industrielles. Par la publicité, la télévision produit la motivation économique à consommer: ainsi, les téléspectateurs apprennent à accepter le travail où ils gagnent l'argent nécessaire à la consommation qui, elle, reproduit le système. Les valeurs de violence et de domination des images du petit écran mènent à une vision simplifiée et dichotomique de la réalité socio-politique.

Les critiques sociaux ont insisté beaucoup sur la quantité impressionnante de scènes de violence montrées au petit écran. On a calculé par exemple que le jeune Nord-Americain de dix-sept ans a été témoin en moyenne de dix-huit mille meurtres depuis qu'il écoute la télévision.[5] Cela, sans doute, contribue à accroître une forme d'insensibilité à l'environnement social. En même temps, ce que l'on oublie souvent d'ajouter, c'est que ces scènes de violence évoquent la plupart du temps des situations sociales marquées par la domination: des riches sur les pauvres, des puissants sur les faibles, des astucieux sur les naïfs, des hommes sur les femmes, des blancs sur les noirs, des parents sur les enfants, de l'Etat et des lois sur les collectivités, des technocrates sur les citoyens. Progressivement, subtilement, les téléspectateurs intériorisent et reproduisent l'Ordre social.

Le dernier axe de construction identitaire de l'imaginaire du téléspectateur concerne ce que l'on pourrait appeler la dimension cosmique-écologique. La télévision fournit des images et des sons situés symboliquement dans un espace/temps spécifique, et qui contribuent à structurer la connaissance perceptive du monde extérieur. La télévision influence la manière dont le téléspectateur pense le rapport entre l'individu, la société et la nature. Du point de vue de la perception de l'espace, on pourrait reprendre ici l'hypothèse de Marcel Rioux[6] concernant la privatisation de l'imaginaire. Il y a repliement objectif du téléspectateur qui individualise ses fantasmes et se désinvestit de la définition des projets collectifs d'émancipation, plutôt laissée aux appareils d'Etat.

Du point de vue de la perception du temps, la télévision valoriserait davantage le présent. Le caractère mosaïque des contenus provoque une perception hachurée du temps. La télévision véhicule une culture de l'éphémère qui ne laisse que peu de prise à la construction d'une mémoire historique par l'ensemble des téléspectateurs considérés comme société. Enfin, en ce qui concerne notre rapport à la nature, la télévision constitue le prolongement du mouvement d'artificialisation de l'environnement quotidien, conséquence de l'industrialisation et de l'urbanisation. L'univers de la télévision est urbain et consommationniste: le téléviseur éloigne physiquement et mentalement le téléspectateur de la possibilité d'expériences directes dans l'environnement naturel et social, expériences directes de contact avec son propre pouvoir personnel et collectif.

Télévision de/dans la crise

L'implantation rapide dans la société, il y a à peine un quart de siècle, du système télévisuel, correspondait à une nouvelle phase de crise et de développement de l'économie capitaliste de croissance. Reprenons ici des éléments de l'analyse des mécanismes économiques de la crise, que propose Jacques Attali.

À chaque fois que le capitalisme entrera en crise, il sera revitalisé par la création d'une nouvelle demande sociale, d'un "besoin nouveau" qui entraîne de nouvelles consommations/destructions de marchandises. Lors de la première crise du capitalisme, de 1873 à 1893, un besoin "d'autonomisation du déplacement", se combinant à l'accroissement des distances suscité par l'urbanisation, provoque la demande d'automobiles. La deuxième crise du capitalisme, de 1929 à 1939, se résorbe d'abord par les nouvelles demandes de l'industrie de guerre, puis, par ce qu'Attali appelle le "besoin d'auto-entretien." Dans le capitalisme d'après-guerre, on assiste ainsi à une nouvelle demande de biens ménagers (réfrigérateur, machine à laver, équipement électro-ménager, téléviseur, etc.) qui se combine à une élévation généralisée du niveau de vie.

Voilà donc le contexte économique dans lequel est née la télévision. La petite boîte à images a été toutefois plus qu'un simple objet de consommation inoffensif; elle devient elle-même porteuse du discours qui produira la demande économique pour les nouvelles marchandises. La télévision devient le système de livraison privilégié des messages publicitaires. C'est la télévision qui apprend aux individus à devenir de bons consommateurs; c'est par la télévision, au rythme hachuré de ses spots publicitaires, que le capitalisme inculque aux citoyens les motivations économiques nécessaires à la consommation des marchandises et, par conséquent, à la reproduction du système.

Le capitalisme en est arrivé maintenant à sa troisième crise. C'est, pour reprendre l'analyse d'Attali, la crise du capitalisme d'auto-entretien. Le nouveau besoin consisterait à s'auto-surveiller. Les mini-ordinateurs deviendraient l'objet de la nouvelle demande économique pour assurer une nouvelle sortie capitaliste de la crise. Les nouvelles technologies télématiques rendent possible une substitution marchande des rapports sociaux originaux. Par exemple, ces technologies permettraient que la relation sociale aux services de santé ou à l'enseignement soit remplacée par une interaction ordinateur/usager. La relation interpersonnelle devient alors pure simulation. La relation humaine est remplacée par la fiction d'une programmation informatique. Le rapport social devient pur rapport marchand, quantifiable en *bits* et en dollars, mais surtout, parfaitement sous contrôle des administrateurs bureaucratiques du Capital et des Etats possédant le contrôle télématique.

La dissémination actuelle d'applications commerciales et industrielles aux nouvelles technologies informationnelles, laisserait donc présager une nouvelle phase de l'économie capitaliste, fondée sur des besoins narcissiques d'auto-surveillance de nos corps et de nos connaissances.

Il n'est plus possible, à l'heure actuelle, d'ébaucher une perspective critique en considérant isolément la télévision. L'avenir technologique indique que s'implanteront progressivement des systèmes combinés intégrant la télévision, l'informatique et les télécommunications. Les systèmes conventionnels de télévision risquent d'être transformés complètement par les nouvelles technologies de l'information et de la télécommunication.

Une question se pose aussitôt: les nouvelles technologies télématiques ne seront-elles utilisées que pour accroître les pouvoirs centraux des appareils administratifs? Nous croyons plutôt que ces innovations techniques devraient susciter auprès des instances politiques responsables des désirs et des volontés d'expérimentations possibles de nouveaux usages technologiques, allant dans le sens d'un accroissement de la qualité relationnelle des rapports humains et d'une décentralisation de l'organisation de société. Il faut bien voir que le progrès technique n'entraîne pas nécessairement un mieux-être social. Ce dernier suppose un projet de société pour lequel les utilisations sociales appropriées des nouvelles technologies ne constituent qu'un aspect.

Il existe au moins deux manières distinctes et opposées d'utilisation stratégique de l'information, à l'échelle d'une société, pour sortir de la crise. La première voie est celle suivie par les appareils sociaux de contrôle, comme les appareils gouvernementaux et les grandes organisations bureaucratiques. Ils utilisent ces technologies informationnelles pour accroître l'efficacité de leur contrôle sur les collectivités et les territoires. Ils ont tendance à favoriser une centralisation des systèmes d'information technique et de contrôle. Leur stratégie informationnelle est instrumentale et manipulatoire, et procède d'un intérêt technique. Le deuxième scénario de sortie télématique de la crise est fondé sur le développement prioritaire des collectivités et des communautés de base. Il consiste à rechercher la revitalisation du tissu social d'origine tout en refusant la destruction technique de l'environnement social, naturel et symbolique. Ici, la stratégie informationnelle se voudrait davantage communicationnelle, c'est-à-dire se donnant pour objectif une meilleure compréhension inter-humaine. Le modèle de société sous-jacent à cette seconde stratégie est celui d'une société où la croissance serait implosive, c'est-à-dire centrée sur la prise en charge du contrôle social du développement économique par les personnes directement soumises aux effets de ce développement.[7]

L'imaginaire social éclaté

Sans adhérer à une problématique qui ferait de la technique le déterminant exclusif des formes sociales, il m'apparaît important de souligner le fait que les nouvelles technologies télématiques représentent potentiellement l'infrastructure d'une nouvelle forme de société. Notre hypothèse générale pourrait se formuler ainsi: en même temps qu'elles sont le produit de l'industrialisation capitaliste, les nouvelles technologies informationnelles peuvent avoir une influence décisive sur l'imaginaire et la structure des rapports sociaux des sociétés où elles sont implantées, indépendamment du fait que ces sociétés sont des démocraties libérales-capitalistes ou des régimes populaires-communistes, et indépendamment de leur niveau et de leur qualité de développement économique. Pour l'instant, nos réflexions concernent d'abord le Québec: petit pays situé à proximité d'un centre de l'économie mondiale capitaliste, il possède simultanément les caractéristiques d'une société fortement industrialisée et économiquement dépendante, et d'une nation politiquement subordonnée.

Comme les autres pays riches du globe, notre société en crise doit, pour s'en sortir, modifier la nature et les réseaux des rapports sociaux qui constituent le tissu sociétal. Il ne fait aucun doute que l'informatisation et la télématique risquent de jouer un rôle décisif dans la transformation de la forme sociale.

La manière dont la télévision a été utilisée jusqu'ici risque de tracer la voie au développement des technologies informationnelles qui lui succéderont. Le système actuel de télévision va s'insérer dans la nouvelle architecture électronique-télématique progressivement mise en place pour gérer la crise.[8]

L'usage de la télévision prend de l'importance au détriment de l'activité de travail et des interactions dans la famille, comme cadre objectif au travers duquel "l'expérience du réel" se constitue. Au dix-neuvième siècle, en Europe, le mouvement ouvrier a contribué à transformer l'imaginaire social prédominant et le système des rapports sociaux. Petit à petit, chez les ouvriers, une conscience de classe a émergé. La classe sociale, d'origine ou

d'appartenance, est devenue le trait identitaire privilegié par lequel les
ouvriers ont donné du sens et du pouvoir à leur propre vie. Ce mouvement
ouvrier a culminé au vingtième siecle en un syndicalisme relativement fort qui
assure aux salariés syndiqués des conditions de vie plus intéressantes.

Ce qui caractérise l'imaginaire social qui a prédominance aujourd'hui,
c'est qu'il est éclaté. Il y a surgissement d'incertitudes multiples quant au sens
que donnent les citoyens à leur propre vie. Il y a crise du consensus social: les
référents assurant la légitimation du pouvoir sont contestés, les modèles de
construction d'un projet (révolutionnaire) de société sont contredits,
renversés, éclatent et s'évanouissent. Baudrillard ira jusqu'à parler d'une crise
et de la mort du sens social.

Ce qu'il faut voir, c'est que la télévision constitue de nos jours un lieu
privilegié de construction de l'imaginaire social. Si ce dernier apparaît éclaté,
il va sans dire que la télévision y est pour quelque chose. On peut penser ainsi
que:

a) l'usage actuel—"explosif"—de la télévision accroît dans l'imaginaire
du téléspectateur la confusion entre la réalité et la fiction;

b) la télévision de masse participe ainsi, en synergie, au mouvement
social généralisé de dissolution des rapports sociaux et de l'imaginaire de ces
rapports.

Vers des alternatives en matière de télévision: que faire?

On constate que jusqu'ici le développement social de la télévision n'a pas contribué à une authentique émancipation des citoyens mais plutôt à la
généralisation de l'aliénation. Si l'on veut que ce moyen technologique devienne un outil favorisant la création, l'imagination et l'autonomie des individus, il devient nécessaire d'intervenir pour en infléchir le développement.
La nature de ces interventions sera évidemment fonction des conceptions
respectives des intervenants concernant l'impact de la télévision dans la
société.

Reprenons ici les diverses conceptions présentées dans l'introduction de
cet article. La perspective fonctionnaliste débouche sur un déterminisme
technologique à la McLuhan, qui fait croire qu'un changement du système
technologique de communication pourrait entraîner un changement de
l'organisation sociale. Ainsi, pour Gene Youngblood, des *usages* inverses des
medias peuvent constituer un moyen pertinent pour inventer un scénario
alternatif de sortie de crise qui ne serait pas fondé sur l'exclusif principe de la
nécessaire croissance de la croissance. La seule manière d'endiguer les effets
néfastes des usages actuels de la télévision qui menacent l'identité individuelle, l'histoire sociale et même l'évolution de l'espèce humaine, consiste
à reconstruire totalement les mass media en inversant radicalement leur
structure et leur fonctionnement. Il doit émerger une nouvelle espèce d'ac-
tivistes politiques qui seraient d'abord des travailleurs culturels dont la tâche
principale consisterait à secouer l'opinion publique en vue d'une transformation radicale nécessaire des usages de la télévision.

Le nouveau système technologique dont rêve Youngblood serait basé sur un principe d'organisation "cybernétique" qui s'oppose à l'actuelle réalité "industrielle." Il trace le portrait d'un système décentralisé, bi-directionnel, à publics spéciaux ou spécialisés, et dont le feedback et le contrôle reviendraient aux usagers. Ainsi, ce système pourrait permettre aux téléspectateurs de se libérer du joug de "l'impérialisme perceptuel" imposé par la forme actuelle de la télévision. Même si Youngblood nous prévient qu'il ne faut pas voir dans son projet la simple description d'une nouvelle "utopie futuriste", force nous est de constater que cette perspective appelle des réserves. J'ai souligné ailleurs que ce projet n'est finalement que la ré-édition de l'utopie mcLuhanienne — fantaisie du "village global électronique." Le projet de Youngblood s'inscrit ainsi dans le prolongement de la problématique de la "guerrilla télévision" de M. Shamberg.

La seconde perspective — marxiste économiste — débouche sur des alternatives en matière de propriété des media et sur l'exploration de formes démocratiques de contrôle de la télévision. On peut penser par exemple aux nombreux projets de "télévision communautaire" et aux groupes d'intervention-vidéo qui cherchent une transformation radicale du contrôle de la télévision. Il semble toutefois que jusqu'ici ces expériences alternatives aient finalement été récupérées par les pouvoirs en place.

Dans ces projets d'utilisation alternative des nouvelles technologies de communication, ne sommes-nous pas piégés au départ par le fait que le développement technologique est contrôlé par des firmes industrielles transnationales et des appareils d'Etat? Comment, par exemple, envisager serieusement le projet d'une "télématique communautaire" quand on sait que le développement actuel de la télématique dépend d'un groupe restreint d'utilisateurs (liés aux grandes administrations des appareils du Capital et de l'Etat) et que ceux-ci pratiquent une auto-sélection des modes d'utilisation ("logiciels") et des banques de données?

La perspective de la sociologie critique postule que la télévision peut devenir un outil de conscientisation pour accroître le pouvoir et élargir l'imaginaire social des individus et des collectivités, au détriment du pouvoir de contrôle des appareils technocratiques. Le fait de vouloir imaginer des alternatives dans ce contexte suppose que les intervenants postulent une capacité potentielle à la télévision d'influencer significativement l'environnement symbolique des téléspectateurs. La difficulté consiste à trouver de nouveaux usages aptes à transformer réellement l'imaginaire. L'alternative consiste ici à subvertir la télévision, à rompre avec le mouvement généralisé d'émiettement de l'imaginaire social et de perte de pouvoir des individus sur leurs propres pratiques sociales.

Concrètement, cela veut dire qu'une véritable transformation des usages de la télévision implique une transformation du mode de vie des usagers. Or, celui-ci ne pourra se transformer "d'un coup" à l'occasion d'un "grand soir" révolutionnaire. . . . Une des pistes à explorer consiste à proposer des transformations ponctuelles et limitées des habitudes d'écoute, en espérant que ces changements partiels s'inscriront en complémentarité avec d'autres changements concernant d'autres aspects de la qualité de vie — travail, alimentation, santé, connaissance de soi, sexualité.

Un travail de sensibilisation est à faire pour que l'écoute de la télévision devienne sélective, ponctuelle et critique. Il serait interessant de favoriser l'écoute critique en groupe et la ré-écoute systématique d'émissions pertinentes. On pourrait songer à des campagnes anti-publicitaires de "déshabituation" de la télévision afin que les individus puissent rompre avec le contexte de passivité suggéré par la télévision de masse. Ce travail d'intervention pourrait connaître une dimension collective par la création d'une agence publique de protection des usagers des medias et par la mise sur pied de regroupements régionaux des usagers.

Des actions pédagogigues particulières pourraient par ailleurs être entreprises auprès des enfants. Il s'agit de proposer à l'enfant de désapprendre à regarder "automatiquement" la télévision; il devient plus intéressant que l'enfant puisse écouter par choix, ponctuellement et sélectivement. On pourra suggérer aussi à l'enfant d'autres occupations plus stimulantes pour sa santé physique et psychique que l'usage de la télévision.

Des usages alternatifs de la télévision, qui transformeraient significativement la relation humain/machine imposée par la forme télévisuelle actuelle, sont non seulement nécessaires: ils demeurent complètement à inventer. . . .

NOTES

1. G. Youngblood, "The Mass Media and the Future of Desire" in *Co-Evolution Quarterly*, No. 16, 1977, pp. 6-17.
2. E. Enriquez, "Interrogation ou Paranoia: Enjeu de l'intervention psychosociologique", *Sociologie et Société*, Vol IX, No. 2, 1977, pp. 79-104.
3. L. Lowenthal, *Literature, Popular Culture and Society* (Englewood Cliffs, N.J.: Prentice Hall, 1961).
4. J. Mander, *Four Arguments for the Elimination of Television* (New York: W. Morrow, 1978).
5. M. Winn, *The Plug-In Drug: Television, Children and the Family* (New York: Viking Press, 1977).
6. M. Rioulx, *Essai de sociologie critique* (Montréal: Hurtubise HMH, 1978).
7. J. Attali, *La Parole et l'outil* (Paris: Alain Moreau, 1975).
8. A. M. Mattelart, *De l'usage des medias en temps de crise* (Paris: Alain Moreau, 1979).

Notes on the Contributors

Douglas Baer is an Assistant Professor in the Department of Communication Studies at the University of Windsor. His current research interests include the mass media and minorities, the role of the mass media in the definition of social "deviance," economic ideologies and the Canadian state, French-English value differences, Canadian nationalism and quantitative research methods. Prior to undertaking his graduate work in Sociology at the University of Waterloo, he was employed as a Policy Analyst in Communications with the Ontario government.

Ron Brunton currently teaches physics and mathematics at Hants West Rural High School in Nova Scotia. An avid musician, Ron was once a sociology teacher at Acadia University.

Debra Clarke obtained her Honours BA at Trent University in 1977 and her MA at McMaster University in 1978. She recently completed a period of study at the Centre for Mass Communication Research, University of Leicester, and is presently writing a doctoral dissertation on Canadian news and current affairs production in the Department of Sociology and Anthropology at Carleton University, Ottawa. Debra is also a member of the research staff of the Federal Cultural Policy Review Committee.

David Crowley is a Professor of Communications in the Faculty of Graduate Studies and Research at McGill University, currently doing research in the area of communication and development.

Michel De Repentigny est professeur au Département d'Information et Communication de l'Université Laval depuis 1974. Il y fait des cours sur l'approche fonctionnaliste pour l'étude des mass-media et pour l'analyse de leurs messages linguistiques et de leurs codes sémiologiques. Il prépare un doctorat en linguistique sous la direction de Conrad Bureau de l'Université Laval. Rédacteur-en-chef de la revue *Communication et Information*, publiée par son Département depuis 1975.

William O. Gilsdorf is an Associate Professor in the Department of Communication Studies at Concordia University, Montreal. He obtained his PhD in Speech Communication, Radio and Television from the University of Michigan in 1972. His research interests are in the areas of Political Communication, Organizational Communication and Mass Communication. He is the recipient of grants from the SSHRCC to study the Liberal party, the media and the 1979 and 1980 federal elections.

Manar Hammad. Né en 1944 à Beyrouth, Liban. Architecte D.P.L.G., Paris, 1972; Doctorat de 3e cycle, Paris, 1976. Travaille avec A. J. Greimas de 1971 à 1979 en sémiotique de l'espace et en sémiotique générale. Directeur scientifique de Groupe 107 de 1972 à 1976 (recherches en sémiotique de l'espace et en sémiotique graphique). Invité au Japon en 1977 comme chercheur au Building Research Institute (Tokyo) pour mener une étude sémiotique de l'habitat japonais. Au Canada depuis 1979 (Professeur invité à l'Université de Montréal, Professeur invité à l'Université du Québec à Montréal, actuellement Professeur à l'Université de Montréal). Travaux d'analyse de l'image et de la télévision.

John Jackson is Professor of Sociology at Concordia University, Sir George Williams Campus, Montreal, and editor (sociology) of the *Canadian Review of Sociology and Anthropology*. He is author of *Community and Conflict* (Toronto: Holt, Rinehart & Winston, 1975) and several articles on ethnic relations and language behaviour.

Gabriel Larocque, B.A. (Montréal), B.Péd. (Université de Montréal), Lic. en pédagogie (Université de Sherbrooke), diplôme de l'E.N.S. de St-Cloud, Doctorat du 3e cycle (Sorbonne); Professeur à l'Université de Sherbrooke et à l'Université de Montréal; Doyen fondateur de la Faculté des Sciences de l'Education de l'Université de Montréal (1965-1970); Directeur-fondateur du laboratoire de Recherche sur la Télévision et l'Enfant; Professeur agrégé, Directeur du Département de Technologie Educationnelle (Université de Montréal); Professeur, Fac. des Sc. psychologiques et pédagogiques, U.L.B. (Bruxelles); Consultant de l'UNESCO, du Ministère des Affaires inter-gouvernementales; Prépare actuellement un volume sur l'imaginaire télévisuel.

John Alan Lee is an Associate Professor of Sociology, Scarborough College, University of Toronto. Author of *Colours of Love,* 1973; *Lovestyles,* 1976; *Getting Sex,* 1978; and with Ted Mann *The RCMP vs. the People,* 1979. Co-founder of the *Gay Academic Union,* University of Toronto; current chairperson of the *Right to Privacy Committee* (Toronto's major gay political action group).

Jim Overton resides in St. John's and has written numerous articles on the situation in Newfoundland. Jim was teaching at Acadia University when he co-wrote his contribution to this volume.

Christopher Plant has a BA Combined Honours in English and Drama, University of Exeter (U.K.) specializing in the use of drama and theatre in education, and in community theatre; MA (Communications), Simon Fraser University, 1980; at present he is working on his PhD in the same department. Prior to coming to Canada in 1978, he spent five years working in the Pacific Islands as a teacher, writer/editor and community activist with the Nuclear Free Pacific movement. For one year he was employed as an Information Officer for the New Hebrides National Party. He has authored several articles on the Pacific Islands, as well as editing two books and translating a third from French. He is currently interested in the role of communication in community and culture, and the use of a biosocial perspective in furthering the discipline.

Serge Proulx a obtenu un doctorat en sociologie de l'Université de Paris, France (1973). Professeur à l'Université du Québec à Montréal depuis

1972, il y fut premier directeur du programme de communication (1974-1977) et co-fondateur du Département des Communications (1975). Auteur de nombreux articles scientifiques ou d'opinions dans les domaines suivants: publicité, pédagogie, télécommunications, télévision, communicologie. Travaille presentement à deux recherches: l'une concerne l'évolution des systèmes de télévision au Québec; l'autre a pour thème les nouvelles formes de rapports sociaux dans les expérimentations socio-culturelles du Québec rural.

Jim Sacouman teaches Sociology at Acadia University and is co-editor of *Underdevelopment and Social Movements in Atlantic Canada*. Unlike Ron Brunton, Jim is not a musician; unlike Jim Overton, he does not reside in Newfoundland.

Liora Salter is on the faculty of the Department of Communication at Simon Fraser University. Before coming to Simon Fraser, she was founder of two community radio stations in Canada and has since written several articles on public-access media. Her current research is on policy process, and a book, *Inquiries in Canada* will be published by the Science Council in 1981. She is co-editor of a collection on Harold Adams Innis, *Culture, Communication and Dependency*.

Bernard Schiele, diplôme de l'Ecole des Beaux-Arts de Montréal (design), Ph.D. (Montréal); Professeur depuis 1975 au Département des Communications de l'Université du Québec à Montréal; Chercheur associé au laboratoire de Recherche sur la Télévision et l'Enfant de l'Université de Montréal; Anime depuis 1976 le groupe d'études inter-disciplinaire et inter-universitaire sur la représentation (G.E.R.); Directeur du projet R.C.I. (évaluation des applications pédagogiques de l'ordinateur) de 1976 à 1978; Responsable des projets intégrés R.C.I.-I.N.R.P. dans le cadre des accords de cooperation franco-québécoise de 1976 à 1978; Co-directeur du projet de recherche sur l'étude des modèles d'émissions télévisuelles d'informations socio-politiques et de vulgarisation scientifique destinées aux adolescents; Prépare actuellement un volume intitulé "Le savoir vide" consacré à l'analyse des fonctions culturelles des moyens de communication de masse.

Marilyn M. Taylor is presently Assistant Professor in the Department of Applied Social Science, Concordia University, Montreal. Her teaching and research interests include: adult learning, specifically experience-based and practice-related learning; life change in adulthood, especially the direction and process of value re-orientations; and innovation in formal social science inquiry. Her doctoral study was completed in Educational Theory, Ontario Institute for Studies in Education, University of Toronto in 1979. She was formerly appointed Assistant Dean of Students at Loyola College in Montreal where she worked with development of para-academic educational programmes and educational innovation.

Donald F. Theall, founding President of the Canadian Communication Association, former Molson Professor and Director of the Graduate Programme in Communications at McGill University, is presently President and Vice-Chancellor of Trent University, a post he assumed in January 1980. He is author of *The Medium is the Rear View Mirror: Understanding McLuhan*, co-editor of *Studies in Canadian Communication*, and has just finished a book entitled *The Ecology of Sense*, which investigates the interaction of art, media and society.

Gaétan Tremblay a complété ses études de doctorat en psychologie sociale à l'Université Louis Pasteur de Strasbourg. Il est actuellement professeur et directeur du Département des Communications à l'Université du Québec à Montréal. Ses activités de recherche portent sur la théorie des communications, les medias communautaires et l'influence socio-culturelle des nouvelles technologies de communication.

George Warskett, educated at London University (Physics) and Queen's University (Mathematics, Economics); employed by the federal government (1973-1978) as an economic researcher (Manpower and Immigration, Department of Communications). He is presently Assistant Professor in the School of Public Administration, Carleton University and on the Editorial Board of *Studies in Political Economy*. His research is in the area of minimum-wage policy, the "Information Economy" and immigration policy, and he is currently working on industrial strategy policy (with Professor Rianne Mahon); aspects of Marxian economic theory; the impact of information technology in offices; the quantitative growth of computerization in Canada (with Department of Communications support); and Optimal Pricing for Regulated Utilities under Incomplete Information (with A. de Fontenay).

Bibliography

Ackermann, W., and R. Zygouris. *Représentation et assimilation de connaissances scientifiques.* Centre d'Etudes et Recherches Psychotechniques, AFPA, 1966.

Adorno, Theodor W. *Introduction to the Sociology of Music.* New York: Seabury Press, 1976.

Altheide, David L. *Creating Reality: How Television News Distorts Events.* Beverly Hills: Sage Publications, 1976.

Anderson, James. "Mass Communications Theory and Research: An Overview," in *Communications Yearbook I*, edited by Brent D. Ruben. New Brunswick, N.J.: Transaction Books, 1977, pp. 279-289.

Ansart, P. "Marx et la théorie de l'imaginaire social," dans *Cahiers Internationaux de Sociologie*, XLV (1968): 99-116.

Arnheim, Rudolf. "The World of the Daytime Serial," in *Mass Communications*, edited by Wilbur Schramm, 2nd edition. Urbana: University of Illinois Press, 1960, pp. 392-411.

Attali, J. *La parole et l'outil.* Paris: PUF, 1975.

Attali, J. "La crise: pourquoi faire?" dans *Le Nouvel Observateur*, 16 janvier 1978.

Bachelard, G. *La formation de l'esprit scientifique.* Paris: PUF, 1970.

Bateson, Gregory. *Steps to an Ecology of Mind.* New York: Ballantine Books, 1975.

Baudrillard, J. *Pour une critique de l'economie politique du signe.* Paris: Gallimard, 1972.

Baudrillard, J. *A l'ombre des majorités silencieuses ou la Fin du social.* Fontenay-Sous-Bois: Utopie, 1978.

Benveniste, Emile. *Problèmes de linguistique générale.* Paris: NRF, 1966.

Benveniste, Emile. *Problèmes de linguistique générale, I, II.* Paris: Gallimard (1966); NRF (1974).

Berger, P., and T. Luckmann. *The Social Construction of Reality.* New York: Doubleday, 1966.

Brake, Mike. *The Sociology of Youth Culture and Youth Subcultures: Sex, Drugs and Rock 'n' Roll.* London: Routledge & Kegan Paul, 1980.

Bremond, C. *Logique du récit.* Paris: Seuil, 1973.

Brym, Robert J. and R. James Sacouman, eds. *Underdevelopment and Social Movements in Atlantic Canada.* Toronto: New Hogtown Press, 1979.

Budd, Richard, Robert K. Thorp and Lewis Donohew. *Content Analysis of Communications.* New York: MacMillan, 1967.

Bureau, Conrad. *Syntaxe fonctionnelle du Français.* Quebec: Presses Universitaires de l'Université Laval, 1978.

Burke, Kenneth. *Philosophy of Literary Forms: Studies in Symbolic Action,* rev. ed. New York: Vintage, 1957.

Burke, Kenneth. *Permanence and Change: An Anatomy of Purpose.* New York: Bobbs Merrill Co., 1965.

Buyssens, Eric. *La communication et l'articulation linguistique.* Bruxelles: Presses Universitaires de Bruxelles, 1970.

Bystrom, John. "Satellite Communications for Social Development," *Educational Broadcasting*, March, 1976.

Camp, Dalton. *Points of Departure.* Canada: Deneau & Greenberg, 1979.

Cappon, Paul. *In Our Own House: Social Perspectives on Canadian Literature.* Toronto: McClelland & Stewart Ltd., 1978.

Carey, James. "Communications and Culture," *Communications Research* 2 (1975): 176-189.

Carpenter, Edmund Snow, and Marshall McLuhan, eds. *Explorations in Communication.* Boston: Beacon Press, 1960.

Castoriadis, C. *L'Institution imaginaire de la société.* Paris: Seuil, 1975.

Chaffee, Steven H. ed. *Political Communication: Issues and Strategies for Research.* Beverly Hills: Sage Publications, 1975.

Chick, John. *Regional Communications and the University of the South Pacific.* Suva: Extension Services, USP, December, 1979.

Clarke, Debra. "The Significance of Mass Media Ownership for the Process of Ideological Reproduction: The Canadian Case." MA Thesis, Department of Sociology, McMaster University, 1978.

Clarke, Harold D., Jane Jenson, Lawrence LeDuc, and Jon H. Pammett. *Political Choice in Canada.* Toronto: McGraw-Hill Ryerson Ltd., 1979.

Clarke, J., C. Critcher and R. Johnson, eds. *Working Class Culture: Essays in History and Theory.* London: Hutchinson, 1979.

Cocking, Clive. *Following the Leaders: A Media Watcher's Diary of Campaign 79.* Toronto: Doubleday, 1980.

Cole, Richard R. "Top Songs in the Sixties: A Content Analysis of Popular Lyrics," *Mass Communications and Youth: Some Current Perspectives,* edited by F. G. Kline and Peter Clarke. London: Sage Publications, 1971, pp. 87-89.

Columbia Broadcasting System (CBS). *Television News Reporting.* New York: McGraw-Hill, 1958.

Couron, J. L. "Le concept de télévision communautaire," dans *Communications* 21 (1974): 66-80.

Cuneo, Carl J. "A Class Perspective on Regionalism," in *Modernization and the Canadian State,* edited by D. Glenday et al. Toronto: Macmillan, 1978, pp. 132-156.

Deleuze, Gilles and Felix Gauttari. *Proust and Signs.* Trans. by Richard Howard. New York: George Braziller, 1972.

Deleuze, Gilles and Felix Gauttari. *Anti-Oedipus: Capitalism and Schizophrenia.* New York: Viking, 1977.

Dewey, John. *Art as Experience.* New York: Capricorn Books, 1958.

Dewey, John. *Experience and Nature.* New York: Dover Publications, 1958.

Dufrenne, Mikel et al., eds. "Aesthetics and the Sciences of Art," in *Main Trends of Research in the Social and Human Sciences,* Part 2, Vol. 1. Paris: Mouton et UNESCO, 1978, pp. 489-855.

Duncan, Hugh D. *Symbols in Society.* New York: Oxford University Press, 1968.

Eagleton, Terry. *Marxism and Literary Criticism.* London: Methuen, 1976.

Edelman, Murray. *Political Language.* New York: Academic Press, 1977.

Elkin, F. and M. B. Hill. "Bicultural and Bilingual Adaptations in French Canada: The Example of Retail Advertising," *Canadian Review of Sociology and Anthropology,* 2 (1965): 132-148.

Elliott, Philip. "Selection and Communication in a Television Production: A Case Study," in *The TV Establishment,* edited by Gaye Tuchman. Englewood Cliffs, N.J.: Prentice-Hall, 1974, pp. 72-90.

Ellison, Harlan. *The Glass Teat.* New York: Ace, 1970.

Enriquez, E. "Interrogation ou Paranoia: enjeu de l'intervention psychosociologique," *Sociologie et Société,* IX (1977): 79-104.

Epstein, Edward Jay. *News from Nowhere.* New York: Random House, 1973.

Fortes, Meyer. *Time and Social Structure and Other Essays.* New York: Humanities Press, 1970.

François, Frédéric, ed. *Linguistique.* Paris: Presses Universitaires de France, 1980.

Freire, Paulo. *Pedagogy of the Oppressed.* Trans. by M. B. Ramos. New York: Seabury Press, 1970.

Frye, Northrop. *The Bush Garden: Essays on the Canadian Imagination.* Toronto: Anansi, 1971.

Gadet, Françoise. "La sociolinguistique n'existe pas: je l'ai rencontrée," *Dialectiques* 20 (1977): 99-117.

Gerbner, G. and L. Gross, "The Scary World of TV's Heavy Viewers," *Psychology Today* (April 1976): 41-89.

Goldmann, A. "Quelques problèmes de sociologie du cinéma," *Sociologie et Société* 8 (1976): 71-80.

Goldmann, Lucien. *Toward a Sociology of the Novel.* London: Tavistock Publications, 1975.

Glasgow University Media Group (GUMG). *Bad News,* Vol. 1. London: Routledge & Kegan Paul, 1976.

Granger, Gilles-Gaston. *Essai d'une philosophie du style.* Paris: Colin, 1968.

Grayson, J. P. and L. M. Grayson. "Class and Ideologies of Class in the English Canadian Novel." *The Canadian Review of Sociology and Anthropology,* 15 (1978): 265-283.

Greimas, A. J. *Sémantique structurale.* Paris: Larousse, 1967.

Greimas, A. J. *Du Sens.* Paris: Seuil, 1971.

Greimas, A. J. *Sémiotique: dictionnaire raisonné.* Paris: Hachette, 1979.

Habermas, J. "Toward a Theory of Communication Competence." *Recent Sociology* 2 (1970): 115-148.

Halberstram, David. *The Powers that Be.* New York: Alfred A. Knopf, 1979.

Hall, Stuart et al. *Policing the Crisis.* London: Macmillan, 1978.

Hamden-Turner, Charles. *Radical Man: The Process of Psycho-Social Development.* Garden City, N.Y.: Doubleday Anchor Books, 1971.

Hamilton, Peter. *Knowledge and Social Structure.* London: Routledge & Kegan Paul, 1974.

Hebdige, Dick. *Subculture: The Meaning of Style.* London: Methuen, 1979.

Hertzler, J. O. *A Sociology of Language.* New York: Random House, 1965.

Hjelmslev, Louis. *Prolégomènes à une théorie du langage.* Paris: De Minuit, 1967.

Holsti, Ole R. *Content Analysis for the Social Sciences and Humanities.* Don Mills: Addison-Wesley, 1969.

Howard, Philip. *New Words for Old.* London: Hamilton, 1977.

Innis, H. A. *The Bias of Communication.* Toronto: University of Toronto Press, 1951.

Innis, H. A. *Empire and Communications.* Toronto: University of Toronto Press, 1972.

Jacquinot, G. *Image et pédagogie.* Paris: PUF, 1977.

Jameson, Frederic. *The Prison House of Language: A Critical Account of Structuralism and Russian Formalism.* Princeton: University Press, 1972.

Johnstone, John W. C. et al. *The News People.* Urbana: University of Illinois Press, 1976.

Kolb, David and Ronald Fry. "Towards an Applied Theory of Experiential Learning," in *Theories of Group Process,* edited by C. Cooper. New York: Wiley & Sons, 1975.

Kraus, Sidney and Dennis Davis. *The Effects of Mass Communication on Political Behaviour.* University Park: Pennsylvania University Press, 1976.

Lafleur, Guy-Antoine. "Référendum d'avril 1972: l'Europe française des débuts de la décennie," *Etudes Internationales* IX (1978): 507-530.

Leiss, William. *The Domination of Nature.* New York: Braziller, 1972.

Leiss, William. *The Limits to Satisfaction*. Toronto: University of Toronto Press, 1976.

Lévi-Strauss, Claude. "The Structural Study of Myth," in *The Structuralists from Marx to Lévi-Strauss*, edited by R. de George and F. de George. Garden City, N.Y.: Doubleday, 1972.

Lewis, George H. "The Sociology of Popular Culture," *Current Sociology* 26 (1978).

Lowenthal, L. *Literature, Popular Culture and Society*. Englewood Cliffs, N.J.: Prentice-Hall, 1961.

Ludes, P. "Towards a Sociology of Alternatives." *Newsletter*, 5 (1979): 6-9, International Society for the Sociology of Knowledge, St. John's, Newfoundland.

MacMurray, John. *Self as Agent*. London: Faber & Faber, 1957.

MacMurray, John. *Persons in Relation*. London: Faber & Faber, 1961.

Mandel, E. *Late Capitalism*. London: New Left Books, 1975.

Mander, J. *Four Arguments for the Elimination of Television*. New York: W. Morrow, 1978.

Mannheim, Karl. *Ideology and Utopia*. New York: Harcourt, Brace & World, 1936.

Marcuse, Herbert. *Eros and Civilization: A Philosophical Inquiry into Freud*. New York: Vintage Books, 1955.

Martinet, André. *La linguistique synchronique: Etudes et recherches*. Paris: Presses Universitaires de France, 1965.

Martinet, André. *Langue et fonction*. Paris: Denoel, 1969.

Martinet, André. *Eléments de linguistique générale*. Paris: Colin, 1970.

Martinet, André. *Studies in Functional Syntax*. Munchen: Wilhelm Fink Verlag, 1975.

Mattelart, A. M. *De l'usage des medias en temps de crise*. Paris: Alain Moreau, 1979.

McCormack, Thelma. *Studies in Communications*. Freewich, Connecticut: JAI Press, 1980.

McLuhan, Marshall. *The Gutenberg Galaxy*. Toronto: University of Toronto Press.

McLuhan, Marshall. *The Medium is the Message* (with Quentin Fiore). New York: Random House, 1967.

Melody, William H., G. Gerbner and Larry Gross, eds. *Communications Technology and Social Policy*. New York: Wiley, 1973.

Melody, William H., Liora Salter and Paul Heyer, eds. *Culture, Communication and Dependency*. Norwood, N.J.: Ablex Press, 1981.

Mezirow, Jack. *Education for Perspective Transformation: Women's Re-entry Programs in Community Colleges*. New York: Centre for Adult Education Teacher's College, Columbia University, 1978.

Mezirow, Jack. "Perspective Transformation: Toward a Critical Theory of Adult Education," public lecture at the University of Northern Illinois, sponsored by the Department of Leadership and Policy Studies, Graduate Colloquium Committee, September 27, 1979.

Mills, C. Wright. *Power, Politics and People*. New York: Ballantine, 1963.

Moscovici, S. *La psychanalyse, son image et son public*. Paris: PUF, 1961.

Mueller, Claus. *The Politics of Communication*. New York: Oxford, 1973.

Nielsen, Greg. "Problematics for the Analysis of Culture and Society," unpublished Master's thesis, Department of Sociology and Anthropology, Concordia University, 1980.

Nimmo, Dan. *Political Communication and Public Opinion in America*. Santa Monica: Goodyear Publishing Company, 1978.

Nora, S. and A. Minc, *L'informatisation de la société*. Paris: Seuil, 1978.

Pecheux, Michel et coll. *Analyse du discours: langue et idéologies*. Paris: Didier-Larousse, 1975.

Penniman, Howard R., ed. *Canada at the Polls: The General Election of 1974*.

Washington, D.C.: American Enterprise Institute for Public Policy Research, 1975.

Piaget, J. *Les relations entre le sujet et l'objet dans la connaissance physique,* dans J. Piaget, *Logique et connaissance scientifique,* Gallimard, Encyclopédie de la Pléiade, 1967.

Piaget, J. *Structuralism.* New York: Harper & Row, 1970.

Pierce, J. R. "Communication." *Scientific American* 227 (1972): 31-41.

Porat, M. *The Information Economy.* U.S. Office of Telecommunications, 1977.

Proulx, S. "Faut-il eliminer la télévision?" *Le Devoir,* Montreal, 7 octobre 1978.

Radcliffe-Brown, A. R. *Structure and Function in Primitive Society.* London: Cohen & West, 1952.

Ricoeur, Paul, and Don Ihde, eds. *The Conflict of Interpretations: Essays in Hermeneutics.* Evanston: Northwestern Univ. Press, 1974.

Rioux, M. *Essai de sociologie critique.* Montréal: Hurtubise HMH, 1978.

Rioux, M. "Pour une sociologie critique de la culture." *Sociologie et Société* XI (1979): 49-55.

Robinson, Gertrude J. "The Politics of Information and Culture during Canada's October Crisis," in *Studies in Canadian Communications,* edited by G. J. Robinson and D. Theall. Montreal: McGill University Press, 1975.

Rogueplo, P. *Le partage du savoir.* Paris: Seuil, 1974.

Seeley, John R. et al. *Crestwood Heights.* Toronto: University of Toronto Press, 1955.

Shamberg, M. *Guerrilla Television.* New York: Holt, Rinehart & Winston, 1971.

Shepherd, John. "Music and Social Control." *Catalyst* 13 (1979): 1-54.

Smythe, Dallas W. *Dependency Road: Communications, Capitalism, Consciousness and Canada.* Norwood, N.J.: Ablex Press, 1981.

Swingwood, Alan. *The Myth of Mass Culture.* London: Macmillan, 1977.

Theall, Donald F. *The Medium is the Rear View Mirror.* Montreal: McGill-Queen's Press, 1971.

Theall, Donald F., and G. J. Robinson, eds. *Studies in Canadian Communication.* Montreal: McGill Programme in Communications.

Theall, Donald F. "The Development of Models of Interpretative Analysis and Structural Analysis to Study the Social and Cultural Effects of Television Advertising on Viewers in the Montreal Area," report to Le Service de la Recherche, Le Ministere des Communications, Gouvernement du Quebec, March, 1978.

Tiger, Lionel. *The Biology of Hope.* New York: Simon & Schuster, 1979.

Tobin, K. and R. Wicker. *The Gay Crusaders.* New York: Paperback, 1972.

Torbert, William. *Learning from Experience toward Consciousness.* New York: Columbia University Press, 1972.

Tracey, Michael. *The Production of Political Television.* London: Routledge & Kegan Paul, 1978.

Tuchman, Gaye, ed. *Hearth and Home: Images of Women in the Mass Media.* Oxford University Press, 1978.

Tuchman, Gaye. *Making News.* New York: Free Press, 1978.

Turk, Austin. "Law as Weapon in Social Conflict," in *The Sociology of Law,* edited by C. E. Reasons and R. M. Rich. Toronto: Butterworths, 1978.

Ullmo, J. *La pensée scientifique moderne.* Paris: Flammarion, 1969.

Wade, Serena E. "Adolescents, Creativity and Media: An Exploratory Study," in *Mass Communications and Youth: Some Current Perspectives,* edited by G. Kline and Peter Clarke. London: Sage Publications, 1971.

Warskett, G. "Information, Competition and Cybernetic Work." *Studies in Political Economy* 5 (1981).

Watzlawick, F., J. Weakland, and R. Fisch. *Change: Principles of Problem Formation and Problem Resolution.* New York: Norton, 1974.

White, Edmund. "The Political Vocabulary of Homosexuality." *The State of the*

Language, edited by L. Michaels and C. Ricks. University of California Press, 1980, pp. 235-246.

Whorf, Benjamin Lee. *Language, Thought and Reality.* Cambridge: MIT Press, 1964.

Williams, Raymond. *Marxism and Literature.* Oxford: Oxford University Press, 1977.

Willis, Paul E. *Profane Culture.* London: Routledge & Kegan Paul, 1978.

Winn, M. *The Plug-in Drug: Television, Children and the Family.* New York: Viking Press, 1977.

Wright, Will. *Six Guns and Society: A Structural Study of the Western.* Berkeley: University of California Press, 1975.

Youngblood, G. "The Mass Media and the Future of Desire." *The Co-Evolution Quarterly* 16 (1977-78): 6-17.